The Father's House
Twenty-Five Selected Sermons on Heaven
by Charles Haddon Spurgeon

Edited by Kerry James Allen

Copyright © 2002 by Fox River Press

Published by
Fox River Press
P.O. Box 1094
Oswego, IL 60543
630-554-1847 Voice Mail
815-886-4144 Voice/FAX
kjallen@ix.netcom.com

Cover design by
Jeff Payne
Sable Visuals
815-462-3689

We welcome your contact, comments, suggestions, and constructive criticisms. Direct them to the address and numbers above. Quantity prices also available.

Many thanks to Bobette Shoger and Tim Zollers for proof reading and computer skills.

Publishers Note: These sermons have been selected from The New Park Street Pulpit and the Metropolitan Tabernacle Pulpit series, originally printed by Passmore and Alabaster, and more recently reprinted by Pilgrim Publications, and are presented here in their entirety, without alteration of sermon titles, Bible texts or versions, or archaic English spelling. Fidelity to the original sermons has been meticulously sought with the exception of the use of a clearer and larger type font (11 point Century Schoolbook).

ISBN 0-9711434-1-2

The Father's House

Twenty-five selected sermons on the subject of Heaven

Charles Haddon Spurgeon

Fox River Press

Oswego, IL

Table of Contents

Preface

The sermons of Charles Haddon Spurgeon have been continuously in print for nearly one hundred and fifty years, as a testimony to their thoroughly Biblical content, fidelity to truth, and marvelous use of the English language. Spurgeon was a wordsmith and literary giant whose sermons were honed to a razor's edge.

His prodigious output is astounding for a man who lived a brief fifty-seven years, with much of that spent in illness. He wrote two to three books every year of his active ministry, and kept an entire printing firm busy with production of just his works. One luminary said that Spurgeon did the life work of fifty men, which may not have been an exaggeration. His magnum opus, of course, is the sixty-three volumes of sermons, begun when he was barely into his twenties and finalized twenty-five years after his death.

In this book, we present yet another offering of the sermons of the most enduring Baptist pastor of all time. What makes this volume of sermons on Heaven different from other topical selections of sermons by Spurgeon, and what is the motivation behind producing these?

My first discovery was that even though small topical books of Spurgeon's sermons have been in print for over one hundred years, in reading many of these "Twelve sermons on..." books (and there are more than four dozen different topical volumes), I didn't feel that these were his best sermons on that given topic. Further investigation of each sermon in at least a dozen of the books that I examined yielded the fact that the selection of sermons had ended with volumes thirty-five to forty in most of them. The problem is that the complete set is sixty-three volumes. Printers have evidently been reprinting these volumes without reading the last twenty-five volumes, which of course contain over one thousand more sermons, many of which never found their way into the "Twelve" series. This "Spurgeon Select Sermon Series" seeks to remedy that by including many of them.

Next, although they are not identical photographic reproductions such as those offered by Pilgrim Publications, the premier distributor of Spurgeon's books in the world today, we have made every effort to retain the strictest adherence to the original words and punctuation. Many archaic old English words will drive the reader to their dictionary (which is not such a bad thing). Only verified misspellings (of which there were very few, amazingly, for the days of setting type by hand) have been changed and corrected. Many of the newer compilations of Spurgeon's sermons have been heavily edited and include updated language, in addition to altering Spurgeon's own words to make him "theologically correct." This usually occurs without any admission of these facts.

Thirdly, as alluded to earlier, the sermons have been selected by meticulously combing the entire New Park Street Pulpit and Metropolitan Tabernacle Pulpit sermon sets (sixty-three volumes total) for every sermon on this topic, and then reading and grading them by their quality. All of Spurgeon is excellent, some of Spurgeon is superlative. This is my admittedly biased selection of the twenty-five best sermons on the subject of Heaven. My main qualification for doing so is ownership of the sixty-three volumes, as well as actually reading them. Very few people will ever assemble and own this massive set (unless procured in a digital format), and fewer still will ever read its nearly 45,000 pages. The reader will benefit from the distillation of literally thousands of hours of reading in the preparation of these volumes of carefully selected sermons.

Finally, they are set in a very readable eleven point Century Schoolbook font. The first seven volumes of

Spurgeon's sermons contain some of his finest material, yet the originals are set in an extremely minute font size that makes reading them very difficult and tiring.

As an interesting aside, a lady in Wisconsin by the name of Diane Dew secured a copy of our previous book by Spurgeon, **The Suffering of Man and the Sovereignty of God,** twenty-five sermons from the book of Job. Being a cancer survivor (as is her son), she enjoyed that book and shared numerous copies with others. She knew I was working on this book, and was anticipating its completion. Just as I was finishing up the proofing, she wrote informing me that she would love to read these sermons as soon as possible because her doctors had given her just weeks to live. She then read these sermons and may be with the Lord by the time you read this. I asked her for her thoughts as she stood on the edge of eternity, and they appear next, after this preface.

Nearly thirty years ago, as a new Christian, someone pointed me to H.A. Ironside as one to read to help ground me in the doctrines of the faith. Reading his entire New Testament commentary set did just that. Six years ago, I drew a bow at a venture (as Spurgeon would say) and read a random volume of Spurgeon's sermons. The experience was bittersweet. I have been everlastingly grateful for the man and his message. My only regret is not having started sooner. Perhaps this book will make it easier for you.

Looking for that Blessed Hope,
Kerry James Allen

xiii

Foreword

"What's heaven like?" my son asked me from his hospital bed in the cancer ward. Caught off guard, I realized I knew next to nothing about the subject. I thought for a moment, then told him, "Heaven will have all of the good things and none of the bad."

After searching the scriptures, I found that was not such a bad answer. Much of what God's Word reveals regarding heaven is about what's not there. There will be no more pain, no more death, no sorrow, no crying, no violence, no darkness, no hunger, no thirst, etc. (Isaiah 65:19-25; Revelation 7:17, 21:4).

I personally became interested in heaven after the passing of my dear mother. I wanted to learn everything the Bible says about the subject. So when doctors told me I had only a few months to live, I was not devastated by the news.

We prepare in great detail when making plans for vacations of just a few days' duration. When planning to relocate to a new community, we research the climate, socioeconomics, real estate prospects, employment opportunities, etc.

However, when it comes to the place of our abode for eternity, many Christians make no preparation but live as though this earth were our permanent home. They spend every spare moment shopping or pursuing vain entertainment.

Then, after spending so much time, money, and effort decorating their homes within and without, they leave to their loved ones the task of ridding their lives of the burden of all that "stuff" accumulated.

Jesus told about a man who spent his entire life accumulating many possessions—who, when he had no more room to store his goods, made plans to build yet another structure in which to store it all. Then one day he was called away, to meet his Maker. Jesus response was, "Then whose shall these things be?"

"Lay not up for yourselves treasures upon earth," Jesus said. Our treasure should be in heaven. That's where our investments should be held, for true security.

Reading Spurgeon's sermons on the subject of heaven has been inspiring and uplifting to my soul. I look forward with great anticipation to the dawning of that new day wherein the Lamb is the Light (Revelation 22:5), where there shall be no more sorrow or pain.

Diane Dew

Introduction

Perhaps nothing reveals man's depravity quite like his views of the afterlife. Punishment is difficult to moderate; so men simply dismiss the concept of Hell completely, yet stubbornly cling to their conception of Heaven with little regard to Divine revelation. Polls show that the percentage of people who believe in a Heaven of bliss always exceeds those who believe in the fires of Hell, in spite of the fact that Christ spoke more of judgment than Heaven.

Among the moral religious, the assumption is that Heaven is the reward for a life of so called "good deeds." For the more depraved religious, it is a place of re-population of other worlds, or being entertained by the sensual pleasures of seventy-two virgins. To the completely irreligious, it is a place where the lusts of the flesh are continually satisfied with more of what passes for fun on earth. To the Bible believer, however, it is the escape from this "penal colony" as Spurgeon called our planet, freedom from sin; rest in Christ; worship of Christ; and service for Christ. The Lord Jesus Christ is Heaven, and to be where Christ is fulfills the longing of the believer in Him.

As Spurgeon states in his sermon *"Heavenly Worship:"* "The divine John was privileged to look within the gates of pearl; and, on turning around to tell us what he saw—observe how he begins—he saith not, 'I saw streets of gold or walls of Jasper;' he saith not, 'I saw crowns, marked their lustre, and saw the wearers.' That he shall notice afterwards. But he begins by saying, 'I looked, and lo, a Lamb!' to teach us that the very first and chief object of attraction in the heavenly state is 'the Lamb of God which taketh away the sins of the world.' Nothing else attracted the Apostle's attention so much as the person of that Divine Being. They have not yet ceased to admire his beauty, and marvel at his wonders and adore his person. 'I looked, and lo, a Lamb!'"

May the Lord so separate us from our idols, our ambitions, and our cares, that our desire for Heaven is not just the nether springs of mansions, relief from pain and suffering, and the new body, but rather, the upper springs of leaning on the breast of the One who has made it all possible.[1]

Charles Spurgeon left the "land of the dying" as he called it, to enter "the land of the living" on January 31, 1892.

"'I shall be home by February,' was, for a long time, the Pastor's reply to everyone who asked him when he thought of being back, and *he was home* in February, in a far more real sense than any of us had supposed when we heard the words."[2]

In Spurgeon's final trip to Mentone, France, he held several brief services at his hotel attended by his wife (her first time in Mentone with him), and less than two dozen other believers. In the last service that he conducted, the song that he chose and sang with the group before he departed for Heaven was *"The Sands Of Time Are Sinking."*

The sands of time are sinking, The dawn of Heaven breaks;
The summer morn I've sighed for—The fair, sweet morn awakes:
Dark, dark hath been the midnight, But dayspring is at hand,
And glory, glory dwelleth in Immanuel's land.

O Christ, He is the fountain, The deep, sweet well of love!
The streams on earth I've tasted, More deep I'll drink above:
There to an ocean fulness, His mercy doth expand,
And glory, glory dwelleth in Immanuel's land.

O I am my Beloved's, And my Beloved's mine!
He brings a poor vile sinner, Into His "house of wine."
I stand upon His merit—I know no other stand,
Not e'en where glory dwelleth in Immanuel's land.

The Bride eyes not her garment, But her dear Bridegroom's face;
I will not gaze at glory, But on my King of grace.
Not at the crown He giveth, But on His pierced hand:
The Lamb is all the glory of Immanuel's land.

This book contains twenty-five of Spurgeon's finest sermons on Heaven and its wonders, carefully selected from the sixty-three volume sermon set. These several months of proofing and work on this book has been to me a "feast of...fat things full of marrow..."[3] If a saint is encouraged in his pilgrimage or a sinner is wooed to the Savior, the labors of this book will be repaid many times over.

What would you do if you learned you had but weeks to live? If you are unconverted "...it is time to seek the Lord."[4] If you are a believer in Jesus Christ, let us "...learn of Him."[5]

If we can help, or if you have been blessed, we would love to hear from you. As *The Sands Of Time Are Sinking* states,

I stand upon His merit—I know no other stand,

Kerry James Allen

[1]Psalm 73:25
[2]Robert Schindler, From The Pulpit To The Palm Branch, (Passmore and Alabaster, 1892), page 40.
[3]Isaiah 25:6
[4]Hosea 10:12
[5]Matthew 11:29

1

Why They Leave Us

"Father, I will that they also, whom thou hast given me, be with me where I am; that they may behold my glory, which thou hast given me: for thou lovedst me before the foundation of the world." **John 17:24**

The prayer of the Saviour rises as it proceeds. He asked for his people that they might be preserved from the world, then that they might be sanctified, and then that they might be made manifestly one; and now he reaches his crowning point—that they may be with him where he is, and behold his glory. It is well when in prayer the spirit takes to itself wings. The prayer that swings to and fro like a door upon its hinges may admit to fellowship; but that prayer is more after the divine pattern which, like a ladder, rises round by round, until it loses itself in heaven.

This last step of our Lord's prayer is not only above all the rest, but it is a longer step than any of the others. He here ascends, not from one blessing which may be enjoyed on earth, to another of higher degree; but he mounts right away from all that is of this present state into that which is reserved for the eternal future. He quits the highest peaks of grace, and at a single stride his prayer sets its foot in glory: "That they also, whom thou hast given me, be with me where I am."

There is this to be noticed also concerning this divine prayer, that not only does it rise as to its subject, but it even ascends as to the place which the Intercessor appears to occupy. Has it not been so with yourselves in prayer at times, that you have hardly known where you were? You

might have cried with Paul, "Whether in the body or out of
the body, I cannot tell."Do not these words of our Lord Jesus
remind you of this? Was he not carried away by the fervour
of his devotion? Where was he when he uttered the words of
our text? If I follow the language I might conclude that our
Lord was already in heaven. He says, "Father, I will that
they also, whom thou hast given me, be with me where I am;
that they may behold my glory." Does he not mean that they
should be in heaven with him? Of course he does; yet he was
not in heaven; he was still in the midst of his apostles, in his
body upon earth; and he had yet Gethsemane and Golgotha
before him ere he could enter his glory. He had prayed
himself into such an exaltation of feeling that his prayer was
in heaven, and he himself was there in spirit. What a hint
this gives to us! How readily may we quit the field of battle
and the place of agony, and rise into such fellowship with
God, that we may think, and speak, and act, as if we were
already in possession of our eternal joy! By the ardour of
prayer and the confidence of faith we may be caught up into
Paradise, and there utter words which are beyond the
latitude of earth, and are dated "from the Delectable
Mountains."

Nor is this all; for still the prayer rises, not only as to its
matter and place, but in a very singular way it also takes to
itself a higher style. Before, our Lord had asked and pleaded;
but now he uses a firmer word: he says, "Father, I will." I
would not force that word so as to make it bear an imperious
or commanding meaning, for the Saviour speaketh not so to
the Father: but still it has a more elevated tone about it than
asking. Our Lord here useth the royal manner rather than
the tone of his humiliation. He speaketh like unto the Son of
God; he addresses the great Father as one who counteth it
not robbery to be equal with him, but exercises the
prerogative of his Eternal Sonship. He saith, "I will." This is
a tone which belongs not to us except in a very modified
degree; but it teaches us a lesson. It is well in prayer, when
the Holy Spirit helpeth us, not only to groan out of the dust
as suppliant sinners, but to seek unto our Father in the
spirit of adoption with the confidence of children, and then
with the promise of God in our hand we may with
consecrated bravery lay hold upon the covenant angel, and
cry, "I will not let thee go, except thou bless me."

Importunity is a humble approach to this divine "I will." The will consecrated, educated, and sanctified, may and must reveal itself in our more spiritual petitions, just as, with equal correctness, it hides away when the pleading is for temporal things, and whispers, "Not as I will, but as thou wilt." The Lord pours upon his pleading servants at times a kind of inspiration by which they rise into power in prayer, and have their will of the Lord. Is it not written, "Delight thyself in the Lord; and he shall give thee the desires of thine heart"? We come at last to feel that the desires of our heart are inspired of his Spirit, and then that we have the petitions which we have asked of him.

There ought to be much for our edification in a text like this, which in subject, place, and style rises to such an elevation. It is the apex of this wonderful pyramid of prayer; the last round of the ladder of light. O Spirit of the Lord, instruct us while we behold it!

I have taken this text because it has taken hold on me. Our beloved brother, Charles Stanford, has just been taken from us. I seem to be standing as one of a company of disciples, and my brethren are melting away. My brethren, my comrades, my delights, are leaving me for the better land. We have enjoyed holy and happy fellowship in days of peace, and we have stood shoulder to shoulder in the battle of the Lord; but we are melting away. One has gone; another has gone; before we look round another will have departed. We see them for a moment, and they vanish from our gaze. It is true they do not rise into the air like the Divine Master from Olivet; yet do they rise, I am persuaded of that: only the poor body descends, and that descent is for a very little while. They rise, to be for ever with the Lord. The grief is to us who are left behind. What a gap is left where stood Hugh Stowell Brown! Who is to fill it? What a gap is left where stood Charles Stanford! Who is to fill it? Who among us will go next? We stand like men amazed. Some of us stood next in the rank with those who have been taken. Why this constant thinning of our ranks while the warfare is so stern? Why this removal of the very best when we so much need the noblest examples? I am bowed down, and could best express myself in a flood of tears as I survey the line of graves so newly digged; but I restrain myself from so carnal a mode of regarding the matter, and look upon it in a clearer light. The

Master is gathering the ripest of his fruit, and well doth he deserve them. His own dear hand is putting his apples of gold into his baskets of silver; and as we see that it is the Lord, we are bewildered no longer. His word, as it comes before us in the text, calms and quiets our spirits. It dries our tears, and calls us to rejoicing as we hear our heavenly Bridegroom praying, "Father, I will that they also, whom thou hast given me, be with me where I am." We understand why the dearest and best are going. We see in whose hand is held the magnet which attracts them to the skies. One by one they must depart from this lowland country, to dwell above, in the palace of the King, for Jesus is drawing them to himself. Our dear babes go home because "he gathereth the lambs with his arm and carrieth them in his bosom"; and our ripe saints go home because the Beloved is come into his garden to gather lilies. These words of our Lord Jesus explain the continual home-going; they are the answer to the riddle which we call death. I am going to talk of how our honoured brethren are not, because God taketh them; and I shall be happy if my words shall prepare us to exercise a holy readiness to see the grand request of our Redeemer fulfilled, even though it cost us many a sorrowful parting.

I. Let us begin as our text begins, and thus the first thought about the continual gathering to the house above will be THE HOME-WORD—the rallying word: "Father." Observe, our Lord had said, "Holy Father," and toward the close of the prayer he said, "O righteous Father"; but in commencing this particular petition he uses the word "Father" by itself alone: this relationship is in itself so dear that it agrees best with the loftiest petition. I like to think of that name "Father," as used in this connection. Is it not the centre of living unity? If there is to be a family gathering and reunion, where should it be but in the father's house? Who is at the head of the table but the father? All the interests of the children unite in the parent, and he feels for them all.

From the great Father the Lord Jesus himself came forth. We do not understand the doctrine of the eternal filiation— we adore the mystery into which we may not pry. But we know that as our Lord Jesus is God-and-man Mediator, he came forth from the Father; and unto the Father's will he submitted himself in so doing. As for us, we come distinctly of that Father; it is he that made us, and not we ourselves;

and, better and brighter fact still, of his own will begat he us by the word of truth. We were born a second time from heaven, and from our Heavenly Father our spiritual life is derived.

The whole of this sermon through, I want to show you that it is right that we should part with our brethren and joyfully permit of their going home; and surely I may at once ask you—What can be more right than that children should go home to their father? From him they came, to him they owe their life; should they not always tend towards him, and should not this be the goal of their being, that they should at last dwell in his presence? To go away from the Father and to live apart from him is the sorrow of our fallen nature as it plays the prodigal; but the coming back to the Father is restoration to life, to peace, to happiness. Yes, all our hopeful steps are towards the Father. We are saved when by believing in the name of Jesus we receive power to become the sons of God. Our sanctification lies in the bosom of our adoption. Because Jesus comes from the Father and leads us back to the Father, therefore is there a heaven for us. Wherefore, whenever we think of heaven let us chiefly think of the Father; for it is in our Father's house that there are many mansions, and it is to the Father that our Lord has gone, that he may prepare a place for us.

"FATHER!" why, it is a bell that rings us home. He who hath the spirit of adoption feels that the Father draws him home, and he would fain run after him. How intensely did Jesus turn to the Father! He cannot speak of the glory wherein he is to be without coupling his Father with it. Brethren, it is in the Father that we live and move and have our being. Is there any spiritual life in the world which does not continually proceed from the life of the great Father? Is it not by the continual outcoming of the Holy Ghost from the Father that we remain spiritual men? And as from him we live, so for him we live, if we live aright. We wish so to act as to glorify God in everything. Even our salvation should not be an ultimate end with any one of us; we should desire to glorify God by our salvation. We look upon the doctrines that we preach, and the precepts which we obey, as means to the glory of God, even the Father.

This is the consummation which the First-born looks for, and to which all of us who are like him are aspiring also,

namely, that God may be all in all: that the great Father
may be had in honour, and may be worshipped in every
place. Since, then, we are from him, and of him, and to him,
and for him, this word "Father" calls us to gather at his feet.
Shall any one of us lament the process? No; we dare not
complain that our choicest brethren are taken up to gladden
the great Father's house. Our brother is gone; but we ask,
"Where is he gone?" and when the answer comes, "He is gone
to the Father," all notion of complaint is over. To whom else
should he go? When the great First-born went away from us,
he told his sorrowing followers that he was going to their
Father and his Father; and that answer was enough. So,
when our friend, or our child, or our wife, or our brother, is
gone, it is enough that he is with the Father. To call them
back does not occur to us; but rather we each one desire to
follow after them.

> "Father, I long, I faint to see
>   The place of thine abode;
> I'd leave thine earthly courts and flee
>   Up to thy seat, my God."

A child may be happy at school, but he longs for the
holidays. Is it merely to escape his lessons? Ah, no! Ask him,
and he will tell you, "I want to go home to see my father."
The same is equally true, and possibly more so, if we include
the feminine form of parentage. What a home-cry is that of
"mother!" The sight of that dear face has been longed and
hungered for by many a child when far away. Mother or
father, which you will; they are blended in the great
Fatherhood of God. Let it but be said that any one has gone
to his father, and no further question is asked as to the right
of his going thither. To the father belongs the first
possession of the child; should he not have his own child at
home? The Saviour wipes our tears away with a
handkerchief which is marked in the corner with this word—
"Father."

II. Secondly, I want your thoughts upon THE HOME
IMPETUS. The force which draws us home lies in the word, "I
will." Jesus Christ, our most true God, veiled in human form,
bows his knee and prays, and throws his divine energy into
the prayer for the bringing home of his redeemed. This one
irresistible, everlastingly almighty prayer carries everything

before it. "Father, I will that they also, whom thou hast given me, be with me where I am," is the centripetal energy which is drawing all the family of God towards its one home.

How shall the chosen get home to the Father? Chariots are provided. Here are the chariots of fire and horses of fire in this prayer. "I will," saith Jesus, "that they be with me"; and with him they must be. There are difficulties in the way—long nights and darkness lie between, and hills of guilt, and forests of trouble, and bands of fierce temptations; yet the pilgrims shall surely reach their journey's end, for the Lord's "I will" shall be a wall of fire round about them. In this petition I see both sword and shield for the church militant. Here I see the eagle's wings on which they shall be upborne till they enter within the golden gates. Jesus saith, "I will"; and who is he that shall hinder the home-coming of the chosen? As well hope to arrest the marches of the stars of heaven.

Examine the energy of this "I will" for a moment, and you will see, first, that it hath the force of *an intercessory prayer*. It is a gem from that wonderful breastplate of jewels which our great High-priest wore upon his breast when he offered his fullest intercession. I cannot imagine our Lord's interceding in vain. If he asks that we may be with him where he is, he must assuredly have his request. It is written, that "he was heard in that he feared." When with strong crying and tears he poured out his soul unto death, his Father granted the requests of his heart. I do not wonder it should be so; how could the best Beloved fail of that which he sought in intercession from his Father God! Mark, then, that the force of irresistible intercession is drawing every blood-bought soul into the place where Jesus is. You cannot hold your dying babe; for Jesus asks for it to be with him. Will you come into competition with your Lord? Surely you will not. You cannot hold your aged father, nor detain your beloved mother, beyond the time appointed; for the intercession of Christ has such a force about it that they must ascend even as sparks must seek the sun.

More than intercession is found in the expression "I will." It suggests the idea of *a testamentary bequest* and appointment. The Lord Jesus is making his last will and testament, and he writes, "Father, I will that they also, whom thou hast given me, be with me." No man who makes his will likes to have it frustrated. Our Saviour's testament will assuredly be carried out in every jot and tittle; and, if for no other reason, yet certainly for this cause, that though he died, and thus made his will valid, yet he lives again to be his own executor, and to carry out his will. When I read in our Lord's testament the words, "Father, I will that they be with me," I ask, "Who is to hold them back?" They must in due time be with him, for the will of the ever blessed Saviour must be carried out: there can be no standing against a force of that kind.

Nor is this all the words read to me, not only like intercession and testamentary decree, but there is a strong expression of *desire, resolve, and purpose.* Jesus desires it, and saith, "I will." It is a deliberate desire—a forcible, distinct, resolute, determined purpose. The will of God is supreme law. It needeth not that he should speak; he doth but will or purpose, and the thing is done. Now read my text: "I will that they be with me"; the Son of God wills it. How are the saints to be hindered from what the Lord wills? They must rise from their beds of dust and silent clay;—they must rise to be with Jesus where he is, for Jesus wills it. By your anxious care you may seek to detain them; you may sit about their bed and nurse them both night and day, but they must quit these dark abodes when Jesus gives the signal. You may clutch them with affectionate eagerness, and even cry in despair, "They shall not go, we cannot bear to part with them"; but go they must when Jesus calls. Take back your naughty hands, which would detain them; for naughty they are if you would rob your Saviour. Would you cross *his* will? Would you set at naught his testament? You could not if you would; you would not if you could. Rather be inclined to go with them than think to resist the heavenly attraction which upraises them. If Jesus saith, "I will," then it is yours to say, "Not as I will, but as thou wilt. They were never so much mine as they are thine. I never had so much right to them as thou hast who hast bought them. They never so truly could be at home with me as they will be at home with thee in thine own bosom; so my will dissolves itself into thy will, and I say with steadfast resignation, 'Let them go.'"

Brothers and sisters, you perceive the forces which are bearing away our beloved ones. I see tender hands reaching after us this morning; they are invisible to sense, but

palpable to faith. Cords of love are being cast about the
chosen, and they are being drawn out secretly from their
fellows. Would you break those bands asunder, and cast
those cords from us? I beseech you, think not so; but let that
pierced hand which bought the beloved ones seek out its own
purchase and bring them home. Should not Jesus have his
own? Do we not bow our knee and pray for Jesus, "Thy will
be done on earth, as it is in heaven?"

III. But now I want to conduct you farther into the text.
We have had the home-word and the home-bringing
impetus, and now let us carefully note THE HOME
CHARACTER. "Father, I will that *they also, whom thou hast
given me,* be with me where I am." The description is—
"They also, whom thou hast given me." The Greek is
somewhat difficult to translate. The translators of the
Revised Version were, no doubt, excellent Greek scholars,
and if they had known a little more English, they might have
come a little nearer to a perfect translation; but they do not
always appear to think the common English reader to be
worthy of their consideration. This is their translation in the
present instance:—"Father, that which thou hast given me,
I will that, where I am they also may be with me." This, to
speak plainly, sounds very like nonsense. It is the translation which a boy would present to his tutor at school, but it
is of small use to the general reader. It is literal, no doubt;
but literalisms are often another proof that the letter killeth.
Translators into the English tongue might have contrived to
have given us words with a meaning in them. I merely quote
the version to show you that there is here a something in the
singular as well as persons in the plural. "Father, I will
concerning *that* which thou hast given me, that *they* may be
with me where I am." Our Lord looked upon those whom the
Father gave him as one—one body, one church, one bride: he
willed that as a whole the church should be with him where
he is. Then he looked again and saw each of the many
individuals of whom the one church is composed, and he
prayed that each, that all of these, might be with him and
behold his glory. Jesus never so prays for the whole church
as to forget a single member; neither does he so pray for the
members individually as to overlook the corporate capacity
of the whole. Sweet thought! Jesus wills to have the whole of
what he bought with his precious blood with him in heaven;

he will not lose any part. He did not die for a part of a church, nor will he be satisfied unless the entire flock which he has purchased shall be gathered around him.

But while the Lord looks at those whom his Father gave him as one body, he looks upon you and me, and each believer here, as a part of that great unity, and his prayer is that all of us may be with him. I believe that he prays as much for the least as for the greatest, as much for Benjamin as for Judah, as much for the despondent as for those who are fully assured. The prayer is one of great breadth and comprehensiveness, but yet it is not the prayer which those who believe in Universalism would put into his mouth. He does not pray that those who die unbelievers may be with him where he is; neither does he will that souls in hell should one day come out of it and be with him in glory. There is no trace of that doctrine in holy writ: those who teach such fables draw their inspiration from some other source. The new purgatory, in which so many have come to believe, is unknown to Holy Scripture. No, our Lord's prayer is distinctly for those whom the Father gave him—for every one of these, but for no others. His "I will" concerns them only.

I feel right glad that there is no sort of personal character mentioned here, but only—"Those whom thou hast given me." It seems as if the Lord in his last moments was not so much looking at the fruit of grace as at grace itself; he did not so much note either the perfections or the imperfections of his people, but only the fact that they were his by the eternal gift of the Father. They belonged to the Father—"thine they were." The Father gave them to Jesus—"thou gavest them me." The Father gave them as a love token and a means of his Son's glorification—"Thine they were and thou gavest them me" and now our Lord pleads that because they were the Father's gift to him he should have them with him. Does anybody raise a cavil as to Christ's right to have those with him who were his Father's, whom his Father gave him, and whom he himself actually took into his own possession? No, they ought to be with him, since they are his in so divine a manner. If I possess a love-token that some dear one has given me I may rightly desire to have it with me. Nobody can have such a right to your wedding-ring, good sister, as you have yourself, and are not Christ's saints, as it

were, a signet upon his finger, a token which his Father gave
him of his good pleasure in him? Should they not be with
Jesus where he is, since they are his crown jewels and his
glory? We in our creature love lift up our hands, and cry,
"My Lord, my Master, let me have this dear one with me a
little longer. I need the companionship of one so sweet, or
life will be misery to me." But if Jesus looks us in the face,
and says, "Is thy right better than mine?" we draw back at
once. He has a greater part in his saints than we can have. O
Jesus, thy Father gave them to thee of old; they are his
reward for the travail of thy soul; and far be it from us to
deny thee. Though blinded by our tears, we can yet see the
rights of Jesus, and we loyally admit them. We cry
concerning our best beloved, "The Lord hath taken away,
and blessed be the name of the Lord." Does not the text
sweetly comfort us in the taking away of one and another,
since it shows how they belong to Christ?

IV. And now, advancing another step, Christ reveals to us
something concerning THE HOME COMPANIONSHIP in the
glory land. Those who are taken away, where are they gone?
The text saith, "I will that they also whom thou hast given
me be with me where I am; that they may behold my glory."

By this language we are impressed with *the nearness of the
saint to Christ in glory*—"that they may be with me." Think
for a moment: when our Lord used these words, and John
took them down, the disciples were with him. They had left
the supper-table where they had feasted together. The
Master had said, "Arise, let us go hence;" and it was in the
very midst of them that the Lord Jesus offered this choice
prayer. Learn, then, that in heaven the saints will be nearer
to Christ than the apostles were when they sat at the table
with him, or heard him pray. That was a nearness which
might consist only in place, and their minds might still be, as
they often were, far away from him: but up in heaven we
shall be one with him in sympathy, in spirit, in conscious
fellowship. We shall be with Jesus in the closest, clearest,
and most complete sense. No fellowship on earth can reach
to the plenitude of the communion which we shall enjoy
above. "With him"—"for ever with the Lord"—this is heaven.
Who would wish to detain from such companionship those
whom we love?

Yet do not drop the thought of place, lest you refine away

the essence of the prayer. Let us see the spiritual clearly, but let us not, on that account, make the sense less real, less matter of fact. To the prayer that his saints may be with him our Lord added the words, "May be with me where I am." Our bodies will rise from the dust, and they must *occupy a place:* that place will be where Jesus is. Even spirits must be somewhere, and that somewhere with us is to be where Jesus is. We are to be, not metaphorically and fancifully, but really, truly, literally with Jesus. We shall enjoy an intense nearness to him in that blessed place which the Father has prepared for him, and which he is preparing for us. There is a place where Jesus is revealed in all the splendour of his majesty, amid angels and glorified spirits; and those whom our Lord's will has taken away from us have not gone into banishment in a mysterious land, neither are they shut up in a house of detention till there is a general jail delivery, but they are with Christ in Paradise. They serve him, and they see his face. Who would be so cruel as to keep a saint from such a fair country? I would desire all good for my children, my relatives, my friends; and what good is better than to be where Jesus is? Are you not glad to hear of the promotion of those you love? Will you quarrel with God because some of your dearest ones are promoted to the skies? The thought of their amazing bliss greatly moderates our natural grief. We weep for ourselves, but as we remember their companionship with the Altogether Lovely One a smile blends with our tears.

Notice the *occupation,* of those who are with Jesus: "That they may behold my glory." I do not wonder that Jesus wants his dear ones to be with him for this purpose, since love always pines for a partner in its joys. When I have been abroad, and have been specially charmed with glorious scenery, I have a hundred times felt myself saying, almost involuntarily, "How I wish that my dear wife could be here! I should enjoy this a hundred times as much if she could but see it!" It is an instinct of affection to seek fellowship in joy. The Lord Jesus is truly human, and he feels this unselfish desire of every loving human heart, and therefore says, "Father, I will that they also, whom thou hast given me, be with me where I am, that they may behold my glory." Our Lord graciously permits his disciples to have fellowship with him in his sufferings, and hence he is all the more desirous

that they should participate in his glory. He knows that
nothing will be a greater joy to them than to see *him* exalted;
therefore he would give them this highest form of delight.
Was not Joseph delighted when he said to his brethren, "Ye
shall tell my father of all my glory in Egypt"; and still more
so when he could actually show his father how great was his
power, how exalted was his rank. It is joy to Jesus to let us
behold his joy, and it will be glory to us to behold his glory.
Should not the redeemed ascend to such blessed delights?
Would you hinder them?

How unselfish it is on our Lord's part to think himself not
fully glorified till we behold his glory! How unselfish he will
make us also, since it will be our glory to see his glory! He
does not say that he is going to take us home, that *we* may be
in glory, but that we may behold *his* glory. His glory is better
to us than any personal glory: all things are more ours by
being his. Glory apart from him were no glory. Beloved, even
as our Lord seems to lose himself in his people, his people
hide themselves away in him. It is his glory to glorify them;
it is their glory to glorify him; and it will be the glory of
glories for them to be glorified together. Who would not go to
this heaven? Who would keep a brother out of it an hour?

Observe the fellowship which exists in the glory land. Read
the verse: "That *they* may behold *my* glory, which *thou* hast
given *me*." What a blending of persons! Where did our Lord's
glory come from? "Thou gavest it me," says Jesus. Hence it is
the Father's glory passed over to the Son. Yet Jesus calls it
"*my* glory," for it is truly his own. The saints are to behold
this, and it will be their glory to see it. Here we have the
Father, and the Elder Brother, and the many brethren, and
a wonderful communism of interests and possessions. It is
ever so in a loving family. There we draw no hard and fast
lines of *meum* and *tuum*. "All thine are mine, and mine are
thine." We ask not whose is this? or whose is that? when we
are at home. If you were to go into a stranger's house, you
would not think of taking this or that; but as your father's
own son you make yourself at home, and no one enquires,
"What doest thou?" Bridegroom and bride do not quarrel
about property whether it be his or hers. Laws have been
made lately to settle different estates for those who are one:
this is well enough when love is gone, but true conjugal love
laughs at all that can make separate that which God hath

joined together. The wife says, "That is mine." "No" saith the
caviller, "it is your husband's." Her answer is, "and therefore
it is mine." In that blessed union into which divine love has
admitted us Christ is ours, and we are Christ's; his Father is
our Father, we are one with him, he is one with the Father;
and hence all things are ours, and the Father himself loveth
us. All this will not only be true in heaven, but it will there
be realized and acted on. So when the Lord brings his people
home, we shall be one with him, and he one with the Father,
and we also in him one with the Father, so that we shall
then find boundless glory in beholding the glory of our Lord
and God. My text has baffled me. I am beaten back by its
blaze of light. Forgive me. I had a thought, but I cannot
express it. The fire of my text burns with such fervent heat
that it threatens to consume me if I draw nearer to it. Easily
could I step into heaven—so I feel at this moment.

V. I must end by speaking of THE HOME ATMOSPHERE.
None of us can wish our departed friends back from their
thrones. Since they have gone to be where Jesus is, and to
enter so fully into the most blissful fellowship with him and
the Father, we would not have them return even for an
instant to this poor country. We only wish that our turn for
migration may come soon. We would not be too long divided
from our fellows. If some of the birds have gone to the sunny
land, let us plume our wings to follow them. There will be
only a little interval between our parting and our everlasting
meeting. Look at the many who died before we came into the
world. Some of them have been in heaven together now for
thousands of years. To them it must seem that they were
only divided by a moment's interval; their continents of
fellowship have made the channel of death seem but a streak
of sea. Soon we shall take the same view of things.

Breathe the home atmosphere. Jesus tells us that the
atmosphere of his home is *love*: "Thou lovedst me before the
foundation of the world." Brethren, can you follow me in a
great flight? Can you stretch broader wings than the condor
ever knew, and fly back into the unbeginning eternity?
There was a day before all days, when there was no day but
the Ancient of Days. There was a time before all time, when
God only was: the uncreated, the only-existent One. The
Divine Three, Father, Son, and Spirit, lived in blessed
consort with each other, delighting in each other. Oh the

intensity of the divine love of the Father to the Son! There was no world, no sun, no moon, no stars, no universe, but God alone; and the whole of God's omnipotence flowed forth in a stream of love to the Son, while the Son's whole being remained eternally one with the Father by a mysterious essential union. How came all this which we now see and hear? Why this creation? this fall of Adam? this redemption? this church? this heaven? How came it all about? It needed not to have been, but the Father's love made him resolve to show forth the glory of his Son. The mysterious volume which has been gradually unfolded before us has only this one design—the Father would make known his love to the Son, and make the Son's glories to appear before the eyes of those whom the Father gave him. This Fall and this Redemption, and the story as a whole, so far as the divine purpose is concerned, are the fruit of the Father's love to the Son, and his delight in glorifying the Son. Those myriads, those white-robed myriads, harping to music infinitely deep, what mean they all? They are the Father's delight in the Son. That he might be glorified for ever, he permitted that he should bear a human body, and should suffer, bleed, and die, so that there might come out of him, as a harvest cometh from a dying and buried corn of wheat, all the countless hosts of elect souls, ordained for ever to a felicity exceeding bounds. These are the bride of the Lamb, the body of Christ, the fullness of him that filleth all in all. Their destiny is so high that no language can fully describe it. God only knows the love of God, and all that it has prepared for those who are the objects of it.

Love wraps up the whole in its cloth of gold. Love is both the source and the channel, and the end of the divine acting. Because the Father loved the Son he gave us to him, and ordained that we should be with him. His love to us is love to the Son. "Not for your sakes do I this, O House of Israel; be ashamed and be confounded." Because of the boundless, ineffable, infinite love of the great Father toward his Son, therefore hath he ordained this whole system of salvation and redemption, that Jesus in the church of his redeemed might everlastingly be glorified. Let our saintly ones go home, beloved, if that is the design of their going. Since all comes of divine love, and all sets forth divine love, let them go to him who loves them—let divine love fulfill its purpose of bringing many sons unto glory. Since the Father once made our Lord perfect by his sufferings, let him now be made perfectly glorious by the coming up of his redeemed from the purifying bath of his atonement. I see them rise like sheep from the washing, all of them gathering with delight at the feet of that great Shepherd of the sheep.

Beloved, I am lost in the subject now. I breathe that heavenly air. Love surrounds all, and conquers grief. I will not cause the temperature to fall by uttering any other words but this—Hold your friends lovingly, but be ready to yield them to Jesus. Detain them not from him to whom they belong. When they are sick, fast and pray; but when they are departed, do much as David did, who washed his face, and ate, and drank. You cannot bring them back again; you will go to them, they cannot return to you. Comfort yourselves with the double thought of their joy in Christ and Christ's joy in them; add the triple thought of the Father's joy in Christ and in them. Let us watch the Master's call. Let us not dread the question—who next, and who next? Let none of us start back as though we hoped to linger longer than others. Let us even desire to see our names in the celestial conscription. Let us be willing to be dealt with just as our Lord pleases. Let no doubt intervene; let no gloom encompass us. Dying is but going home; indeed, there is no dying for the saints. Charles Stanford is gone! Thus was his death told to me— "He drew up his feet and smiled." Thus will you and I depart. He had borne his testimony in the light, even when blind. He had cheered us all, though he was the greatest sufferer of us all; and now the film has gone from the eyes, and the *anguish* is gone from the heart, and he is with Jesus. He smiled. What a sight was that which caused that smile! I have seen many faces of dear departed ones lit up with splendour. Of many I could feel sure that they had seen a vision of angels. Traces of a reflected glory hung about their countenances. O brethren, we shall soon know more of heaven than all the divines can tell us. Let us go home now to our own dwellings; but let us pledge ourselves that we will meet again. But where shall we appoint the trysting place? It would be idle to appoint any spot of earth, for this assembly will never come together again in this world. We will meet with Jesus, where he is, where we shall behold his glory. Some of you cannot do this. Turn from your evil ways.

Turn to the right, where stands that cross, and keep straight on, and you will come to Jesus in glory. Blessed be the name of the Lord! Amen.

2

Fallen Asleep

"...some are fallen asleep."   **1 Corinthians 15:6**

Writing concerning the brethren who had seen the Lord Jesus Christ after his resurrection, and of whom "above five hundred" were present at one time, Paul said that, at the date when he was writing this Epistle, "the greater part" remained alive, "but," he added, "some are fallen asleep."

We might have thought that God, in great mercy, would have preserved the lives of those five hundred brethren to an extreme old age, that, in every part of the globe, there might be extant, as long as possible, someone who would be able to say, "I beheld the Son of God when he was upon the earth. I heard him preach. I saw him die on the cross, and then I looked upon him again after he had risen from the grave;" for every one of these witnesses was worth his weight in gold to the Christian religion. Wherever such a man lived, he must have been, under the blessing of God, the means of convincing many people of the truth of our glorious faith. Yet, dear friends, it does not appear that these invaluable brethren were spared by the shafts of death. These witnesses of Christ's resurrection died as other men did. They had no immunity from death, and no extreme old age was granted to them, for the apostle, writing not so very long after the event, said, "Some are fallen asleep."

From this fact, I gather that lives, which appear to us to be extremely necessary, may not be so regarded by God. Your

own observation will, I am sure, agree with mine, that the
Lord sometimes takes away from us those whom we can
least spare. Those, who seemed to be the pillars of the
church, have been suddenly removed. The fathers amongst
us, those who have been the bravest confessors of the faith,
or the most useful servants of the Saviour, have been called
away. This should teach us,—if we are wise enough to learn
the lesson,—to regard the most invaluable person in our own
Israel as being only lent to us by the Lord, for a season, and
liable to be summoned to higher service at any moment.
Possibly, God takes some men away from us because we
think them absolutely needful. He will not let us trust in an
arm of flesh; and if he is so condescending as to use human
feebleness, and then we go and confide in the feebleness, and
suppose that God's strength is tied up to it, in secret jealousy
he removes the instruments that he has used, that men may
learn not to glory in their fellow-men, or to make idols out of
their Christian brethren and fathers.

It is probable that these witnesses of Christ's resurrection
enjoyed a large measure of reverence from the members of
the Christian Church. Had they lived very long, they might
have been regarded with a superstitious and almost
idolatrous reverence. God intended that his Church should
increasingly live by faith, not by sight; so, while she was in
her infancy he gave her the prop of miracles and also the
support of living witnesses; but when she had somewhat
increased in strength, he no longer gave the power to work
miracles, but left her to rest upon his Word alone; and as she
further progressed, he, in a few years, took away the earthly
witnesses of Christ's life, and death, and resurrection, that
the Eternal Spirit, working through the Word, might stand,
to all time, as the living and unfailing Witness of the fact
that Jesus lived, and died, and "rose again the third day
according to the Scriptures."

The lesson for us all to learn is just this, let us not set too
much store by any of God's servants; and, especially, let us
never reckon that we are essential to the carrying on of his
work. The fly upon the chariot wheel was easily to be
dispensed with, and so are we. Like shadows have we come;
like shadows shall we go. We may be missed; I hope we shall
all live so that many will miss us when we are gone; but they
will brush their tears away, and both the world and the

Church—and especially the Church—will continue to go on without us. While Jesus lives, whoever may die, we shall never have to say, "My father, my father, the chariot of Israel, and the horsemen thereof;" but still shall the Church of God flourish and increase, for the Spirit of God is with her.

Paul wrote, "Some are fallen asleep." Of course, all the witnesses, who saw Christ personally, have long ago fallen asleep; but, among ourselves, it is also true that "some are fallen asleep;" and the truth is impressed upon us more and more forcibly every week. I never expect now to come to this place, on two succeeding Sabbaths, without hearing that some one or other of our friends has departed. Our death-rate, for many years, has been wonderfully small, for God seems to have favoured us by sparing us to one another. We must not forget that, in past days, more of our number were young than is the case with us now; and as we all march onwards towards the inevitable river, the deaths will naturally be more numerous among us than they have been. They are beginning to be so already, and I am continually hearing of one or another of our most useful brethren or sisters being "called home." Almost every day, this truth is impressed upon me: "Some are fallen asleep." I suppose that, all the year round, almost as regularly as the clock ticks, about two a week of our church-members, beside others out of the congregation, are taken up to dwell in the Master's presence. So my subject concerns us just as much as it did those of whom and to whom the apostle wrote.

I. Now, coming to the text, I call your attention, first, to THE FIGURE HERE USED: "Some are fallen asleep."

In the heathen part of the catacombs of Rome, the inscriptions over the place where their dead were buried are full of lamentation and despair. Indeed, the writers of those inscriptions do not appear to have been able to find words in which they could express their great distress, their agony of heart, at the loss of child, or husband, or friend. They pile the mournful words together, to try to describe their grief. Sometimes, they declare that the light has gone from their sky now that their dear ones are taken from them. "Alas! alas!" says the record, "dear Caius has gone, and with him all joy is quenched for ever, for I shall see him no more." Heathenism is hopeless to afford any comfort to the

bereaved. But when you come into that part of the
catacombs which was devoted to Christian sepulture,
everything is different. There you may constantly read these
consoling words, "He sleeps in peace." There is nothing
dreadful or despairing in the inscriptions there; they are
submissive, they are cheerful, they are even thankful;
frequently, they are victorious, and the most common
emblem is not the quenched torch, as it is on the heathen
side, where the light is supposed to have gone out for
ever,—but the palm branch, to signify that the victory
remains eternally with the departed one. It is the glory of
the Christian religion to have let light into the sepulchre, to
have taken the sting away from death, and, in fact, to have
made it no more death to die.

The figure here used is that of falling asleep; it describes
first the act, and then the state: "Some are fallen asleep."
That is the act of death. Having fallen asleep, they remain
so; that is the state of death. For a Christian to die, is,
according to Scripture, *an act of the most natural kind,* for it
is but to fall asleep. What that act really is, in its literal
meaning, I cannot fully explain to you, though I know by
long personal experience; and all of you know, and will soon
know again if you are permitted to fall asleep to-night and to
wake in the morning. Yet you never knew exactly when you
went to sleep. You have often wanted to go to sleep, but you
could not; and probably nobody has ever gone to sleep while
he has tried to do so; but it is when all idea of forcing
slumber has gone from us that gradually we pass into a state
of unconsciousness. Such, perhaps, is death;—the sinking
away, and becoming unconscious of this world, and asleep to
it, though happily conscious of another world, and sweetly
awake to it. That is the act of falling asleep.

Then, after the act of falling asleep, which is death, comes
the state of sleep, in which rest is the main ingredient. Are
believers then asleep? Yes, and no. Never make a figure run
on four legs when it was only meant to go on two. Some
people, when they get hold of a metaphor, want to make it
have as many feet as a centipede, and they seek to draw all
sorts of parallels which were never intended to be drawn.
The fact is, that the saints sleep, first, as to their bodies.
There they lie in the cemetery,—which means, the sleeping-
place,—till dawns the bright illustrious day when those

bodies shall wake again. As for their souls, they are asleep as to this world; their memory and their love are things of the past; they are alike unknowing and unknown as far as this earth is concerned. As to that other world, we read that they shall be "for ever with the Lord." Our Saviour said to the penitent thief, "To-day shalt thou be with me in paradise;" and the prayer of Christ for his people was, that we might be with him where he is,—not to be asleep,—but to behold his glory, the glory which the Father had given him. Hence, the word "sleep" is not to be regarded as implying that the souls of the departed lie in a state of un-consciousness. It is nothing of the kind; it is unconsciousness as to the things of time and sense, but a blessed consciousness as to another and a fairer and brighter and better world than this. Even while I am in this mortal state, when I am asleep, though I may be unaware of anything that is happening in my bedroom, yet, full often, in my sleep, my mind is soaring on the wings of eagles, mounting up to heaven, or diving into the depths, conscious of dreamland, and of the spirit land, though unconscious of the present world for the time being.

The meaning of the term is evidently this,—as sleep brings to us rest, the blessed ones, who have fallen asleep in Christ, are perfectly at rest. It is delightful for a man, who has worked very hard all day, to forget his toils, and fall asleep. Well did Young write, in his *Night Thoughts,* concerning—

"Tired nature's sweet restorer, balmy sleep."

In his sleep, the prisoner in the dungeon forgets his manacles; the slave in the galley forgets his bondage; the poor man forgets his poverty; and he who dreads the approach of danger, drinks a draught of the waters of Lethe, and remembers his fears no more. What a blessing sleep is to this poor, weary frame and to the throbbing brain! The saints in heaven have a better rest than sleep can give, but sleep is the nearest word we can find to describe the state of the blessed. They have no poverty, no toil, no anguish of spirit, no remorse, no struggling with indwelling sin, no battling with foes without and fears within. "They rest from their labours, and their works do follow them." Oh, what a sweet thing to fall asleep, if this be what it is,—to enjoy perfect repose, and to be beyond the reach of all influences

which make life here to be so sorrowful! "Some are fallen
asleep;" that is, they have entered into their rest.

By falling asleep, again, is meant *a state of security*. The
man who is in the battle may be wounded, and may die; but
he who has gone up to his chamber to sleep is supposed
there to be at peace, and out of the reach of danger, though
that is not always the case. But, in those heavenly chambers
where the Lord shall hide away his people, they shall be
perfectly secure. They will never have to keep watch against
"the arrow that flieth by day," or "the pestilence that walketh
in darkness." They are out of gunshot of the enemy. As Dr.
Payson said, when he was dying, "The battle is fought;" so is
it with them, the battle is fought, and the victory is won for
ever. Therefore have they ascended to the hill-tops of glory,
and to the chambers of eternal rest; and there they sleep
while we still struggle hand to hand with the enemy, with
many a deadly thrust, and many an ugly wound. God be
praised that there is a place of safety for all the soldiers of
the cross! "Some are fallen asleep," and so shall we, in due
time, if we are fighting under the banner of Emmanuel, God
with us.

Now let us learn, from this figure of falling asleep, a little
about death; and, especially, about a Christian's death. I
learn from it, first, that *the act is not a painful one, nor even
a disagreeable one*. As I have said before, I cannot really tell
what falling asleep is, for in the very act we ourselves pass
out of the consciousness of it; but, as far as one has watched
children falling asleep, there certainly is no appearance of
any pain, for usually they drop off into slumber very happily,
and that is how God's people shall do when they fall asleep
in Jesus. Do not regard your departure out of the world as a
thing to be surrounded with horror; do not conjure up
hobgoblins, and evil spirits, and darkness, and terror. "The
valley of the shadow of death," of which David spoke, I do not
think was ever meant to be applied to dying, for it is a valley
that he walks through, and he comes out again at the other
side of it; and it is not the valley of death, but only of "the
shadow of death." I have walked through that valley many a
time,—right through from one end of it to the other, and yet
I have not died. The grim shadow of something worse than
death has fallen over my spirit, but God has been with me,
as he was with David, and his rod and his staff have

comforted me; and many here can say the same, and I believe that, often, those who feel great gloom in going through "the valley of the shadow of death," feel no gloom at all when they come to the valley of death itself. There has generally been brightness there for the most sorrowful spirits; and those who, before coming there, have grovelled in the dust, have been enabled to mount as on eagles' wings when they have actually come to the place of their departure into the future state.

The more you think this matter over, the more clearly will it appear to you that there cannot be any pain in death; all pain must be connected with life, it is the living who suffer. In death, we forget all pain. That gentle touch, that divine love-pat that shall end all pain and sorrow, is the thing which men usually call death, but which the apostle rightly calls sleep. There is nothing to be dreaded in it; it may be altogether unattended with pain; I believe that, full often, it is so. To fall asleep is a very natural act, and so it is for us to die. A little child has been playing in the field gathering buttercups and daisies all day long; but, at last, tired right out, he drops asleep upon his mother's lap; what could he do better? So, though we may be unwilling to die, the time will come when we shall have finished our life,—work or play, whichever you may please to call it,—and we shall fall asleep upon the bosom of our God; what better thing could we do? There is a dear old friend of mine, now in heaven; and when he came to this house, one Sabbath-day, I said to him, "Our old friend So-and-so has gone home." The one to whom I spoke was an old man himself, one of our most gracious elders, and he looked at me in a most significant way, and his eyes twinkled as he said, "He could not do better, dear Pastor; he could not do better; and you and I will do the same thing one of these days. We also shall go home!" Our aged friend, as I told you, has himself gone home since that time, and now I may say of him, "He could not have done better." Why! that is where good children always go at night,—home. If they ran away, where would they go? When our night comes, beloved children of God, you and I also must go home; do we feel at all afraid of such a prospect? If so, surely our love to our Heavenly Father, and to our Elder Brother, and to our home above, must be growing somewhat cold.

And then, again, *if we did not die, we should wish to do so.*
Certainly, when people cannot sleep, that is the very thing
they crave for. There have, perhaps, been times when you
have been ready to take something which would help to keep
you awake when you have needed to do some special work,
or to watch over some precious sick one; but when night
follows night, and there has been no sleep for you, you do not
want anything to keep you awake then, but you long for
sleep. "Oh, that I could sleep!" you cry. We regard it, always,
as a bad symptom when the sufferer says, "I cannot sleep."
The disciples said, concerning Lazarus, "If he sleep, he shall
do well;" and they spoke wisely, although they misunderstood the meaning of the word sleep in that
connection; and, surely, we shall do well when we fall asleep
in Jesus. It shall become to us the most blessed thing that
God himself can send us. Oh, if we could not die, it would be
indeed horrible! Who wants to be chained to this poor life for
a century or longer? There came to me one, of whom I may
tell the story, for he is dead now; and he said that, if I would
do his bidding, I should live for ever here, for he had
discovered a great secret by which men need never die. I
said to him, "Sir, you seem to me like a man of seventy, and
I should say that you are getting on towards death yourself."
He replied, "Oh, no! I expect some little rash will come out
all over me, in a few years, and then I shall be quite young
again, and start living for another hundred years." He told
me that the people would believe his teaching when he had
been here six or seven hundred years, and I answered that I
thought it was very likely that they would! He offered to
share his great secret with me, dear good man that he was;
but I replied, "I would not give a button with the shank off to
know it; why should I want to live in this wretched penal
colony for ever?" He talked to me for some little time, and
when he found that he could make no impression on me, to
consummate his madness, he asked me to go outside my
door with him; he lifted up the knocker, and rapped two or
three times, saying very solemnly, "Too late! Too late! Ye
cannot enter now." He said that he had shut me out of the
blessing of being here for ever; so I said to him, "I am very
much obliged to you for doing me such a kindness." He
printed books, and gave lectures on the subject, being fully
persuaded in his own mind that he would never die; but he

has died, I knew he would, and I told him so. He said it was my want of faith which made me talk like that, but he himself was confident that he should never die. Oh, what an awful thing it would be if that man's fad could be a fact! Superstition declares it to be the curse upon "the wandering Jew" that he should never die. God be thanked that such a curse has never fallen upon us! No, unless the Lord should come first, we shall fall asleep in him; and what a blessed thing it must be to fall asleep on the bosom of Christ! The child may be afraid to be put to bed in the dark, but it never fears to fall asleep upon its mother's breast; and we might dread to be laid to rest out there in the cold cemetery, all alone, but we do not fear to sleep in Jesus. Such a state as that is a thing to be desired, not to be dreaded.

II. Now let us come to our second point, THE THOUGHTS AROUSED BY THIS FIGURE: "Some are fallen asleep."

First, thinking about the many who have fallen asleep, let me ask,—*How did you treat them?* If your conscience pricks you concerning that matter, I want you to act towards the living saints in such a way as you would like to have done supposing you never see them again. When there has been an angry meeting or parting,—when there have been hard words spoken,—when there have been unkind thoughts,—when you could not enjoy true fellowship with some Christian friend, suppose that, the next morning, somebody came round to your house, and said, "Brother So-and-so is dead," you would feel deeply pained to think that he had fallen asleep after you had so treated him. People who have killed their minister by their unkindness,—and there have been, alas! many who have done so;—those who have killed other persons,—and there have been many of that sort, who have vexed and worried other people into their graves;—may well think, with great sorrow, "Some are fallen asleep, but we did not treat them with the love and kindness we ought to have shown to them." Think over that matter, dear friends, and see to it that no such regrets shall be possible to you.

"Some are fallen asleep." Then, *who is to fill their place?* Many have already gone from us this year, and others keep on going. Sunday-school teachers go: who will be "baptized for the dead," by taking their places in the ranks, and filling the gap? Hear this, ye church-members who are doing

nothing for Christ! "Some are fallen asleep." Let that little
sentence be a clarion call to you to wake up, and go, and
occupy the vacant positions, that the work of Christ may
know no lack in any part of his vineyard. Rouse ye! Rouse ye!
you who are asleep in another sense, and now that so many
are being taken away from us, dig up the talent that has
been wrapped in a napkin, and buried in the earth, and put
it out to blessed usury by employing it in the Master's
service.

"Some have fallen asleep." *Then you and I also will fall
asleep before long.* It cannot be a long while for some of you
who are getting grey or white; it may be a very short time for
some of us who have scarcely reached the middle of life; and
even you young folk may soon fall asleep, too, for I have seen
a child asleep in the morning as well as at night, and so have
you. Oh! let us not live in this world as if we thought of
staying here for ever; but let us try to be like a pious Scotch
minister, who was very ill, and, being asked by a friend
whether he thought himself dying, answered, "Really, friend,
I care not whether I am or not; for, if I die, I shall be with
God; and if I live, he will be with me." There is not much to
choose between those two blessed states; but let us recollect,
by the memory of every one who has fallen asleep, that the
time of our own departure is coming by-and-by, and it may
be very soon!

But, as for those who have fallen asleep in Jesus, we need
not fret or trouble ourselves about them. To cut their faces,
in token of their mourning for the dead, was natural to the
heathen; well might they torture themselves in their
hopeless grief, for they believed the separation to be eternal.
But as for us, when children go upstairs to bed, do their
elder brothers and sisters, who sit up later, gather together,
and cry because the other children have fallen asleep? Ah,
no! they feel that they have not lost them, and they expect to
meet again in the morning; and so do we! Therefore, let us
not weep and lament to excess concerning the dear ones who
are fallen asleep in Christ, for all is well with them. They are
at rest: shall we weep about that? They are enjoying their
eternal triumph: shall we weep about that? They are as full
of bliss as they can possibly be: shall we weep about that? If
any of your sons and daughters were taken away from you to
be made into kings and queens in a foreign land, you might

shed a tear or two at parting, but you would say, "It is for their good; let them go." And do you grudge your well-beloved their crown of glory, and all the bliss which God has bestowed upon them? If the departed could speak to us, they would say, "Bless God for us. Do not sit down and mourn because we have entered into his glory; but rather rejoice because we are with him where he is." Wherefore, let us comfort one another with these words.

III. Lastly, brethren, let us think, for just a minute or two, of THE HOPES CONFIRMED BY THIS FIGURE: "Some are fallen asleep."

First, then, *they are still ours.* If they were really dead, we might say that we had lost them; but as they have only fallen asleep, they are still ours. Wordsworth proclaimed a great truth in that simple little poem of his, "We are seven." There were some of the family buried in the churchyard, but the girl still declared that they were seven, and so they were. Did you ever notice, concerning Job's children, that when God gave him twice as much substance as he had before, he gave him only the same number of children as he formerly had? The Lord gave him twice as much gold, and twice as much of all sorts of property, but he only gave him the exact number of children that he had before. Why did he not give the patriarch double the number of children as well as twice the number of cattle? Why, because God reckoned the first ones as being his still. They were dead to Job's eye, but they were visible to Job's faith. God numbered them still as part of Job's family; and if you carefully count up how many children Job had, you will find that he had twice as many in the end as he had in the beginning. In the same way, consider your friends who are asleep in Christ as still yours,—not lost, any one of them, and say of them "Some are fallen asleep." "Our membership has been diminished," says somebody. Yes, it has been, according to the church-book, and the figures as we reckon them here; but it has not really been diminished. I have, by faith, seen our brethren and sisters flying, like doves to their windows, and ascending to heaven from this place. Every week, some of them are going to the land beyond the skies. My soul has often rejoiced as I have thought of the spiritual children whom God has given me. I might almost claim that great promise which was made to Abraham, "Look now toward heaven, and tell the

stars, if thou be able to number them: and he said unto him,
So shall thy seed be;" for, if they have not reached the
number of the stars yet, they are no more to be reckoned
than are the stars. As I remember how many of them have
already reached the better land, I do not think of them as
lost, for they only fell asleep here, to wake in the presence of
Jesus. Their sleeping bodies also shall wake again when the
resurrection trumpet sounds. No matter what has become of
the particular particles of dust of which those bodies were
composed, the essence of each individual shall be preserved
by omnipotent power, and out of it shall spring an undying
body, remodelled, and fashioned like unto Christ's glorious
body, and the soul shall enter it, and that soul shall be here
again at the coming of Christ, for when he shall come in his
glory, them also who sleep in Jesus will he bring with him,
"wherefore," again I say unto you, "comfort one another with
these words."

This is our last thought, *we shall meet again those who
have fallen asleep.* We said, "Adieu" to them, and so
committed them to God's keeping. We said, "Good-bye," that
is, "God be with you;" and God has been with them. We said,
"Farewell," and they have fared well; and we shall see how
well they have fared to be with Christ, for we shall see them
again. I believe that we shall know them, and have
communion with them, and shall admire Christ's grace in
them, and that it shall be part of our heaven to come not
only "to Jesus the Mediator of the new covenant," but also
"to the general assembly and church of the firstborn, who
are written in heaven."

Now I have finished my discourse, but how far is there any
comfort to some of you in all that I have said? Some of you
work very hard: have you any hope of rest in heaven? If not,
I do pity you, from the very depths of my heart. Some of you
fare very hard: have you any hope of better fare with Christ
for ever? If not, I do indeed pity you, more than I can tell. To
go, from poverty and misery here, to a place where there
shall be no hope for you for ever, will be dreadful indeed. If
there were no hell, I could not endure the thought of being
shut out of heaven; for, to be with Christ, to be with the
Father, to be with the Holy Spirit, to miss the company of
gracious and just men for ever, would be a hell that might
well make men gnash their teeth in torment. Oh, may God

save us all through faith which is in Christ Jesus! May we be
saved to-night; and then it will not matter how soon anyone
may say of us also, "They have fallen asleep," for all will be
well with us for ever. God bless you, dear friends, for Christ's
sake! Amen.

3

The Heaven Of Heaven

"And they shall see his face..."   **Revelation 22:4**

The Italians so much admire the city of Naples, that their proverb is, "See Naples and die;" as if there remained nothing more to be seen after that fair bay and city had been gazed upon. To behold the far fairer sight mentioned in the text men might well be content to die a thousand times. If it shall please God that we shall depart this life before the Master's appearing, we may laugh at death and count it to be gain, seeing that it introduces us to the place where we shall see his face. "Thou canst not see my face and live," said the Lord of old; but that was true of mortals only, and refers not to immortals who have put on incorruption: in yonder glory-land they see the face of God and yet live; yea, the sight is the essence and excellence of their life. Here that vision might be too overpowering for the soul and body, and might painfully separate them with excess of delight, and so cause us death; but up yonder the disembodied spirit is able to endure the blaze of splendour, and so will the body also when it shall have been refined and strengthened in its powers by resurrection from the dead. Then these eyes, which now would be smitten with blindness should they look upon the superlative glory, shall be strengthened to behold eternally the Lord of angels, who is the brightness of his Father's glory and the express image of his person.

Brethren and sisters, regard the object of our expectations!

See the happiness which is promised us! Behold the heaven
which awaits us! Forget for awhile your present cares: let all
your difficulties and your sorrows vanish for a season; and
live for awhile in the future which is so certified by faithful
promises that you may rejoice in it even now! The veil which
parts us from our great reward is very thin: hope gazes
through its gauzy fabric. Faith, with eagle eyes, penetrates
the mist which hides eternal delights from longing eyes.
"Eye hath not seen, nor ear heard, neither have entered into
the heart of man, the things which God hath prepared for
them that love him; but he hath revealed them unto us by
his Spirit, for the Spirit searcheth all things, even the deep
things of God;" and we, in the power of that Spirit, have
known, believed, and anticipated the bliss which every
winged hour is bringing nearer to us.

While our Lord was here below it would have been a great
delight to spiritual minds to have seen his face. I can
scarcely imagine, but perhaps some of you mothers can,
what must have been the joy that flooded the heart of Mary,
when for the first time she gazed upon the lovely face of the
holy child Jesus. I suppose the infant Jesus to have
possessed an extraordinary beauty. A soul absolutely perfect
as his was, must surely have been enshrined in a body
perfect in its symmetry, and attractive in its features. The
overshadowing Spirit, by whose miraculous agency he was
conceived of the Virgin, would scarcely have created an
uncomely body at all, and much less would he have
fashioned an unlovely body for so delightful a person as the
only Begotten of the Father. Methinks, as his virgin mother
looked upon him, and as the wise men and the shepherds
gazed into that dear face, they might all have said with the
spouse of old, "Thou art fairer than the children of men."
That manger held an unrivalled form of beauty: well may
painters strain their art to paint the mother and her
wondrous child, for the spectacle brought shepherds from
their flocks, sages from the far-off land, and angels from
their thrones—heaven and earth were alike intent to see his
face.

It would have been no small joy, methinks, to have seen
the face of Jesus of Nazareth in the years of his maturity,
when his countenance beamed with joy. "At that hour Jesus
rejoiced in spirit, and said, Father, I thank thee." One would

like to have basked in the radiance of a sinless smile: it was a vision fit only for the pure in heart to have traced the fair marks of joy upon the face of Jesus; and such a joy, so spiritual, so refined, so heavenly, so divine! "Father, I thank thee:" blessing God for that eternal decree of election by which he has hidden the things of the kingdom from the wise and prudent, and has revealed them unto babes, and saying, "Even so, Father, for so it seemed good in thy sight." Equally rare must have been the vision which Peter and James, and John beheld, when they looked into that Saviour's face, and saw it transfigured, beams of light flashing from its every feature, and his whole person made to glow with a superhuman splendour. The favoured spectator might well be content to die upon that mount; it was enough to have lived to have beheld his glory so divinely revealed.

Beloved, have you not sometimes felt as I have, that you could have wished to have seen the Well-beloved's face even in its grief and agony? It was not long before the beauty of Jesus began to be marred by his inward griefs and his daily hardships. He appears to have looked like a man of fifty when he was scarcely thirty. The Jews said, "Thou art not yet fifty years old, and hast thou seen Abraham?" His visage was more marred, we are told, than that of any man, and his form more than the sons of men; for he took upon himself our sickness and bare our sorrows, and all this substitutionary grief ploughed deep furrows upon that blessed brow, and made the cheeks to sink, and the eyes to become red with much weeping. Yet fain would I have gazed into the face of the Man of Sorrows; fain would I have seen those eyes which were "as the eyes of doves by the rivers of waters, washed with milk and fitly set;" those founts of pity, wells of love, and springs of grief; fain would I have adoringly admired those cheeks which were as beds of spices, as sweet flowers, and those lips like lilies, dropping sweet-smelling myrrh; for all the suffering that he suffered could not take away from that marred visage its majesty of grace and holiness, nor withdraw from it one line of that mental, and moral, and spiritual beauty which were peculiar to the perfect man. O how terribly lovely that beloved face must have looked when it was covered with the crimson of the bloody sweat, when the radiant hues of his rosy sufferings suffused the lily of his perfection! What a vision

must that have been of the Man of Sorrows, when he said,
"My soul is exceeding sorrowful, even unto death"! What
must it have been to have looked into his face, when his
brow was girt about with the crown of thorns, when the ruby
drops followed each other down those bruised cheeks which
had been spit upon by the shameful mouths of the scorners?
That must have been a spectacle of woe indeed! But,
perhaps, yet more ghastly still was the face of the Redeemer
when he said, "I thirst!" when, in bitterest anguish, he
shrieked, "My God, my God, why hast thou forsaken me!"
Then, indeed, the sun of the universe suffered a horrible
eclipse; then the light of heaven for awhile passed under a
black tempestuous cloud. That face in such a condition we
have not seen, nor shall see; yet, beloved, we shall see his
face.

I could have wished to have been with Mary, and the holy
women, and Joseph, and Nicodemus, when they took his
blessed body from the cross and laid it in the tomb. O for one
gaze into that poor pale dead face—to have seen how death
looked when mirrored in that matchless clay; and how Jesus
appeared when conquered and yet conquering, vanquished
and yet victor, yielding up his body to the spoiler, to be laid
for awhile in the treasure-house of the tomb, and yet
bursting all the bars of the spoiler's den!

But, brethren, there was a glorious change, no doubt, in
the face of our Lord when it was seen by divers brethren
after the resurrection. It was the same face, and they knew
him to be the same Christ. Did they not put their fingers into
the nail-prints and thrust their hand into his side? Did they
not know him to be veritable flesh and bone as they saw him
eat the piece of fish and of an honeycomb? But the face was
restored to its former majesty and radiance, for I suppose it
to have beamed with the dawn-flashes of that light which
now flames forth from it, of which John says, "His face was
as the sun shining in its strength." There were, we believe,
some soft unveilings of that unexampled glory which
glorified saints, day without night, are perpetually beholding
in heaven. That face was for the last time seen when he
ascended and the clouds concealed him. Then, gazing
downward, and scattering benedictions with both his hands,
he appointed his disciples to be his witnesses, and bade
them go and preach his gospel, for he would be with them

alway, even unto the end of the world. Such was the face of
Christ on earth, and the remembrance may serve to inspire
in us a holy panting after the beatific vision which the Lord
hath promised us, and of which we are now about to speak
as the Holy Ghost may graciously give us utterance.

First, this morning, I purpose, brethren, to bring before
your minds *the beatific vision itself*—"They shall see his
face;" then secondly, we shall dwell for a moment upon *the
surpassing clearness of the vision*—"They shall *see* his
face"—in a sense more than usually emphatic; then thirdly,
upon *the privileges, choice and precious, which are involved
in the vision;* and lastly, we shall have a word or two upon
those favoured ones who shall enjoy the sight—"They,"— and
none other—"*They* shall see his face."

I. First, then, THE BEATIFIC VISION.

"They shall see his face." It is the chief blessing of heaven,
the cream of heaven, the heaven of heaven, that the saints
shall there *see Jesus.* There will be other things to see. Who
dare despise those foundations of chrysolite and chrys-
oprasus and jacinth? Who shall speak lightly of streets of
glassy gold and gates of pearl? We would not forget that we
shall see angels, and seraphim, and cherubim; nor would we
fail to remember that we shall see apostles, martyrs, and
confessors, together with those whom we have walked with
and communed with in our Lord while here below. We shall
assuredly behold those of our departed kindred who sleep in
Jesus, dear to us here and dear to us still—"not lost, but
gone before." But still, for all this, the main thought which
we now have of heaven, and certainly the main fulness of it
when we shall come there, is just this: we shall see Jesus.
We shall care little for any of those imaginary occupations,
which have such charms for a certain class of minds that
they could even find a heaven in them. I have read fanciful
periods in which the writer has found celestial joys to consist
in an eternal progress in the knowledge of the laws of God's
universe. Such is not my heaven. Knowledge is not
happiness, but on the contrary, is often an increase of
sorrow.

Knowing, of itself, does not make men happy nor holy. For
mere knowing's sake, I would as soon not know as know, if I
had my choice: better to love an ounce than to know a pound;
better a little service than much knowledge. I desire to know

what God pleases to teach me; but beyond that, even
ignorance shall be my bliss. Some have talked of flitting
from star to star, seeing the wonders of God throughout the
universe, how he rules in this province of his wide domain,
how he governs in that other region of his vast dominion. It
may be so, but it would be no heaven to me. So far as I can at
present judge, I would rather stop at home, and sit at the
feet of Christ for ever than roam over the wide creation.

> "The spacious earth and spreading flood
> Proclaim the wise and powerful God,
> And thy rich glories from afar
> Sparkle in every rolling star.
>
> Yet in Christ's looks a glory stands,
> The noblest wonder of God's hands;
> He, in the person of his Son,
> Has all his mightiest works outdone."

If Jesus were not infinite we should not speak so; but since
he is in his person divine, and as to his manhood, so nearly
allied to us that the closest possible sympathy exists
between us, there will always be fresh subjects for thought,
fresh sources for enjoyment, for those who are taken up with
him. Certainly, brethren and sisters, to no believer would
heaven be desirable if Jesus were not there, or, if being
there, they could not enjoy the nearest and dearest
fellowship with him. A sight of him first turned our sorrow
into joy; renewed communion with him lifts us above our
present cares, and strengthens us to bear our heavy
burdens: what must heavenly communion be? When we have
Christ with us we are content on a crust, and satisfied with
a cup of water; but if his face be hidden the whole world
cannot afford a solace, we are widowed of our Beloved, our
sun has set, our moon is eclipsed, our candle is blown out.
Christ is all in all to us here, and therefore we pant and long
for a heaven in which he shall be all in all to us for ever; and
such will the heaven of God be. The Paradise of God is not
the Elysium of imagination, the Utopia of intellect, or the
Eden of poetry; but it is the heaven of intense spiritual
fellowship with the Lord Jesus—a place where it is promised
to faithful souls that "they shall see his face."

In the beatific vision it is Christ whom they see; and
further, it is his *face which they behold.* They shall not see

the skirts of his robe as Moses saw the back parts of
Jehovah; they shall not be satisfied to touch the hem of his
garment, or to sit far down at his feet where they can only
see his sandals, but they "shall see his face;" by which I
understand two things: first, that they shall literally and
physically, with their risen bodies, actually look into the face
of Jesus; and secondly, that spiritually their mental faculties
shall be enlarged, so that they shall be enabled to look into
the very heart, and soul, and character of Christ, so as to
understand him, his work, his love, his all in all, as they
never understood him before. They shall literally, I say, see
his face, for Christ is no phantom; and in heaven though
divine, and therefore spiritual, he is still a man, and
therefore material like ourselves. The very flesh and blood
that suffered upon Calvary is in heaven; the hand that was
pierced with the nail now at this moment grasps the scepter
of all worlds; that very head which was bowed down with
anguish is now crowned with a royal diadem; and the face
that was so marred is the very face which beams resplendent
amidst the thrones of heaven. Into that selfsame
countenance we shall be permitted to gaze. O what a sight!
Roll by, ye years; hasten on, ye laggard months and days, to
let us but for once behold him, our Beloved, our hearts' care,
who "redeemed us unto God by his blood," whose we are, and
whom we love with such a passionate desire, that to be in his
embrace we would be satisfied to suffer ten thousand deaths!
They shall actually see Jesus.

Yet the spiritual sight will be sweeter still. I think the text
implies that in the next world our powers of mind will be
very different from what they are now. We are, the best of
us, in our infancy as yet, and know but in part; but we shall
be men then, we shall "put away childish things." We shall
see and know even as we are known; and amongst the great
things that we shall know will be this greatest of all, that we
shall know Christ: we shall know the heights, and depths,
and lengths, and breadths of the love of Christ that *passeth*
knowledge. O how delightful it will be then to understand
his everlasting love; how without beginning, or ever the
earth was, his thoughts darted forward towards his dear
ones, whom he had chosen in the sovereignty of his choice,
that they should be his for ever! What a subject for delightful
meditation will the covenant be, and Christ's suretyship

engagements in that covenant when he undertook to take
the debts of all his people upon himself, and to pay them all,
and to stand and suffer in their room! And what thoughts
shall we have then of our union with Christ—our federal,
vital, conjugal oneness! We only talk about these things now,
we do not really understand them. We merely plough the
surface and gather a topsoil harvest, but a richer subsoil lies
beneath. Brethren, in heaven we shall dive into the lowest
depths of fellowship with Jesus. "We shall see his face," that
is, we shall see clearly and plainly all that has to do with our
Lord; and this shall be the topmost bliss of heaven.

In the blessed vision the saints see Jesus, and they see him
clearly. We may also remark that *they see him always;* for
when the text says "They shall see his face," it implies that
they never at any time are without the sight. Never for a
moment do they unlock their arm from the arm of their
Beloved. They are not as we are—sometimes near the
throne, and anon afar off by backslidings; sometimes hot
with love, and then cold with indifference; sometimes bright
as seraphs, and then dull as clods—but for ever and ever
they are in closest association with the Master, for "they
shall see his face."

Best of all, they see his face as it is now in all its glory.
John tells us what that will be like: In his first chapter he
says, "His head and his hairs were white like wool, as white
as snow," to mark his antiquity, for he is the Ancient of days.
"And his eyes were as a flame of fire; and his countenance
was as the sun shineth in his strength." Such is the vision
which the redeemed enjoy before the throne; their Lord is all
brightness, and in him there is nothing to weep over,
nothing to mar his glory. Traces there doubtless are upon
that wondrous face, of all the griefs he once endured, but
these only make him more glorious. He looks like a lamb
that has been slain and wears his priesthood still; but all
that has to do with the shame, and the spitting, and
slaughter, has been so transformed that the sight is all
blissful, all comforting, all glorious; and in his face there is
nothing to excite a tear or to beget a sigh. I wish my lips
were unloosed and my thoughts were free, that I could tell
you something more of this sight, but indeed it is not given
unto mortal tongues to talk of these things; and I suppose
that if we were caught up to see his face and should come

back again, yet should we have to say like Paul, that we had heard and seen that which it was not lawful for us to utter. God will not as yet reveal these things fully to us, but he reserves his best wine for the last. We can but give you a few glimpses, but O beloved, wait a little, it shall not be long ere you also shall see his face!

II. Secondly, we turn to another thought, THE SURPASSING CLEARNESS OF THAT VISION.

"They shall *see* his face." The word "see" sounds in my ears with a clear, full, melodious note. Methinks we see but little here. This, indeed, is not the world of sight; "we walk by faith, not by sight." Around us all is mist and cloud. What we do see, we see only as if men were trees walking. If ever we get a glimpse of the spirit-world, it is like yonder momentary lightning-flash in the darkness of the tempest, which opens for an instant the gates of heaven, and in the twinkling of an eye they are closed again, and the darkness is denser than before, as if it were enough for us poor mortals to know that there is a brightness denied to us as yet.

The saints see the face of Jesus in heaven, because they are purified from sin. The pure in heart are blessed: they shall see God, and none others. It is because of our impurity which still remains that we cannot as yet see his face, but their eyes are touched with eye-salve, and therefore they see. Ah, brethren, how often does our Lord Jesus hide himself behind the clouds of dust which we ourselves make by our unholy walking. If we become proud, or selfish, or slothful, or fall into any other of our besetting sins, then our eye loses its capacity to behold the brightness of our Lord; but up yonder they not only do not sin, but they cannot sin; they are not tempted, and there is no space for the tempter to work upon, even could he be admitted to try them; they are without fault before the throne of God; and, surely, this alone is a heaven—to be rid of inbred sin, and the plague of the heart, and to have ended for ever the struggle of spiritual life against the crushing power of the fleshly power of death. They may well see his face when the scales of sin have been taken from their eyes, and they have become pure as God himself is pure.

They surely see his face the more clearly because all the clouds of care are gone from them. Some of you while sitting here to-day have been trying to lift up your minds to

heavenly contemplation, but you cannot; the business has
gone so wrong this week; the children have vexed you so
much; sickness has been in the house so sorely; you yourself
feel in your body quite out of order for devotion—these
enemies break your peace. Now they are vexed by none of
these things in heaven, and therefore they can see their
Master's face. They are not cumbered with Martha's cares;
they still occupy Mary's seat at his feet. When shall you and
I have laid aside the farm, and the merchandise, and the
marrying, and the burying, which come so fast upon each
other's heels, and when shall we be for ever with the Lord—

> "Far from a world of grief and sin,
>   With God eternally shut in"?

Moreover, as they have done with sins and cares, so have
they done with sorrows. "There shall be no more death,
neither sorrow, nor crying, neither shall there be any more
pain, for the former things are passed away." We are none of
us quite strangers to grief, and with some of us pain is an
inseparable companion; we dwell in the smoky tents of
Kedar still. Perhaps it is well that we should so be tried
while we are here, for sanctified sorrow refines the soul; but
in glory there is no affliction, for the pure gold needeth not
the furnace. Well may they then behold Christ when there
are no tears to dim their eyes, no smoke of this world to rise
up between them and their Beloved, but they are alike free
from sin, and care, and sorrow. They see his face right
gloriously in that cloudless atmosphere, and in the light
which he himself supplies.

Moreover, the glorified see his face the more clearly
because there are no idols to stand between him and them.
Our idolatrous love of worldly things is a chief cause of our
knowing so little of spiritual things. Because we love this
and that so much, we see so little of Christ. Thou canst not
fill thy life-cup from the pools of earth, and yet have room in
it for the crystal streams of heaven. But they have no idols
there—nothing to occupy the heart; no rival for the Lord
Jesus. He reigns supreme within their spirits, and therefore
they see his face.

They have no veils of ignorance or prejudice to darken
their sight in heaven. Those of us who most candidly
endeavor to learn the truth are nevertheless in some degree

biased and warped by education. Let us struggle as we may, yet still our surroundings will not permit us to see things as they are. There is a deflection in our vision, a refraction in the air, a something everywhere which casts the beam of light out of its straight line so that we see rather the appearance than the reality of truth. We see not with open sight; our vision is marred; but up yonder, among the golden harps, they "know, even as they are known." They have no prejudices, but a full desire to know the truth: the bias is gone, and therefore they are able to see his face. O blessed thought! One could almost wish to sit down and say no more, but just roll that sweet morsel under one's tongue, and extract the essence and sweetness of it. "They see his face." There is no long distance for the eye to travel over, for they are near him; they are in his bosom; they are sitting on his throne at his right hand. No withdrawals there to mourn over: their sun shall no more go down. Here he stands behind our wall; he showeth himself through the lattices; but he hides not himself in heaven. O when shall the long summer days of glory be ours, and Jesus our undying joy for ever and ever? In heaven they never pray—

> "Oh may no earthborn cloud arise
> To hide thee from thy servant's eyes;"

but for ever and for aye they bask in the sunlight, or rather, like Milton's angel, they live in the sun itself. They come not to the sea's brink to wade into it up to the ankles, but they swim in bliss forever. In waves of everlasting rest, in richest, closest fellowship with Jesus, they disport themselves with ineffable delight.

III. The third part of the subject which commands our attention this morning is THE MATCHLESS PRIVILEGE WHICH THIS VISION INVOLVES.

We may understand the words "they shall see his face" to contain five things. They mean, first, *certain salvation*. The face of Jesus Christ acts in two ways upon the sons of men: with some it is a face of terror—"Before his face heaven and earth fled away." It is written concerning him, "Who may abide the day of his coming? and who shall stand when he appeareth? for he is like a refiner's fire, and like fullers' soap." A sight of Christ's face will be to the ungodly eternal destruction from the presence of the Lord. But if there are

some men who shall see his face, who shall sit down and
delight themselves in gazing upon the face of the great
Judge upon the throne, then those persons are assuredly
saved; they are abiding the day of his coming; they are
dwelling with the eternal flame without being consumed;
they are resting on the bosom of our God who is a consuming
fire; and yet, like the burning bush of old, though glowing
with the glory they are not consumed by the heat. O happy
men, who can live where others must expire; who can find
their heaven where a carnal world must eternally find its
hell! This is the first thing in the text. "They shall see his
face;" then they are everlastingly safe. The second privilege
is, they shall have a *clear knowledge* of him. I have dwelt
upon that thought before, and merely mention it to complete
the summary. To look into the face of Christ signifies to be
well acquainted with his person, his office, his character, his
work. So the saints in heaven shall have more knowledge of
Christ than the most advanced below. As one has said, the
babe in Christ admitted to heaven discovers more of Christ
in a single hour than is known by all the divines of the
assemblies of the church on earth. O yes, our catechisms and
our creeds, and even our Bible—all these reveal but very
little of what we shall discover when we shall see his face.
Our text implies also *conscious favour*. Was not that the old
benediction, "The Lord lift up his countenance upon you"?
He has lifted it up upon the glorified, and they see it world
without end. Here it is our joy of joys to have the Lord
smiling upon us, for if he be with us who can be against us?
If we know that he loves us, and that he delights in us, it
mattereth not to us though earth and hell should hate us,
and men cast out our names as evil. In heaven, then, they
have this to be their choice privilege. They are courtiers who
stand always in the monarch's palace, secure of the
monarch's smile. They are children who live unbrokenly in
their father's love, and know it, and rejoice to know it
evermore.

The fourth privilege involved in the text is that of *close
fellowship*. They are always near to Jesus. They are never
hoping that they are with him, and yet fearing that they are
not; they have none of those inward struggles which make
life so unhappy to some of us; they never say—

"'Tis a point I long to know;"

But they see his face and are in hourly communion with their Lord. Perfect spirits are always walking with the Lord, for they are always agreed with him. In glory they are all Enochs, walking with God. There for ever and for ever they lie in the bosom of Jesus, in the nearest possible place of communion with him who redeemed them with his blood.

And this involves a fifth privilege, namely, *complete transformation.* "They shall be like him, for they shall see him as he is." If they see his face they shall be "changed from glory to glory" by this face-to-face vision of the Lord. Beholding Christ, his likeness is photographed upon them; they become in all respects like him as they gaze upon him world without end.

Thus have I very briefly mentioned the privileges involved in seeing Christ face to face.

IV. We must conclude by noting WHO THEY ARE TO WHOM THIS CHOICE BOON IS AFFORDED BY THE DIVINE MERCY.

"They shall see his face." Who are they? They are all his elect, all his redeemed, all his effectually called ones, all the justified, all the sanctified. They are the tens of thousands and myriads who have died in Jesus, of whom the Spirit saith, "Blessed are the dead which die in the Lord." Thank God we are not strangers to those who now behold his face. As we look back to the associations of our youth, and to the friendships of our manhood, we remember many whose privilege it has been to precede us, and to know long before us the things which we desire and expect so soon to learn. Some are taken away to see his face while yet young. We bless God that our babes shall have the same heaven as our holy sires; they shall not be placed in the back settlements of Canaan, but they shall with equal clearness see the face of Jesus. Those dear boys and girls who learnt to love Christ and made a profession of his name in their youth, were never spared to reach the ripeness of manhood and womanhood, but they shall equally see his face with the gravest and most reverend fathers of the church. I read of no secondary joys. Whoever may have invented the doctrine of degrees in heaven I do not know, but I believe there is as much foundation for it in Scripture as there is for the doctrine of purgatory, and no more. All the saints shall see

their Master's face. The thief dying on the cross was with
Christ in paradise, and Paul could be no more. I like
sometimes to think of heaven in the same way as old Ryland
did when he wrote his rhyming letter from Northampton—

> "They all shall be there,
> The great and the small:
> For I shall shake hands
> With the blessed St. Paul."

Doubtless so we shall. Whether dying young or old, whether
departing after long service of Christ, or dying immediately
after conversion as with the thief, of all the saints shall it be
said in the words of the text, "They shall see his face." What
more can apostles and martyrs enjoy?

Do you regret that your friends have departed? Do you
lament that wife, and husband, and child, and father, and
grandparent, have all entered into their rest? Be not so
unkind, so selfish to yourself, so cruel to them. Nay, rather,
soldier of the cross, be thankful that another has won the
crown before you, and do you press forward to win it too. Life
is but a moment: how short it will appear in eternity. Even
here hope perceives it to be brief; and though impatience
counts it long, yet faith corrects her, and reminds her that
one hour with God will make the longest life to seem but a
point of time, a mere nothing, a watch in the night, a thing
that was and was not, that has come and gone.

So we will close our sermon by observing that they who see
his face already make only a part of the great "they" who
shall see his face, for many of us here below are on the way
to the same reward. So many as have felt the burden of sin,
and have come to the cross-foot and looked to those five
crimson founts, the wounds of Jesus; so many as can say,
"He is all my salvation and all my desire;" so many as can
serve him feeling that for them to live is Christ; so many as
shall fight day by day against sin, and shall overcome
through the blood of the Lamb; so many as by the eternal
Spirit's power shall be kept by faith unto salvation—so many
shall see his face. It is mine to hope to see it, and it is yours
too. Beloved, the hope shall not be disappointed, it maketh
not ashamed; we shall see his face, and that vision shall
yield us perfect bliss.

I fear my text is not true of all here assembled. Just this

word with the unconverted: I am afraid you may almost say with Balaam, "I shall see him but not now, I shall behold him but not nigh." For every eye shall see him, and they also which crucified him; and what will they say when they see him? These ungodly ones, what will they do? They shall cry to the rocks, "Hide us;" and to the mountains, "Cover us from the face of him that sitteth on the throne." Ah, my dear hearer, what a dreadful thing it will be if that very face which is the heaven of your mother, and the heaven of your husband, or the heaven of your wife and of your child, should be the hell to you from which you shall desire to be hidden. Now it must be the case unless first of all you seek his face on earth. Certain Greeks said to the disciples, "Sir, we would see Jesus." I wish you had that same desire this morning in a spiritual sense, for he himself has said, "Look unto me, and be ye saved, all the ends of the earth." If you see him now by simple faith as your Saviour, you shall see him at the last as your King, your Friend, your Beloved; but you must first see him to trust him here, or you shall not see him to rejoice in him hereafter.

"Ye sinners, seek his grace,
Whose wrath ye cannot bear:
Fly to the shelter of his cross,
And find salvation there."

May God, even our own God, bless you for Jesus' sake. Amen.

4

Preparation For Heaven

"Now he that hath wrought us for the selfsame thing is God, who also hath given unto us the earnest of the Spirit."

2 Corinthians 5:5

How very confidently Paul contemplates the prospect of death! He betrays no trembling apprehensions. With the calmness and serenity, not merely of resignation and submission, but of assurance, and courage, he appears joyous and gladsome, and even charmed with the hope of having his body dissolved, and being girt about with the new body which God hath prepared for his saints. He that can talk of the grave and of the hereafter with such intelligence, thoughtfulness, faith, and strong desire as Paul did, is a man to be envied. Princes might well part with their crown for such a sure and certain hope of immortality. Could emperors exchange their treasures, their honours, and their dominions, to stand side by side with the humble tent-maker in his poverty, they would be great gainers. Were they but able to say with him, "We are always confident, and willing rather to be absent from the body, and to be present with the Lord," they might well barter earthly rank for such a requital. This side heaven, what can be more heavenly than to be thoroughly prepared to pass through the river of death? On the other hand, what a dreary and dreadful state of mind must they be in who, with nothing before them but to die, have no hope and see no outlet—the pall and the shroud their last adorning; the grave and the sod their destination. Without hope of rising again in a better future, or realising a better heritage than that which should know us no more ere long; no prospects of seeing God face to face with rejoicing; well may men dislike any reference to death. So they shrink from the thought of it; far less can they tolerate its being talked of in common conversation. No marvel that they recoil from the shade of mortality when they are so ill-prepared to face the reality of the soul's departure. But, dear friends, since it is so desirable to be ready to depart, it cannot be inexpedient sometimes to talk about it; and on my part the more so, because there is a proneness in all our minds to start aside from that grave topic which, as God shall help us, shall be our subject this evening—preparation for the great hereafter. "For," saith the Apostle, "God hath wrought us for this self-same thing"; he has prepared us for the dropping of the present body, and the putting on of the next, and he has "given us the earnest of his Spirit."

Our three departments of meditation will be—*the work of preparation itself; the Author of it;* and *the seal which he sets to it,* the possession of which may resolve all scruples as to whether we are prepared or not.

I. THE WORK OF PREPARATION stands first. Is it not almost universally admitted that some preparation is absolutely essential? Whenever the death of a friend or comrade is announced, you will hear the worst-instructed say, "I hope, poor man, he was prepared." It may be but a passing reflection or a common saying. Yet everybody will give expression to it, "I hope he was ready." Whether the words be well understood or not, I do not know; but the currency given to them proves a unanimous conviction that some preparation is necessary for the next world. And, in truth, this doctrine is in accordance with the most elementary facts of our holy religion. Men by nature need something to be done for them before they can enter heaven, and something to be done in them, something to be done with them, for by nature they are enemies to God. Dispute it as ye will, God knows best. He declares that we are enemies to him, and alienated in our hearts. We need, therefore, that some ambassador should come to us with terms of peace, and reconcile us to God. We are debtors as well as enemies to our Creator—debtors to his law. We owe him what we cannot pay, and what he cannot pardon. He must exact obedience, and we cannot render it. He must, as God, demand perfection of us, and we, as men, cannot bring him that perfection. Some mediator, then, must come in to pay the debt for us, for we cannot pay it, neither can we be exempted from it. There must be a substitute who shall stand between us and God, one who shall undertake all our liabilities and discharge them, and so set us free, that the mercy of God may be extended to us. In addition to this, we are all criminals. Having violated the law of God, we are condemned already. We are not, as some vainly pretend, introduced to this world on probation; but our probation is over; we have forfeited all hope; we have broken the law, and the sentence is gone out against us, and we stand by nature as condemned criminals, tenants of this world during the reprieve of God's mercy, in fear of a certain and terrible execution, unless someone come in between us and that punishment; unless some gracious hand bring us a free pardon; unless some voice divine plead and prevail for us that we may be acquitted. If this be not done for us, it is impossible that we should entertain any well-grounded hope of entering heaven. Say, then, brethren and sisters, has this been done for you? I know that many of you can answer, "Blessed be God, I have been reconciled to him through the death of his Son; God is no enemy of mine, nor I of his; there is no distance now between me and God; I am brought near to him, and made to feel that he is near to me, and that I am dear to him." Full many here present can add, "My debts to God are paid; I have looked to Christ, my Substitute; I have seen him enter into suretyship engagements for me, and I am persuaded that he has discharged all my liabilities; I am clean before God's bar; faith tells me I am clean." And, brethren, you know that you are no longer condemned. You have looked to him who bore your condemnation, and you have drunk in the spirit of that verse, "There is, therefore, now no condemnation to them that are in Christ Jesus, who walk not after the flesh, but after the Spirit." Surely this is a preparation for heaven. How could we enter there if our debts were not discharged? How could we obtain the divine favour eternally if we were still condemned criminals? How could we dwell for ever in the presence of God if we were still his enemies? Come, let us rejoice in this, that he hath wrought us for this self-same thing, having championed our cause from the cradle to the grave.

Preparation for heaven consists still further in *something that must be wrought in us,* for observe, brethren, that if the Lord were to blot out all our sins we should still be quite incapable of entering heaven unless there was a change wrought in our natures. According to this Book, we are dead by nature in trespasses and sins—not some of us, but all of us; the best as well as the worst; we are all dead in trespasses and sins. Shall dead men sit at the feasts of the Eternal God? Shall there be corpses at the celestial banquets? Shall the pure air of the New Jerusalem be defiled with the putrefaction of iniquity? It must not, it cannot be. We must be quickened; we must be taken from the corruption of our old nature into the incorruption of the new nature, receiving the incorruptible seed which liveth and abideth for ever. Only the living children can inherit the promises of the living God, for he is not the God of the dead, but of the living; we must be made living creatures by the new-creating power of grace, or else we cannot be made meet for glory. By nature we are all worldly. Our thoughts go after earthly things. We "mind earthly things," as the Apostle says. We seek after the world's joys; the world's maxims govern us; the world's fears alarm us; the world's hopes and ambitions excite us. We are of the earth, earthy, for we bear the image of the first Adam. But, brethren, we cannot go to heaven as worldly men; for there would be nothing there to gratify us. The gold of heaven is not for barter to use, nor for covetousness to hoard. The rivers of heaven are not for commerce, neither are they to be defiled by men. The joys and glories of heaven are all spiritual, all celestial.

> "Pure are the joys above the skies
> And all the region peace."

Such peace is of a heavenly kind, and for heavenly minds. Carnal spirits, greedy, envious spirits—what would they do in heaven? If they were in the place called heaven, they could not be in the state called heaven, and heaven is more a state than a place. Though it is probably both, yet it is mainly the former, a state of happiness, a state of holiness, a state of spirituality, which it would not be possible for the worldly to reach. The incongruity of such a thing is palpable. Therefore, you see, brethren, the Holy Spirit must come and give us new affections. We must have a fresh object set

before us. In fact, instead of minding the things that are
seen, we must come to love and to aspire to the things that
are not seen. Our affections, instead of going downwards to
things of earth, must be allured by things that are above,
where Christ sitteth at the right hand of God. In addition to
our spiritual death and worldliness, we are all unholy by
nature. Not one of us is pure in the sight of God. We are all
defiled and all defiling, but in heaven they are "without fault
before the throne of God." No sin is tolerated there; no sin of
thought, or word, or deed. Angels and glorified spirits
delight to do God's will without hesitation, without demur,
without omission; and we, like them, must be holy, or we
cannot enter into their sacred fellowship.

> "Those holy gates for ever bar
> Pollution, sin, and shame;
> None shall obtain admission there
> But followers of the Lamb."

But what a change must come over the carnal man to make
him holy! Through what washings he must pass! What can
wash him white, indeed, but that far-famed blood of the Son
of God? Through what purification he must pass! What,
indeed, can purify him at all but the refining energy of God
the Holy Ghost? He alone can make us what God would have
us to be, renewed in his image in holiness and righteousness.

That a great change must be wrought in us, even ungodly
men will confess, since the idea of the heaven of the
Scriptures has always been repulsive, never agreeable, to
unconverted men and women. When Mahomet would charm
the world into the belief that he was the prophet of God, the
heaven he pictured was not at all the heaven of holiness and
spirituality. His was a heaven of unbridled sensualism,
where all the passions were to be enjoyed without let or
hindrance for endless years. Such the heaven that sinful
men would like; therefore, such the heaven that Mahomet
painted for them, and promised to them. Men in general, be
they courtly, or be they coarse in their habits, when they
read of heaven in the Scriptures with any understanding of
what they read, curl their lips and ask contemptuously, Who
wants to be everlastingly psalm-singing? Who could wish to
be always sitting down with these saints talking about the
mighty acts of the Lord and the glorious majesty of his

kingdom? Such people cannot go to heaven, it is clear; they have not character or capacity to enter into its enjoyment. I think Whitefield was right. Could a wicked man be admitted into heaven, he would be wretched there; being unholy, he must be unhappy. From sheer distaste for the society of heaven, he might fly to hell for shelter. With the tumult of evil passions in his breast, he could not brook the triumph of righteousness in the city of the blest. There is no heaven for him who has not been prepared for it by a work of grace in his soul. So necessary is this preparation—a preparation for us, and a preparation in us. And if we ever have such a preparation, beyond all question we *must have it on this side of our death*. It can only be obtained in this world. The moment one breathes his last, it is all fixed and settled. As the tree falleth, so it must lie. While the nature is soft and supple it is susceptible of impression, stamp what seal you may upon it; once let it grow cold and hard, fixed and frigid, you can do so no more, it is proof against any change. While the iron is flowing into the mould you can fashion it into what implement you please; let it grow cold, in vain you strive to alter its form. With pen of liquid ink in your hand you write what you will on the paper, but the ink dries, the impress remains, and where is the treachery that shall tamper with it? Such is this life of yours. It is over, all over with you for eternity, beyond alteration or emendation, when the breath has gone from the body. Your everlasting state is fixed then.

> "There are no acts of pardon passed
> In the cold grave to which we haste;
> But darkness, death, and long despair
> Reign in eternal silence there."

We have no intimation in the Word of God that any soul dying in unbelief will afterwards be converted to the faith. Nor have we the slightest reason to believe that our prayers in this world can at all affect those who have departed this life. The masses of priests are fictions, without the shadow of divine authority. Purgatory, or "Pick-purse," as old Latimer used to call it, is an invention for making fat larders for priests and monks, but the Scriptures of truth give it no countenance. The Word of God says, "He that is holy, let him be holy still; he that is filthy, let him be filthy still." Such as

you are when death comes to you, such will judgment find
you, and such will the eternal reward or the eternal
punishment leave you, world without end. Preparation is
needed, and the preparation must be found before we die.

Moreover, we ought to know—for *it is possible for a man to
know whether he is thoroughly prepared.* Some have said
not, but they have usually been persons very little
acquainted with the matter. The writings of those grand old
divines of the Puritan period abundantly prove how
thoroughly they enjoyed the assurance of faith. They did not
hesitate to express themselves in such language as the
Apostle used: "We *know* that if this earthly house of our
tabernacle be dissolved, we have a house not made with
hands, eternal in the heavens." They were wont to speak as
Job doth when he saith, "I *know* that my Redeemer liveth."
And, indeed, many of the children of God among us at this
present time are favoured with a confident, unstaggering
confidence that, let their last hour come when it may, or let
the Lord himself descend from heaven with a shout, there
will be nothing but joy and peace for them—no cause of
trembling, nothing that can give them dismay. Why, some of
us live from year to year in constant assurance of our
preparation for the bliss that awaiteth and the rest that
remaineth for God's people. Beloved, God has not so left us
in such a dubious case that we always need to be enquiring,
"Am I his, or am I not?" He has given us good substantial
grounds to go upon to make sure work of it. He tells us that
"he that believeth and is baptized shall be saved"; if we have
been obedient to these two commands, we shall be saved, for
our God keepeth his word. He tells us that such believers,
patiently continuing in well-doing, inherit eternal life. If we
are kept by his grace, walking in his fear, we may rest
assured that we shall come to the ultimate end of such a life,
namely, the glory which abideth for the faithful. We need not
harbour endless questionings. What miserable work it is to
stand in any doubt on this matter. Let us not be satisfied till
we are sure and confident that heaven will be ours. Alas!
how many put off all thoughts of being prepared to die! They
are prepared for almost anything except the one thing for
which it is most needful to be ready. If the summons should
come to some of you at this moment, how dread it would be!
Were we to see an angel hovering in the air, and should we

have intelligence by a message from the clouds that someone
of us must, on a sudden, leave his body behind him and
appear before God, what cowering down, what trembling,
what muttering of forgotten prayers there would be with
some of you! You are not ready. You never will be ready, I
fear. The carelessness in which you have lived so long has
become habitual. One would think you had resolved to die in
your sins. Have you never heard the story of Archaeus, the
Grecian despot, who was going to a feast, and on the way a
messenger brought him a letter, and seriously importuned
him to read it? It contained tidings of a conspiracy that had
been formed against him, that he should be killed at the
feast. He took the letter, and put it into his pocket. In vain
the messenger urged that it was concerning serious matters.
"Serious matters to-morrow," said Archaeus, "feasting to-
night." That night the dagger reached his heart while he had
about him the warning which, had he heeded it, would have
averted the peril. Alas! too many men say, "Serious things
to-morrow!" They have no misgiving that, when their sport is
over, they will have alike the leisure and the leanings for
these weighty matters. Were it not wiser, sirs, to let these
grave affairs come first? Might ye not, then, find some better
sport of nobler character than all the froth and frivolity to
which fashion leads on? A holy merriment and a sacred
feasting that well become immortal spirits. How vain and
grovelling the mirth which reduces men to children, pleased
with a rattle, tickled with a straw; then brings them down to
drivelling fools, and degrades them often till they become
worse than brutes. I wish I could imprint a solemn thought
on the mind of some careless individuals. Reck ye not that
time is short, that life is precarious, that opportunities cross
your path at lightning speed, that hope flatters those on
whom the fangs of death are fixed; that there is no vestibule
in which to fit your frame of mind; that the shock will always
come sudden at last. What sentence more trite; what
sentiment more prevalent; yet what solemnity more
neglected than this, "Prepare to meet your God"! Propound
it, profess it, preach it as we may, the most of men are
unprepared. They know the inevitable plight, they see the
necessity of preparation, but they postpone and
procrastinate, instead of preparing. God grant you may not
trifle, any of you, until your trembling souls are launched

into that sphere unknown, but not unfeared, and read your doom in hell. Now:—

II. AS TO THE AUTHOR OF THIS PREPARATION FOR DEATH, the text saith, "He that hath wrought us for the self-same thing *is God.*" It is God alone, then, who makes men fit for heaven. He works them to the self-same purpose. Who made Adam fit for Paradise but God? And who must make us fit for the better Paradise above but God? That we cannot do it ourselves is evident. According to the Scriptures, we are dead in trespasses and sins. Can the dead start from the grave of their own accord? Do ye think to see coffins opened and grave-stones uplifted by the natural energy of corpses? Such things were never dreamed of. The dead shall surely rise, but they shall rise because God raises them. They cannot vitalise their inert frames, neither can the dead in sin quicken themselves and make themselves fit for the presence of God. Conversion, which prepares us for heaven, is a new creation. That word "creation" puts all the counsel, the conceit, and the contrivance of man into the background. If anyone saith that he can make a new heart, let him first go and make a fly. Not until he has created such a winged insect let him presume to tell us that he can make a man a new creature in Christ Jesus. And yet to make a fly would not demonstrate that a fly could make itself; and it would offer but a feeble pretext for that wonderful creation which is supposed in a man's making himself a new heart. The original creation was the work of God, and the new creation must likewise be of God. To take away a heart of stone and give a heart of flesh is a miracle. Man cannot do it; if he attempts it, it shall be to his own shame and confusion. The Lord must make us anew. Have not we, who know something of the Lord's working in us, this self-same thing, been made to feel that it is all of his grace? What first made us think about eternal things? Did we, the stray sheep, come back to the fold of our own accord? No; far from it.

> "Jesus sought me when a stranger,
> Wandering from the fold of God."

And ever since we have been living men in Christ Jesus. To whom must we ascribe our preservation and our progress? Must we not attribute every victory over sin, and every advance in the spiritual life, to the operation of God, and nothing at all to ourselves? A poor simpleton once said, "Twas God and I did the work." "Well, but, Charlie, what part did you take in it?" "Sure, then," said he, "I did all I could to stop the Lord, and he beat me." I suppose, did we tell the simple truth, we should say much the same. In the matter of our salvation we do all we can to oppose it—our old nature does—and he overcomes our evil propensities. From first to last, Jesus Christ has to be the Author and the Finisher of our salvation, or it never would have been begun, and it never would have been completed.

Think, beloved, of what fitness for heaven is. To be fit for heaven a man must be perfect. Go, you who think you can prepare yourselves, be perfect for a day. The vanity of your own mind, the provocation of this treacherous world, and the subtle temptation of the devil, would make short work of your empty pretensions. You would be blown about like chaff. Creature perfection, indeed! Was ever anything so absurd? Men have boasted of attaining it, but their very boastings have proved that they possessed it not. He that gets nearest to perfection is the very man who sighs and cries over the abiding infirmities of his flesh. No, if perfection is to be reached—and it must be, or we shall not be fit for heaven—by the operation of God it must be wrought. Man's work is never perfect; it is always marred on the wheel. His best machinery may still be improved upon; his finest productions of art might still be excelled. God alone is perfect, and he alone is the Perfecter. Blessed be God, we can heartily subscribe to this truth, "He that hath wrought us for the self-same thing is God."

But what shall I say to those of you, my friends, who have no acquaintance with God? You certainly cannot be fitted for heaven. Your cause is not committed to him. He is doing nothing for you. He has not begun the good work in you. You live in this world as if there were no God. The thought, the stupendous thought of his "Being" does not affect you. You would not act any differently if there were twenty Gods, or if there were no God. You utterly ignore his claims on your allegiance, and your responsibility to his law. Virtually in thought and deed you are without God in the world. Poor forlorn creature, thou hast forgotten thy Creator. Poor wandering soul, thou hast fallen out of gear with the universe; thou hast become alienated from the great Father

who is in heaven. I tremble at the thought. To be on the wide
sea without rudder or compass; to be lost in the wilderness,
where there is no way! Cheerless as thy condition is,
remember this: Though thou seest not God, God sees thee.
God sees thee now; he hears thee now. If thou breathe but a
desire towards him, that desire shall be accepted and
fulfilled. He will yet begin to work in thee that gracious
preparation which shall make thee meet to be a partaker of
the inheritance of the saints in light. And now, thirdly:—

III. LET THE SEAL OF THIS PREPARATION be briefly, but
attentively considered.

The Apostle says, "He that hath wrought us for the self-
same thing is God, who also hath given unto us *the earnest of
the Spirit.*" Masters frequently pay during the week a part of
the wages which will be due on Saturday night. God gives
his Holy Spirit, as it were, to be a part of the reward which
he intends to give to his people, when, like hirelings, they
have fulfilled their day. Our country friends just before
harvest go out into the fields, and they pick half a dozen ears
that are ripe, braid the ends, and hang them up over the
mantleshelf as a kind of earnest of the harvest. So God gives
us his Holy Spirit to be in our hearts as an earnest of
heaven; and as the ears of wheat are of the same quality and
character as the harvest, so the gift of the Holy Spirit is the
antepast of heaven. When you have him, you have a plain
indication to your soul of what heaven will be. You have a
part of heaven —"a young heaven," as Dr. Watts somewhere
calls it, within you.

Ask yourself, then, dear hearer, this question, "Have I
received the earnest of the Spirit?" If so, you have the
preparation for heaven; if not, you are still a stranger to
divine things, and you have no reason to believe that the
heaven of the saints will be your heritage. Come, now, have
you received the Holy Spirit? Do you reply "How may I
know?" Wherever the Holy Spirit is, he works certain graces
in the soul—repentance, to wit. Hast thou ever repented of
sin? I mean, dost thou hate it? Dost thou shun it? Dost thou
grieve to think thou shouldst once have loved it? Is thy mind
altogether changed with regard to sin, so that what once
seemed pleasure now is pain, and all the sweetness of sin is
poison to thy taste? Where the Holy Spirit is, repentance is
followed by the whole train of graces, all in a measure, not

any in perfection, for there is always room to grow in grace
and in the knowledge of Jesus Christ. Such is *patience,*
which submits to the Lord's will; such, too, the gracious
disposition of *forgiveness,* which enables us to bear injuries
and to forgive those that vex us; such, likewise, that holy
courage which is not ashamed to own our Lord, or to defend
his cause. In fact, where the Holy Ghost is bestowed, all the
graces of the Spirit will be communicated in some degree.
Though they will all need to grow, yet there will be the seeds
of them all. Where the Holy Spirit is, there will be the joy.
No delight can be more animating or more elevating than
that which springs from the indwelling of God in the soul.
Think of God coming to abide in this poor bosom! Why, were
a cross of diamonds or pearls glittering on your breast, some
might envy you the possession of such a treasure; but to
have God within your breast is infinitely better. God
dwelleth in us, and we in him. Oh! sacred mystery! Oh! birth
of joy unspeakable! Oh! well of bliss divine that maketh
earth like heaven! Hast thou ever had this joy—the joy of
knowing that thou art pardoned; the joy of being sure that
thou art a child of God; the joy of being certain that all
things work together for thy good; the joy of expecting that
ere long, and the sooner the better, thou shalt be for ever
beyond gunshot of fear, and care, and pain, and want?
Where the Spirit of God is, there is more or less of this joy,
which is the earnest of heaven.

This gift, moreover, will be conspicuously evidenced by a
living faith in the Lord Jesus Christ. The Holy Ghost is not
in you if you rely on anything but Jesus; but if, as a poor
guilty sinner, you have come to him, partaken of his gracious
pardon, kissed his blessed feet, and are now depending upon
him alone, you have received the Holy Ghost, and you have
got the antepast of heaven.

Brethren and sisters, it is intensely desirable that we
should seek more to be consciously filled with the Holy
Spirit. We get easily contented with a little spiritual
blessedness. Let us grow more covetous of the best gifts. Let
us crave to be endued with the Holy Spirit, and to be
baptized in the Holy Ghost and in fire. The more we get of
him the more assurance we shall have of heaven for our
peace, the more foretastes of heaven for our happiness, and
the more preparation for heaven in lively hope.

Thus have I shown you the need of preparation, the Author of preparation, and the great seal which proves the verity of that preparation. If your honest conscience allows your humble claim to have received this sacred token of salvation, how happy you should be! Do not be afraid to be happy. Some Christians seem to court the gloom of despondency as if they dared not bask in the sunshine of heaven. I have sometimes heard people say that they have *not enjoyed themselves*. No, dear friends; pity, methinks, if any of us ever should. It would be a poor kind of enjoyment if we merely enjoyed ourselves. But, oh! it is delightful when you can enjoy your God, and when you can enjoy the mercies that are in him, and the promises that are in him, and the blessings which, through him, come to you. When you gather round the table of the Lord's love, do not be afraid to partake of the feast. There is nothing put there to be looked at. There is no confectionery spread out for show. If you dare conclude that you are living in Christ, and living on Christ, do not be afraid to sing as you go home:—

> "Now I can read my title clear,
> To mansions in the skies;
> I bid farewell to every fear,
> And wipe my weeping eyes."

It will be a blessing to your family for you to be happy. You may find that something has gone wrong while you have been away. Go home as happy as you can be, and you will be better able to bear the cares and vexations that must and will befall you. Keep your spirit well worked up to the fear of the Lord, and the enjoyment of his presence. Then, if some little cross matter should come to disquiet you, you can say, "Who am I that I should be vexed and chafed, or lose my temper, or be cast down about such a matter as this? This is not my sphere of well-being; this is not my heaven; this is not my God."

> "If thou shouldst take them all away,
> Yet should I not repine;
> Before they were possess'd by me,
> They were entirely thine."

"Nor would I speak a murmuring word,
Though the whole world were gone;
But seek enduring happiness,
In thee, and thee alone."

But, oh! suppose you feel persuaded and honestly admit that you are not prepared to die, not made meet for heaven. Do not utterly despair, but be grateful that you live where the gospel is preached. "Faith cometh by hearing, and hearing by the Word of God." Be much in hearing the Word, and be much in earnest prayer that the hearing may be blessed to your soul. Above all, give diligence to that divine command which bids thee trust in Jesus Christ, whom he hath sent. Eternal life lies in the nutshell of that one sentence, "Believe in the Lord Jesus Christ, and thou shalt be saved." All that is asked of you—and even that grace gives you—is simply to trust in him who, as Son of God, died for the sins of men. God give you that faith, and then may you meet death with joy, or look forward to the coming of the Lord with peace, whichever may be your lot. Amen.

5

"For Ever With The Lord"

"...to be with Christ; which is far better." **Philippians 1:23**

The apostle was confined in the guard-room of the
Prætorium. It is very probable that he had a soldier
chained to his right hand, and another to his left, and it is
very possible that this position suggested to him the
expression, "I am in a strait betwixt two." He was literally
held by two forces, and he was mentally in the same
condition, exercised with two strong desires, influenced by
two master passions, and he did not know to which he
should yield. He says, "Between the two I am in perplexity,"
or, as some render it, "I am straitened by the pressure of the
two things." Picture yourself sitting in a gloomy dungeon, a
captive in the hands of the cruel tyrant Nero, and under the
supervision of the infamous præfect Tigellinus, the most
detestable of all Nero's satellites. Conceive yourself as
expecting soon to be taken out to death—perhaps to such a
horrible death as the refined cruelty of the monster had
often devised—as, for instance, to be smeared over with
bituminous matter and burned in the despot's garden, to
adorn a holiday. What would be your feelings? If you were
not a Christian I should expect you to tremble with the fear
of death, and even if you were a believer, I should not marvel
if the flesh shrunk from the prospect. Paul was an utter
stranger to any feeling of the kind. He had not the slightest
dread of martyrdom. He calls his expected death a

departure, a loosing of the cable which holds his ship to the shore, and a putting forth upon the main ocean. So far from being afraid to die, he stands fully prepared, he waits patiently, and even anticipates joyfully the hour when his change shall come. On the other hand, I can readily imagine that amidst the miseries of a wretched prison, subject to frequent insults from a rude soldiery, you might be seized with a desire to escape from life. Good men have felt the power of that feeling. Elijah said, "Let me die: I am no better than my fathers." Job sighed to be hidden in the grave, and oftentimes under far less afflictions than those which vexed the apostle, good men have said, "Would God this life were at an end, and these miseries over; I am a-weary, I am a-weary; when will death release me?" I see nothing of that feeling in the apostle; he is not restive under the chain; there is not a trace of impatience about him. He admits, and joyfully admits it, that to be with Christ is far better; but upon consideration he sees reasons for his remaining here, and therefore he cheerfully submits to whatever may be the Lord's will. He does not choose, his mind is so wrapt up with God, and free from self, that he cannot choose. What a blessed state of heart to be in! One might be willing to wear Paul's chain on the wrist to enjoy Paul's liberty of mind. He is a freeman whom the Lord makes free, and such a man Nero himself cannot enslave. He may confine him in the military prison, but his soul walks at liberty through the earth, yea, and climbs among the stars. Paul, instead of being either weary of life or afraid of death, sits down and coolly considers his own case, as calmly indeed as if it had been the case of some one else. Do you observe how he weighs it? He says, to depart and to be with Christ is, in itself considered, far better, he therefore desires it; but looking round upon the numerous churches which he had formed, which in their feebleness and exposure to many perils needed his care, he says, on the other hand, "To abide in the flesh is more needful for you." He holds the balance with unquivering hand, and the scales quietly vibrate in equilibrium: one rises and then the other, gently swaying his heart by turns. He is in a strait, a blessed strait betwixt two, and he does not say that he knew not which of two things to avoid, or which to deprecate, but his mind was in such a condition that either to live or to die seemed equally desirable, and he says, "What I shall *choose* I wot not." It is a poor choice, to choose to live in a dungeon, and an equally poor business, as men judge it, to choose to die, but the apostle regards both of them as choice things, so choice that he does not know which to select. He deliberates as coolly and calmly as if he were not at all concerned about it: and indeed it is fair to say he was not at all concerned about it, he was moved by a higher concern than any which had to do with himself, for his main object was the glory of God. He desired the glory of God when he wished to be with Christ, he desired the same when he was willing to remain with Christ's people, and to labour on.

His mind, as we have seen, hung in an equilibrium between two things, but he is clear enough upon one matter, namely, that considering his own interests only, it would greatly increase his happiness to depart and to be with Christ. He had said the same before, when he declared that, "To die is gain." He had no doubt that to be loosed from the body and suffered to fly away to Jesus, would be a great boon to him. Of that assurance we will now speak.

I. The first thing to which I shall call your attention is THE APOSTLE'S CERTAINTY CONCERNING THE DISEMBODIED STATE: "Having a desire to depart, and to be with Christ; which is far better." Now, the apostle was an eminently conscientious man. At the time when he was a Jewish teacher, whatever else he might not be, he was very conscientious—he verily thought that he did God service in persecuting the Christians; and throughout the whole of his subsequent career, in every incident of his history we mark him as pre-eminently a man guided by conscience. If he believed a thing to be right, he attended to it; and if anything struck him as being wrong, he could not be persuaded to countenance it. He would not do or say that which he did not fully believe to be right and true. It is a grand thing to meet with a witness of this order, for his testimony can be relied on. What such a man affirms we may be quite certain is correct, so far as he knows.

And withal, the apostle was eminently cool. He was a man of well-balanced reason. I should think that logic greatly preponderated amongst his faculties. John has a warm and glowing heart, and one does not wonder that he is rather a warm lover of Jesus than a systematic unfolder of doctrine;

Peter is impulsive, and when he writes he writes with force, but it is not the force of reasoning. Paul is calm, collected; you never find him excited beyond the bounds of reason. He is as orderly, correct, and argumentative as a Grecian sage. He is enthusiastic to a white heat, but withal he still holds himself well in hand. The coursers of his imagination can outstrip the wind, but he always holds the reins with a strong hand, and knows how to turn them, or to make them stand still at his pleasure. It is a great thing to receive the testimony of a man who is both conscientious to tell what he believes to be true, and calm and logical to form a clear judgment as to what is really fact.

Now this man, Paul, was convinced that there is a future state for believers, he was quite sure about it, and he believed it to be a future conscious state, which commenced the moment they died, and was beyond measure full of blessedness. He did not believe in purgatorial fires through which believers' souls must pass; much less did he believe the modern and detestable heresy which some have broached, that like the body the soul of the saint dies until the resurrection; but he was wont to speak of being "absent from the body and present with the Lord," and here he speaks about departing not to sleep or to lie in the cold shade of oblivion till the trumpet should arouse him, but to depart and immediately to be with Christ, which is far better. What had made this very conscientious and very collected man come to this conclusion? I suppose he would have replied first, that he had been converted by a sight of the Lord Jesus Christ. On the road to Damascus, while desperately set against the religion of Jesus, the Lord himself had appeared to him, so that he had seen Jesus with his own eyes, and had heard him speak. About that sight and sound he had no question: he was sure that he had seen the Lord Jesus and heard his voice. He was so certain of this that he was led to give up his position in society, which was a very elevated one, to lose his repute, which he greatly valued, to be rejected by his countrymen whom he loved with more than ordinary patriotism, and to run continual risk of death for the sake of the truth to which he was a witness. He was content to be made the offscouring of all things for the love of that once despised Saviour who, out of the windows of heaven, had looked down upon him in mercy. Now, he was quite sure that Jesus Christ came from somewhere, and went back to some place or other. He felt sure that there must be a place where the man Jesus Christ dwelt, and he felt quite certain that wherever that might be it would be a place of happiness and glory. Recollecting the prayer of the Lord Jesus, which John had recorded, "Father, I will that they also whom thou hast given me be with me where I am, that they may behold my glory," he was quite certain that as soon as saints died they would be where their glorious Lord Jesus was, and would share his honours.

Remember, also, that this judicious and truthful witness tells us that he had on other occasions distinct evidence of the disembodied state. He informs us that he was caught up into the third heaven, and there heard things which it was not lawful for a man to utter. He observes that he does not understand how he went there, but of the fact he is quite sure. His body was here on earth still alive, and yet his spirit was caught away into heaven; the question with him was, whether he was in the body or out of the body, and I dare say his metaphysical mind often tried to untie that knot. His soul must have remained in the body to keep the body alive, and if so, how could it go up to heaven; and yet into heaven he was quite clear that he had entered. At last the apostle came to the conclusion that whether in the body or out of the body he could not tell, but God knew. This, however, he was sure of, that he had been caught up into paradise, or the third heaven, and therefore there was a paradise; he had heard words which it was not possible for him to utter, therefore there was a place where glorious words were to be heard, and glorious words to be said, and he was quite sure, not merely as a matter of belief; but as a matter of observation, that there was a place into which disembodied spirits go, where they are with Jesus, their Lord, which is far better. It is clear that it would not be far better for a saint to die and sleep till the resurrection than it would be to work on here. It would be evidently by far a better thing for saints to continue in life till Christ came, than to lie dormant in oblivion; yet he says it is far better for them to depart, and the ground of his judgment lies in the fact that there is a place of real happiness, of intense joy, where it is far better for the disembodied spirit to be than for it to remain here in the body. About this Paul expressed no sort of doubt. There

was such a state; it was a state of great joy, so that even to
him who was one of the greatest apostles, the most useful of
the saints, and the most honoured with his Master's blessing
—even to him to depart and to be with Christ, would be far
better.

I want you also to notice that he does not express any sort
of doubt about his own entrance into a state of felicity so
soon as he should depart. He does not say, as I am afraid
some here would have done, "It would be far better,
certainly, for me to die if I were sure I should then be with
Christ." Oh, no; he had risen above such hesitation. Dear
brethren, it is a wretched state to be in to be saying, "It
would be sweet for me to depart if, indeed, these glories were
for me." He had got beyond all doubt as to whether eternal
bliss would be his; he was sure of that, and why are we not
sure, too? Why do we hesitate where he spoke so
confidently? Had Paul something to ground his confidence
upon which we have not? Do you suppose that Paul reckoned
he should be saved because of his abundant labours, his
earnest ministry, and his great successes? Far from it; know
ye not what he himself said, "God forbid that I should glory
save in the cross of our Lord Jesus Christ"? As for anything
that he had ever done, he declared that he trusted to be
found in Christ, not having his own righteousness, which
was of the law, but the righteousness which is of God by
faith. Now, where Paul built we build, if we build aright; our
hope is founded upon the righteousness of Christ, upon the
grace of God, upon the promise of our heavenly Father. Well,
I dare to say it, he, the chief of the apostles, had not a
solitary grain of advantage over any one of us as to the basis
and essence of his hope. Mercy, grace, atoning blood, the
precious promise; these alone he built on, for other
foundation can no man lay. If Paul was sure of eternal bliss,
I would be sure of it too; nay, I am; are you, beloved? Are you
equally as sure of being with Christ as Paul was? You should
be, for you have the same reason for certainty as the apostle
had, if indeed you are believing in the Lord Jesus. God is not
a God of perhapses, and ifs, and buts, but he is a God of
shalls and wills, of faithful truth and everlasting verities.
"He that believeth on him is not condemned." "There is,
therefore, now no condemnation to them that are in Christ
Jesus." "He that believeth and is baptized, shall be saved."

"Who shall lay anything to the charge of"—what? Paul, the apostle? No, but "of God's elect"? Of all of them, of any one of them whom you shall please to select, however humble, however obscure; they are all safe in Jesus. He is made sin for us that we might be made the righteousness of God in him, and we may, each one of us, cry, "I know whom I have believed, and am persuaded that he is able to keep that which I have committed to him until that day." So much, then, concerning the apostle's certainty as to the disembodied state, its happiness, and his own possession of it before long.

II. It is very interesting to notice THE APOSTLE'S IDEA OF THAT STATE. He says, "To be with Christ." It is a one-sided idea, and it is almost a one-worded description of it. "To be with Christ." I have no doubt Paul had as enlarged ideas as to what the state of disembodied spirits would be as the most intelligent and best read Christian that ever lived. I have no doubt he would have said, "Yes, there is fellowship among the saints: we shall sit down with Abraham, and Isaac, and Jacob in the kingdom of heaven: it will be certainly as true in heaven as it is on earth that we have fellowship one with another." I have no doubt, he believed that heaven was a place of a far clearer knowledge than any we possess below: he said so once—"Here I know in part, but there shall I know even as I am known." Some Christians have entertained the idea that they shall gaze upon the various works of God in distant parts of his universe, and enjoy infinite happiness in beholding the manifold wisdom of God—very possible, and if it will conduce to their happiness—very probable. Perhaps Paul believed all that, but we do not know whether he did or not. Here it is plain that he gives us only one idea. He was a man of great mind and much information, but here he gives us only one idea—for my part, one that perfectly satisfies me, and I think one which charms and fills to overflowing the heart of every believer. He describes the disembodied state as "to be with Christ." A very exclusive idea! No, a very inclusive idea—for it takes in all the heaven which the largest mind can conceive. It does seem to omit a great many things, but I dare say Paul felt that they were such trifles that it did not matter about forgetting them.

Being with Christ is so great a thing that he mentioned it alone. I think he did this first, because his love was so concentrated upon Christ that he could think of nothing else in connection with going away to heaven. There is a wife here, perhaps, and her husband has accepted an appointment in India. He has been long away, and the years of his forced absence have been weary to her. She has had loving messages from him and kind letters, but often has she sighed, and her heart has looked out of the windows towards the east, yearning for his return; but now she has received a letter entreating her to go out to her husband, and without hesitation she has resolved to go. Now, if you ask her what she is going to India for, the reply will be, "I am going to my husband." But she has a brother there. Yes, she will see him, but she does not tell you that; her great thought is that she is going to her husband. She has many old friends and companions there, but she is not drawn to the far-off land by desire for their company, she crosses the sea for the sake of her beloved. But her husband has a handsome estate there, and he is wealthy, and has a well-furnished house and many servants. Yes, but she never says, "I am going out to see my husband's home," or anything of that kind. She is going to her husband. That is the all-absorbing object. There may be other inducements to make the voyage, but to be with her beloved is the master object of her journey. She is going to the man she loves with all her soul, and she is longing for the country, whatever that country may be, because he is there. It is so with the Christian, only enhanced in a tenfold degree. He does not say, "I am going to the songs of angels, and to the everlasting *chorales* of the sanctified," but, "I am going to be with Jesus." It would argue unchastity to Christ if that were not the first and highest thought. To come back to the figure—and it is one which Christ himself would approve of, for he continually uses the metaphor of marriage in relation to himself and the soul—if that woman did regard as the first thing in that journey out to the East, the sight of some other person, or the mere enjoyment of wealth and possessions, it would argue that she had little love to her husband, that she was not such a wife as she ought to be. And if it could be so that the Christian should have some higher thought than being with Christ, or some other desire worth mentioning in the same day with it, it would look as if he had not presented himself as a chaste virgin to Christ, to be his and his alone. I see, therefore, why Paul calls the disembodied state a being with Christ, because his love was all with his Lord.

And, no doubt, there was this further reason amongst others—he was persuaded that heaven could not be heaven if Christ was not there. Oh, to think of heaven without Christ! It is the same thing as thinking of hell. Heaven without Christ! It is day without the sun; existing without life, feasting without food, seeing without light. It involves a contradiction in terms. Heaven without Christ! Absurd. It is the sea without water, the earth without its fields, the heavens without their stars. There cannot be heaven without Christ. He is the sum total of bliss; the fountain from which heaven flows, the element of which heaven is composed. Christ is heaven and heaven is Christ. You shall change the words and make no difference in the sense. To be where Jesus is is the highest imaginable bliss, and bliss away from Jesus is inconceivable to the child of God. If you were invited to a marriage feast, and you were yourself to be the bride, and yet the bridegroom were not there—do not tell me about feasting. In vain they ring the bells till the church tower rocks and reels, in vain the dishes smoke and the red wine sparkles, in vain the guests shout and make merry: if the bride looks around her and sees no bridegroom, the dainties mock her sorrow and the merriment insults her misery. Such would a Christless heaven be to the saints. If you could gather together all conceivable joys, and Christ were absent, there would be no heaven to his beloved ones. Hence it is that heaven is to be where Christ is.

> To dwell with Christ, to feel his love,
> Is the full heaven enjoyed above;
> And the sweet expectation now,
> Is the young dawn of heaven below.

And, beloved, just to be with Christ is heaven—that bare thing. Excuse my using such words; I only want to make the sense the stronger. That bare thing, just to be with Christ is all the heaven a believer wants. The angels may be there or not, as they will, and the golden crowns and harps present or absent as may be, but if I am to be where Jesus is, I will find angels in his eyes, and crowns in every lock of his hair; to me the golden streets shall be my fellowship with him, and the harpings of the harpers shall be the sound of his voice. Only to be near him, to be with him—this is all we want. The apostle does not say, "to be in heaven, which is far better:" no, but, "to be with Christ; which is far better," and he adds no description; he leaves the thoughts just as they are, in all their majestic simplicity. "To be with Christ; which is far better."

But what is it to be with Christ, beloved? In some sense we are with Christ now, for he comes to us. We are no strangers to him. Even while we are in this body we have communion with Jesus; and yet it must be true that a higher fellowship is to come, for the apostle says, that while we are present in the body we are absent from the Lord. There is a sense in which, so long as we are here, we are absent from the Lord; and one great saint used to say upon his birthday that he had been so many years in banishment from the Lord: to abide in this lowland country, so far from the ivory palaces, is a banishment at the very best. All that we can see of Christ here is through a glass darkly; face to face is true nearness to him, and that we have not reached as yet.

What will it be, then, to be with Christ? Excuse me if I say it will be, first of all, exactly what it says, namely, to be with him. I must repeat that word—it is heaven only to be with him. It is not merely what comes out of being with him, his company itself is heaven. Why, even to have seen Jesus in his flesh was a privilege:—

> "I think when I read that sweet story of old,
> When Jesus was here among men,
> How he took little children like lambs to his fold,
> I should like to have been with him then.
> I wish that his hands had been placed on my head,
> That his arms had been thrown around me,
> And that I might have seen his kind look when he said,
> 'Let the little ones come unto me.'"

I think I should have found a little heaven in gazing on that blessed form. But our text speaks of a different sort of being with him, for there were people near him here in body who were a long way off from him in spirit. The text speaks of being with him in the spirit when the soul shall have shaken itself loose of the flesh and blood, and left all its slough behind it, and gone right away, to bask in the glory of Jesus, to participate in the nature of Jesus; and, best of all, to abide near to his person, with the God-man Mediator, who is Lord of all.

Still, there will flow out of that nearness the following things among many others. We shall enjoy, first of all, a clearer vision of him. Oh, we have not seen him yet! Our views of him are too dim to be worth calling sights. The eyes of faith have looked through a telescope and seen him at a distance, and it has been a ravishing vision; but when the eyes of the soul shall really see him—him, and not another, him for ourselves, and not another for us, oh, the sight! Is not the thought of it a burning coal of joy? The sight of his very flesh will charm us, his wounds still fresh, the dear memorials of his passion still apparent. The perception of his soul will also delight us, for our soul will commune with his soul, and this is the soul of communion. The sight of his Godhead, so far as created spirit can see it, will also ravish us with joy.

And then we shall have a brighter knowledge of him. Here we know in part—we know the names of his offices, we know what he has wrought, we know what he is working for us; but there those offices will shine in their splendour, and we shall see all that he did for us in its real weight and value; we shall comprehend then the height and depth, and know the love of Christ which passeth knowledge, as we do not know it at this hour.

And with that will come a more intimate intercourse. Our soul will lean her head on Jesus' bosom, our heart will get into his heart and hide herself in his wounds. What must it be to speak to him as our soul will speak to him, as our spirit nature will commune with his inmost nature, his spirit speaking to our spirits, without a veil between! We shall not see him looking down from the windows, but we shall rest in his arms, in a far more intimate intercourse than any we can enjoy this side the grave. To-day I see him through the grating of my prison-windows, and my heart is ready to leap out of my body; what will it be when his left hand shall be under my head, and his right hand shall embrace me?

And then, beloved, when we shall be with him it will be unbroken fellowship. There will be no sin to blind our eyes to his charms, or to entice us away from his love. Blessed be God, there will be no Monday mornings to recall us to the world, but our sacred Sabbath will last on for ever. Doubts,

backslidings, and spiritual chills will then be gone for ever.
No more shall we cry, "Saw ye him whom my soul loveth?"
but we shall hold him, and never let him go. There will be no
need even for the spirit to fall asleep, and so suspend its joy;
it will find its true rest in constant communion with Jesus. It
is possible to live in fellowship with Jesus here always;
possible, but, oh, how few ever reach it! but there we shall all
have reached it, the very lowest amongst us, and we shall be
with the Lord for ever.

And then we shall have a sight of his glory, and though I
put this after a sight of himself, yet, remember, our Lord
thinks much of it. He prayed, "Father, I will that they also
whom thou hast given me be with me where I am, that they
may behold my glory." We have seen something of his
shame, and have been partakers in the reproach that is
poured upon his gospel; but we shall see him then with silver
sandals on the feet that once were mired by the clay of earth,
and a crown of gold upon the once thorn-pierced brow. We
shall see him when his hands shall gleam as with gold rings
set with beryl, and look no more like a malefactor's hand
nailed to the cruel wood. Then shall we say—

> His body's like bright ivory
> With sapphires overlaid,
> His limbs like marble pillars
> In golden sockets stayed.

Then looking on his face we shall understand Solomon's
Song, when he said, "His countenance is as Lebanon,
excellent as the cedars; his voice is most sweet, yea, he is
altogether lovely." One would wish to leap right away out of
this body to behold him in his glory.

And then, beloved, we shall share in the glory too, for his
joy will be our joy, his honour will be our honour. Our spirits
which wrestled hard here below, and had to strive against a
thousand outward enemies, and inward doubts and fears,
will then be all light, and joysome, and gladsome, full of the
life of God, and beaming with ecstatic bliss. The Lord grant
us to know this in due season, and so we shall if, indeed, we
are believers in Jesus. So you see Paul's one idea was that he
should be with Jesus; that was all; he cared little for
anything else.

III. Very briefly, let us consider THE APOSTLE'S ESTIMATE OF THIS DISEMBODIED STATE. He says, "To be with Christ; *which is far better.*" Now, the Greek has a triple comparative. We could not say "far more better" in our language, but that would be a fair translation. We will therefore read, "It is far rather preferable," or it is much better to be with Christ away from the body, than it would be to abide here. Now, you must recollect that Paul does not claim for the disembodied state that it is the highest condition of a believer, or the ultimate crown of his hopes. It is a state of perfection so far as it goes; the spirit is perfect, but the entire manhood is not perfect while the body is left to moulder in the tomb. One half of the saint is left behind in the grave; corruption, earth, and worms have seized upon it, and the grand concluding day of our manifestation can only come when the redemption of the body is fully achieved. The fulness of our glory is the resurrection, for then the body will be united to our spirit, and perfected with it. At present the saints who are with Jesus are without their bodies, and are pure spirits; their humanity is in that respect maimed; only half their manhood is with Jesus; yet even for that half of the manhood to be with Christ is far better than for the whole of their being to be here in the best possible condition. Now, the apostle does not say, that to be with Christ is far better than to be here, and to be rich, young, healthy, strong, famous, great, or learned: Paul never thinks of putting those petty things into contrast with being with Christ. He had got above all that. There was he sitting chained in the dungeon, the poorest man in the emperor's dominions, and often, I have no doubt—for he was getting on to be "such an one as Paul the aged," and wrote particularly about an old cloak he had left at Troas—often he felt rheumatic pains shooting through him; and he did not find this life to have many attractions of wealth or ease, though he might have had them if he had chosen them as his portion. He had given them all up, and counted them as insignificant trifles, not to be mentioned at all, for Jesus' sake. He is not speaking of the low joys of this world; he is far above such considerations; but he does mean that to be with Christ is infinitely superior to all the joys of Christians. Anything that the most of Christians know about Christ and heavenly joys and heavenly things is very poor compared with being with

Christ. But he meant more than that; he meant that the highest joys which the best taught believer can here possess are inferior to being with Christ. For, let me say, Paul was no obscure believer; he was a leader among the followers of Christ. Could he not say, "Thanks be unto God, who always maketh us to triumph in every place"? He knew the graces of the Holy Spirit, he had them abundantly; he was head and shoulders above the tallest Christian here; he had the highest experience of any man out of heaven, and it was that which he contrasted with being with Christ, and he said that the most that we could get here of heavenly things was not to be compared with being with Christ. That was far, far, far better. And truly, brethren, so it is. Thanks be to God for all the mercies of the pilgrimage, for all the dropping manna and the following stream; but oh, the wilderness with all its manna, is nothing compared with the land that floweth with milk and honey. Let the road be paved with mercy, it is not so sweet as the Father's house of the many mansions to which it leads. It is true that in the battle our head is covered, the wings of angels oft protect us, and the Spirit of God himself nerves our arm to use the sword; but who shall say that the victory is not better than the battle? The warrior who has won the most of victory will tell you that the gladdest day will be when the sword rattles back into the scabbard, and the victory is won for ever. Oh, the wooing of Christ and the soul, this is very sweet: the rapturous joys we have had in the love-making between Christ and us, we would not exchange with emperors and kings, even if they offered us their crowns; but the marriage day will be better far, the glorious consummation of our soul's highest desire, when we shall be with our Wellbeloved where he is. Far better, said the apostle, and he meant it; far better it is.

He did not say—and I want you to notice this again— though he might have said it, "We shall be better in condition; no poverty there, no sickness there;" he did not say, "We shall be better in character;" he might have said it: there will be no sin, no depravity, no infirmity, no temptation there. He did not say, "We shall be better in employment," though surely it will be better to wait on the Master, close at his hand, than to be here amongst sinners and often amongst cold-hearted saints. He did not say, "We shall have better society there," though, truth to tell, it will be better to be with the perfect than with the imperfect. Neither did he say we should see fairer sights there, though we shall see the city that hath foundations of jasper, whose light is the light of the Lamb's own presence. But he did say, "To be with Christ." He summed it up there. The bare being with Christ would be far better. And so it will be. Our spirit longs for it.

Yet mark you, for all that, he said he felt a pull the other way. He had a twitch towards stopping on earth, as well as a pull towards going to heaven, for he said, "To abide in the flesh is more needful for you." How I love Paul for thinking of the churches here when he had got heaven before him. Anthony Farindon says it is like a poor beggar woman outside the door, and she carries a squalling child, and some one says, "You may come in and feast, but you must leave the babe outside;" and she is very hungry, and she wants the feast; but she does not like to leave the babe, and so she is in a strait betwixt two. Or, he says again, it is like a wife who has children at home, five or six little ones, and her husband is on a journey, and suddenly there comes a letter which says that he wants her, and she must go to him, but she may do as she thinks best. She desires to go to her husband, but who will take care of the last little babe, and who is to see to all the rest? and so she is in a strait betwixt two. She loves him and she loves them. So stood the apostle, and oh! it is blessed to think of a man having such a love for Christ that for Christ's sake he loves poor souls well enough to be willing to stop out of heaven awhile. "Oh," says he, "it is all gain for me to go to heaven; for me to die is far better; yet there are some poor sinners who need to be called, some poor trembling saints to be comforted, and I do not know which is the best;" and the apostle stands puzzled; he does not know which it shall be. There we leave him. May we get into the same blessed embarrassment ourselves.

The last word shall be this. Concerning our beloved friends gone from us, we do not sorrow as those who are without hope; what is more, we do not sorrow at all. If we chance to sorrow, it is for ourselves, that we have lost their present company, but as for them it is far better with them; and if the lifting of our little finger could bring them back again, dear as they are to us, we would not be so cruel as to subject them again to the troubles of this stormy sea of life. They are

safe landed. We will go to them, we would not have them
return to us.

Then, with regard to ourselves, if we have believed in
Jesus we are on our journey home, and all fear of death is
now annihilated. You notice the apostle does not say
anything at all about death, he did not think it worth
mentioning; in fact, there is no such thing to a Christian. I
have heard of people being afraid of the pains of death.
There are no pains of death: the pain is in life. Death is the
end of pain. It is all over. Put the saddle on the right horse.
Do not blame death for what he does not do. It is life that
brings pain: death to the believer ends all evil. Death is the
gate of endless joy, and shall we dread to enter there? No,
blessed be God, we will not.

And this points us to the fountain of bliss while we are
here, for if heaven is to be with Christ, then the nearer we
get to Christ here, the more we shall participate in that
which makes the joy of heaven. If we want to taste heaven's
blessed dainties while here below, let us walk in unbroken
fellowship with him—so we shall get two heavens, a little
heaven below, and a boundless heaven above, when our turn
shall come to go home. Oh, I wish you were all on the way to
being with Christ. If you do not go to be with Christ, where
can you go? Answer that question, and go to Jesus now by
humble faith, that afterwards he may say, "Come; ye did
come on earth, now come again, ye blessed of my Father,
inherit the kingdom prepared for you from before the
foundation of the world."

6

Heavenly Rest

"There remaineth therefore a rest to the people of God."
Hebrews 4:9

The Apostle proved, in the former part of this and the latter part of the preceding chapter, that there was a rest promised in Scripture called the rest of God. He proved that Israel did not attain that rest; for God sware in his wrath, saying, "They shall not enter into my rest." He proved that this did not merely refer to the rest of the land of Canaan; for he says that after they were in Canaan, David himself speaks again in after ages concerning the rest of God, as a thing which was yet to come. Again he proves, that "seeing those to whom it was promised did not enter in, because of unbelief, and it remaineth that some must enter in, therefore," saith he, "there remaineth a rest to the people of God."

"My rest," says God: the rest of God! Something more wonderful than any other kind of rest. In my text it is (in the original) called the *Sabbatism*—not the Sabbath, but the rest of the Sabbath—not the outward ritual of the Sabbath, which was binding upon the Jew, but the inward spirit of the sabbath, which is the joy and delight of the Christian. "There remaineth therefore"—because others have not had it, because some are to have it—"There remaineth therefore a rest to the people of God."

Now, this rest, I believe, is partly enjoyed on earth. "We that have believed do enter into rest;" for we have ceased

from our own works, as God did from his. But the full
fruition and rich enjoyment of it remains in the future and
eternal state of the beatified on the other side the stream of
death. Of that it shall be our delightful work to talk a little
this morning. And oh! if God should help me to raise but one
of his feeble saints on the wings of love to look within the
veil, and see the joys of the future, I shall be well contented
to have made the joy-bells ring in one heart at least, to have
set one eye flashing with joy, and to have made one spirit
light with gladness. The rest of heaven! I shall try first to
exhibit it and then to *extol it.*

I. First, I shall try to EXHIBIT the rest of heaven; and in
doing so I shall exhibit it, first by way of contrast, and then
by way of comparison.

1. To begin, then, I shall try to exhibit heaven *by way of
contrast.* The rest of the righteous in glory is now to be
contrasted with certain other things.

We will contrast it, first, *with the best estate of the
worldling and the sinner.* The worldling has frequently a
good estate. Sometimes his vats overflow, his barns are
crammed, his heart is full of joy and gladness; there are
periods with him when he flourishes like a green bay tree,
when field is added to field, and house to house, when he
pulls down his barns and builds greater, when the river of
his joy is full, and the ocean of his life is at its flood with joy
and blessedness. But ah! beloved, the state of the righteous
up there is not for a moment to be compared with the joy of
the sinner;—it is so infinitely superior, so far surpassing it,
that it seems impossible that I should even try to set it in
contrast. The worldling, when his corn and his wine are
increased, has a glad eye and a joyous heart; but even then
he has the direful thought that *he may soon leave his wealth.*
He remembers that death may cut him down, that he must
then leave all his fair riches behind him, and sleep like the
meanest of the land in a narrow coffin, six feet of earth his
only heritage. Not so the righteous man: he has obtained an
inheritance which is "undefiled, and that fadeth not away."
He knows that there is no possibility of his losing his joys;

> "He is securely blessed,
> Has done with sin, and care, and woe,
> And doth with Jesus rest."

He has no dread of dissolution, no fear of the coffin or the shroud, and so far the life of heaven is not worthy to be put in comparison with the life of the sinner. But the worldling, with all his joys, always has *a worm at the root* of them. Ye votaries of pleasure! the flush upon your cheek is frequently but a painted deception. Ah! ye sons and daughters of gaiety! the light foot of your dance is not in keeping with the heavy woe of your miserable spirits. Do you not confess that if by the excitement of company you for awhile forget the emptiness of your heart, yet silence, and the hour of midnight, and the waking watches of your bed, bid you sometimes think that there must be something more blessed than the mere wanderings of gaiety in which you now are found? You are trying the world some of you; speak then! Do you not find it empty? Might it not be said of the world, as an old philosopher said of it, when he represented a man with it in his hands smiting it and listening to its ringing? Touch it, touch it! make it ring again; it is empty. So it is with the world. You know it is so; and if you know it not as yet, the day is coming when after you have plucked the sweets you shall be pricked with the thorn, and when you shall find that all is unsatisfactory that does not begin and end with God. Not so the Christian in heaven. For him there are no nights; and if there be times of solitude and rest, he is ever filled with ecstatic joy. His river floweth ever full of bliss, without one pebble of sorrow over which it ripples; he has no aching conscience, no "aching void the world can never fill." He is supremely blessed, satisfied with favour, and full with the goodness of the Lord. And ye know, ye worldlings, that your best estates often bring you great anxiety, *lest they should depart from you.* You are not so foolish yet as to conceive that riches endure for ever. You men of business are frequently led to see that riches take to themselves wings and fly away. You have accumulated a fortune; but you find it is harder to retain than it is to get. You are seeking after a competence; but you find that you grasp at shadows that flit away—that the everlasting vicissitudes of business and the constant changes of mankind are causes of prudent alarm to you, for you fear that you shall lose your gods, and that your gourd shall be eaten by the worm, and fall down, and your shadow shall be taken away. Not so the Christian. He lives in a house that can never hasten to decay; he wears a crown,

the glister of which shall never be dim; he has a garment
which shall never wax old; he has bliss that never can depart
from him, nor he from it. He is now firmly set, like a pillar of
marble in the temple of God. The world may rock, the
tempest may sway it like the cradle of a child; but there,
above the world, above the perpetual revolution of the stars,
the Christian stands secure and immovable; his rest
infinitely surpasseth yours. Ah! ye shall go to all the fabled
luxuries of eastern monarchs, and see their dainty couches
and their luscious wines. Behold the riches of their
pleasantry! How charming is the music that lulls them to
their sleep! How gently moves the fan that wafts them to
their slumber! But ah!

> "I would not change my blest estate
> For all the world calls good or great;
> And whilst my faith can keep her hold
> I envy not the sinner's gold"—

I reckon that the richest, highest, noblest condition of a
worldly man is not worthy to be compared with the joy that
is to be revealed hereafter in the breasts of those who are
sanctified. O ye spendthrift mortals, that for one merry
dance and a giddy life will lose a world of joys! O fools that
catch at bubbles and lose realities! O ten thousand times
mad men, that grasp at shadows and lose the substance!
What! sirs, do you think a little round of pleasure, a few
years of gaiety and merriment, just a little time of the
tossing about, to and fro, of worldly business, is a
compensation for eternal ages of unfading bliss! Oh! how
foolish will you conceive yourselves to be, when you are in
the next state, when cast away from heaven you will see the
saints blessed? I think I hear your mournful soliloquy, "Oh!
how cheaply did I sell my soul! What a poor price did I get
for all I have now lost! I have lost the palace and the crown,
and the joy and bliss for ever, and am shut up in hell! And
for what did I lose it? I lost it for the lascivious wanton kiss;
I lost it for the merry drunken song; I lost it for just a few
short years of pleasures, which, after all, were only painted
pleasures!" Oh! I think I see you in your lost estates, cursing
yourselves, rending your hair, that you should have sold
heaven for counters, and have changed away eternal life for
pitiful farthings, which were spent quickly, and which

burned your hand in the spending of them! Oh! that ye were wise, that ye would weigh those things, and reckon that a life of the greatest happiness here is nothing compared with the glorious hereafter: "There remaineth a rest to the people of God."

Now let me put it in *more pleasing contrast.* I shall contrast the rest of the believer above with the miserable estate of the believer sometimes here below. Christians have their sorrows. Suns have their spots, skies have their clouds, and Christians have their sorrows too. But oh! how different will the state of the righteous be up there, from the state of the believer here! Here the Christian has to suffer anxiety. He is anxious to serve his Master, to do his best in his day and generation. His constant cry is—"Help me to serve thee, O my God," and he looks out, day after day, with a strong desire for opportunities of doing good. Ah! if he be an active Christian, he will have much labour, much toil, in endeavouring to serve his Master; and there will be times when he will say, "My soul is in haste to be gone; I am not wearied of the labour, I am wearied in it. To toil thus in the sun, though for a good Master, is not the thing that just now I desire." Ah! Christian, the day shall soon be over, and thou shalt no longer have to toil; the sun is nearing the horizon; it shall rise again with a brighter day than thou hast ever seen before. There, up in heaven, Luther has no more to face a thundering Vatican; Paul has no more to run from city to city, and continent to continent; there Baxter has no more to toil in his pulpit, to preach with a broken heart to hard hearted sinners; there no longer has Knox to "cry aloud and spare not" against the immoralities of the false church; there no more shall be the strained lung, and the tired throat, and the aching eye; no more shall the Sunday school teacher feel that his sabbath is a day of joyful weariness; no more shall the tract distributor meet with rebuffs. No, there, those who have served their country and their God, those who have toiled for man's welfare, with all their might, shall enter into everlasting rest. Sheathed is the sword, the banner is furled, the fight is over, the victory won; and they rest from their labours.

Here, too, the Christian is always *sailing onward,* he is always in motion, he feels that he has not yet attained. Like Paul he can say "Forgetting the things that are behind, I

press forward to that which is before." But there his weary
head shall be crowned with unfading light. There the ship
that has been speeding onward shall furl its sails in the port
of eternal bliss. There he who, like an arrow, has sped his
way shall be fixed for ever in the target. There we who like
fleeting clouds were driven by every wind, shall gently distil
in one perennial shower of everlasting joy. There is no
progress, no motion there; they are at rest, they have
attained the summit of the mountain, they have ascended to
their God and our God. Higher they cannot go; they have
reached the *Ultima Thule,* there are no fortunate islands
beyond; this is life's utmost end of happiness; and they furl
their sails, rest from their labours, and enjoy themselves for
aye. There is a difference between the progress of earth and
the perfect fixity of the rest of heaven.

Here, too, the believer is often the subject of *doubt and
fear.* "Am I his or am I not?" is often the cry. He trembleth
lest he should be deceived; at times he almost despairs, and
is inclined not to put his name down as one of the children of
God. Dark insinuations are whispered into his ears; he
thinks that God's mercy is clean gone for ever, and that he
will not be mindful of him any more. Again, his sins sometimes upbraid him, and he thinks God will not have mercy
on him. He has a poor fainting heart; he is like Ready-to-
halt, he has to go all his way on crutches; he has a poor
feeble mind, always tumbling down over a straw, and
fearing one day he shall be drowned in a cart-rut. Though
the lions are chained he is as much afraid of them as if they
were loose. Hill Difficulty often afrights him; going down
into the valley of humiliation is often troublesome work to
him; but there, there are no hills to climb, no dragons to
fight, no foes to conquer, no dangers to dread. Ready-to-halt,
when he dies, will bury his crutches, and Feeblemind will
leave his feebleness behind him; Fearing will never fear
again; poor Doubting-heart will learn confidently to believe.
Oh, joy above all joys! The day is coming when I shall "know
as I am known," when I shall not want to ask whether I am
his or not, for in his arms encircled, there shall be no room
for doubt. Oh! Christian, you think there are slips between
your lips and that cup of joy; but when you grasp the handle
of that cup with your hand, and are drinking draughts of
ineffable delight, then you will have no doubt or fear.

"There you shall see his face,
And never, never sin;
There from the rivers of his grace,
Drink endless pleasures in."

Here, too, on earth, the Christian has to *suffer;* here he has
the aching head and the pained body; his limbs may be
bruised or broken, disease may rack him with torture; he
may be an afflicted one from his birth, he may have lost an
eye or an ear, or he may have lost many of his powers; or if
not, being of a weakly constitution, he may have to spend the
most of his days and nights upon the bed of weariness. Or if
his body be sound, yet what suffering he has in his mind!
Conflicts between depravity and gross temptations from the
evil one, assaults of hell, perpetual attacks of divers kinds,
from the world, the flesh, and the devil. But there, no aching
head, no weary heart; there no palsied arm, no brow
ploughed with the furrows of old age; there the lost limb
shall be recovered, and old age shall find itself endowed with
perpetual youth; there the infirmities of the flesh shall be
left behind, given to the worm and devoured by corruption.
There they shall flit, as on the wings of angels, from pole to
pole, and from place to place, without weariness or anguish;
there they shall never need to lie upon the bed of rest, or the
bed of suffering; for day without night, with joy unflagging,
they shall circle God's throne rejoicing, and ever praise him
who hath said, "The inhabitants there shall never be sick."

There, too, they shall be free from *persecution.* Here
Sicilian Vespers, and St. Bartholomew, and Smithfield, are
well-known words; but there shall be none to taunt them
with a cruel word, or touch them with a cruel hand. There
emperors and kings are not known, and those who had
power to torture them cease to be. They are in the society of
saints; they shall be free from all the idle converse of the
wicked, and from their cruel jeers set free for ever. Set free
from persecution! Ye army of martyrs, ye were slain, ye were
torn asunder, ye were cast to wild beasts, ye wandered about
in sheep skins and goats' skins, destitute, afflicted, and
tormented. I see you now, a mighty host. The habiliments
you wear are torn with thorns; your faces are scarred with
sufferings; I see you at your stakes, and on your crosses; I
hear your words of submission on your racks, I see you in
your prisons, I behold you in your pillories—but

> "Now ye are arrayed in white,
> Brighter than the noonday-sun;
> Fairest of the sons of light,
> Nearest the eternal throne."

These are they, who "for their Master died, who love the cross and crown;" they waded through seas of blood, in order to obtain the inheritance; and there they are, with the blood-red crown of martyrdom about their heads, that ruby brightness, far excelling every other. Yes, there is no persecution there. "There remaineth a rest for the people of God."

Alas! in this mortal state the child of God is also subject to *sin;* even he faileth in his duty, and wandereth from his God; even he doth not walk in all the law of his God blameless, though he desireth to do it. Sin now troubleth him constantly; but there sin is dead; there they have no temptation to sin, from without or from within, but they are perfectly free to serve their Master. Here the child of God has sometimes to weep repentingly of his backslidings; but there they never shed tears of penitence, for they have never cause to do so.

And last of all, here, the child of God has to wet the cold ashes of his relatives with *tears;* here he has to bid adieu to all that is lovely and fair of mortal race; here it is he hears, "Earth to earth, and dust to dust, and ashes to ashes," while the solemn music of the dust upon the coffin lid beats doleful time to those words. Here is the mother buried, the child snatched away, the husband rent from the bosom of a loving wife, the brother parted from the sister. The plate upon the coffin, the last coat of arms of earth, earth's last emblems are here ever before our eyes. But there never once shall be heard the toll of the funeral bell; no hearse with plumes has ever darkened the streets of gold; no emblems of sorrow have ever intruded into the homes of the immortal; they are strangers to the meaning of death; they cannot die—they live for ever; having no power to decay, and no possibility of corruption. Oh! rest of the righteous, how blest art thou, where families shall again be bound up in one bundle, where parted friends shall again meet to part no more, and where the whole church of Christ united in one mighty circle, shall together praise God and the Lamb throughout eternal ages.

Brethren, I have tried thus to set the rest of the righteous in the way of contrast; I feel I have failed. Poor are the words I can utter to tell you of immortal things. Even holy Baxter himself, when he wrote of the "Saint's Rest," paused and said, "But these are only tinklings compared with the full thunders of heaven." I cannot tell you, dear friends, nor can mortal tell, what God hath prepared for them that love him.

2. And now I shall try very briefly to exhibit this contrast *in the way of comparison.* The Christian hath some rest here, but nothing compared with the rest which is to come.

There is the *rest of the church.* When the believer joins the church of God, and becomes united with them, he may expect to rest. The good old writer of the "Pilgrim's Progress," says, that when the weary pilgrims were once admitted to the house Beautiful, they were shown to sleep in a chamber called "peace," or "rest." The church-member at the Lord's table has a sweet enjoyment of rest in fellowship with the saints; but ah! up there the rest of church fellowship far surpasses anything that is known here; for there are no divisions there, no angry words at the church meetings, no harsh thoughts of one another, no bickerings about doctrine, no fightings about practice. There Baptist, and Presbyterian, and Independent, and Wesleyan, and Episcopalian, serving the same Lord, and having been washed in the same blood, sing the same song, and are all joined in one. There pastors and deacons never look coolly on each other; no haughty prelates there, no lofty-minded ministers there, but all meek and lowly, all knit together in brotherhood; they have a rest which surpasseth all the rest of the church on earth.

There is, again, a rest of *faith* which a Christian enjoys; a sweet rest. Many of us have known it. We have known what it is, when the billows of trouble have run high, to hide ourselves in the breast of Christ, and feel secure. We have cast our anchor deep into the rocks of God's promise, we have gone to sleep in our chamber and have not feared the tempest, we have looked at tribulation, and have smiled at it; we have looked at death himself, and have laughed him to scorn; we have had such trust by Christian faith that, dauntless and fearless, nothing could move us. Yes, in the midst of calumny, reproach, slander and contempt, we have said, "I shall not be moved, for God is on my side." But the rest up there is better still, more unruffled, more sweet, more perfectly calm, more enduring, and more lasting than even the rest of faith.

And, again, the Christian sometimes has the blessed rest of *communion.* There are happy moments when he puts his head on the Saviour's breast—when, like John, he feels that he is close to the Saviour's heart, and there he sleeps. "God giveth his beloved sleep;" not the sleep of unconsciousness, but the sleep of joy. Happy, happy, happy are the dreams we have had on the couch of communion; blessed have been the times, when, like the spouse in Solomon's song, we could say of Christ, "His left hand was under my head, and with his right hand did he embrace me."

> "But sweeter still the fountain head,
> Though sweet may be the stream;"

When we shall have plunged into a very bath of joy, we shall have found the delights even of communion on earth to have been but the dipping of the finger in the cup, but the dipping of the bread in the dish, whereas heaven itself shall be the participation of the whole of the joy, and not the mere antepast of it. Here we sometimes enter into the portico of happiness, there we shall go into the presence chamber of the King; here we look over the hedge and see the flowers in heaven's garden, there we shall walk between the beds of bliss, and pluck fresh flowers at each step; here we just look and see the sunlight of heaven in the distance, like the lamps of the thousand-gated cities shining afar off, but there we shall see them in all their blaze of splendour; here we listen to the whisperings of heaven's melody, borne by winds from afar; but there, entranced, amidst the grand oratorio of the blessed, we shall join in the everlasting hallelujah to the great Messiah, the God, the I AM. Oh! again I say, do we not wish to mount aloft, and fly away, to enter into the rest which remaineth to the people of God?

II. And now, yet more briefly, and then we shall have done. I am to endeavour to EXTOL this rest, as I have tried to EXHIBIT it. I would extol this rest for many reasons; and oh! that I were eloquent, that I might extol it as it deserves! Oh! for the lip of angel, and the burning tongue of cherub, to talk now of the bliss of the sanctified and of the rest of God's people!

It is, first, a *perfect* rest. They are wholly at rest in heaven.

Here rest is but partial. I hope in a little time to cease from every-day labours for a season; but then the head will think, and the mind may be looking forward to prospective labour, and whilst the body is still, the brain will yet be in motion. Here, on Sabbath days a vast multitude of you sit in God's house, but many of you are obliged to stand, and rest but little except in your mind, and even when the mind is at rest the body is wearied with the toil of standing. You have a weary mile perhaps, many miles, to go to your homes on the Sabbath day. And let the Sabbatarian say what he will, you may work on the Sabbath day, if you work for God; and this Sabbath day's work of going to the house of God is work for God, and God accepts it. For yourselves you may not labour, God commands you to rest, but if you have to toil these three, these four, these five, these six miles, as many of you have done, I will not and I must not blame you. "The priests in the sanctuary profane the Sabbath, and are blameless." It is toil and labour, it is true, but it is for a good cause—for your Master. But there, my friends, the rest is perfect; the body there rests perpetually, the mind too always rests; though the inhabitants are always busy, always serving God, yet they are never weary, never toil-worn, never fagged; they never fling themselves upon their couches at the end of the day, and cry, "Oh! when shall I be away from this land of toil?" They never stand up in the burning sunlight, and wipe the hot sweat from their brow; they never rise from their bed in the morning, half refreshed, to go to labourious study. No, they are perfectly at rest, stretched on the couch of eternal joy. They know not the semblance of a tear; they have done with sin, and care, and woe, and with their Saviour rest.

Again, it is a *seasonable* rest. How seasonable it will be for some of you! Ye sons of wealth, ye know not the toils of the poor; the horny-handed labourer, perhaps, you have not seen, and you know not how he has to tug and to toil. Among my congregation I have many of a class, upon whom I have always looked with pity; poor women who must rise to-morrow morning with the sun, and begin that everlasting "stitch, stitch," that works their finger to the bone. And from Monday morning till Saturday night, many of you, my members, and multitudes of you, my hearers, will not be able to lay aside your needle and your thread, except when,

tired and weary, you fall back on your chair, and are lulled
to sleep by your thoughts of labour! Oh! how seasonable will
heaven's rest be to you! Oh! how glad will you be, when you
get there, to find that there are no Monday mornings, no
more toil for you, but rest, eternal rest! Others of you have
hard manual labour to perform; you have reason to thank
God that you are strong enough to do it, and you are not
ashamed of your work; for labour is an honour to a man. But
still there are times when you say, "I wish I were not so
dragged to death by the business of London life." We have
but little rest in this huge city; our day is longer, and our
work is harder than our friends in the country. You have
sometimes sighed to go into the green fields for a breath of
fresh air; you have longed to hear the song of the sweet birds
that used to wake you when you were lads; you have
regretted the bright blue sky, the beauteous flowers, and the
thousand charms of a country life. And, perhaps, you will
never get beyond this smoky city, but remember, when you
get up there, "sweet fields arrayed in living green" and
"rivers of delight" shall be the place where you shall rest,
you shall have all the joys you can conceive of in that home
of happiness; and though worn and weary, you come to your
grave, tottering on your staff; having journeyed through the
wilderness of life, like a weary camel, which has only
stopped on the Sabbath to sip its little water at the well, or
to be baited at the oasis, there you will arrive at your
journey's end, laden with gold and spices, and enter into the
grand caravanserai of heaven, and enjoy for ever the things
you have wearily carried with you here.

And I must say, that to others of us who have not to toil
with our hands, heaven will be a seasonable rest. Those of us
who have to tire our brain day after day will find it no slight
boon to have an everlasting rest above. I will not boast of
what I may do, there may be many who do more; there may
be many who are perpetually and daily striving to serve
God, and are using their mind's best energies in so doing.
But this much I may say, that almost every week I have the
pleasure of preaching twelve times; and often in my sleep do
I think of what I shall say next time. Not having the
advantage of laying out my seven shillings and sixpence in
buying manuscripts, it costs me hard diligent labour to find
even something to say. And I sometimes have a difficulty to

keep the hopper full in the mill; I feel that if I had not now and then a rest I should have no wheat for God's children. Still it is on, on, on, and on we must go; we hear the chariot wheels of God behind us, and we dare not stop; we think that eternity is drawing nigh, and we must go on. Rest to us now is more than labour, we want to be at work; but oh! how seasonable it shall be, when to the minister it shall be said—

> "Servant of God, well done!
> Rest from thy loved employ;
> The battle fought, the victory won,
> Enter thy Master's joy."

It will be seasonable rest. You that are weary with state cares, and have to learn the ingratitude of men; you that have sought honours, and have got them to your cost, you seek to do your best, but your very independence of spirit is called servility, whilst your servility would have been praised! You who seek to honour God, and not to honour men, who will not bind yourselves to parties, but seek in your own independent and honest judgment to serve your country and your God; you, I say, when God shall see fit to call you to himself, will find it no small joy to have done with parliaments, to have done with states and kingdoms, and to have laid aside your honours, to receive honours more lasting amongst those who dwell for ever before the throne of the Most High.

One thing, and then once more, and then farewell. This rest, my brethren, ought to be extolled, because it is *eternal.* Here my best joys bear "mortal" on their brow; here my fair flowers fade; here my sweet cups have dregs and are soon empty; here my sweetest birds must die, and their melody must soon be hushed; here my most pleasant days must have their nights; here the flowings of my bliss must have their ebbs, everything doth pass away, but there everything shall be immortal; the harp shall be unrusted, the crown unwithered, the eye undimmed, the voice unfaltering, the heart unwavering, and the being wholly consolidated unto eternity. Happy day, happy day, when mortality shall be swallowed up of life, and the mortal shall have put on immortality!

And then, lastly, this glorious rest is to be best of all commended for its *certainty.* "There remaineth a rest to the people of God." Doubting one, thou hast often said, "I fear I shall never enter heaven." Fear not; all the people of God shall enter there; there is no fear about it. I love the quaint saying of a dying man, who, in his country brogue, exclaimed, "I have no fear of going home; I have sent all before me; God's finger is on the latch of my door and I am ready for him to enter." "But," said one "are you not afraid least you should miss your inheritance?" "Nay," said he, "nay; there is one crown in heaven that the angel Gabriel could not wear; it will fit no head but mine. There is one throne in heaven that Paul the apostle could not fill; it was made for me, and I shall have it. There is one dish at the banquet that I must eat, or else it will be untasted, for God has set it apart for me." O Christian, what a joyous thought! thy portion is secure; "there remaineth a rest." "But cannot I forfeit it?" No; it is entailed. If I be a child of God I shall not lose it. It is mine as securely as if I were there.

> "Come, Christian, mount to Pisgah's top,
> And view the landscape o'er."

Seest thou that little river of death, glistening in the sunlight, and across it dost thou see the pinnacles of the eternal city? Dost thou mark the pleasant suburbs and all the joyous inhabitants? Turn thine eye to that spot. Dost thou see where that ray of light is glancing now? There is a little spot there; dost thou see it? That is thy patrimony; that is thine. Oh, if thou couldst fly across thou wouldst see written upon it, "This remaineth for such an one, preserved for him only. He shall be caught up and dwell for ever with God." Poor doubting one; see thine inheritance; it is thine. If thou believest in the Lord Jesus thou art one of the Lord's people; if thou hast repented of sin thou art one of the Lord's people; if thou hast been renewed in heart thou art one of the Lord's people, and there is a place for thee, a crown for thee, a harp for thee. No one else shall have it but thyself, and thou shalt have it ere long. Just pardon me one moment if I beg of you to conceive of yourselves as being in heaven. Is it not a strange thing to think of—a poor clown in heaven? Think, how will you feel with your crown on your head? Weary matron, many years have rolled over you. How changed will be the scene when you are young again. Ah, toil-worn labourer, only think when thou shalt rest for aye.

Canst thou conceive it? couldst thou but think for a moment, of thyself as being in heaven now, what a strange surprise would seize thee. Thou wouldst not so as much say, "What! are these streets of gold? What! are these walls of jasper?" "What, am I here? in white? Am I here, with a crown on my brow? Am I here singing, that was always groaning? What! I praise God that once cursed him? What! I lifting up my voice in his honour? Oh, precious blood that washed me clean! Oh, precious faith that set me free! Oh, precious Spirit that made me repent, else I had been cast away and been in hell! But oh! what wonders! Angels! I am surprised; I am enraptured! Wonder of wonders! Oh! gates of pearls, I long since heard of you! Oh! joys that never fade, I long since heard tell of you! But I am like the Queen of Sheba; the half has not yet been told me. Profusion, oh profusion of bliss!—wonder of wonders!—miracle of miracles! What a world I am in! And oh! that I am here, this is the topmost miracle of all!" And yet 'tis true, 'tis true; and that is the glory of it. It is true. Come, worm, and prove it; come, pall; come shroud; come, and prove it. Then come wings of faith, come, leap like a seraph; come, eternal ages, come, and ye shall prove that there are joys that the eye hath not seen, which the ear hath not heard, and which only God can reveal to us by his spirit. Oh! my earnest prayer is, that none of you may come short of this rest, but that ye may enter into it, and enjoy it for ever and ever. God give you his great blessing, for Jesus sake! Amen.

7

No Tears In Heaven

"...and God shall wipe away all tears from their eyes."
Revelation 7:17

It is an ill thing to be always mourning, sighing, and complaining concerning the *present*. However dark it may be, we may surely recall some fond remembrances of the *past*. There *were* days of brightness, there were seasons of refreshing from the presence of the Lord. Be not slow to confess, O believing soul, that the Lord has been thy help! and though now thy burden be very heavy, thou wilt find an addition to thy strength in the thought of seasons long since past, when the Lord lightened thy load, and made thy heart to leap for joy. Yet more delightful will it be to expect the *future*. The night is dark, but the morning cometh. Over the hills of darkness the day breaketh. It may be that the road is rough, but its end is almost in view; Thou hast been clambering up the steep heights of Pisgah, and from the brow thereof thou mayest view thy glorious heritage. True the tomb is before thee, but thy Lord has snatched the sting from death, and the victory from the grave. Do not, O burdened spirit, confine thyself to the narrow miseries of the present hour, but let thine eye gaze with fondness upon the enjoyment of the past, and view with equal ardour the infinite blessings of old eternity, when thou wast not, but when God set thee apart for himself, and wrote thy name in his book of life; and let thy glance flash forward to the future eternity, the mercies which shall be thine even here on earth, and the glories which are stored up for thee beyond the skies. I shall be well rewarded this morning if I shall minister comfort to one heavy spirit by leading it to remember the glory which is yet to be revealed.

Coming to our text, we shall observe, in the first place, that as God is to wipe away tears from the faces of the glorified, *we may well infer that their eyes will be filled with tears till then;* and in the second place, it is worthy of reflection that as God never changes, *even now he is engaged in drying tears from his children's eyes;* and then, coming right into the heart of the text, we shall dwell upon the great truth, *that in heaven Divine Love removes all tears from the glorified;* and so we shall close, by making some *inquiry as to whether or not we belong to that happy company.*

I. Our first subject of meditation is the inference that tears ARE TO FILL THE EYES OF BELIEVERS UNTIL THEY ENTER THE PROMISED REST. There would be no need to wipe them away if there were none remaining. They come to the very gates of heaven weeping, and accompanied by their two comrades, sorrow and sighing; the tears are dried, and sorrow and sighing flee away. The weeping willow grows not by the river of the water of life, but it is plentiful enough below; nor shall we lose it till we change it for the palm-branch of victory. Sorrow's dewdrop will never cease to fall until it is transformed into the pearl of everlasting bliss.

> "The path of sorrow, and that path alone,
> Leads to the place where sorrow is unknown."

Religion brings deliverance from the curse, but not exemption from trial.

The ancients were accustomed to use bottles in which to catch the tears of mourners. Methinks I see three bottles filled with the tears of mourners. The first is *a common bottle,* the ordinary lachrymatory containing griefs incidental to all men, for believers suffer even as the rest of the race. *Physical pain* by no means spares the servants of God. Their nerves, and blood-vessels, and limbs, and inward organs, are as susceptible of disease as those of unregenerate men. Some of the choicest saints have lain longest on beds of sickness, and those who are dearest to the heart of God have felt the heaviest blows of the chastening rod. There are pains which, despite the efforts of patience, compel the tears to wet the cheeks. The human frame is capable of a fearful degree of agony, and few there be who have not at some time or other watered their couch with tears because of the acuteness of their pains. Coupled with this, there are *the losses and crosses of daily life.* What Christian among you trades without occasional difficulties and serious losses? Have any of you a lot so easy that you have nothing to deplore? Are there no crosses at home? Are there no troubles abroad? Can you travel from the first of January to the last of December without feeling the weariness of the way? Have you no blighted field, no bad debt, no slandered name, no harsh word, no sick child, no suffering wife to bring before the Lord in weeping prayer? You must be an inhabitant of another planet if you have had no griefs, for man is born to trouble as the sparks fly upwards. No ship can navigate the Atlantic of earth without meeting with storms, it is only upon the Pacific of heaven that all is calm for evermore. Believers must through much tribulation, inherit the kingdom of heaven. "Trials must and will befall." *Death* contributes to our woes; the heirs of immortality are often summoned to gather around the tomb. Who hath not lost a friend? If Jesus wept, expect not that we shall be without the tears of bereavement; the well-beloved Lazarus died, and so will our choicest friends. Parents will go before us, infants will be snatched from us, brothers and sisters will fall before the scythe of death. Impartial foe of all, thou sparest neither virtue nor vice, holiness nor sin; with equal foot thou treadest on the cherished loves of all! The Christian knows also *disappointments* as bitter and as keen as other men. Judas betrays Christ, Ahithophel is a traitor to David. We have had our Ahithophels, and we may yet meet with our Judas. We have trusted in friends, and we have found their friendships fail. We have leaned upon what seemed a staff, and it has pierced us like a spear. You cannot, dear friends, traverse the wilderness of this world without discovering that thorns and thistles grow plenteously in it, and that, step as you may, your feet must sometimes feel their power to wound. The sea of life is salt to all men. Clouds hover over every landscape. We may forget to laugh, but we shall always know how to weep. As the saturated fleece must drip, so must the human race, cursed by the fall, weep out its frequent griefs.

I see before me *a second bottle,* it is *black and foul,* for it contains tears distilled by the force of the fires of sin. This bottle holds more than the first, and is far more regularly filled. Sin is more frequently the mother of sorrow than all the other ills of life put together. Dear brothers and sisters, I am convinced that we endure more sorrow from our sins than from God's darkest providence. Mark our rebellious *want of resignation!* When a trouble comes it is not the trial which makes us groan so much as our rebellion against it. It is true the ox goad is thrust into us, but we kick against it, and then it hurts us far more. Like men with naked feet we kick against the pricks. We head our vessel against the stream of God's will, and then murmur because the waves beat violently upon us. An unsubdued will is like a maniac's hand which tears himself. The chastisements which come directly from our heavenly Father are never so hard to bear as the frettings and fumings of our unhumbled self-will. As the bird dashes against the wires of its cage and breaks its own wing, even so do we. If we would take the cross as our gracious Father gives it, it would not gall our shoulders, but since we revolt from it and loathe the burden, our shoulders grow raw and sore, and the load becomes intolerable. More submission, and we should have fewer tears. There are the tears, too, of *wounded, injured pride,* and how hot and scalding they are! When a man has been ambitious and has failed, how he will weep instead of standing corrected, or gathering up his courage for a wiser venture. When a friend has spoken slightingly of us, or an enemy has accused us, how we have had to put our fingers to our hot eye-lids to keep the tears from streaming out, and have felt all the while as full of wretchedness as we well could be. Ah, these are cruel and wicked tears. God wipe them away from our eyes now! certainly he must do it before we shall be able to enter heaven. How numerous, too, are the tears of *unbelief!* We manufacture troubles for ourselves by anticipating future ills which may never come, or which, if they do come, may be like the clouds, all "big with mercy," and "break with blessings on our head." We get supposing what we should do if such-and-such a thing occurred, which thing God has determined never shall occur. We imagine ourselves in positions where Providence never intends to place us, and so we feel a thousand trials in fearing one. That bottle, I say,

ought never to carry within it a tear from a believer's eyes,
and yet it has had whole floods poured into it. Oh, the
wickedness of mistrust of God, and the bitterness with which
that distrust is made to curse itself. Unbelief makes a rod for
its own back; distrust of God is its own punishment; it brings
such want of rest, such care, such tribulation of spirit into
the mind, that he who loves himself and loves pleasure, had
better seek to walk by faith and not by sight. Nor must I
forget the scalding drops of anger *against our fellow-men,*
and of petulance and irritation, because we cannot have our
way with them; these are black and horrid damps, as
noisome as the vaults of Tophet. May we ever be saved from
such unholy tears. Sometimes, too, there are streams which
arise from *depressed spirits,* spirits desponding because we
have neglected the means of grace and the God of grace. The
consolations of God are small with us because we have been
seldom in secret prayer; we have lived at a distance from the
Most High, and we have fallen into a melancholy state of
mind. I thank God that there shall never come another tear
from our eyes into *that* bottle when eternal love shall take us
up to dwell with Jesus in his kingdom.

We would never overlook the *third bottle,* which is the true
crystal lachrymatory into which holy tears may drop, tears
like the *lachrymae Christi,* the tears of Jesus, so precious in
the sight of God. Even these shall cease to flow in heaven.
Tears of *repentance,* like glistening dewdrops fresh from the
skies, are stored in this bottle; they are not of the earth, they
come from heaven, and yet we cannot carry them thither
with us. Good Rowland Hill used to say, repentance was
such a sweet companion that the only regret he could have in
going to heaven, was in leaving repentance behind him, for
he could not shed the tears of repentance there. Oh, to weep
for sin! It is so sweet a sorrow that I would a constant
weeper be! Like a dripping well, my soul would ever drop
with grief that I have offended my loving, tender, gracious
God. Tears for *Christ's injured honour* and slightedness
glisten in the crystal of our third bottle. When we hear
Jesus' name blasphemed among men, or see his cause driven
back in the day of battle, who will not weep then? Who can
restrain his lamentations? Such tears are diamonds in
Christ's esteem; blessed are the eyes which are mines of
such royal treasure. If I cannot win crowns I will at least

give tears. If I cannot make men love my Master, yet will I weep in secret places for the dishonour which they do him. These are holy drops, but they are all unknown in heaven. Tears of *sympathy* are much esteemed by our Lord; when we "weep with those that weep" we do well; these are never to be restrained this side the Jordan. Let them flow! the more of them the better for our spiritual health. Truly, when I think of the griefs of men, and above all, when I have communion with my Saviour in his suffering, I would cry with George Herbert,—

> "Come all ye floods, ye clouds, ye rains,
> Dwell in my eyes! My grief hath need
> Of all the watery things that nature can produce!
> Let every vein suck up a river to supply my eyes,
> My weary, weeping eyes, too dry for me,
> Unless they get new conduits, fresh supplies,
> And with my state agree."

It were well to go to the very uttermost of weeping if it were always of such a noble kind, as fellowship with Jesus brings. Let us never cease from weeping over sinners as Jesus did over Jerusalem; let us endeavour to snatch the firebrand from the flame, and weep when we cannot accomplish our purpose.

These three receptacles of tears will always be more or less filled by us as long as we are here, but in heaven the first bottle will not be needed, for the wells of earth's grief will all be dried up, and we shall drink from living fountains of water unsalted by a tear: as for the second, we shall have no depravity in our hearts, and so the black fountain will no longer yield its nauseous stream; and as for the third, there shall he no place amongst celestial occupations for weeping even of the most holy kind. Till then, we must expect to share in human griefs, and instead of praying against them, let us ask that they may be sanctified to us; I mean of course those of the former sort. Let us pray that tribulation may work patience, and patience experience, and experience the hope which maketh not ashamed. Let us pray that as the sharp edge of the graving tool is used upon us it may only remove our excrescences and fashion us into images of our Lord and Master. Let us pray that the fire may consume nothing but the dross, and that the floods may wash away nothing but defilement. May we have to thank God that though before we were afflicted we went astray, yet now have we kept his word; and so shall we see it to be a blessed thing, a divinely wise thing, that we should tread the path of sorrow, and reach the gates of heaven with the tear drops glistening in our eyes.

II. Secondly, EVEN HERE IF WE WOULD HAVE OUR TEARS WIPED AWAY WE CANNOT DO BETTER THAN REPAIR TO OUR GOD.

He is the great tear wiper. Observe, brethren, that God can remove every vestige of grief from the hearts of his people by granting them complete resignation to his will. Our selfhood is the root of our sorrow. If self were perfectly conquered, it would be equal to us whether love ordained our pain or ease, appointed us wealth or poverty. If our will were completely God's will, then pain itself would be attended with pleasure, and sorrow would yield us joy for Christ's sake. As one fire puts out another, so the master passion of love to God and complete absorption in his sacred will quenches the fire of human grief and sorrow. Hearty resignation puts so much honey in the cup of gall that the wormwood is forgotten. As death is swallowed up in victory, so is tribulation swallowed up in complacency and delight in God.

He can also take away our tears by constraining our minds to dwell with delight upon the end which all our trials are working to produce. He can show us that they are working together for good, and as men of understanding, when we see that we shall be essentially enriched by our losses, we shall be content with them; when we see that the medicine is curing us of mortal sickness, and that our sharpest pains are only saving us from pains far more terrible, then shall we kiss the rod and sing in the midst of tribulation, "Sweet affliction!" sweet affliction! since it yields such peaceable fruits of righteousness.

Moreover, he can take every tear from our eye in the time of trial by shedding abroad the love of Jesus Christ in our hearts more plentifully. He can make it clear to us that Christ is afflicted in our affliction. He can indulge us with a delightful sense of the divine virtue which dwells in his sympathy, and make us rejoice to be co-sufferers with the angel of the covenant. The Saviour can make our hearts leap for joy by re-assuring us that we are written on the palms of his hands, and that we shall be with him where he is. Sick beds become thrones, and hovels ripen into palaces when Jesus is made sure to our souls. My brethren, the love of Christ, like a great flood, rolls over the most rugged rocks of afflictions, so high above them that we may float in perfect peace where others are a total wreck. The rage of the storm is all hushed when Christ is in the vessel. The waters saw thee, O Christ, the waters saw thee and were silent at the presence of their king.

The Lord can also take away all present sorrow and grief from us by providentially removing its cause. Providence is full of sweet surprises and unexpected turns. When the sea has ebbed its uttermost it turns again and covers all the sand. When we think the dungeon is fast, and that the bolt is rusted in, he can make the door fly open in a moment. When the river rolls deep and black before us he can divide it with a word, or bridge it with his hand. How often have you found it so in the past? As a pilgrim to Canaan you have passed through the Red Sea, in which you once feared you would be drowned; the bitter wells of Marah were made sweet by God's presence; you fought the Amalekite, you went through the terrible wilderness, you passed by the place of the fiery serpents, and you have yet been kept alive, and so shall you be. As the clear shining cometh after rain, so shall peace succeed your trials. As fly the black clouds before the compelling power of the wind, so will the eternal God make your griefs to fly before the energy of his grace. The smoking furnace of trouble shall be followed by the bright lamp of consolation.

Still, the surest method of getting rid of present tears, is communion and fellowship with God. When I can creep under the wing of my dear God and nestle close to his bosom, let the world say what it will, and let the devil roar as he pleases, and let my sins accuse and threaten as they may, I am safe, content, happy, peaceful, rejoicing.

> "Let earth against my soul engage,
> And hellish darts be hurled;
> Now I can smile at Satan's rage,
> And face a frowning world."

To say, "My Father, God," to put myself right into his hand, and feel that I am safe there; to look up to him though it be with tears in my eyes and feel that he loves me, and then to put my head right into his bosom as the prodigal did, and sob my griefs out there into my Father's heart, oh, this is the death of grief, and the life of all consolation. Is not Jehovah called the God of all comfort? You will find him so, beloved. He has been "our help in ages past;" he is "our hope for years to come." If he had not been my help, then had my soul perished utterly in the day of its weariness and its heaviness. Oh, I bear testimony for him this day that you cannot go to him and pour out your heart before him without finding a delightful solace. When your friend cannot wipe away the tear, when you yourself with your strongest reasonings, and your boldest efforts cannot constrain yourself to resignation; when your heart beats high, and seems as if it would burst with grief, then ye people pour out your hearts before him. God *is* a refuge for us. He is our castle and high tower, our refuge and defence. Only go ye to him, and ye shall find that even here on earth God shall wipe away all tears from your eyes.

III. Now we shall have to turn our thoughts to what is the real teaching of the text, namely, THE REMOVAL OF ALL TEARS FROM THE BLESSED ONES ABOVE.

There are many reasons why glorified spirits cannot weep. These are well known to you, but let us just hint at them. *All outward causes of grief are gone.* They will never hear the toll of the knell in heaven. The mattock and the shroud are unknown things there. The horrid thought of death never flits across an immortal spirit. They are never parted; the great meeting has taken place to part no more. Up yonder they have no losses and crosses in business. "They serve God day and night in his temple." They know no broken friendships there. They have no ruined hearts, no blighted prospects. They know even as they are known, and they love even as they are loved. No pain can ever fall on them; as yet they have no bodies, but when their bodies shall be raised from the grave they shall be spiritualized so that they shall not be capable of grief. The tear-gland shall be plucked away; although much may be there that is human, at least the tear-gland shall be gone, they shall have no need of that organ; their bodies shall be unsusceptible of grief; they shall rejoice for ever. Poverty, famine, distress, nakedness, peril, persecution, slander, all these shall have ceased. "The sun shall not light on them, nor any heat." "They shall hunger no more, neither thirst any more," and therefore well may their tears cease to flow.

Again, *all inward evils will have been removed by the perfect sanctification wrought in them by the Holy Ghost.* No evil of heart, of unbelief in departing from the living God, shall vex them in Paradise; no suggestions of the arch enemy shall be met and assisted by the uprisings of iniquity within. They shall never be led to think hardly of God, for their hearts shall be all love; sin shall have no sweetness to them, for they shall be perfectly purified from all depraved desires. There shall be no lusts of the eye, no lusts of the flesh, no pride of life to be snares to their feet. Sin is shut out, and they are shut in. They are for ever blessed, because they are without fault before the throne of God. What a heaven must it be to be without spot, or wrinkle, or any such thing! Well may *they* cease to mourn who have ceased to sin.

All fear of change also has been for ever shut out. They know that they are eternally secure. Saints on earth are fearful of falling, some believers even dream of falling away; they think God will forsake them, and that men will persecute and take them. No such fears can vex the blessed ones who view their Father's face. Countless cycles may revolve, but eternity shall not be exhausted, and while eternity endures, their immortality and blessedness shall co-exist with it. They dwell within a city which shall never be stormed, they bask in a sun which shall never set, they swim in a flood-tide which shall never ebb, they drink of a river which shall never dry, they pluck fruit from a tree which shall never be withered. Their blessedness knows not the thought, which would act like a canker at its heart, that it might, perhaps, pass away and cease to be. They cannot, therefore, weep, because they are infallibly secure, and certainly assured of their eternal blessedness.

Why should they weep, when every desire is gratified? They cannot wish for anything which they shall not have. Eye and ear, heart and hand, judgment, imagination, hope, desire, will, every faculty shall be satisfied. All their capacious powers can wish they shall continually enjoy. Though "Eye hath not seen, nor ear heard the things which God hath

prepared for them that love him," yet we know enough, by
the revelation of the Spirit, to understand that they are
supremely blessed. The joy of Christ, which is an infinite
fulness of delight, is in them. They bathe themselves in the
bottomless, shoreless sea of Infinite Beatitude.

Still, dear friends, this does not quite account for the fact,
that all tears are wiped from their eyes. I like better the text
which tells us that *God* shall do it, and I want you to think
with me, of fountains of tears which exist even in heaven, so
that the celestial ones must inevitably weep if God did not by
a perpetual miracle take away their tears. It strikes me, that
if God himself did not interfere by a perpetual outflow of
abundant consolations, the glorified have very deep cause
for weeping. You will say, "How is this?" Why, in the first
place, if it were not for this, *what regrets they must have for
their past sins*. The more holy a man is, the more he hates
sin. It is a token of growth in sanctification, not that
repentance becomes less acute, but that it becomes more and
more deep. Surely, dear friends, when we shall be made
perfectly holy, we shall have a greater hatred of sin. If on
earth we could be perfectly holy, why, methinks we should
do little else than mourn, to think that so foul, and black,
and venomous a thing as sin had ever stained us; that we
should offend against so good, so gracious, so tender, so
abundantly loving a God. Why, the sight of Christ, "the
Lamb in the midst of the throne," would make them
remember the sin from which he purged them; the sight of
their heavenly Father's perfection would be blinding to
them, if it were not that by some sacred means, which we
know not, God wipes away all these tears from their eyes;
and though they cannot but regret that they have sinned, yet
perhaps they know that sin has been made to glorify God by
the overcoming power of Almighty grace; that sin has been
made to be a black foil, a sort of setting for the sparkling
jewel of eternal, sovereign grace, and it may be that for this
reason they shed no tears over their past lives. They sing,
"Unto him that hath loved us, and washed us from our sins
in his blood:" but they sing that heavenly song without a tear
in their eyes; I cannot understand how this may be, for I
know I could not do so as I now am; let this be the best
reason, that God has wiped away the tears from their eyes.

Again, do you not think, beloved, that the thought of *the*

vast expense of shame and woe which the Saviour lavished
for their redemption must, in the natural order of things, be
a constant source of grief? We sing sometimes that hymn
which reminds us of the angelic song before the throne, and
in one of its verses the poet says:—

> "But when to Calvary they turn,
>   Silent their harps abide;
> Suspended songs a moment mourn
>   The God that loved and died."

Now, that is natural and poetical, but it is not true, for you
know very well that there are no suspended songs in heaven,
and that there is no mourning even over Christ "that loved
and died." It seems to me, that if I were thoroughly
spiritualized and in such a holy state as those are in heaven,
I could not look at the Lamb without tears in my eyes. How
could I think of those five wounds; that bloody sweat in
Gethsemane; that cruel crowning with the thorns in
Gabbatha; that mockery and shame at Golgotha—how could
I think of it without tears? How could I feel that he loved *me*
and gave himself for *me,* without bursting into a passion of
holy affection and sorrow? Tears seem to be the natural
expression of such hallowed joy and grief—

> "Love and grief my heart dividing,
>   With my tears his feet I'll bathe."

I must think it would be so in heaven, if it were not that by
a glorious method, I know not how, God shall wipe away
even those tears from their eyes. Does it not need the
interference of God to accomplish this wonder?

Is there not another cause for grief, namely, *wasted
opportunities.* Beloved, when we once ascend to heaven,
there will be no more feeding of Christ's hungry people; no
giving drink to the thirsty; no visiting his sick ones, or his
imprisoned ones; no clothing of the naked; there will be no
instructing the ignorant; no holding forth the Word of God
among "a crooked and perverse generation." It has been
often and truly said, if there could be regrets in heaven,
those regrets would be, that we have wasted so many
opportunities of honouring Christ on earth, opportunities
which will then be past for ever. Now in heaven their hearts
are not steeled and hardened, so that they can look back

upon sins of omission without sorrow. I believe there will be
the tenderest form of conscience there, for perfect purity
would not be consistent with any degree of hardness of
heart. If they be sensitive and tender in heart, it is
inevitable that they should look back with regret upon the
failures of the life below unless some more mighty emotion
should overwhelm that of contrition. I can say, beloved, if
God would take me to heaven this morning, if he did not
come in, and by a special act of his omnipotence, dry up that
fountain of tears, I should almost forget the glories of
Paradise in the midst of my own shame, that I have not
preached more earnestly, and have not prayed more
fervently, and laboured more abundantly for Christ. That
text, to which we heard a reference from a dear brother
during the week, where Paul says, "I call God to witness that
for the space of three years I ceased not night and day with
tears, to warn every one of you," is a text that we cannot any
of us read without blushes and tears; and in heaven,
methinks, if I saw the Apostle Paul, I must burst out into
weeping, if it were not for this text, which says that "God
shall wipe away all tears," and these among them. Who but
the Almighty God could do this!

Perhaps, again, another source of tears may suggest itself
to you; namely, *regrets in heaven for our mistakes, and
misrepresentations, and unkindnesses towards other
Christian brethren.* How surprised we shall be to meet in
heaven some whom we did not love on earth! We would not
commune with them at the Lord's table. We would not own
that they were Christians. We looked at them very askance
if we saw them in the street. We were jealous of all their
operations. We suspected their zeal as being nothing better
than rant, and we looked upon their best exertions as having
sinister motives at the bottom. We said many hard things,
and felt a great many more than we said. When we shall see
these unknown and unrecognized brethren in heaven will
not their presence naturally remind us of our offences
against Christian love and spiritual unity? I cannot suppose
a perfect man, looking at another perfect man, without
regretting that he ever ill-treated him: it seems to me to be
the trait of a gentleman, a Christian, and of a perfectly
sanctified man above all others, that he should regret having
misunderstood, and misconstrued, and misrepresented one

who was as dear to Christ as himself. I am sure as I go round among the saints in heaven, I cannot (in the natural order of things) help feeling "I did not assist you as I ought to have done. I did not sympathize with you as I ought to have done. I spoke a hard word to you. I was estranged from you;" and I think you would all have to feel the same; inevitably you must, if it were not that by some heavenly means, I know not how, the eternal God shall so overshadow believers with the abundant bliss of his own self that even that cause of tears shall be wiped away.

Has it never struck you, dear friends, that if you go to heaven and *see your dear children left behind unconverted,* it would naturally be a cause of sorrow? When my mother told me that if I perished she would have to say "Amen" to my condemnation, I knew it was true and it sounded very terrible, and had a good effect on my mind; but at the same time I could not help thinking, "Well, you will be very different from what you are now," and I did not think she would be improved. I thought "Well, I love to think of your weeping over me far better than to think of you as a perfect being, with a tearless eye, looking on the damnation of your own child." It really is a very terrible spectacle, the thought of a perfect being looking down upon hell, for instance, as Abraham did, and yet feeling no sorrow; for you will recollect that, in the tones in which Abraham addressed the rich man, there is nothing of pity, there is not a single syllable which betokens any sympathy with him in his dreadful woes; and one does not quite comprehend that perfect beings, God-like beings, beings full of love, and everything that constitutes the glory of God's complete nature, should yet be unable to weep, even over hell itself; they cannot weep over their own children lost and ruined! Now, how is this? If you will tell me, I shall be glad, for I cannot tell you. I do not believe that there will be one atom less tenderness, that there will be one fraction less of amiability, and love, and sympathy—I believe there will be more—but that they will be in some way so refined and purified, that while compassion for suffering is there, detestation of sin shall be there to balance it, and a state of complete equilibrium shall be attained. Perfect acquiescence in the divine will is probably the secret of it; but it is not my business to guess; I do not know what handkerchief the Lord will use, but I know that he will wipe *all* tears away from their faces, and these tears among them.

Yet, once again, it seems to me that spirits before the throne, taking, as they must do, a deep interest in everything which concerns the honour of the Lord Jesus Christ, *must feel deeply grieved when they see the cause of truth imperilled, and the kingdom of Christ, for a time put back.* Think of Luther, or Wickliffe, or John Knox, as they see the advances of Popery just now. Take John Knox first, if you will. Think of him looking down and seeing cathedrals rising in Scotland, dedicated to the service of the Pope and the devil. Oh, how the stern old man, even in glory, methinks, would begin to shake himself; and the old lion lash his sides once more, and half wish that he could come down and pull the nests to pieces that the rooks might fly away. Think of Wickliffe looking down on this country where the gospel has been preached so many years and seeing monks in the Church of England, and seeing spring up in our national establishment everywhere, not disguised Popery as it was ten years ago, but stark naked Popery, downright Popery that unblushingly talks about the "Catholic Church," and is not even Anglican any longer. What would Wickliffe say? Why, methink as he leans over the battlements of heaven, unless Wickliffe be mightily altered, and I cannot suppose he is (except for the better, and that would make him more tender-hearted and more zealous for God still), he must weep to think that England has gone back so far, and that on the dial of Ahaz the sun has beat a retreat. I do not know how it is they do not weep in heaven, but they do not. The souls under the altar cry, "How long? how long? how long?" There comes up a mighty intercession from those who were slaughtered in the days gone by for Christ: their prayer rises, "How long? how long? how long?" and God as yet does not avenge his own elect though they cry day and night unto him. Yet that delay does not cost them a single tear. They feel so sure that the victory will come, they anticipate so much the more splendid a triumph because of its delay, and therefore they do both patiently hope and quietly wait to see the salvation of God. They know that without us they cannot be made perfect, and so they wait till we are taken up, that the whole company may be completed, and that then the soul may be dressed in its body, and they may be perfected in their bliss: they wait but they do not weep. They wait and they cry, but in their cry no sorrow has a place. Now I do not understand this, because it seems to me that the more I long for the coming of Christ, the more I long to see his kingdom extended, the more I shall weep when things go wrong, when I see Christ blasphemed, his cross trampled in the mire, and the devil's kingdom established; but the reason is all in this, *"God* shall wipe away all tears from their eyes."

I thought I would just indicate to you why it says that God does it. It strikes me that these causes of tears could not be removed by an angel, could not be taken away by any form of spiritual enjoyment apart from the direct interposition of Almighty God. Think of all these things and wonder over them, and you will recall many other springs of grief which must have flowed freely if Omnipotence had not dried them up completely; then ask how it is that the saints do not weep and do not sorrow and you cannot get any other answer than this—God has done it in a way unknown to us, for ever taking away from them the power to weep.

IV. And now, beloved, SHALL WE BE AMONG THIS HAPPY COMPANY?

Here is the question, and the context enables us to answer it. "They have washed their robes, and made them white in the blood of the Lamb." There is their character. "Therefore are they before the throne of God." The blood is a sacred argument for their being there, the precious blood. Observe, "they washed their robes." It was not merely their feet, their worst parts, but they washed their robes, their best parts. A man's robes are his most honoured attire, he puts them on, and he does not mind our seeing his robes. There may be filthiness beneath, but the robes are generally the cleanest of all. But you see they washed even them. Now it is the mark of a Christian that he not only goes to Christ to wash away his black sins, but to wash his duties too. I would not pray a prayer unwashed with Jesus' blood; I would not like a hymn I have sung to go up to heaven except it had first been bathed in blood; if I would desire to be clothed with zeal as with a cloak, yet I must wash the cloak in blood; though I would be sanctified by the Holy Spirit and wear imparted righteousness as a raiment of needlework, yet I must wash even that in blood. What say you, dear friends? have you washed in blood? The meaning of it is, have you trusted in the atoning sacrifice? "Without shedding of blood there is no remission of sin." Have you taken Christ to be your all in all? Are you now depending on him? If so, out of deep distress you shall yet ascend leaning on your Beloved to the throne of God, and to the bliss which awaiteth his chosen. But if not, "there is none other name," there is no other way. Your damnation will be as just as it will be sure. Christ is "the way," but if ye will not tread it ye shall not reach the end; Christ is "the truth," but if you will not believe him, you shall not rejoice; Christ is "the life," but if you will not receive him you shall abide among the dead, and be cast out among the corrupt. From such a doom may the Lord deliver us, and give us a simple confidence in the divine work of the Redeemer, and to him shall be the praise eternally. Amen.

8

Departed Saints Yet Living

"Now that the dead are raised, even Moses shewed at the bush, when he calleth the Lord the God of Abraham, and the God of Isaac, and the God of Jacob. For he is not a God of the dead, but of the living: for all live unto him." Luke 20:37-38

During the past week the church of God, and the world at large, have sustained a very serious loss. In the taking home to himself by our gracious Lord of the Earl of Shaftesbury, we have, in my judgment, lost the best man of the age. I do not know whom I should place second, but I certainly should put him first—far beyond all other servants of God within my knowledge—for usefulness and influence. He was a man most true in his personal piety, as I know from having enjoyed his private friendship; a man most firm in his faith in the gospel of our Lord Jesus Christ; a man intensely active in the cause of God and truth. Take him whichever way you please, he was admirable: he was faithful to God in all his house, fulfilling both the first and second commands of the law in fervent love to God, and hearty love to man. He occupied his high position with singleness of purpose and immovable steadfastness: where shall we find his equal? If it is not possible that he was absolutely perfect, it is equally impossible for me to mention a single fault, for I saw none. He exhibited scriptural perfection, inasmuch as he was sincere, true, and consecrated. Those things which have been regarded as faults by the loose thinkers of this age are prime virtues in my esteem. They called him *narrow;* and in this they bear unconscious testimony to his loyalty to truth. I rejoiced greatly in his integrity, his fearlessness, his adherence to principle, in a day when revelation is questioned, the gospel explained away, and human thought set up as the idol of the hour. He felt that there was a vital and eternal difference between truth and error; consequently, he did not act or talk as if there was much to be said on either side, and, therefore, no one could be quite sure. We shall not know for many a year how much we miss in missing him; how great an anchor he was to this drifting generation, and how great a stimulus he was to every movement for the benefit of the poor. Both man and beast may unite in mourning him; he was the friend of every living thing. He lived for the oppressed; he lived for London; he lived for the nation; he lived still more for God. He has finished his course; and though we do not lay him to sleep in the grave with the sorrow of those that have no hope, yet we cannot but mourn that a great man and a prince has fallen this day in Israel. Surely, the righteous are taken away from the evil to come, and we are left to struggle on under increasing difficulties.

It must always be so. The godly must die, even as others. Though our life be perfectly consecrated, yet it cannot for ever be continued in this world. It is appointed unto men once to die, and that appointment stands. We expect the present rule to last till he shall come who shall destroy the last enemy. We are not troubled with Sadducean doubts; to us, seeing that Christ rose from the dead, it is a matter of certainty that all his followers must rise also; and seeing that Jesus ever liveth, it is equally a matter of certainty to us that all the saints are still living, for he hath said, "Because I live, ye shall live also." Yet, if no infidelity is permitted to creep into our brain and disturb our belief, it may penetrate into our heart, and cause us great sadness. We who believe in Jesus should rise into an atmosphere more clear and warm than that of the sepulchre; for the Lord Jesus hath "abolished death, and brought life and incorruption to light through the gospel." We are not now sitting in the shadow of death, for eternal light has sprung up. Children of God, it is in the highest degree proper that you should think of things as your Father thinks of them; and he saith that "all live unto God." Let us correct our phraseology by that of Scripture, and speak of departed saints as inspiration speaks of them. Then shall we come back to the simple child's talk which Wordsworth so sweetly turned into rhyme—"Master, we are seven"; and in our family we shall number brothers, and sisters, and friends, whose bodies lie in the churchyard, and shall speak of those who have crossed the border, and passed within the veil, as still our own. Like Jesus, we shall say, "Our friend Lazarus sleepeth"; like Paul, we shall speak of them as absent from the body but present with the Lord, and regard them as part and parcel of the one family in heaven and earth.

Our text was fashioned in a place which has the air of death, burial, and resurrection about it. The voice came to Moses in the desert. This was a strange place for Moses: the living, active, well-instructed mind of Moses, mighty in all the wisdom of Egypt, and full of noble thoughts concerning the living God, was buried in a desert. It is singular to see the foremost mind of the age in the remotest part of the desert, hidden away among sheep. He who was a born king is here feeding a flock. It is death to Moses. Rest assured that Moses cannot be kept in this living tomb; he must rise to life and leadership. While there is a God and a providence Moses cannot continue in obscurity. There are certainties wrapped up in him which cannot fail. A man need not be a prophet to stand at Horeb and prognosticate that Moses will emerge from the desert, and shake Egypt by his resurrection.

While Moses is in the desert he is thinking about another case of death, burial, and resurrection, namely, Israel in Egypt. The people of God, the favoured nation of Jehovah, with whom he had entered into covenant, saying, "I will be their God, and they shall be my people"—these were in Egypt, ground down by relentless oppression, begrimed with brick-earth, and black and blue with the blows of task-masters. It has come to this, that they are compelled to cast their male children into the river, and so to be the destroyers of their own race. The children of Israel have become a herd of slaves; yet they are God's elect people, God's favoured family. It does not require a prophet to declare that this death in Egypt cannot last; the elect nation must live, and rise, and go forth free to serve the Lord. No, Israel; thou shalt never perish! The voice must yet be heard: "Thus saith the Lord, Let my people go, that they may serve me."

And so, while Moses in the desert is thinking of Israel in

Egypt, he sees a bush, and that bush is all ablaze. An ordinary bush upon the heath needs only to be touched with a match: in one moment there is a puff of flame, and then all is over; nothing is left but a trace of ashes. Yet here was an extraordinary thing—a bush that continued to burn, and was not consumed. Here was life in the midst of death, continuance in the midst of destruction. This was an emblem of God abiding with a people, and yet suffering them to live; or of the fires of affliction being rendered harmless to the chosen of God. He who then spoke to Moses was the God of life, the God who could sustain in the midst of destruction, the God who could preserve even a bush from being devoured by the intense fury of flame. Said I not truly that the surroundings of Moses and the bush all favour a display of life in death, and resurrection out of death?

Now we come to the central matter. Out of the midst of the bush there came a voice, a mysterious and divine voice, which said, "I am the God of Abraham, and the God of Isaac, and the God of Jacob." From this voice our divine Lord teaches us to gather this fact: that God's people live when they appear to have been long dead—for he who cannot be the God of the dead, or non-existent, still avows himself to be the God of the long-buried patriarchs. Our Lord proved from that utterance at the bush the continued life of the Lord's chosen, and also their resurrection: how did he do this?

I. We will not go straight to the answer, but we will beat about the bush a little, that the reasoning may the more gently enter our minds. I would say, first, that in these words we have A GLORIOUS RELATIONSHIP DECLARED. Moses calleth the Lord "The God of Abraham, and the God of Isaac, and the God of Jacob."

The glorious Lord did at the bush as good as say, *"These three men have chosen me to be their God."* So they had; through the grace of God they had deliberately chosen to part with their natural kindred in the country of the Chaldees, and to journey to a land of which they knew nothing except that God had promised that they should afterwards receive it for an inheritance. Abraham, Isaac, and Jacob were three very different characters; yet this was common to the three—that they believed God, and took him to be their God alone. They nestled in the bosom of Jehovah while the rest of the world went after their idols. In all their troubles they flew to Jehovah; for the supply of all their needs they resorted alone to him. They were men who had through divine grace deliberately attached themselves unto Jehovah the Most High throughout the whole of their lives. It is a sublime sight to see a man trust in God as Abraham did, and obey the Lord fully as he did in the matter of Isaac, when he accounted God to be able to raise him up even from the dead. Surely there must be everlasting life in a being who could thus confide in Jehovah. I call you to admire the fact that God called the patriarchs into the noble position of following the Lord fully, of fixed and settled choice. Being men of like passions with ourselves, they nevertheless cast in their lot with the Lord, and for his sake preferred the life of strangers and pilgrims on the earth to the comforts of settled residence in Ur of the Chaldees, and to the sinful pleasures of Canaan. We also take this God to be our God, even the God of Abraham, of Isaac, and of Jacob. There is a nobility about the choosers of the true God which will surely secure them from annihilation.

Next, these three men had learned to *commune with God.* How wondrously had Abraham spoken with God! Full many a spot was consecrated as "the place where he stood before the Lord." Isaac also walked in the fields at eventide; and, doubtless, there entered into secret fellowship with God. The Lord also appeared unto him at night, and led him to build an altar and call upon the name of Jehovah. The good old man even in his blindness found solace in communion with the Lord God Almighty. Jacob also was favoured with heavenly visitations. We can never forget that mystic dream at Bethel, nor the wrestling at Jabbok, nor the many times when he turned to the God of his father Abraham, and his father Isaac, and God spake with him as a man speaketh with his friend. It is a wonderful thing that the Lord should thus commune with men. He does not thus show himself to the beasts which perish; he does not thus reveal himself to the lifeless stones of the field. Those are strangely honoured beings with whom God enters into close communion as he did with these three men. I argue from it that these beings cannot dissolve into a handful of dust and cease to be. Can those eyes cease to be which have seen the Lord? Can these souls perish which have conversed with the Eternal? We think not so. But just now I ask you only to meditate upon the glories to which the patriarchs were lifted up, when they were permitted to be the friends of God.

What was still more notable, the Lord *entered into covenant with them.* He made a covenant with Abraham, Isaac, and Jacob, which he remembered, saying, "Surely, blessing I will bless thee, and in multiplying I will multiply thee." You know how the Lord swore to give unto the seed of Abraham a goodly heritage, a land that flowed with milk and honey. Now, it is a wonderful thing that God should enter into compact with man. Doth he make an everlasting covenant, ordered in all things and sure, with mere insects of an hour? Especially, would he give his Son Jesus to die to seal the everlasting covenant by his heart's blood with mere shadows who are but for a little time and then cease to be? I am sure it is not so. If God makes men capable of entering into everlasting covenant with himself, there lies within that fact the clear suggestion that he imparts to them an existence which is not for to-day and to-morrow, but for eternity. Still, I wish you mainly to regard the glory into which manhood is lifted up when God enters into gracious covenant with it.

Moreover, to go further, these men were not only in covenant with God, but *they had lived in accordance with that covenant.* I do not mean that they had lived perfectly in accord with it, but that the main strain of their lives was in conformity with their covenant relationship to God. For the sake of that covenant Abraham quitted Ur of the Chaldees, and dwelt no longer in the land of Haran, but became a sojourner with God in the land of Canaan. For the sake of this he sent away his firstborn after the flesh, seeing it was said, "In Isaac shall thy seed be called." "By faith he sojourned in the land of promise, as in a strange country, dwelling in tabernacles with Isaac and Jacob, the heirs with him of the same promise." These faithful men had respect to the recompense of the reward, and, therefore, they were not mindful of the country from whence they came out, neither sought opportunity to return. Jacob, the most faulty of the three, greatly as he erred in his conduct to his brother Esau, was evidently actuated by an intense faith in the covenant birthright, so that he ventured all things to obtain it. In his old age and death he was anxious not to be confounded with the Egyptians, or separated from the chosen household, and, therefore, he said unto Joseph, "But I will lie with my fathers, and thou shalt carry me out of Egypt, and bury me in their buryingplace." This he made Joseph swear; for he must make sure of it. He was aiming at the promise, despite the errors that he committed in so doing. Now, doth God enter into covenant with men and help men to live in accordance with that covenant, and after all shall they miss the blessing? Shall it end in nothing? Hiding beneath the shadow of God's wing, shall they, after all, perish? It cannot be: they must live to whom God is God.

For this was the covenant, that *they should have God to be their God,* and that they should be God's people. O brothers, I do not know how to speak on such a blessing as this, though I live in the daily enjoyment of it. This God is our God. All that the Lord is, and all that he can do, he hath given over to us, to be used on our behalf: the fulness of his grace and truth, the infinity of his love, the omnipotence of his power, the infallibility of his wisdom—all, all shall be used on our behalf. The Lord has given himself over to his people to be their inheritance; and on the other hand, we, poor weak feeble creatures as we are, are taken to be the peculiar treasure of the living God. "They shall be mine, saith the Lord of hosts, in that day when I make up my jewels." "The Lord's portion is his people: Jacob is the lot of his inheritance." We are God's heritage, we are God's jewels, we are God's children, we are dear to him as the apple of his eye. We are to him as the signet upon his hand and the crown upon his head. He cannot have chosen for his portion a mass of corruption, or a handful of brown dust; yet that is what the body comes to in death. He cannot have chosen for his heritage that which will melt back into mother earth, and be no more found; this cannot be. The covenant hath within it the sure guarantee of eternal life. Oh what an honour it is that God should even say to you and to me—"I will be your God, and you shall be my people. Beyond the angels, beyond heaven, beyond all my other creatures, I reserve you unto myself. I have loved you with an everlasting love. I will rest in my love to you. I will rejoice over you with singing." In this the Lord has highly exalted his covenanted ones, and raised them to great nearness to himself, and thus to glory and honour. What hath God wrought! What is man that God is thus mindful of him, or the son of man that he thus visits him! Angels are nowhere as compared with men, yea, cherubim with all their burning bliss and consecrated ardour cannot match with men who are in covenant with God. Blessed above all other beings are those who have Jehovah to be their God, and who are themselves the Lord's choice, and care, and delight. Each one of these points, if well thought out, will go to strengthen our belief that the saints must live, must live for ever, and are at this moment living unto God.

II. We now come to that matter more distinctly under our second head: here is ETERNAL LIFE IMPLIED; for "God is not the God of the dead, but of the living."

It is implied first in *the very fact of the covenant of grace.* As I have asked before—Doth the eternal God covenant with creatures that shall live only to threescore years and ten, and then shall go out like a candle-snuff? How can he be a God to them? I understand how he can be a helper and a friend to men of brief existence, but I see not how he can be a God. Must they not partake in his eternity if it be truly said, "I will be your God"? How can the Lord be an eternal blessing to an ending being? He has power, and he will give me strength sufficient; he hath wisdom, and he will give me as much of his wisdom as I am capable of receiving; must he not also cause me to partake of his immortality? How is he a God to me if he suffers me to be blotted out of existence? When David said in dying, "Yet hath he made with me an everlasting covenant," his comfort lay in his belief that he should live in the everlasting age to enjoy the fruit of that covenant. How could there be an everlasting covenant with a creature who would cease to exist?

But next, *this covenant was made up of promises of a very peculiar order;* for in very deed the covenant that God made with Abraham was not altogether, or even mainly, concerning things temporal. It was not the land of Canaan alone of which the Lord spake to Abraham, but the patriarchs declared plainly that they desired "a better country, that is, an heavenly" (Hebrews xi. 16). Even when they were in Canaan they were still looking for a country; and the city promised to them was not Jerusalem; for, according to Paul in the eleventh of the Hebrews, they still were looking for "a city which hath foundations, whose builder and maker is God." They did not find in their earthly lives the complete fulfillment of the covenant; for they received not the promises, but saw them afar off, and were persuaded of them. The temporal blessings which God gave to them were not their expected portion; but they took hold upon invisible realities, and lived in expectation of them. They were evidently actuated by faith in something spiritual, something everlasting; and they believed that the covenant which God had made with them concerned such things. I have not the time to go into this subject; you get it more fully explained to you in the Epistle to the Hebrews; but so it was, that the covenant blessings were of an order and a class that could not be compassed within the space of this present mortal life: the outlook of covenant promises was towards the boundless sea of eternity. Now, if the Lord made with them a covenant concerning eternal blessings, these saints must live to enjoy those blessings. God did not promise endless blessings to the creatures of a day.

More especially, beloved, it is to be remembered that *for the sake of these eternal things the patriarchs had given up transient enjoyments*. Abraham might have been a quiet prince in his own country, living in comfort; but for the sake of the spiritual blessing he left Chaldea, and came to wander in the pastures of Canaan, in the midst of enemies, and to dwell in tents in the midst of discomforts. Isaac and Jacob were "heirs with him also of the same promises;" but they entered not into the pursuits of the people; they dwelt alone, and were not numbered among the nations. Like Moses himself, to whom God spake, they "counted the reproach of Christ greater riches than the treasures of Egypt." They quitted kith and kin, and all the advantages of settled civilized life, to be rangers of the desert, exiles from their fatherland. They were the very types and models of those who have no abiding city here; therefore, for certain, though they died in hope, not having received the promise, we cannot believe that God deceived them. Their God was no mocker of them, and therefore they must live after death. They had lived in this poor life for something not seen as yet; and if there be no such thing, and no future life, they had been duped and cozened into a mistaken self-denial. If there be no life to come, the best philosophy is that which saith, "Let us eat and drink; for to-morrow we die." Since these men put this life in pawn for the next, they were sadly

mistaken if there be no such life. Do you not see the force of
our Saviour's reasoning?—God, who has led his people to
abandon the present for the future, must justify their choice.

Besides, *the Lord had staked his honour and his repute
upon these men's lives.* "Do you want to know," saith he, "who
I am? I am the God of Abraham, of Isaac, and of Jacob. If you
want to know how I deal with my servants, go and look at
the lives of Abraham, and Isaac, and Jacob." My brethren, as
far as the earthly lives of the patriarchs can be written in
human records, they are certainly full of God's
lovingkindness; but still there is nothing so remarkably
joyous and majestic about them from a natural point of view
as to make the Lord's dealings with them appear to be
specially wonderful. Others who feared not God have been as
rich, and powerful, and honourable as they. Especially is the
life of Jacob ploughed and cross-ploughed with affliction and
trial. He spake the truth when he summed up his life in the
words, "Few and evil have the days of the years of my life
been." Does the Lord intend us to judge of his goodness to his
servants from the written life of Jacob? or from the career of
any one of his servants? The judgment must include the ages
of an endless blessedness. This life is but the brief preface to
the volume of our history. It is but the rough border, the
selvage of the rich cloth of our being. These rippling streams
of life come not to an end, but flow into the endless, shoreless
ocean of bliss. Abraham, Isaac, and Jacob have long been
enjoying felicity, and shall enjoy it throughout eternity. God
is not ashamed to be called their God if you judge of the
whole of their being; he would not have spoken thus if the
visible were all, and there were no future to counterbalance
the tribulations of this mortal life. God is not the God of the
short-lived, who are so speedily dead; but he is the living
God of an immortal race, whose present is but a dark
passage into a bright future which can never end.

Yet further, to bring out the meaning here, *God cannot be
the God of the non-existent.* The supposition is too absurd.
Our Saviour does not argue about it, but he says so most
peremptorily! God is not the God of the dead—that cannot
be! If Abraham, and Isaac, and Jacob are reduced to a
handful of ashes, God cannot be at this moment their God.
We cannot take a dead object to be our God, neither can
Jehovah be a God to lifeless clay. God is not the God of

putrefaction and annihilation. God is not the God of that which has ceased to be. We have but to put the idea into words to make it dissolve before the glance of reason. A living God is the God of living men; and Abraham, Isaac, and Jacob are still alive.

This even goes far to show that the bodies of these saints shall yet live. God reckons his covenanted ones to be alive. He saith, "The dead are raised." He reckons them to be raised; and as he reckons nothing falsely, it is said by way of anticipation. "Thy dead men shall live." Inasmuch as a portion of these chosen ones is still in the earth, God, who reckons things that are not as though they were, looks upon their bodies as possessing life, because they are to possess life so soon. God is not only the God of Abraham's soul, but of Abraham as a whole, his body, soul, and spirit. God is the God of Abraham's body; we are sure of that, because the covenant seal was set upon the flesh of Abraham. Where the doubt might be, there is the confirming seal, namely, in his mortal body. There was no seal set upon his soul, for the soul had life, and could not see death; but it was set upon his body, which would die, to make sure that even *it* would live. At this day we have baptism and the holy supper to be seals as to the body. I have sometimes thought to myself that it were better if there were no water baptism, seeing it has become the nest of so much superstition; and the Lord's Supper, with all its blessed uses, has been so abused that one is apt to think that without outward ordinances there might be more spiritual religion; but the Lord intends that the materialism of man, and of creation, shall be uplifted; and that the body shall be raised incorruptible, and therefore has he given seals which touch the outward and material. The water wherein the body is washed, and the bread and wine whereby the body is nourished, are tokens that there cometh to us, not only spiritual and invisible blessings, but even such as shall redeem and purify our mortal body. The grave cannot hold any portion of the covenanted ones: eternal life is the portion of the whole man. God is the God of our entire manhood, spirit, soul, and body; and all live unto him in their entirety. The whole of the covenant shall be fulfilled to the whole of those with whom that covenant was made.

This is good reasoning to those who have gone beyond

mere reason, and have ascended into the realm of faith. May
the Holy Spirit grant unto us to be among them!

III. Thirdly, and very briefly, beloved friends: my text not
only declares glorious relationship, and implies eternal life,
but it also unveils somewhat scantily, but still sufficiently,
what the glorious life must be. Look then and see the
GLORIOUS LIFE UNVEILED.

It is clear that they live *personally*. It is not said, "I am the
God of the whole body of the saints in one mass." But "I am
the God of Abraham, Isaac, Jacob." God will make his people
to live individually. My mother, my father, my child, each
will personally exist. God is the God of saints, as living
distinct lives: Abraham is Abraham, Isaac is Isaac, Jacob is
Jacob. The three patriarchs were not all melted into one
common Abraham, nor Isaac into one imaginary Isaac;
neither was any one so altered as to cease to be himself.
Abraham, Isaac, and Jacob are all literally living as actual
men, and the same men as they used to be. Jacob is Jacob,
and not an echo of Abraham; Isaac is Isaac, and not a
rehearsal of Jacob. All the saints are existent in their
personality, identity, distinction, and idiosyncrasy.

What is more, the patriarchs are *mentioned by their
names;* and so it is clear they are known: they are not three
anonymous bodies, but Abraham, Isaac, and Jacob. Many
enquire, "Shall we know our friends in heaven?" Why should
we not? The saints in heaven are never spoken of in
Scripture as moving about anonymously; but their names
are spoken of as written in the book of life. Why is this? The
apostles knew Moses and Elias on the Mount, though they
had never seen them before. I cannot forget old John
Ryland's answer to his wife: "John," she said, "will you know
me in heaven?" "Betty," he replied, "I have known you well
here, and I shall not be a bigger fool in heaven than I am
now; therefore I shall certainly know you there." That seems
to be clear enough. We read in the New Testament, "They
shall sit down with Abraham, Isaac, and Jacob in the
kingdom of heaven;" not sit down with three unknown
individuals in iron masks, or three impersonalities who
make a part of the great *pan,* nor three spirits who are as
exactly alike as pins made in a factory; but Abraham, Isaac,
and Jacob. That is clear enough in the text.

That glorious life, while it is a personal and a known life,

is also *free from all sorrow,* and misery, and earthly
grossness. They are neither married nor given in marriage,
neither shall they die any more; but they are as the angels of
God. It is a life of perfect blessedness, a life of hallowed
worship, a life of undivided glory. Oh, that we were in it! Oh,
that we may soon reach it! Let us think of the many who are
enjoying it now, and of those who have attained to it during
the last few days. I am sure they are at home in every golden
street, and fully engaged in the adoration and worship of
their Lord. Those saints who have been in glory now these
thousands of years cannot be more blest than the latest
arrivals. Within a very short space you and I shall be among
the shining ones. Some of us may spend our next Sabbath
with the angels. Let us rejoice and be glad at the bare
thought of it. Some of us are not doomed to live here through
another winter: we shall pass beyond these autumn fogs into
the golden light of the eternal summer before another
Christmas-day has come. Oh the joy which ought to thrill
through our souls at the thought of such amazing bliss!

And now, taking the whole subject together, I want to say
a few familiar things about the influence which all this
ought to have upon us.

Concerning those that have gone before us, we gather from
this whole text that *they are not lost.* We know where they
are. Neither have they lost anything, for they are what they
were, and more. Abraham has about him still everything
that is Abrahamic; he is Abraham still. And Isaac has
everything about him that properly belongs to Isaac; and
Jacob has all about him that makes him God's Israel. These
good men have lost nothing that really appertained to their
individuality, nothing that made them precious in the sight
of the Lord. They have gained infinitely; they have
developed gloriously. They are Abraham, and Isaac, and
Jacob now at their best; or rather they are waiting till the
trumpet of the resurrection shall sound, when their bodies
also shall be united to their spirits, and then Abraham, and
Isaac, and Jacob will be completely Abraham, and Isaac, and
Jacob, world without end. We are by no means deprived of
our dear ones by their death: they *are;* they are themselves;
and they are ours still. As Abraham is not lost to Isaac, nor
to Jacob, nor to God, nor to himself; so are our beloved ones
by no means lost to us. Do not let us think of them then as if

they were lost. I know your sorrows make an excursion to
the grave, to look there for the deceased ones. You want to
lift that coffin lid, and to unwrap the shroud. Oh, do not so,
do not so! He is not here; the real man has gone. He may be
dead to you for a while, but he lives unto God. Yes, the dead
one liveth, he liveth unto God. Do but anticipate the passage
of that little time, which is almost gone while I am speaking
of it, and then your Saviour's angels shall sound their golden
trumpets, and at the welcome noise the grave shall open its
portals, and resign its captives. "Thy brother shall rise
again." Wherefore, comfort one another with these words.
Shaftesbury is as much Shaftesbury as ever, and even more
so. We have parted with the earl, but the saint liveth: he has
gone past yonder veil into the next room, and there he is
before the Lord of Hosts. He has gone out of this dim, dusky,
cloudy chamber into the bright, pearly light that streameth
from the throne of God and of the Lamb. We have nothing to
sorrow about in reference to what he is or where he is. So,
too, your valued parents, and beloved children, and choice
friends—they are yours still. Herein is great cause for
thankfulness. Put aside your sackcloth, and wear the
garments of hope; lay down the sackbut, and take up the
trumpet. Draw not the beloved bodies to the cemetery with
dreary pomp, and with black horses; but cover the coffin
with sweet flowers, and drape the horses with emblems of
hope. It is the better birthday of the saint, yea, his truer
wedding-day. Is it sad to have done with sadness? Is it
sorrowful to part with sorrow? Nay rather, when joy
beginneth to our friends, where glory dwelleth in
Immanuel's land, we may in sympathy sing, as it were, a
new song, and tune our harps to the melodies of the
glorified.

I want you also to recollect that *the departed have not
become members of another race;* they have not been
transferred into another family; they are still men, still
women, still of our kindred dear; their names are in the
same family register on earth, and in heaven. Oh, no, no! do
not dream that they are separated, and exiled; they have
gone to the home country: we are the exiles; they it is who
are at home. We are *en route* for the fatherland; they are not
so far from us as we think. Sin worked to divide them from
us, and us from them, while we were here together; but since

sin is now taken away from them, one dividing element is gone. When it is also removed from us, we shall be nearer to each other than we could have been while we were both sinful. Do not let us think of them as sundered far, for we are one in Christ.

And *they are not gone over to the other side in the battle.* Oh, do not speak of them as dead and lying on the battle-field: they live, they live in sympathy with our divine conflict. They have marched through the enemy's country; they have fought their fight and taken possession of their inheritance. They are still on our side, though we miss them from the daily service. When you number up the hosts of God, you must not forget the godlike bands that have fought the good fight, and kept the faith, and finished their course. They are in the armies of the Lord, though not at this moment resisting unto blood. The hundred and forty-four thousand sealed unto the Lord include in their ranks all who are with God, whether here or in heaven.

> "One family we dwell in him,
> One church, above, beneath,
> Though now divided by the stream,
> The narrow stream of death."

Our sacramental host marches onward to the New Jerusalem. Certain of the legionaries have forded the dividing flood. I see them ascending the other side! The hither bank of the river is white with their rising companies. Lo! I hear the splash of the ranks before us as they steadily pass down into the chill stream; in deep silence we see them solemnly wading through the billows. The host is ever marching on, marching on. The much dreaded stream lies a little before us: it is but a silver streak. We are to the margin come. We shudder not at the prospect. We follow the blessed footsteps of our Lord and his redeemed. We are all one army still: we are not losing our men; they are simply ascending from the long campaign to take their endless rewards at the Lord's right hand.

What then? Why, then, *we will take up their work.* If they have gone into the upper chamber to rest, we will make up their lack of service in this lower room. The work they did was so human that we will not allow a stitch to drop, but take it up where they left it, and persevere in earnest. They are in glory, but they were not glorified when they were here. The work they did was done by men of such infirmities as ours; so let us not fear to go on where they left off, and perpetuate the work which they rejoiced in. There lies the plough in the furrow, and the oxen are standing still, for Shamgar, the champion, is gone. Will no one lay hold of the plough handles? Will nobody urge the oxen with the goad? Young men, are you idling? Here is work for you. Are you hiding yourselves? Come forward, I pray you in the name of the great Husbandman, and let the fields be tilled, and sown with the good seed. Who will fill the gap made by death? Who will be baptized for the dead? Who will bear the banner now that a standard-bearer has fallen? I hope some consecrated voice will answer, "Here am I; send me."

For, last of all, brethren, *we may expect the same succours as they received who have gone before.* Jehovah saith that he is the God of Abraham, the God of Isaac, and the God of Jacob; but he also saith, "I am the God of your father." The father of Moses had the Lord to be his God. That God is the God of my father, blessed be his name. As I took the old man by his hand yesterday, at the age of seventy-six, I could not but rejoice in all the faithfulness of the Lord to him and to his house. He was the God of my father's father also; I cannot forget how the venerable man laid his hands upon his grandchild, and blessed him; and the blessing is with him still. Yes, and he is the God of my children, and he shall be the God of my children's children; for he keepeth covenant to thousands of them that love him. Wherefore take courage, men and brethren! This God is your God. He is a God to you, and you are a people to him. Act as his true servants. Live as those that are elect. If you are his choice, be choice characters. The chosen should be the best, should they not? The elect should be especially distinguished above all others by their conversation and their fervent zeal for him that chose them. As you shall rise from among the dead, because the Lord Jesus hath redeemed you from among men, so stand up from among the dead and corrupt mass of this world, and be alive unto God, through Jesus Christ your Lord. What manner of people ought ye to be who serve the living God? Since the living God hath manifested himself so wonderfully to you, ought you not to live unto him to the utmost? God bless you for Jesus' sake. Amen.

9

The Hope Laid Up In Heaven

"For the hope which is laid up for you in heaven, whereof ye heard before in the word of the truth of the gospel."

Colossians 1:5

Three graces should be always conspicuous in Christians—faith, love, and hope. They are each mentioned by Paul in the opening verses of the epistle from which our text is taken. These lovely graces should be so conspicuous in every believer as to be spoken of, and consequently heard of even by those who have never seen us. These flowers should yield so sweet a perfume that their fragrance may be perceived by those who have never gazed upon them. So was it with the saints at Colosse. Paul says, "We give thanks to God and the Father of our Lord Jesus Christ, praying always for you, since we *heard* of your faith in Christ Jesus, and of the *love* which ye have to all the saints, for the *hope* which is laid up for you in heaven." May our characters be such as can be reported of without causing us to blush; but that can never be the case if these essential virtues are absent. If these things be in us and abound we shall not be barren or unfruitful, but if they be lacking we are as withered branches. We should, therefore, be rich in faith, which is the root of every grace; and to this end we should daily pray, "Lord, increase our faith." We should strive to be full even to overflowing with love, which is of God, and makes us like to God; and we should also abound in hope, even that heavenly hope which causeth a man to purify himself in readiness for the inheritance above. See ye to it that neither of these three divine sisters are strangers to your souls, but let faith, hope, and love take up their abode in your hearts.

Note, however, the special character of each of these graces as it exists in the Christian. It is not every faith and love and hope that will serve our turn, for of all precious things there are counterfeits. There is a kind of *faith* in all men, but ours is *faith in Christ Jesus,* faith in him whom the world rejects, whose cross is a stumblingblock, and whose doctrine is an offence. We have faith in the man of Nazareth, who is also the Son of God, faith in him who having made atonement by his own blood once for all, is now exalted to his Father's right hand. Our confidence is not placed in ourselves, nor in any human priest nor in the traditions of our fathers, nor in the teachings of human wisdom, but alone in Christ Jesus. This is the faith of God's elect.

The *love* of Christians, too, is also special, for while a Christian man is moved by universal benevolence and desires to do good unto all men, yet he has a special love *unto all the saints,* and these the world loves not, because it loves not their Lord. The true believer loves the persecuted, the misrepresented, and despised people of God for Christ's sake. He loves them all, even though he may think some of them to be mistaken in minor matters; he has love to the babes in grace as well as to the grown saints, and love even to those saints whose infirmities are more manifest than their virtues. He loves them not for their station, or for their natural amiability, but because Jesus loves them, and because they love Jesus. You see the faith is in Christ Jesus, but the love extends beyond Christ himself to all those who are in union with him: while hope takes a still wider sweep, and includes the eternal future in its circuit; thus do our graces increase in range as well as in number.

Our *hope,* too, upon which we are to speak this morning, is special, because it is a hope which is laid up for us in heaven; a hope, therefore, which the worldling cares not one whit about. He hopes that to-morrow may be as this day, and yet more abundant, but he cares nothing for the land where time has ceased to flow. He hopes for riches, or he hopes for fame; he hopes for long life and prosperity; he hopes for pleasure and domestic peace; the whole range of his hope is within the compass of his eye: but our hope has passed beyond the sphere of sight, according to the word of the apostle, "What a man seeth, why doth he yet hope for? But if we hope for that we see not, then do we with patience wait for it." Ours is a hope which demands nothing of time, or earth, but seeks its all in the world to come. It is of this hope that we are about to speak. May the Holy Spirit lead us into a profitable meditation upon it.

The connection of our text seems to be this: the apostle so much rejoiced when he saw the saints at Colosse possessing faith, love, and hope, that he thanked God and prayed about them. He saw these seals of God upon them, these three tokens that they were a really converted people, and his heart was glad. All the faithful ministers of Christ rejoice to see their people adorned with the jewels of faith, and love, and hope; for these are their ornament for the present, and their preparation for the future. This I believe to be the connection, but yet from the form of the language it is clear that the apostle intended to state that their love to the saints was very much produced in them by the hope which was laid up in heaven. You notice the word "for," which stands there: "The love which ye have to all the saints for," or *on account of,* or *because of,* "the hope which is laid up for you in heaven." There can be no doubt that the hope of heaven tends greatly to foster love to all the saints of God. We have a common hope, let us have a common affection: we are on our way to God, let us march in loving company; we are to be one in heaven, let us be one on earth. One is our Master and one is our service; one is our way and one is our end; let us be knit together as one man. We all of us expect to see our Well-beloved face to face, and to be like him; why should we not even now love all those in whom there is anything of Christ? Brethren, we are to live together for ever in heaven: it is a pity we should quarrel. We are for ever to be with Jesus Christ, partakers of the same joy, of the same glory, and of the same love; why should we be scant in our love to each other? On the way to Canaan we have to fight the same enemy, to publish the same testimony, to bear the same trials, and to fly to the same helper: therefore let us love one another. It were not difficult to show that the hope which is laid up in heaven should be productive of love among the saints on earth. This connection of my text with the clause immediately before it does not at all prevent its being regarded in the sense which I first mentioned, namely, that it was a subject for joy with the apostle that the Colossians had faith and love and hope; for he would rejoice none the less because their faith was fostered by their hope. It commendeth these sweet graces, that they are so wonderfully intertwisted with each other and dependent upon one another. There would be no love to the saints if there were not faith in Christ Jesus, and if there were not faith in Christ Jesus there would be no hope laid up in heaven. If we had no love it would be certain that we had no true faith, and if we had no hope, faith would be assuredly absent. If we entertain one of the graces we must receive her sisters, for they cannot be separated. Here are three brilliants set in the same golden setting, and none must break the precious jewel. "Now abideth faith, hope and love, these three," and blessed is he who hath them abiding in his own heart.

Now we will let faith and love stand by for a little while, and we will talk about hope, the hope mentioned in our text, the hope which is laid up for you in heaven. First, *it is a very marvellous hope;* secondly, *it is a very secure hope;* and thirdly, *it is a very powerfully influential hope.* May the Holy Ghost bless these three thoughts to us all.

I. First, then, we speak of our hope which is laid up for us in heaven as A VERY MARVELLOUS HOPE, and it is so, if we only consider that *it is a great act of grace that sinners should have a hope at all.* That when man had broken his Maker's law there should remain a hope for him is a thought which should make our hearts leap with gratitude. Do you not recollect when you felt it to be so? When sin lay heavily upon your conscience, Satan came and wrote over the lintel of your door, "NO HOPE," and the grim sentence would have stood there to this day had not a loving hand taken the hyssop, and by a sprinkling of precious blood removed the black inscription. "Wherefore remember that at that time ye were without Christ, having no hope, and without God in the world." That was our condition once; and it is a marvellous thing that it should be thoroughly changed, and that assurance should have taken the place of despair. In our carnal estate many false hopes, like will-o'-the-wisps, danced before us, deceived us, and led us into bogs of presumption and error, but we really had no hope. This is a dreadful condition for a man to be in: it is, indeed, the very worst of all; never is the storm so terrible as when in the howling of the winds the man distinctly hears the words *"No hope."* Yet into the thick darkness of NO HOPE we once steered our course, and each time we tried to rely upon good works, outward ceremonies, and good resolutions, we were disappointed anew, and the words rung into our souls with dread monotony, "No hope, no hope," until we were fain to lie down and die. Now, sinners though we be, we have a hope. Ever since by faith we looked to Jesus on the cross, a hope full of glory has taken possession of our hearts. Is not this a marvellous thing?

More marvellous still is it *that our hope should venture to be associated with heaven.* Can there be heaven for such as we are? It seems almost presumptuous for a sinner who so richly deserves hell even to lift up his eyes towards heaven. He might have some hope of purgatory, if there were such a region, but a hope of heaven, is not that too much? Yet, brethren, we have no fear of hell or of purgatory now, but we expect to taste the joys laid up in heaven. There is no purgatory for anyone, and there is no hell for saints, heaven awaits all believers in Jesus. Our hope is full of glory, for it has to do with the glory of Christ, whom we hope to behold. Dost thou expect then, thou who wast black with lust, that thou shalt sit among the angels? "Ay, that I do," saith the believer, "and nearer to the throne than they." And thou who hast plunged into every form of uncleanness, dost thou expect to see God, for none but the pure in heart can behold him? "Aye, that I do," saith he, "and not only to see him, but to be like his Son, when I see him as he is." What a divine hope is this! Not that we shall sit down on heaven's doorstep, and hear stray notes of the songs within, but that we shall sing with the happy band; not that we shall have an occasional glance within the gates of pearl, and feel our hearts hankering after the unutterable joys within the sacred enclosure, but we shall actually and personally enter into the halls of the palace, and see the king in his beauty in the land which is very far off. This is a brave hope, is it not? Why, she aspireth to all that the best of saints have received, she looketh for the same vision of glory, the same ecstasy of delight; she even aspireth to sit upon the throne of Christ, according to the promise, "To him that overcometh will I grant to sit with me in my throne, even as I also overcame, and am set down with my Father in his throne." Hope reckons to be among the overcomers, and to partake in their enthronement. This is marvellous hope for a struggling believer to entertain; yet it is not presumption, but confidence warranted by the word of God. Is it not a miracle of love that such poor creatures as ourselves should be enabled thus to hope in God?

This hope is the more marvellous because *it is so substantial*. In our text the apostle scarcely seems to be speaking of the grace of hope, since that can hardly be said to be laid up in heaven, but dwells in our bosoms: he rather speaks of the object of hope, and yet it is clear that in his mind the grace of hope as well as the object must have been intended, because that which is laid up in heaven is not a hope except to those who hope for it; it is clear that no man has a hope laid up in heaven, unless he has hope within himself. The truth is that the two things—the grace of hope and its object—are here mentioned under one term, which may be intended to teach us that when hope is wrought in the heart by the Holy Ghost, it is the thing hoped for, even as faith is the thing believed, because it realizes and secures it. Just as faith is the substance of things hoped for, and the evidence of things not seen, so is hope the substance of the thing it expects, and the evidence of the thing it cannot see. Paul in this case, as in many others, uses language rather according to the theological sense which he would convey than according to the classical usage of the Greek tongue. The words of a heathen people must be somewhat strained from their former use if they are to express divine truth, and Paul does thus stretch them to their utmost length in this case. The hope of the true believer is so substantial that Paul even speaks of it as though it were the thing itself; and were laid up in heaven. Many a man hath a hope of wealth, but that hope is a different thing from being wealthy. There is many a slip 'twixt the cup and the lip,' saith the old proverb, and how true it is! A man may have a hope of old age, yet he may never reach even middle life, and thus it is clear that the hope of long life is not in itself longevity; but he that hath the divine hope which grows out of faith and love hath a hope which shall never be disappointed, so that the apostle speaks of it as being identical with the thing hoped for, and describes it as laid up in heaven. What a marvellous hope is this which long before its realization is treated as a matter of actual attainment, and spoken of as a treasure reserved in the coffers of heaven!

One marvellous point about our hope is this, that *it is the subject of divine revelation*. No one could ever have invented this hope, it is so glorious as to baffle imagination. The prince of dreamers could never have dreamed it, nor the master of the art of logic have inferred it by reason: imagination and understanding are both left upon the ground, while the Bible idea of heaven soars upward like a strong-winged angel. The eternal hope had to be revealed to us; we should never have known it else, for the apostle says, "Whereof ye heard before in the word of the truth of the gospel." That a sinful man should have a hope of enjoying the perfect bliss of Paradise is a thing not to be thought of, were it not that the Lord hath promised it. I say again, imagination's utmost stretch had never reached to this, neither could we have had the presumption to suppose that such a bliss could be in store for men so unworthy and undeserving, had we not been assured thereof by the word of God. But now the word of God hath opened a window in heaven and bidden us look therein and hope for the time when we shall drink of its living fountains of waters, and go no more out for ever.

This is marvellous, and it is even more marvellous to think that *this hope came to us simply by hearing*. "Whereof ye heard before in the word of the truth of the gospel." "Faith cometh by hearing," and hope comes by faith; and so the divine hope of being in heaven came to us by hearing,—not by working, not by deserving, not by penance and sacrifice, but simply by hearkening diligently unto the divine word, and believing unto life. We heard that the pierced hand of Jesus had opened the kingdom of heaven to all believers, and we believed, and saw a way of entrance into the holiest by his blood. We heard that God had prepared for them that love him joys indescribable, and we believed the message, trusting in his Son. Our confidence is in the word which we have heard, for it is written, "Hear and your soul shall live"; and we find that by hearing our confidence is strengthened, and our heart filled with inward assurance and joyful expectation, therefore do we love the word more and more.

Will we not prize to the uttermost that sacred word which
has brought us such a hope? Yes, that we will; till we
exchange hearing for seeing, and the message of Jesus for
Jesus himself, we will always lend a willing ear to the
testimony of Jesus.

This hope is marvellous, once more, because *the substance
of it is most extraordinary.* Brethren, what is the hope which
is laid up for us in heaven? It would need many a sermon to
bring out all the phases of delight which belong to that hope.
It is the hope of *victory,* for we shall overcome every foe, and
Satan shall be trodden under our feet. A palm of victory is
prepared for our hands, and a crown for our heads. Our life
struggle shall not end in defeat, but in complete and eternal
triumph, for we shall overcome through the blood of the
Lamb. Nor do we hope for victory only: but in our own
persons we shall possess *perfection.* We shall one day cast off
the slough of sin, and shall be seen in the beauty of our
new-born life. Truly, "it doth not yet appear what we shall
be," but when we think of the matchless character of our
Lord Jesus, we are overjoyed by the assurance that "we shall
be like him." What an honour and a bliss for the younger
brethren to be like the firstborn! To what higher honour
could God himself exalt us? I know not of aught which could
surpass this. Oh, matchless joy to be as holy, harmless, and
undefiled as our own beloved Lord! How delightful to have
no propensity to sin remaining in us nor trace of its ever
having been there; how blissful to perceive that our holy
desires and aspirations have no weakness or defect
remaining in them. Our nature will be perfect and fully
developed, in all its sinless excellence. We shall love God, as
we do now, but oh how much more intensely! We shall
rejoice in God, as we do now, but oh what depth there will be
in that joy! We shall delight to serve him, as we do now, but
there will then be no coldness of heart, no languor of spirit,
no temptation to turn aside. Our service will be as perfect as
that of angels. Then shall we say to ourselves without fear of
any inward failure, "Bless the Lord, O my soul, and all that
is within me bless his holy name." There will be no recreant
affection then; no erring judgment, no straying passion, no
rebellious lust: there will remain nothing which can defile,
or weaken, or distract. We shall be perfect, altogether
perfect. This is our hope—victory over evil and perfection in

all that is good. If this were all our hope it would be marvellous, but there is more to be unfolded.

We expect to enjoy *security* also from every danger. As there will be no evil in us, so there will be none around us or about us to cause us alarm. No temporal evil, such as pain, bereavement, sorrow, labour, or reproach shall come near us: all will be security, peace, rest, and enjoyment. No mental evil will intrude upon us in heaven; no doubts, no staggering difficulties, no fears, no bewilderments will cause us distress. Here we see through a glass darkly, and we know in part, but there shall we see face to face, and know even as we are known. Oh, to be free from mental trouble! What a relief will this be to many a doubting Thomas! This is a marvellous hope. And then no spiritual enemy will assail us, no world, no flesh, no devil will mar our rest above. What will you make out of it, ye tried ones? Your Sabbaths are very sweet now on earth, but when they are over you have to return to yon cold world again; but there your Sabbath shall never end, and your separation from the wicked will be complete. It will be a strange sensation for you to find no Monday morning, no care to be renewed, no toil to be encountered, no harness to be buckled on afresh; above all, no sin to be dreaded, no temptation to be escaped. Heaven is so peaceful that the storms of earth are there unknown, the stirrings of the flesh are never felt, and the howlings of the dog of hell are never heard. There all is peace and purity, perfection and security for ever.

With this security will come perfect *rest:* "Yea, saith the Spirit, for they rest from their labours." Heavenly rest is quite consistent with *continual service,* for, like the angels, we shall rest on the wing, and find it rest to serve God day and night. But there you shall not toil till the sweat bedews your face, neither shall the sun smite you, nor any heat. No weary limb nor fevered brain shall follow upon the blessed service of the glory-land. It is a paradise of pleasure, and a palace of glory; it is a garden of supreme delights, and a mansion of abiding love; it is an everlasting *sabbatismos,* a rest which never can be broken, which evermore remaineth for the people of God; it is a kingdom where all are kings, an inheritance where all are heirs. My soul panteth for it. Is not this a charming hope? Did I not say well when I declared it to be marvellous?

Nor is this all, brethren, for we expect to enjoy in heaven a *happiness* beyond compare. Eye hath not seen it, nor ear heard it, nor hath the heart conceived it; it surpasses all carnal joy. We know a little of it, for the Lord hath revealed it unto us by the Spirit, who searcheth all things, even the deep things of God; yet what we know is but a mere taste of the marriage feast: enough to make us long for more, but by no means sufficient to give us a complete idea of the whole banquet. If it be so sweet to preach about Christ, what must it be to see him and be with him? If it be so delightful to be ravished by the music of his name, what must it be to lie in his bosom? Why, if these few clusters of Eshcol which are now and then brought to us are so sweet, what will it be to abide in the vineyard, where all the clusters grow? If that one bucketful from the well of Bethlehem tasted so sweetly that we scarce dared to drink it, but poured it out before the Lord as a thankoffering, what a joy will it be to drink at the well-head without stint for ever? O to be eternally at the right hand of God, where there are pleasures for evermore! This is our hope, and yet there is more, for we have the hope of everlasting *fellowship* with Christ. I would give ten thousand worlds, if I had them, to have one glimpse of that dear face, which was marred with sorrow for my sake; but to sit at my Lord's feet and look up into his countenance, and hear his voice, and never, never grieve him, but to participate in all his triumphs and glories for ever and for ever,—what a heaven will this be? Then shall we have fellowship with all his saints, in whom he is glorified, and by whom his image is reflected; and thus shall we behold fresh displays of his power and beamings of his love. Is not this surpassing bliss? Said I not well when I declared that ours is a marvellous hope? Had I eloquence and could pile on goodly words, and could a poet assist me with his sweetest song, to tell of the bliss and joy of the eternal world, yet must preacher and poet both confess their inability to describe the glory to be revealed in us. The noblest intellect and the sweetest speech could not convey to you so much as a thousandth part of the bliss of heaven. There I leave the first head. It is a very marvellous hope.

II. Secondly, let us remark that IT IS A MOST SECURE HOPE. It is so according to the text, because *it is laid up or secured.* The recent calamities which have occurred in connection with the Glasgow City Bank will make business men very careful where they lay up their treasures; but no one can entertain any fear of the safety of that which God himself takes under his charge. If your hope is laid up with him it becomes sinful to doubt its security. It is "laid up," the text says, and this means that it is hidden in a safe place like a treasure which is well secured. We find it hard to lay up our valuables safely in this world because thieves break through and steal; the iron safe, the strong room, and all sorts of inventions are employed to preserve them from felonious grip; but when God becomes the guardian of our treasure he lays it up where none can touch it, and neither man nor devil can steal it. Our hope is laid up just as crowns and wreaths were laid up at the Grecian games for those who gained them: no one could snatch them away from their rightful owners, but the rewards were safely retained for the winners, to be distributed when the contest was over. You see not as yet your hope, beloved, but it is laid up: it is hidden with Christ in God, and made as safe as the throne of God himself.

Notice the next word, it is laid up *"for you."* It is something to have your hope laid up, but it is much better to have it laid up for yourself. "Laid up *for you"*; that is, for you whose faith is in Christ Jesus, and who have love to all the saints. There is a crown in heaven which will never be worn by any head but yours; there is a harp in glory that never will be touched by any finger but yours. Make no mistake about it; it is laid up in heaven *for you*, "reserved in heaven *for you*, who are kept by the power of God, through faith unto salvation." "For you";— "Fear not, little flock; for it is your Father's good pleasure to give *you* the kingdom." Lay the stress there, and get honey out of it. "Laid up for *you*."

Where is it laid up? The next word tells us. "Laid up for you *in heaven*," "where," says the Saviour as though he were expounding the text, "neither moth nor rust doth corrupt." This means that no process of decay will cause your treasure to become stale and worn out; no secret moth will eat the garments of heaven's courtiers, and no rust will tarnish the brightness of their crowns. Our Lord adds, "Nor do thieves break through nor steal." We cannot imagine a burglar's breaking through the walls of heaven. We could not imagine Satan himself undermining the bastions of the New

Jerusalem, or leaping over the bulwarks which guard the city of the Great King. If your hope is laid up in heaven it must be perfectly safe. If your hope lies in the bank, it may break: if it lies in an empire, it may melt away; if it lies in an estate, the title-deeds may be questioned; if it lies in any human creature, death may bereave you; if it lies in yourself, it is deceitful altogether: but if your hope is laid up in heaven, how secure it is. Be glad, and bless the Lord.

To show how secure is our hope, the apostle tells us that we have an indisputable certificate and guarantee for it. He says, "We heard of it in the word of the truth of the gospel." Notice these three emphatic words—"In *the word* of *the truth* of *the gospel.*" First, "In the word." What word is that? Man's word? Man's words are so much wind. But this is God's word, the same word that made heaven and earth, a word of power which cannot fail and of truth which cannot lie. You first hear of this blessed hope through the word of God, and that word is the best of evidence. You know how a person will say, "My word for it"—here you have God's word for it. We take a good man's word freely; and will we not take God's word much more readily? You have the word of God for the sure hope that believers in Christ Jesus shall be blessed for ever: is not this security enough?

Our text goes on to say, "the word *of the truth*": so, then, it is not a word of guess, conjecture, or of probable inference, but of infallible truth. My brethren of the modern school, my wise brethren, have a word of excogitation, and outcome, and development; but the word the apostle preached was "the word of *the truth*"—something positive, dogmatic, and certain. Ugly as the word may sound, the Lord grant that we may never be ashamed of the thing *called* dogmatism nowadays, which is none other than faith in God's truth. We believe the word of God not only to be true, but to be "the word of the truth." "Let God be true and every man a liar." There may be other true things in the world, but God's word is the essence of truth, *the* truth beyond all things else that may be true, for he hath said, "Heaven and earth shall pass away, but my word shall never pass away." The apostle saith in another place, "All flesh is as grass, and all the glory of man as the flower of grass. The grass withereth, and the flower thereof falleth away; but the word of the Lord endureth for ever. And this is the word which by the gospel is preached unto you."

Note the next word, "The word of the truth of *the gospel,*" or of the good news. That is to say, the sum and substance of the good news is to be found in this glorious hope. If you extract the essence of the gospel, and get *the* truth, which is the central germ of the glad tidings, you come at that blessed hope most sure and steadfast, which entereth into that within the veil.

Now, then, before your God-created hope can fail the word of God will have to be broken, but the word of God cannot be broken: the truth will have to fail, but the truth abideth for ever, and is by force of its own nature eternal; and the gospel will have to be disproved, but that cannot be, since the glory of God is made to hang upon it. Ye have heard it, then, "in the word of the truth of the gospel," what better assurance do you need? Hold to it and rejoice in it, and you shall never be ashamed of your hope.

III. I close by saying that IT IS A MOST POWERFULLY INFLUENTIAL HOPE. Brethren, I have already said to you that this hope is *the parent and nurse of love,* because the text says, "The love which ye have to all the saints for the hope which is laid up for you in heaven." Now, that is no trifling fountain of action which leads believing hearts to love, since love is always a working grace. Oh, for more love in this distracted world. Whatsoever in this world promotes Christian love is to be admired, and since the hope that we shall be for ever together before the throne of God lifts us above the little disagreements of society, and makes us affectionate to each other, it is a thing to cultivate with care.

Love is one part of the powerful operation of hope upon ourselves, but *hopefulness affects others also.* Where the hopefulness of saints is conspicuous, it leads ministers and gracious people to give thanks to God. Paul says, "We give thanks to God and the Father, praying always for you since we heard of your hope." I do not know a greater delight that a minister can have than the thought of all his people entering the bliss of heaven, and of his meeting them all there. We hardly have time to know each other here below; we have loved each other in the Lord, and we have striven together in the service of God, and some of us are old fellow-soldiers now, after many years of Christian warfare, how pleasant it will be to dwell together above world without end! Some have gone home whom we dearly loved, and would almost have detained if we could; and there are others among us who in the order of nature will soon be translated; happy are we because we cannot long be separated. The age of some among us prophesies their speedy departure, and foreshadows that they will soon go over to the majority: but it is a most blessed reflection that all of us who are in Christ shall meet together above. We shall have ample room and verge enough for fellowship when we have reached eternity, and what will our joy be then! Perhaps some of you will say to me when we converse in heavenly language,—"You remember talking to us concerning the blessed hope on that fine Lord's-day morning, but you did not know much about it. We said then, 'The half has not been told us'; but now we perceive you did not tell us the one-hundredth part. Still we were glad to share in the joy of what little we did know, and in the blessed hope of knowing so much more." Oh yes, dear friends, because the hope of heaven in us helps to make other people thank God on our account, it is a sweet grace and mightily influential, and the more we have of it the better.

Moreover, hearing of their hope, *led the apostle to pray,* and if you will follow me in reading the words which succeed the text, you will see what he desired for his friends at Colosse. In the ninth verse you will see what he prayed for. He says, "For this cause we also, since the day we heard it, do not cease to pray for you, and to desire that ye might be filled with the knowledge of his will in all wisdom and spiritual understanding." Having believed in Jesus, and loving his people, you are going to heaven; and so Paul says "I desire that you be filled with the knowledge of his will," and well may he so desire, since to do that will is the joy and business of heaven. Is not our prayer, "Thy will be done on earth as it is in heaven"? Brethren, let us learn the will of the Lord now, and so be educated for the skies. Here we are to go through our apprenticeship, that we may be able to take up our freedom as citizens of the New Jerusalem. Here we are at school, preparing to take our degree above among the instructed saints of God. Are we to enter heaven ignorant of what the will of the Lord is? Surely we ought to know something of the ways of the place, something of the rules of the court. This part of our life below is intended to be a prelude to our life above, a preparation for perfection. Here below we undergo the tuning of the instruments. It is not meet that there should be discordant scrapings and screwings of strings in heaven. No, let us do all that here. Let us have our harps tuned below, so that when we reach the orchestra of the skies we may take our right place, and drop into the right note directly. A good hope should make you eager to know the will of the Lord. It should purify you even as Christ is pure, and make you anxious to begin the perfect service of heaven while yet you linger below.

Then the apostle prays "that ye might walk worthy of the Lord unto all pleasing." Is it not fit that you who are to rise to Enoch's heaven should walk as he did, and have this testimony, that you please God? You are going to dwell at God's right hand, where there are pleasures for evermore, would not you wish to do all you can to please your Lord before you see him? You are a son of a king: you have not put on your glittering array as yet; your crown is not yet on your head; but surely you wish to behave yourself as becometh one who is fore-ordained for so much honour and glory. If a son is in a distant country and is coming home, he begins to think "What can I take home? What can I do to please the beloved father whom I am soon to see?" Begin, beloved, to see what you can do to please God, because you are so soon to enter into his pleasure, and dwell with those that wear white robes, "for they are worthy."

Next he says, "Being fruitful in every good work." Why, if there is to be such a rich reward of grace, let us bear all the gracious fruit we can, and if the time of working is so soon to be over, let us be instant in every holy labour while yet the season is with us. Who wants to go into heaven empty-handed? Who wishes to spend the time of his sojourning here in idleness? Oh no; let us seek to be fruitful to the glory of God so that we may have an abundant entrance into the kingdom.

The apostle further adds, "Increasing in the knowledge of God." If I am going to dwell with God, let me know somewhat of him; let me search his word and see how he has revealed himself; let me endeavour to have fellowship with him and his Son Jesus that I may know him. How can I enter heaven as a total stranger to him who is the king of it? Is not the knowledge of God as needful as it is desirable?

Those who have a good hope of heaven will not rest without knowing the Lord, from the least even to the greatest of them. If anyone were to make you a present of a great estate, no matter in what country it might be situated, you would feel an interest in the land and its neighbourhood, and before nightfall you would be found enquiring about the place. No matter how rustic the neighbourhood or remote the locality, you would set your thoughts towards it if you knew the estate to be yours. As a usual thing, one of the driest documents in all the world is a rich man's will. If you have ever heard one read you will know how it proses on and on in that rigmarole fashion dear to lawyers: but if you are present when it is read to the family, please notice how "my son John's" eyes clear up when it comes to the clause which concerns himself, and how even the aged countenance of "my faithful servant Jane" brightens when her small legacy is mentioned. Everyone is on the alert when his own interests are affected. Even so, he that hath a hope in heaven and an interest in Christ's great testament, will at once take an interest in divine things, and will desire to increase in the knowledge of God.

Once again, the apostle says, "strengthened with all might, according to his glorious power, unto all patience and longsuffering with joyfulness." A hope of heaven is a mighty strengthener for bearing the ills of life and the persecutions of the adversary. "It will soon be over," says a man who looks for heaven, and therefore he is not over-weighted with grief. "It is an ill lodging," said the traveller, "but I shall be away in the morning." Well may we be strengthened with all might by the hope of heaven: it is but reason that the exceeding weight of glory should cast into the shade this light affliction, which is but for a moment.

You will say, "But have you not wrought this part of the chapter into your subject without any warrant?" No. Here is my warrant in the next verse: "Giving thanks unto the Father, which has made us meet to be partakers of the inheritance of the saints in light." I have been following the evident track of the apostle's thoughts. The Lord gives us a hope of glory, and then he gives us a meetness for it, and that meetness is largely wrought in us by the Holy Spirit through the instrumentality of our hope. Cultivate, then, your hope, dear brethren. Make it to shine so plainly in you that your minister may hear of your hopefulness and joy; cause observers to take note of it, because you speak of heaven, and act as though you really expected to go there. Make the world know that you have a hope of heaven: make worldlings feel that you are a believer in eternal glory, and that you hope to be where Jesus is. Often surprise them as they see what they call your simplicity, but what is in truth only your sincerity, while you treat as matter of fact the hope laid up for you in heaven. The Lord grant it for Jesus Christ's sake. Amen.

10

The Christian's Manifestation

"Beloved, now are we the sons of God, and it doth not yet appear what we shall be: but we know that, when he shall appear, we shall be like him; for we shall see him as he is." 1 John 3:2

The text mentions "now", and then passes on to the future, and speaks of *"yet."* It does, however, speak of "now"; and, after all, despite our trials, there is much to make us happy in our present condition. "Beloved, *now* are we the sons of God." Our manifold temptations and infirmities cannot make us lose the blessings that come to us through our adoption into the family of God. "Happy art thou, O Israel: who is like unto thee, O people saved by the Lord?" To-day, even to-day, we are the blessed of the Lord, and we find in godliness the blessing of "the life that now is."

Yet, beloved, for all that, we are still forced to cry,—

"Alas for us if thou wert all,
And nought beyond, O earth!"

If this were all our life, it would have been better for us not to have lived. Woe unto us if we had to live here always! Young says,—

"Were there no death, e'en fools might wish to die;"—

and, certainly, wise men would do so; for, brethren, this is a life of distractions, cares, anxieties, disappointments, and, what is worse, it is a life of sins, and sorrows, and bitter repentances for wrong-doing. This life is to us a traveller's life, with all the inconveniences that we meet with in travelling. We are here to-day, and we are gone to-morrow. Sometimes the heat consumes us, and at other times the cold bites us. We are like men at sea; we have not yet cast our anchor, nor furled our sails, nor reached the port whither we are bound; and the sea on which we are sailing is rough, and tempest-tossed, and beset with rocks, and shoals, and quicksands. Our soul is often half a wreck, and longs for the desired haven, where "the wicked cease from troubling," and "the weary be at rest." Ours is a soldier's life; we have to be constantly fighting, or else continually upon our guard. Think not, thou who hast just buckled on thy harness, that thou hast won the victory; for the good soldiers of Jesus Christ must fight from morn till eve, from youth's gay morning till the eve of grey old age.

I would not paint life in sadder colours than it needs, but I dare not shut my eyes to the fact that this is a sad world, and that our path is one of sorrow, for it is "through much tribulation" that we "enter into the kingdom of God."

> "The path of sorrow, and that path alone,
> Leads to the land where sorrow is unknown."

It is to that other and better land that I would, for a little while, bear away your thoughts. We shall borrow the wings of our text; and, like the eagle, soar towards heaven.

We will begin with this sentence: "IT DOTH NOT YET APPEAR WHAT WE SHALL BE."

What we are to be, we can scarcely guess. Indeed, we cannot guess at all merely by the use of our senses. "Eye hath not seen, nor ear heard, neither have entered into the heart of man, the things which God hath prepared for them that love him. But God hath revealed them unto us by his Spirit;" but only to our spirit. Flesh and blood, as they are, cannot inherit the kingdom of God, and cannot even guess what that kingdom is like. This is not the place where the Christian is to be seen. This is the place of his veiling; heaven is the place of his manifestation. This is the place of his night; yonder is the place of his day. Our portion is on the other side of the river: our days of feasting are not yet. Some of the reasons why "it doth not yet appear what we shall be" may be as follows. First, *our Master was, to a great extent, concealed and hidden, and we must expect to be as he was.* Is it not written, in this very Epistle, "As he is, as are we in this world"? Jesus said to his followers when he was here upon earth, "The disciple is not above his master, nor the servant above his lord. It is enough for the disciple that he be as his master, and the servant as his lord." My brethren, see that man, wearing a coat "without seam, woven from the top throughout;"—the carpenter's son, the heir of poverty, the companion of the humblest classes of mankind. Can you see in him God over all, blessed for ever? If you can, you are not looking with the eyes of your flesh, I am sure; for, in that manner, you cannot detect the glory of the Lord Jesus Christ beneath so humble a garb. The veil which the Saviour cast about himself was not so thick but that some rays of his glory burst through when he trod the waves, and rebuked the winds, and raised the dead; but, still, it was sufficiently dense, for he cried, "The foxes have holes, and the birds of the air have nests; but the Son of man hath not where to lay his head." You will see that Christ was concealed as you recollect that, although, as Dr. Watts says,—

"All riches are his native right,"—

yet, when he had to pay the temple tax, he had to work a miracle that Peter might be able to catch the fish which had the exact amount required in its mouth. He was so poor that he had to live upon the charity of his followers. Would you have believed that *he* was the Lord of all creation if you had seen him up on yonder lonely mountain's side without a bed to rest upon, or sitting wearily upon Jacob's well at Sychar, and asking a sinful woman to give him a little water to drink? The Saviour was, indeed, masked and hidden so that the vulgar eye could not detect his glory. Only such men eagle-eyed as John were able to say, "We beheld his glory, the glory as of the only-begotten of the Father, full of grace and truth." Our Lord's wisdom, and grace, and power, and all his other illustrious attributes were concealed beneath the veil of our inferior clay. Dr. Watts was right, as I reminded you just now, when he wrote,—

"Worthy is he that once was slain,
The Prince of Peace that groan'd and died;
Worthy to rise, and live, and reign
At his almighty Father's side."

"Power and dominion are his due
Who stood condemned at Pilate's bar;
Wisdom belongs to Jesus too,
Though he was charged with madness here."

"All riches are his native right,
Yet he sustained amazing loss;
To him ascribe eternal might,
Who left his weakness on the cross."

So fully did he veil his glory that some even ventured to call
him Beelzebub, and to say that he was a gluttonous man and
a wine-bibber!

Now, Christian, as you think of all this, do you wonder if
worldlings do not know you, and only speak of you to slander
you? Do you wonder if your integrity is questioned, and your
most manifest virtue is mis-represented, and if the grace
which really is within you is cavilled at and despised? How
should the world know you when the Saviour himself was
not discovered? As the bright gleams of his divine glory were
almost wholly concealed, surely the weaker gleams of your
earthly and human glory must be altogether hidden. That,
perhaps, is the first reason why "it doth not yet appear what
we shall be."

I think I may also remark, brethren, that *we are not yet fit
to let it appear what we shall be.* "The son in the house," says
one, "is treated as if he were a servant, and even worse than
if he were a servant. A servant is not chastised; he may do
many wrong things, and yet escape without a stripe, yet it is
not so with the son. Why does not his father give him the
honour and dignity which belong to his sonship?" Simply
because he is at present only a child, and he must be treated
as a child, for a time, in order that he may be fitted to adorn
his sonship. It would spoil him to receive at once all that is
to be his when he enters upon his inheritance. He is the heir
to all his father's estates, yet he has to be thankful to his
father for even a penny, and he receives his pittance week by
week, as though he were a poor pensioner upon his father's
bounty or a beggar at his door. Why does not the father give
this heir to large estates a thousand pounds? Why does he
not entrust him with a great store of wealth? Because he is
in his nonage; and if he were trusted with a large sum of
money, at so early an age, he might grow profligate, and so
be unfitted to use his wealth aright if he should reach riper

years.

Brethren, you and I, if we are believers in the Lord Jesus
Christ, are kings;—not only sons of God, but kings who are
to reign with him for ever. Then, why are we not treated like
kings? You know that, in some earthly royal families, it is
thought best for the prince, the heir-apparent to the throne,
that he should be a soldier or a sailor, and serve his country
in that capacity, so that, when he comes to the throne, he
may understand how to wield his sceptre for the good of all
classes of his subjects. So, Christian, is it with you. You are
so childish at present; you have so lately begun to learn the
nature of divine things; you are so uninstructed; you know
but in part, and you know that part so badly, that it would
not be fitting that your greatness should be revealed to you
at present. You must be held back for a while till you have
been better trained in the Holy Spirit's school, and then it
shall appear what you shall be.

A third reason why it doth not yet appear what we shall be
is, I think, because *this is not the world in which the
Christian is to appear in his glory;* for, if he did, his glory
would be lost in this world. The multitudes climbed to the
tops of the trees, or the roofs of the houses, whence they
might see Caesar or Pompey returning with the spoils of
war, and the multitudes still clap their hands when a
warrior has overcome his country's enemies, and so become
a great man. But the world cares little or nothing about
self-denial, about Christian love, about consecration and
devotion to Christ and his cause; yet these things are the
glory of a Christian. That moral excellence, that spiritual
worth which flashes from the eyes of the holy angels and the
saints in glory, is almost unappreciated here. Your Master
had this glory, though it was usually veiled while he was
here below; yet the people cried out, "Away with him, away
with him, crucify him;" and if you had here, to its full extent,
the glory which will be revealed in you in heaven, people
would say the same concerning you. This is not the world in
which you are to display your full honours. When a king is
journeying through a foreign country, he does not wear his
crown, nor the rest of his regalia; he often travels *incognito;*
and even when he reaches his own country, he does not put
on his royal robes for fools to admire at every village wake
and fair. He is not a puppet-king, strutting upon the stage to

show himself to the common people; but he reserves his
grandeur for great public occasions and grand court
ceremonies. In this poor sinful world, you Christians would
be out of place if you could be what you shall yet be. You also
must go, *incognito,* through this world to a large extent; but,
by-and-by, you shall take off the travel-worn garments that
you have worn during your earthly pilgrimage, and put on
your beautiful array, and be manifested to the whole
universe as a son or a daughter of "the King eternal,
immortal, invisible."

And, to close this part of the subject, "It doth not yet
appear what we shall be," because *this is not the time for the
display of the Christian's glory.* If I may use such an
expression, time is not the time for the manifestation of a
Christian's glory. Eternity is to be the period for the
Christian's full development, and for the sinless display of
his God-given glory. Here, he must expect to be unknown; it
is in the hereafter that he is to be discovered as a son of the
great King. At present, it is with us as it is with the world
during the winter. If you had not seen the miracle wrought
again and again, you would not guess, when you look upon
those black beds in the garden, or when you walk over that
snowy and frosty covering, crisp and hard beneath your feet,
that the earth will yet be sown with all the colours of the
rainbow, and that it will be gemmed with flowers of
unspeakable beauty. No, the winter is not the time when the
beauty of the earth is to be best seen; and, Christian, you
also must pass through your winter season. Ay, but let that
wintry weather once be over, let the bleak December winds
howl into your ears, let the cold and cheerless January come
and go, let, "February fill-dyke" also pass; and, behold, the
springtime cometh. I might also say that grey hairs come
upon your head, like the snowdrops appear upon the earth,
as the harbingers of spring and of summer, and your soul
shall yet blossom "with joy unspeakable and full of glory,"
and all the graces and excellences of the Christian shall be
revealed in you. It is winter with you now, but the summer
cometh.

If you stand, as many of you have often done, at the
seaside, you have noticed that, at certain hours of the day,
there is a long expanse of mud, or of dry sand, and it may not
seem to one who sees it for the first time as though the sea

had ever rolled over it, or that it ever will. Ah, but "it doth not yet appear" what it will be. It is ebb-tide now; but wait till the flood comes, and then you will see the whole of that black mire or that yellow sand glistening in the sunshine. So, the flood of glory is rising, Christian; can you not see the breakers in the distance, the white crests of the incoming waves? God's great sea of eternity draws nearer and nearer; can you not hear the booming of that mighty flood? Soon shall your ransomed spirit float and bathe in that sea of glory, where not a single wave shall cause you a moment's grief or pain. This is not the time, Christian, in which you are to be fully revealed. You are, to-day, like that ugly shrivelled seed; there is no beauty in it that you should desire it. Ay, but wait a little while; and when the sweetly-perfumed flower shall shed its fragrance on the air, and make the gazer pause to admire the matchless colours with which God has been pleased to paint it, then shall its full glory be known and seen. At present, you are in your seed stage, and your sowing time is coming. Tremble not that it is so. There will be a time for your poor flesh to sleep in the silent grave; but, at the voice of the archangel, and the blast of the trumpet of the resurrection, you shall arise. Just as the flower rises in spring, the dead body, which was put into the tomb, shall rise incorruptible, in the image of the Saviour.

So, you see, "it doth not yet appear what we shall be," because the Lord Jesus Christ was not fully revealed here, because we are not fit to appear in glory, because we are not here in the midst of the men and women who should see us in our glory, and because it is not yet the right time for us thus to appear. "To every thing there is a season, and a time to every purpose under the heavens;" but this is not the time for the full manifestation of Christians; and, therefore, "it doth not yet appear what we shall be; but we know that, when he shall appear, we shall be like him, for we shall see him as he is."

Having spent so much time over the previous clause, we will merely hint at the teaching of the next words of the text: "BUT WE KNOW THAT, WHEN HE SHALL APPEAR."

So, then, *it is quite certain that Christ will appear.* John does not stop to prove it. He speaks of it as though it were perfectly understood that Christ would again appear, and he mentions what is to be the nature of that appearing.

Christ will appear in person. This is what the two angels declared to the disciples after his ascension, "This same Jesus, which is taken up from you into heaven, shall so come in like manner as ye have seen him go into heaven;" that is, as the incarnate God, he will come back from heaven.

When he comes, *he will appear full of happiness.* There will be no more sorrow to wrinkle his brow, no more furrows to be ploughed on his back, no fresh wounds to be made in his hands or his feet, no more offering of a sacrifice for sin; but he will come to rejoice with his people for ever.

Further, when he comes, *he will appear in his glory;*—not as the man of Nazareth, to be despised, and spit upon, but as "The mighty God, The everlasting Father, The Prince of Peace." If any of you are tempted to ask, "When will he come?" I give you his own assurance, "Surely I come quickly;" so go your way, and pray, as John did, "Even so, come, Lord Jesus;" yet do not forget Paul's inspired sentences, "But of the times and the seasons, brethren, ye have no need that I write unto you. For yourselves know perfectly that the day of the Lord so cometh as a thief in the night. For when they shall say, Peace and safety; then sudden destruction cometh upon them, as travail upon a woman with child; and they shall not escape," Christ is coming, beloved, literally coming,—not figuratively, and by his Spirit, but literally, actually, really.

> "Lo! he comes with clouds descending
> Once for favour'd sinners slain."

He is coming in glory, to dwell in the midst of his saints for ever. This is our blessed hope, "the glorious appearing of the great God and our Saviour Jesus Christ, who gave himself for us, that he might redeem us from all iniquity, and purify unto himself a peculiar people, zealous of good works."

Now, passing on, "We know that, when he shall appear, WE SHALL BE LIKE HIM; FOR WE SHALL SEE HIM AS HE IS."

There are other passages, in his Word, where we are distinctly told that his manifestation will be coincident with our manifestation. Here, we are told that, "when he shall appear, we shall be like him;" and the reason given for this is, "for we shall see him as he is."

Let us, while pondering the text, then, meditate upon this

great truth: "We shall be like him." This afternoon,
meditating upon this glorious assurance that I shall be like
Christ,—and I fully believe that I shall be like him,—it did
seem to me as if it were almost too good to be true. Yet it is
true that *we are to be like Christ,* first, *as to our body.* Here,
we are like the first Adam; of the earth, earthy. But we shall,
one day, have a body like that of the second Adam, a
heavenly body. Like the first Adam, we are mortal now; like
the second Adam, we shall be immortal by-and-by. Christ's
body is not now subject to any pains, or to any decay or
disease; neither shall our body be. It is quite true that "flesh
and blood cannot inherit the kingdom of God;" yet it will be
this very body of ours that will inherit the kingdom of God,
only that which is corruptible in it, that which is mere flesh
and blood, will then have been removed. As the apostle Paul
writes to the Corinthians, in that wonderful chapter about
the resurrection, "It is sown a natural body; it is raised a
spiritual body." It is "a spiritual body" which the Lord Jesus
Christ has to-day. I cannot imagine how glorious the Saviour
is in heaven; but I always think of him, even when he was
upon this earth, as being far fairer than any artist ever
depicted him. I have gazed a long while upon many
paintings of Christ, both in England and abroad; but I have
never yet seen one which appeared to me to be equal even to
my ideal of the Saviour. I have looked, and I have said, "Oh,
no! he was far fairer than that; there must have been more
beauty in his face than even that great master has
portrayed." Well, brethren, if that is true concerning him as
he was when among the sons of men, how true it must be
concerning him as he is now! He is fairer than all the fair
spirits that surround the heavenly throne. He is "the rose of
sharon, and the lily of the valleys." Amongst the shining
seraphim and cherubim, none can be compared with him;
and, Christian, you are to be like him. Whatever are the
characteristics of the Saviour's glorified body, they are to be
the characteristics of your body also. You are to have an
immortal body, a spiritual body, a body incapable of pain,
and suffering, and decay, a body which shall be suited to
your emancipated spirit, a body having a wider range than
this limited earthly sphere, having greater powers of
locomotion, perhaps flying, swiftly as light, from world to
world, or possibly having the power even to outrun the

lightning's flash. I do not know how wondrous Christ's glorified body is; but I do know that, "when he shall appear, we shall be like him (even in body); for we shall see him as he is."

But, far more important than that, *we shall also be like Christ in soul.* Have the eyes of your spiritual understanding or sanctified imagination ever looked upon Christ's spotless, perfectly-developed soul; that equably-adjusted spirit, in which no one power or passion was too prominent or predominant; but in which his whole being was beautifully moulded and rounded, according to the perfect pattern of moral excellence and beauty? Now, beloved, you are to be just like that;—not quick in temper, as perhaps you now are, but meek and lowly as he was;—not haughty, and prone to pride, but humble and gentle as he was;—not selfish and self-seeking, but as disinterested and as tender to others as he was; in fact, perfection's own self. It was said of Harry the Eighth that, if all the histories of all the tyrants who ever lived had been lost, you might have composed them all with the material from the life of that execrable monster; and I will venture to say that, if all the biographies of all the good men and holy angels that have ever existed could be blotted out of existence or memory, they might all be written again with the material from the life of our Lord Jesus Christ, for in him dwelleth all excellence and all goodness. What a joy it is to us to know that we shall be like him! Brethren and sisters in Christ, this blessed truth is enough to make you stand up or even leap in the exuberance of your joy. I have heard of our enthusiastic Welsh friends dancing during some of their preachers' sermons; and if it be this or a similar truth which makes them dance, who can wonder at it? "We shall be like him,"—like him in soul, with no more infirmities of temper, or sloth, or undue haste. Our human nature shall be rid of all its rags, and we shall be perfect, even as our Father in heaven is perfect. Oh, that the blessed day had already come, and that we were like our Lord! But "we shall be like him; for we shall see him as he is."

> "Nor doth it yet appear
> How great we must be made;
> But when we see our Saviour here,
> We shall be like our Head."

Time fails me to say what I should have liked to have said; yet I ought to add that *we shall be like Christ,* not only in body and in soul, but *also in condition.* We shall be with him where he is, and we shall be as happy as he is, as far as our capacity for happiness goes. We shall be crowned even as he is crowned, and we will sit upon thrones even as he sits upon his Father's throne. He shall lead us to living fountains of water, and be our constant Companion, never going away from us again. He shall call us his brethren, and we shall share in his honour and glory. The joy of which we shall partake shall be his joy, and it will be in us that our joy may be full. O Christian, think lofty thoughts concerning thy Lord in glory, and remember that thou shalt be like him! I cannot help repeating that quaint little ditty which Rowland Hill was so fond of humming over in his old age,—

> "And when I'm to die, 'Receive me,' I'll cry,
> For Jesus hath loved, I cannot tell why;
> But this I do find, we too are so joined,
> He'll not live in glory and leave me behind."

So, "we shall be like him;" and the reason why we shall be like him is thus given by John, "FOR WE SHALL SEE HIM AS HE IS."

How is it that we shall be like him because of that? Partly, *by reflection.* Perhaps you are aware that, in the olden time, looking-glasses (if I may use an Irishism,) were not looking-glasses at all, for they were made of polished brass. If a person looked into such a mirror when the sun was shining upon that mirror, not only would the mirror itself be bright, but it would also throw a reflection on the face of the person who was looking into it. This is only according to the laws of light. When a man looks into a bright mirror, it makes him also bright, for it throws its own light upon his face; and, in a much more wonderful fashion, when we look at Christ, who is all brightness, he throws some of his brightness upon us. When Moses went up into the mount, to commune with God, his face shone because he had received a reflection of God's glory upon his face. He had looked into the blazing light of Deity, as far as a created eye could look there; and, therefore, that light was so brilliantly reflected in his own face that Aaron and the people were afraid to draw near him, and he had to cover his face with a veil while he spoke to them.

Further, beloved, we get to be like Christ by seeing him *in type and symbol,* as through a glass darkly. The Lord's supper is one of the glasses; believers baptism is another; the preaching of the Word is another; the Bible itself is another of these glasses. It is only a partial reflection of Christ that we get from all these glasses; yet, as we look at it, as Paul writes to the Corinthians, "We all, with open face beholding as in a glass the glory of the Lord, are changed into the same image from glory to glory, even as by the Spirit of the Lord," or, "by the Lord the Spirit."

But, brethren, if there be such a sanctifying influence about the very reflection of Jesus Christ, *what a wondrous power it must have upon us when we see him as he is!* When we shall gaze upon him with unveiled vision, and see him as he is, do you wonder that John says that, then, "we shall be like him; for we shall see him as he is?" Oh, that amazing sight, that unique sight of Jesus as he is! It would be worth while to die a thousand painful deaths in order to get one brief glimpse of him as he is. I do not think that Rutherford exaggerated when he talked of swimming through seven hells to get at Christ if he could not get at him anyhow else. A distant view of him, as we have seen him "leaping upon the mountains, skipping upon the hills," has so ravished our souls that we have scarcely known whether we have been in the body or out of the body. When we have heard his voice, we have longed to be with him. The very thought of him has made us, like the dove separated for a while from her mate, long to cleave the air with rapid wing, and fly home to our dovecote, and to our blessed Noah. What must it be to be there? What must it be to see our Saviour as he is?

In some of the houses not far from here, I noticed some linnets in cages, in which there were tufts of grass, or small branches of trees as perches for the poor prisoners; yet they were singing away right merrily. I suppose that grass and those fragments of trees were meant to remind them, in this great, dirty, smoky Babylon, that there are green fields and wide forests somewhere. I thought, as I looked upon them, "Ah, you poor birds are very like what I myself am!" My Master has put me in a little cage, and bidden me bide here for a while; and he has given me my little tuft of grass as an earnest of my inheritance in the—

"Sweet fields beyond the swelling flood."

He graciously sends me a few comforts on the way. Ah! but that poor little tuft of grass, what is it in comparison with the fields and the hedges which are the proper home of the singing birds which have their liberty? And, Christian, you do not know what it will be for you to have your cage door opened, that you may fly away to that blessed land where the true birds of Paradise for ever warble, from their joyful throats, the loudest praises to the great King who has set them free for ever. Let us begin the music here; let us try even now to anticipate that happy day as we sing of—

"Jerusalem the golden,
With milk and honey blest;"—

where—

"The daylight is serene;"—

and where—

"The pastures of the blessed
Are deck'd in glorious sheen."

I leave my text with you who love the Lord. As for you who do not love him, I dare not give it to you. Oh, that you did love him, and that you did trust him! He waiteth to be gracious. Seek ye his face, and he will be found of you. Fly to him, and he will not reject you. Trust in him, and he will wash you from all your sins, and bring you to his presence in eternal glory, to go no more out for ever. May he give you this unspeakable blessing, for his love's sake! Amen.

11

The Two Pivots

"...I am the God of thy father, the God of Abraham, the God of
Isaac, and the God of Jacob."   Exodus 3:6
"...wherefore God is not ashamed to be called their God: for he
hath prepared for them a city."   Hebrews 11:16

You recollect, dear friends, that Paul is writing to the
Hebrews concerning Abraham, Isaac, and Jacob, and he
says, "God is not ashamed to be called their God." Then,
when you turn back to our text in Exodus, you find that God
was called their God at the burning bush; and, oftentimes,
on other occasions, he is called the God of Abraham, the God
of Isaac, and the God of Jacob. We must not forget that, at
the time when God appeared to Moses, in the desert, in the
bush that burned, but was not consumed, the condition of
the descendants of Abraham, Isaac, and Jacob was very
terrible. They were slaves to the Egyptians; they were an
oppressed and downtrodden race; their male children were
taken from them, and cast into the river. They were entirely
in Pharaoh's hands. They were a degraded people, as all
slaves gradually become; and they were unable, of
themselves, to rise out of that degradation; yet, at that very
time, God was not ashamed to be called their God. There,
with Israel in bondage, Jehovah, whose name is the great I
AM,—a name which makes all heaven bright with ineffable
glory,—did not disdain to say to Moses, "I am the God of
Abraham, the God of Isaac, and the God of Jacob." I do not
wonder that the apostle should note it, as a remarkable
thing, that he was not ashamed to be called their God.

I have been looking into this text very earnestly, and

trying to find out exactly what was the meaning of the Holy
Spirit in it; and I think I have discovered a clue in two words
which it contains;—first, "Wherefore": *"Wherefore* God is not
ashamed to be called their God;"—and next, "for": *"For* he
hath prepared for them a city." As a door hangs upon two
hinges, so my golden text turns upon these two pivots,
"wherefore" and "for."

I. I shall ask you to keep your Bibles open at the 11th of
Hebrews, that you may see, first, "WHEREFORE" it is that
God is not ashamed to be called the God of his people. Look
at the 13th verse: "These all died in faith, not having
received the promises, but having seen them afar off, and
were persuaded of them, and embraced them, and confessed
that they were strangers and pilgrims on the earth;" and so
on. "Wherefore God is not ashamed to be called their God."

To begin with, then, the Lord was not ashamed to be called
his people's God *because they had faith in him.* You read
here of Abraham, Sarah, Isaac, Jacob, and then Paul says,
"These all died in faith." If a man believes in God, trusts
him,—believes that his promise is true, and that he will
keep it,—believes that God's command is right, and
therefore ought to be obeyed,—God is never ashamed to be
called that man's God. He is not the God of unbelievers, for
they act contrary to his will. They set up their own will in
opposition to his; many of them even doubt his existence,
they deny his power, they distrust his love; wherefore, he is
not called their God; but when a man comes to trust God,
and to accept his Word, from that moment God sees in that
man the work of his grace, which is very precious in his eyes,
and he is not ashamed to be called that man's God.

Notice that it is said, "These all died in faith," so that they
did not believe in God for a little while, and then become
unbelievers; but, throughout the whole of their lives, from
the moment when they were called by God's grace, they
continued to believe him, they trusted him till they came to
their graves; so that this epitaph is written over the
mausoleum where they all lie asleep, "These all died in
faith." Ah! my beloved brothers and sisters, it is very easy to
say, "I believe," and to get very enthusiastic over the notion
that we have believed; but so to believe as to persevere to the
end,—this is the faith which will save the soul. "He that
shall endure unto the end the same shall be saved." The

faith that many waters cannot drown and the fiercest fires cannot burn,—the faith that plods on throughout a long and weary life,—the faith that labours on, doing whatever service God appoints it,—the faith that waits patiently, expecting the time when every promise of God shall be fulfilled to the letter when its hour has come,—that is the faith which, if it be in a man, makes him such a man that God is not ashamed to be called his God. I put it to every one of you, have you a faith that will hold on and hold out,—not a faith that starts with a fine spurt, but a faith that runs from the starting-place to the goal? Some of you, I know, have believed in God these twenty, thirty, forty, or even fifty years. Just before I came to this service, I stood by the bedside of a dear brother who is the nearest to Job of any man I ever saw, for he is covered from head to foot with sore blains; I might almost say, "wounds, and bruises, and putrefying sores;" and yet he is as happy as anyone among us, joyful and cheerful as he talks about the time when he shall be "with Christ, which is far better." Oh, that is the faith we want! "These all died in faith," "wherefore God is not ashamed to be called their God." He is not the God of apostates, for he hath said, "If any man draw back, my soul shall have no pleasure in him." If he has put his hand to the plough, and looks back, he is not worthy of the kingdom. It is the man who steadily, and perseveringly, resting in his God, and believing him against all that may be said by God's foes, holds on until he sees the King in his beauty in the land which is very far off. Of such a man it may be truly said that God is not ashamed to be called his God.

Now let us come back to the Scripture; we cannot do better than keep close to it, for our text is only to be understood by the context. Scripture is the best interpreter of Scripture. The locks of Scripture are only to be opened with the keys of Scripture; and there is no lock in the whole Bible, which God meant us to open, without a key to fit it somewhere in the Bible, and we are to search for it until we find it. Now read on in the 13th verse: "These all died in faith, not having received the promises." That is to say, the things that God promised to them, he did not give them in their mortal life, and they did not always expect that he would do so. *They were a waiting people.* God loves those who are like himself; I am not now speaking of his love of benevolence, for with that love he loved us even when we were dead in trespasses and sins, but I am speaking of the love of complacency, which makes him not ashamed to be called our God. In that sense, God loves those who are like himself, and God is a waiting God; he is never in a hurry. How wondrous is the leisure of the Eternal! When he is coming to help his people, he is quick indeed: "He rode upon a cherub, and did fly: yea, he did fly upon the wings of the wind." But, oftentimes, he waits and tarries till some men count it slackness; but he does not reckon time as we do. With God, a day is as a thousand years, and a thousand years as one day. So, being himself a waiting God, he loves a waiting people; he loves a man who can take the promise, and say, "I believe it; it may never be fulfilled to me in this life, but I do not want that it should be. I am perfectly willing that it should be fulfilled when God intends that it should be." Abraham saw Christ's day afar off, but he never saw Christ; yet he rejoiced in the promise of which he did not receive the fulfillment. Isaac did not see Christ, except in a vision of the things that were long afterwards to come to pass. Jacob did not hear that joyful sound, which—

> "Kings and prophets waited for,
> And sought, but never found."

But they were perfectly willing to wait, and God was not ashamed to be called the God of such a waiting people. You remember Mr. Bunyan's description of the two children, Passion and Patience. Passion would have his best things now, and he had them; but he soon spoiled them, misused them, and abused them. But Patience would have his best things last; and, as Bunyan very prettily says, "There is nothing to come after the last." Therefore, when Patience got his best things, they lasted on for ever and for ever. God loves not the passion, but he loves the patience. "The husbandman waiteth for the precious fruit of the earth, and hath long patience for it;" and I would fain imitate him. "My soul, wait thou only upon God; for my expectation is from him." The worldly man lives in the present; but that is a poor way of living, worthy only of the beasts that perish. Look on the sheep and bullocks in the pasture; what kind of life is theirs? They also live in the present. If they have grass enough for to-day, they are perfectly satisfied. The butcher's knife has no terrors for them; neither do they, in the cold of winter, look forward to the bright days of summer. They cannot look before them; and God loves not men who are like the beasts of the field; he is ashamed to be called their God. But he loves the man who gets to live in eternity, for God himself lives there. To God, there is no past, present, or future; he sees all at a single glance. And when a man comes to feel that he is not living simply in to-day which will so soon end, but that he is living in the eternity which will never end, when he is rejoicing in the covenant, "ordered in all things, and sure," made from before the foundation of the world,—when a man feels that he is living in the future as well as the present, that his vast estates are on the other side of Jordan, that his chief joy is up there where Christ sits at the right hand of God, and that his own heart has gone up there where his treasure is, for "where your treasure is, there will your heart be also,"—when the affection is set, not upon things below, but upon things above,—that is the man whom God loves, because he has learned how to live in God's atmosphere, in God's own eternity. He has risen above the beggarly elements of time and space. He is not circumscribed by Almanacks, and days, and months, and years; his thoughts range right away from that glorious declaration, "I have loved thee with an everlasting love," to those endless, dateless periods when still the everlasting love of God shall be the constant delight of his people.

I see, then, why it is written that "God is not ashamed to be called their God," because they are content to live without having received the promises, but to keep on patiently waiting, with a holy, joyful confidence, till the hour of God's gracious purpose shall arrive, and the promise shall be fulfilled.

Now read on in the 13th verse, and see whether this description fits yourself, dear friend: "But having seen them afar off." So *they were a far-seeing people.* God, you know, sees everything; and he loves people who can see afar off. The gods of the heathen have eyes, but they see not; and the psalmist says, "They that make them are like unto them." So they that worship a blind god are a blind people; but they that worship a seeing God, are themselves made to see, for they are numbered with the pure in heart who shall see God. It is a grand thing when a man can see infinitely further than these poor eyes can carry, and far beyond the range of the strongest telescope,—when he can see beyond death,—and see beyond the judgment-seat,—and see right into heaven, and there behold the Lamb leading his glorified flock to the living fountains of waters, and the saints, with tearless eyes, for ever bowing before the throne of God and the Lamb. God is not ashamed to be called the God of the people who can do this. God is ashamed to be called the God of you blind people, whose eyes have never been opened; but when he opens your eyes, then he becomes your God, and he is not ashamed to be so called, for he it is that gives us this blessed power to see. Until spiritual sight is thus bestowed upon us, we are blind; but when God has given us sight, then he is not ashamed to own us as his children, nor is he ashamed to own that he himself is our God. I appeal to you whom I am now addressing, and ask whether you can see God's promises afar off? There are some who say, "A bird in the hand is worth two in the bush." Yes, it may be so with the poor birds that sing here; but, for my part, I am willing to wait till I can have the one in the bush, if it is in the bush that burned with fire because God was there. You may have the bird in the hand, if you will. You will soon pluck off its feathers; it will speedily die in your hand, and there will come an end to it; but there are other birds which, as yet, we cannot reach, but which are really ours; and if we cannot at present grasp them, we are willing to wait God's time, because we can see that they will be in our hands in the future, we can already see them "afar off." Unhappy is the man who sees nothing but what he calls "the main chance," or who sees nothing but that which is within a few feet of him. Wretched indeed is he who lives only to get money, or to gain honour,—whose whole life is spent in the pursuit of personal comfort, but who never had his eye opened enough to see the things eternal, and who never was able to set a value upon anything but what could be paid for with pounds, shillings, and pence. Beloved, have you seen the promises afar off? Has the Lord opened your eyes to see eternal things? Then it is written concerning you also, "Wherefore God is not ashamed to be called their God."

Now pass on to the next sentence, for every word is fruitful with meaning: "and were persuaded of them, and embraced them." *They were people who rejoiced in things unseen.* You will find that, in the Revised Version, the words "persuaded of them" are left out, and very properly so, for there is no doubt whatever that they were not in the original, but were added by somebody who wished to explain the meaning to us. The Greek is properly rendered, "but having seen them afar off, greeted them;" but I like, even better, the translation "embraced them." It means that, as for the things which are promised to us, if we are believers, like Abraham, Isaac, and Jacob, we have, from afar, seen those promised things, and we have welcomed them; or, to use our Authorized Version, we have "embraced them." We have pressed them to our bosom, we have hugged them to our heart, we have loved them in our very soul, we have rejoiced in them; they have filled our spiritual nature full of music, and all the bells of our being are ringing merry peals because of the blessed promises of our God.

Now, when a man is of that mind, God is not ashamed to be called his God. Let me, then, ask you, dear friend,—What is it that you are embracing? Is it some earthly thing? Does your heart love and cling to that which you can see, and touch, and handle? Is that your chief delight? Then God is ashamed to be called your God, because you are an idolater; you are worshipping some created thing. But if you can say of Christ, "He is all my salvation, and all my desire," then God is not ashamed to be called your God. Remember what David said: "Delight thyself also in the Lord; and he shall give thee the desires of thine heart;" for God is able to give to a man his desires when all his heart is delighting in his God; and God is not ashamed to be called his God. The Lord's love is not set upon merely material objects; the infinite heart of God loves truth, and righteousness, and purity, and everything that is holy and glorious. And if your heart does the same, God is not ashamed to be called your God; but if you do not love these things, you have neither part nor lot in God, but you are a stranger to him: and, though I speak this solemn truth in gentle language, I pray that it may drop like caustic upon your spirit, and burn its way into your very soul. What an awful thing it must be to be without God,—to have no part nor lot in him,—never to be able to say, "My God, my Father," but only to speak of him as a God,—an unknown God, another man's God, but no God to you! May it not be so with you, brethren! If you can say that you have seen the promises from afar, and have by faith embraced them, then God is not ashamed to be called your God.

Pass on to the next sentence: "and confessed that they were strangers and pilgrims on the earth." *They owned that they were not at home here.* Abraham never built a house; Isaac never lived anywhere but in a tent; and though Jacob tried to dwell in a settled habitation, he got into trouble through it, and he was bound still to be a tent-dweller. The reason why they lived in tents was because they wanted to show to all around them that they did not belong to that country. There were great cities with walls which, as men said, reached to heaven; but they did not go to dwell in those cities. You remember that Lot did, yet he was glad enough to get out again,—"saved, yet so as by fire;" but Abraham, Isaac, and Jacob kept away from other men, for they were commanded to dwell alone, and not to be numbered among the nations. Nor were they; they kept themselves apart from other people as strangers and sojourners here below, so, for that very reason, God is not ashamed to be called their God. Remember how David says to the Lord, "I am a stranger with thee, and a sojourner, as all my fathers were." That is a very singular expression: "a stranger with thee;"—blessed be God, not "a stranger *to* thee;" but, "a stranger *with* thee." That is to say, God is a stranger here; it is his own world, and he made it; but when Christ, who is the Son of God, and the Creator of the world, came into it, "he came unto his own, and his own received him not;" and they soon made him feel that the only treatment which he would receive at their hands was this: "This is the heir; come, let us kill him, that the inheritance may be ours." There was no man, who ever lived, who was a truer man than was Christ the Lord; but there never was a man who was more unlike the rest of men. He was a homely man, a home-loving man, to the last degree; yet he was never at home. This world was not his rest; he had nowhere even to lay his head; and what was true naturally, was also true spiritually. This world offered Christ no rest whatever. Now, dear friends, how is it with us? Do we belong to this world, or to the unseen? How do you feel about this matter? Do you feel at home here? I think that, often, we are compelled to cry, with the psalmist, "Woe is me, that I sojourn in Mesech, that I dwell in the tents of Kedar!" We wish to do good to others as far as we can; we are men of peace, but when we speak, they are for war; and we realize the truth of our Lord's words, "A man's foes shall be they of his own household." The more a man comes right straight out for God, the more opposition he is sure to meet with. Be half-asleep, and nobody will say much against you; but wake up, and be active for God, and for his Christ, and you will soon discover that the seed of the serpent has the serpent's venom in it still, and it hates the seed of the woman as much as ever it did. It must be so; therefore always feel that you are only a stranger here, and that your business is to go through this world, as a traveller passes through a foreign country. He does not speak the language of the people, he does not follow their customs, he is not one of the citizens of the land; he is just a temporary dweller here below, and he is on his journey home. If that is the kind of man you are, God is not ashamed to be called your God; but he is not the God of the earthworms that only want to burrow down into the soil. He is not the God of those who build their nests, and say, "Here would we live for ever." He is not the God of the man who can say, "Give me a knife and fork, and plenty to eat and drink; give me suitable clothes to wear in the day, and a nice soft bed to sleep on at night; give me wealth, give me fame; that is all I want, and I will let heaven go to anyone who wants it." Jehovah is not the God of Esau, who sells his birthright for a mess of pottage; but he is the God of Abraham, of Isaac, and of Jacob, who have a heritage that they cannot see, and who count the land in which they dwell to be a place of strangers and of sojourners; and they think of themselves as only strangers and sojourners in it.

Now read on a little further: "For they that say such things declare plainly that they seek a country." The word translated "country" might, I think, be better rendered "fatherland." "They who say that they are strangers here declare plainly that they seek a "fatherland." The word is sometimes translated "their own country." "A prophet is not without honour, save in his own country." It is the same word here in the Greek. *It signifies that they sought their own country,—their fatherland.* Wherefore, God, who is the Father of all his people, and whose heaven is their fatherland, is not ashamed to be called their God. Now, dear friends, are you seeking a fatherland? I put the question to

every hearer here,—Are *you* looking for a fatherland? Sir
Walter Scott wrote,—

> "Breathes there the man, with soul so dead,
> Who never to himself hath said,
> 'This is my own, my native land!'
> Whose heart hath ne'er within him burned,
> As home his footsteps he hath turned
> From wandering on a foreign strand?"

So said the patriot poet, and we have said it, too, for we are
patriots; but yet I venture to say that this is not my home,
this is not my fatherland.

> "I'm but a stranger here;
> Heaven is my home."

My fatherland lies out of sight, beyond the everlasting hills,
where God dwells, and where Christ sits at the right hand of
the Father. Now, the men who, by grace, have been brought
to say this, "We are out of our own country, we are seeking a
fatherland," these are the people of whom it is written,
"Wherefore God is not ashamed to be called their God."

Paul goes on to say, "And truly, if they had been mindful of
that country from whence they came out, they might have
had opportunity to have returned." Brethren, this is another
characteristic of believers, *we have left the world as our
home, and joy, and comfort, to seek a better country; but we
may go back if we like.* There is no compulsion to keep a man
a Christian, but the compulsion of love. He who is enlisted in
the army of Christ may desert if he pleases, but the blessed
grace of God will hold us so that we shall do no such thing.
We have plenty of opportunities to return. Oh, how many
invite us to turn back! I know how they beckon some of you
who have lately come out on the Lord's side. Sometimes it is
a female voice that would charm you, and there is a great
fascination about it, and you have to mind what you are
doing lest you become unequally yoked together. Sometimes
it is the voice of the world promising you wealth,—offering
you a better situation, perhaps, if you will go back; but, like
Moses, you esteem "the reproach of Christ greater riches
than the treasures in Egypt." You have plenty of opportunities to return. There are back entrances to Satan's
kingdom; he does not ask you to come in at the front door, he
lets you sneak in again by the back gate. If you want to go

into slavery again, there are many opportunities of returning; but if you are made by Christ to be, in this respect, like God, immutable, so that you say, "I cannot turn; I cannot change; I must be what Christ has made me; I must stand fast for truth and for holiness, and stand fast as long as I live, so help me, my God,"—if you are able to talk like that, then God is not ashamed to be called your God. Abraham, Isaac, and Jacob, you can get back to the old country whenever you like. But they never will go back; the deep dividing river rolls between them and that land, even as, to-day, there rolls between some of us and the world the stream in which we have been buried with Christ, and, by God's grace, we shall never cross it again; and, because of that holy determination, God is not ashamed to be called our God.

I finish up my remarks upon the word "wherefore," which is very full of matter, by noticing how the apostle says, "But now they desire a better country, that is, an heavenly." That is to say, *instead of going back, we are pressing forward towards heavenly things.* "God is a Spirit: and they that worship him must worship him in spirit and in truth." "The Father seeketh such to worship him." That is, those who are spiritual, who are seeking after heavenly things with all their heart, these are they whom God loves, for God is spiritual; God is heavenly; and when he has made us spiritual, and made us pant after heavenly things, then he is not ashamed to be called our God.

I have put these points before you as briefly as I could, wishing every moment to be examining myself, and asking you to examine yourselves. Have you a life within you which makes you pant and pine after heavenly things? Whatever you have in this world, do you hold it with a loose hand? Do you feel that it is not your real riches,—it is not your true treasure? You know that Abraham, Isaac, and Jacob were all rich men. God blessed them, and gave them a great increase to all that they had; but, still, they did not live simply to gather riches; they did not make them their chief delight. If you had asked them, they would have told you that they were inheritors of a mysterious covenant, by which God had bound himself to be their God, and the God of their seed; and in that covenant was included the promise that Christ himself should come out of their loins, and for him they waited, and he was the hope of their spirit. Now, dear friends, if that be the case with you also, you can understand the meaning of my text, "Wherefore God is not ashamed to be called their God."

II. I must give but a few minutes to the second part of the text, yet it wants a good deal of thought, for it says, "for he hath prepared for them a city." The second pivot-word is "FOR."

Now go back again to the text in Exodus, "I am the God of Abraham, the God of Isaac, and the God of Jacob." Yet Paul says, "These all died;" and we know that our Lord said to the Sadducees, "God is not the God of the dead, but of the living." Is he not ashamed to be called the God of Abraham, and Isaac, and Jacob, seeing that they all died? No; because they are not dead, though they died, "for he hath prepared for them a city." *These men, though they lived, and died, and passed out of this world without having received the heritage, are not dead.* There is the glory of the matter. When they lay a-dying, the devil might have come, and said to them, "Now, what have you got by your covenant with God? You left father, and mother, and everything that you had, and went and lived the separated life, and now you are dying out here; what have you got? Nothing but some little holes in the Cave of Machpelah, into which they will push your bodies; that is all that you have got." Oh, but the devil does not know; or if he does, he is a liar, for they gained everything by that life of faith, for they still live, and God has prepared for them a city. They have entered that city now. Abraham, Isaac, and Jacob are at the very head of the celestial company, for our Lord said, "Many shall come from the east, and west, and shall sit down with Abraham, and Isaac, and Jacob in the kingdom of heaven." And, by-and-by, Machpelah shall yield up her dead; and Abraham, and Sarah, and Isaac, and Jacob shall live again in the fullest sense, for their bodies as well as their souls shall live again; and Joseph's bones, which he would not suffer to lie in Egypt,—for he would not let the Egyptians have a scrap of him,—shall live;—and thus, in their flesh, shall they see God, and shall rejoice before him. Therefore, God is not ashamed to be called the God of these people who all died in faith, because they are still living, and they shall continue to live for ever and ever.

Somebody may perhaps say that these people did not

receive the promises. Well, they did not literally receive the
fulfillment of them. They did not see Christ; they did not
witness the descent of the Holy Ghost; they did not hear the
gospel preached. They did not see those wonders that they
looked for, so is not God ashamed to be called the God of
people who did not receive the promises after all? No,
because "he hath prepared for them a city." *They have
received the promises now;* and they shall receive them yet
more and more. God will yet cause the believer's life to be all
blessing. Do not be afraid of the consequences of trusting in
Christ; you may have the rough side of the road here; but
what we sang, just now, is quite true,—

> "Afflictions may press me, they cannot destroy,
> One glimpse of his love turns them all into joy;
> And the bitterest tears, if he smile but on them,
> Like dew in the sunshine, grow diamond and gem.
>
> Let doubt, then, and danger my progress oppose,
> They only make heaven more sweet at the close:
> Come joy or come sorrow, whate'er may befall,
> An hour with my God will make up for them all."

If God gave to his children here gall and wormwood to
drink,—ay, if they never had anything but aches and pains
from the moment of their conversion till they died, yet they
would have the best of the bargain, after all, for there is an
eternity of bliss in the heaven which is prepared for them.

But, further, these people were a sort of gipsies, always
moving about, and living in tents, different from everybody
else. Yes, *they were strangers among the people where they
dwelt;* and men often say of us now, that we cannot be
content to go on as other people do. Those patriarchs were
strangers, odd folk, peculiar people. Is not God ashamed to
be called their God? No; because, now, they have gone where
they are all right, for their manners and customs are exactly
suitable to the place. A very dear old woman, whom I visited
when she was dying, said to me, "One thing comforts me, sir,
I do not think that God will ever send me among the wicked,
for I never could get on in their company. The best times I
have ever had were when I could sit with a few of the Lord's
people, and hear them talk about him; and though I could
not always be sure that I was myself a Christian, yet I was
very like them, and I was very happy when I was with them.
I think I shall go to my own company, sir." Yes, dear soul,

and so she did; and if we are strangers here, we are going to that company where we shall not be at all strangers. They will understand our language when once we get across the river into the King's own country. "Wherefore God is not ashamed to be called their God," because they speak the language which he speaks, the language of his own courts; and he is not ashamed to say, "These are my people, and I own them before you all."

Notice, yet again, that *these people were seekers and desirers all their lives:* "They seek a country;" "they desire a better country." Is this a right state of heart for a Christian, —to be always seeking and always desiring? Well, brethren, that is the state in which I often am, and I wish still to keep in that condition,—always seeking, always desiring. Whenever God gives me any spiritual blessing, I always seek some more; and if he gives me more, I seek for more still. And if he gives me my heart's desire, I pray him to enlarge my heart, that I may desire some greater boon. For, in spiritual things, we may be as covetous as ever we like; and we may say, "Not as though I had already attained, either were already perfect: but I follow after, if that I may apprehend that for which also I am apprehended of Christ Jesus. Brethren, I count not myself to have apprehended: but this one thing I do, forgetting those things which are behind, and reaching forth unto those things which are before, I press toward the mark for the prize of the high calling of God in Christ Jesus." And God is not ashamed to be called the God of those who are thus seeking and desiring, because he has laid up for them all that they seek, and he has prepared for them all that they desire. I should be ashamed to set a poor person desiring if I could not gratify the desire; I should be ashamed to set a man seeking if I knew that he could not get what he sought after; but because God has prepared a city for these seekers and desirers, he is not ashamed to be called their God. As I stood, this evening, by the bedside of the dear brother whom I mentioned to you, a little while ago, I could not help saying, "Here is a poor soul covered with boils and blains, but God is not ashamed to be called his God." And there may be a child of God who is very poor indeed, with hardly sufficient garments to cover him, but God is not ashamed to be called his God. Perhaps his own brother is ashamed to be called his brother; I have even known cases where men have been so wicked as to be ashamed of their own parents, because they were not so well off as themselves; but God is never ashamed of his poor people. Ay, and if God's people are persecuted, and ill-used, if they are covered with mud from head to foot, or if they are cast into prison, God is not ashamed to be called their God. In those days when God permitted his people to be fastened up to the cross, or when others were taken to the stake and burnt, and everybody hissed at them, and cast out their name as evil, and said that they were the offscouring of all things; God was not ashamed to be called their God. I am almost ashamed to say what I am going to say; I really feel my very heart blush that I should have to say it. I have known some professors who have been ashamed to call God their God. Is it not strange that the glorious God of heaven and earth should call a worm his own, and take mean wretches such as we are, and say, "I am not ashamed to be called their God," and yet that some of these creatures should be so miserably cowardly that they are ashamed to be called the people of God? Oh, write his name on your foreheads! Never be ashamed of it. Ashamed of God? Ashamed of Jesus? Ashamed of the truth? Ashamed of righteousness? I do not wonder that there is such a text as this,—"The fearful"—that is the cowardly—"and unbelieving...shall have their part in the lake which burneth with fire and brimstone: which is the second death." If you really do love the Lord, come out, and show yourself on his side; and if he is not ashamed of you, and if your prayer be, "Lord, remember me when thou comest into thy kingdom," own him as your Lord and Saviour now. You who are not members of any Christian church,—you who have believed in Christ, or think you have, and yet have never confessed him,—you who are hiding like rats behind the wainscot, come out, and confess Christ. What are you at? How can you be soldiers of the cross, and followers of the Lamb, if you fear to own his cause, and blush to speak his name? Come out of your hiding-places! May God the Holy Spirit draw or drive you out at once! If anything could do it, surely, it should be such a blessed fact as this, that you are numbered amongst those of whom it is said that "God is not ashamed to be called their God."

God bless you, dear friends, for Jesus' sake! Amen.

12

Citizenship In Heaven

"For our conversation is in heaven; from whence also we look for the Saviour, the Lord Jesus Christ." **Philippians 3:20**

There can be no comparison between a soaring seraph and a crawling worm. Christian men ought so to live that it were idle to speak of a comparison between them and the men of the world. It should not be a comparison but a contrast. No scale of degrees should be possible; the believer should be a direct and manifest contradiction to the unregenerate. The life of a saint should be altogether above, and out of the same list as the life of a sinner. We should compel our critics not to confess that moralists are good, and Christians a little better; but while the world is darkness, we should manifestly be light; and while the world lieth in the Wicked One, we should most evidently be of God, and overcome the temptations of that Wicked One. Wide as the poles asunder, are life and death, light and darkness, health and disease, purity and sin, spiritual and carnal, divine and sensual. If we were what we profess to be, we should be as distinct a people in the midst of this world, as a white race in a community of Ethiopians; there should be no more difficulty in detecting the Christian from the worldling than in discovering a sheep from a goat, or a lamb from a wolf. Alas! the Church is so much adulterated, that we have to abate our glorying, and cannot exalt her character as we would. "The precious sons of Zion, comparable to fine gold, how are they esteemed as earthen pitchers, the work of the hands of the potter!" O for the time when "our conversation shall be in heaven," and the ignoble life of the man, whose god is his belly and whose end is destruction, shall be rebuked by our unworldly, unselfish character. There should be as much difference between the worldling and the Christian as between hell and heaven, between destruction and eternal life. As we hope at last that there shall be a great gulf separating us from the doom of the impenitent, there should be here a deep and wide gulf between us and the ungodly. The purity of our character should be such, that men must take knowledge of us that we are of another and superior race. God grant us more and more to be most clearly a chosen generation, a royal priesthood, a holy nation, a peculiar people, that we may show forth the praises of him who has called us out of darkness into his marvellous light.

Brethren, to-night I exhort you to holiness, not by the precepts of the law; not by the thunderings from Sinai; not by the perils or punishments which might fall upon you if you are unholy; but by the privileges to which you have been admitted. Gracious souls should only be urged by arguments from grace. Whips are for the backs of fools, and not for heirs of heaven. By the honourable citizenship which has been bestowed upon you, I shall beseech you to let your conversation be in heaven, and I shall urge that most prevailing argument, that the Lord Jesus Christ cometh, and therefore we should be as men that watch for our Lord, diligently doing service unto Him, that when He cometh he may say unto us, "Well done, good and faithful servants." I know that the grace which is in you will freely answer to such a plea.

Our text, I think, might be best translated thus—"Our citizenship is in heaven." The French translation renders it, "As for us, our burgessship is in the heavens." Doddridge paraphrases it, "But we converse as citizens of heaven, considering ourselves as denizens of the New Jerusalem, and only strangers and pilgrims upon earth."

I. The first idea which is suggested by the verse under consideration is this: if our citizenship be in heaven, then WE ARE ALIENS HERE; we are strangers and foreigners, pilgrims and sojourners in the earth, as all our fathers were. In the words of Sacred Writ, "Here we have no continuing city," but "we desire a better country, that is an heavenly." Let us illustrate our position. A certain young man is sent out by his father to trade on behalf of the family: he is sent to America, and he is just now living in New York. A very fortunate thing it is for him that his citizenship is in England; that, though he lives in America and trades there, yet he is an alien, and does not belong to that afflicted nation; for he retains his citizenship with us on this side the Atlantic. Yet there is a line of conduct which is due from him to the country which affords him shelter, and he must see to it that he does not fail to render it. Since *we* are aliens, we must remember to behave ourselves as aliens should, and by no means come short in our duty. We are affected by the position of our temporary country. A person trading in New York or Boston, though a freeman of the city of London, will find himself very much affected by the trade of the Dis-United States: when the merchants of his city suffer, he will find himself suffering with them, the fluctuations of their money-market will affect his undertakings, and the stagnation of commerce will slacken his progress; but if prosperity should happily return, he will find that when the coffers of their merchants are getting full, his will be the better; and the happy development of trade will give buoyancy to his own ventures. He is not of the nation, and yet every trembling of the scale will affect him; he will prosper as that nation prospers, and he will suffer as that nation suffers; that is to say, not as a citizen, but as a trader. And so we in this country find that, though we are strangers and foreigners on earth, yet we share all the inconveniences of the flesh. No exemption is granted to us from the common lot of manhood. We are born to trouble, even as others, and have tribulation like the rest. When famine comes we hunger; and when war rages we are in danger; exposed to the same clime, bearing the same burning heat, or the same freezing cold; we know the whole train of ills, even as the citizens of earth know them. When God in mercy scatters liberally with both his hands the bounties of his providence, we take our share, though we are aliens, yet we live upon the good of the land, and share the tender mercies of the God of Providence. Hence we have to take some interest in it; and the good man, though he be a foreigner, will not live even a week in this foreign land without *seeking to do good* among the neighbours with whom he dwells. The good Samaritan sought not only the good of the Samaritan nation, but of the Jews. Though there was no sort of kinship among them (for the Samaritans were not, as we have often heard erroneously said, first cousins or relations to the Jews; not a drop of Jewish blood ever ran in the Samaritans' veins; they were strangers brought from Assyria; they had no relation to Abraham whatever) yet the good Samaritan, finding himself travailing between Jericho and Jerusalem, did good to the Jew, since he was in Judea. The Lord charged his people by his servant Jeremiah, "Seek the peace of the city whither I have caused you to be carried away captives, and pray unto the Lord for it: for in the peace thereof shall ye have peace." Since we are here, we must seek the good of this world. "To do good and to communicate forget not." "Love ye your enemies, and do good, and lend, hoping for nothing again; and your reward shall be great, and ye shall be the children of the Highest: for he is kind unto the unthankful and to the evil." We must do our utmost while we are here to bring men to Christ, to win them from their evil ways, to bring them to eternal life, and to make them, with us, citizens of another and a better land; for, to tell the truth, we are here as recruiting sergeants for heaven; here to give men the enlisting money, to bind upon them the blood-red colours of the Saviour's service, to win them to King Jesus, that, by-and-bye, they may share his victories after having fought his battles.

Seeking the good of the country as aliens, we must also remember that it behooves aliens to *keep themselves very quiet*. What business have foreigners to plot against the government, or to intermeddle with the politics of a country in which they have no citizenship? An Englishman in New York had best be without a tongue just now; if he should criticise the courage of the generals, the accuracy of their despatches, or the genius of the President, he might meet with rather rough usage. He will be injudicious indeed, if he cannot leave America to the Americans. So, in this land of ours, where you and I are strangers, we must be orderly sojourners, submitting ourselves constantly to those that are in authority, leading orderly and peaceable lives, and, according to the command of the Holy Ghost through the apostle, "honouring all men, fearing God, honouring the king;" "submitting ourselves to every ordinance of man for the Lord's sake." I cannot say that I delight in political Christians; I fear that party-strife is a serious trial to believers, and I cannot reconcile our heavenly citizenship with the schemes of the hustings and the riot of the polling-booth. You must follow your own judgment here, but for my part, I am a foreigner even in England, and as such I mean to act. We are simply passing through this earth, and should bless it in our transit, but never yoke ourselves to its affairs. An Englishman may happen to be in Spain—he wishes a thousand things were different from what they are, but he does not trouble himself much about them: says he, "If I were a Spaniard I would see what I could do to alter this government, but, being an Englishman, let the Spaniards see to their own matters. I shall be back to my own country by-and bye, and the sooner the better." So with Christians here; they are content very much to let the potsherds strive with the potsherds of the earth; their politics concern their own country, they do not care much about any other; as *men* they love liberty, and are not willing to lose it even in the lower sense; but, spiritually, their politics are spiritual, and as citizens they look to the interest of that divine republic to which they belong, and they wait for the time when, having patiently borne with the laws of the land of their banishment, they shall come under the more beneficent sway of him who reigns in glory, the King of kings, and Lord of lords. If it be possible, as much as lieth in you, live peaceably with all men, and serve your day and generation still, but build not your soul's dwelling place here, for all this earth must be destroyed at the coming of the fiery day.

Again, let us remember that as aliens *we have privileges as well as duties*. The princes of evil cannot draft us into their regiments; we cannot be compelled to do Satan's work. The king of this world may make his vassals serve him, but he cannot raise a conscription upon aliens. He may order out his troops to this villany, or to that dastard service, but the child of God claims an immunity from all the commands of Satan; let evil maxims bind the men that own their sway, we are free, and own not the prince of the power of the air. I know that men of this world say we must keep up appearances; we must be respectable; we must do as others do; we must swim with the tide; we must move with the crowd; but not so the upright believer: "No," says he, "Do not expect me to fall in with your ways and customs; I am in Rome, but I shall not do as Rome does. I will let you see that I am an alien, and that I have rights as an alien, even here in this foreign land. I am not to be bound to fight your battles, nor march at the sound of your drums." Brethren, we are soldiers of Christ; we are enlisted in *his* army; and as aliens here, we are not to be constrained into the army of evil. Let lords and lands have what masters they will, let us be free, for Christ is our Master still. The seven thousand whom God has reserved, will not bow the knee to Baal. Be it known unto thee, O world, that we will not serve thy gods, nor worship the image which thou hast set up. Servants of God we are, and we will not be in bondage unto men.

As we are free from the conscription of the State, we must remember, also, that we are *not eligible to its honours.* I know you will say that is not a privilege; but it is a great boon if looked at aright. An Englishman in New York is not eligible for the very prickly throne of the President; I suppose he could not well be made a governor of Massachusetts or any other State, and, indeed, he may be well content to renounce the difficulties and the honour too. So also, the Christian man here is not eligible to this world's honours. It is a very ill omen to hear the world clap its hands, and say, "Well done" to the Christian man. He may begin to look to his standing, and wonder whether he has not been doing wrong when the unrighteous give him their approbation. "What, did I do wrong," said Socrates, "that yonder villain praised me just now?" And so may the Christian say, "What, have I done wrong, that So-and-so spoke well of me, for if I had done right he would not; he has not the sense to praise goodness, he could only have applauded that which suited his own taste." Christian men, ye must never covet the world's esteem; the love of this world is not in keeping with the love of God. "If any man love the world the love of the Father is not in him." Treat its smiles as you treat its threats, with quiet contempt. Be willing rather to be sneered at than to be approved, counting the cross of Christ greater riches than all the treasures of Egypt. O harlot world, it were a sad dishonour to be thy favourite. Tire thy head and paint thy face, thou Jezebel, but thou art no friend of ours, nor will we desire thy hollow love.

The men of this world were mad to raise us to their seats of honour, for we are aliens and citizens of another country. When the Pope sent a noted Protestant statesman a present of some silver goblets, he returned them with this answer— "The citizens of Zurich compel their judges to swear twice in the year that they will receive no presents from foreign princes, therefore take them back." More than twice in the year should the Christian resolve that he will not accept the smiles of this world, and will do no homage to its glory. "We fear the Greeks even when they bear gifts." Like the Trojans of old, we may be beguiled with presents even if un-conquered in arms. Forswear then the grandeur and honour of this fleeting age. Say in life, what a proud cardinal said in death, "Vain pomp and glory of the world, I hate ye." Pass through Vanity-Fair without trading in its vanities; crying, in answer to their "What will ye buy?"—"We buy the truth." Take up the pilgrim's song and sing it always—

> "The things eternal I pursue,
> And happiness beyond the view
> Of those who basely pant
> For things by nature felt and seen;
> Their honours, wealth, and pleasures mean,
> I neither have nor want.
>
> Nothing on earth I call my own:
> A stranger to the world unknown,
> I all their goods despise;
> I trample on their whole delight,
> And seek a country out of sight,—
> A country in the skies."

Furthermore, as aliens, *it is not for us to hoard up this world's treasures.* Gentlemen, you who know the exchange of New York, would you hoard up any extensive amount of Mr. Chase's green backed notes? I think not. Those stamps which officiate in the States in lieu of copper coinage I should hardly desire to accumulate; perhaps the fire might consume them, or if not, the gradual process of wear and tear which they are sure to undergo might leave me penniless ere long. "No, sir," says the British trader, "I am an alien; I cannot very well accept payment in these bits of paper, they are very well for you; they will pass current in your state, but my riches must be riches in England, for I am

going there to live directly; I must have solid gold, old
English sovereigns, nothing else but these can make me
rich." Brethren, so it is with us. If we are aliens, the
treasures of this world are like those bits of paper, of little
value in our esteem; and we should lay up our treasure in
heaven, "where neither moth nor rust doth corrupt, and
where thieves do not break through nor steal." The money of
this world is not current in Paradise; and when we reach its
blissful shore, if regret can be known, we shall wish that we
had laid up more treasure in the land of our fatherhood, in
the dear fatherland beyond the skies. Transport thy jewels
to a safer country than this world; be thou rich toward God
rather than before men. A certain minister collecting for a
chapel, called upon a rich merchant, who generously gave
him fifty pounds. As the good man was going out with
sparkling eye at the liberality of the merchant, the
tradesman opened a letter, and he said, "Stop a minute, I
find by this letter, I have lost this morning a ship worth six
thousand pounds." The poor minister trembled in his shoes,
for he thought the next word would be, "Let me have the fifty
pound cheque back." Instead of it, it was "Let me have the
cheque back a moment," and then taking out his pen he
wrote him a cheque for five hundred pounds. "As my money
is going so fast, it is well," said he, "to make sure of some of
it, so I will put some of it in God's bank." The man, you doubt
not, went his way astonished at such a way of dealing as
this, but indeed that is just what a man should do, who feels
he is an alien here, and his treasure is beyond the sky.

> "There is my house and portion fair;
> My treasure and my heart are there,
>   And my abiding home:
> For me my elder brethren stay,
> And angels beckon me away,
>   And Jesus bids me come."

II. It is our comfort now to remind you that although
aliens *on earth,* WE ARE CITIZENS IN HEAVEN.

What is meant by our being citizens in heaven? Why, first
that *we are under heaven's government.* Christ the king of
heaven reigns in our hearts; the laws of glory are the laws of
our consciences; our daily prayer is, "Thy will be done on
earth as it is in heaven." The proclamations issued from the

throne of glory are freely received by us, the decrees of the Great King we cheerfully obey. We are not without law to Christ. The Spirit of God rules in our mortal bodies, grace reigns through righteousness, and we wear the easy yoke of Jesus. O that he would sit as king in our hearts, like Solomon upon his throne of gold. Thine are we, Jesus, and all that we have; rule thou without a rival.

As citizens of the New Jerusalem, *we share heaven's honours.* The glory which belongs to beatified saints belongs to us, for we are already sons of God, already princes of the blood imperial; already we wear the spotless robe of Jesus' righteousness; already we have angels for our servitors, saints for our companions, Christ for our brother, God for our Father, and a crown of immortality for our reward. We share the honours of citizenship, for we have come to the general assembly and Church of the firstborn, whose names are written in heaven. "Beloved, now are we the sons of God, and it doth not yet appear what we shall be: but we know that, when he shall appear, we shall be like him; for we shall see him as he is."

As citizens, *we have common rights in all the property of heaven.* Those wide extensive plains we sung of just now are ours; ours yon harps of gold and crowns of glory; ours the gates of pearl and walls of chrysolite; ours the azure light of the city that needs no candle nor light of the sun; ours the river of the water of life, and the twelve manner of fruits which grow on the trees planted at the side thereof; there is nought in heaven that belongeth not unto us, for our citizenship is there. "Things present, or things to come; all are ours; and we are Christ's; and Christ is God's."

And as we are thus under heaven's government, and share its honours and partake of its possessions, so we to-day *enjoy its delights.* Do they rejoice over sinners that are born to God—prodigals that have returned? So do we. Do they chant the glories of triumphant grace? We do the same. Do they cast their crowns at Jesus' feet? Such honours as we have, we cast there too. Do they rejoice in Him? So also do we. Do they triumph, waiting for his second advent? By faith we triumph in the same. Are they to-night singing "Worthy the Lamb?" We also have sung the same tune, not to such glorious notes as theirs, but with as sincere hearts; with minstrelsy not quite so splendid, but we hope as sincere, for the Spirit gave us the music, which we have, and the Spirit gave them the thunders of their acclamations before the throne. "Our citizenship is in heaven."

Brethren, we rejoice to know also that as the result of our being citizens, or rather I ought to have said as the cause of it, our *names are written in the roll* of heaven's free-men. When, at last, the list shall be read, our names shall be read too; for where Paul and Peter, where David and Jonathan, where Abraham and Jacob shall be found, we shall be found too; numbered with them we were in the divine purpose, reckoned with them we were in the purchase on the cross, and with them shall we sit down for ever at the tables of the blessed. The small and the great are fellow-citizens and of the same household. The babes and the perfect men are recorded in the same great registry, and neither death nor hell can erase a single name.

Our citizenship then is in heaven. We have not time to extend that thought. John Calvin says of this text, "It is a most abundant source of many exhortations, which it were easy for any one to elicit from it." We are not all Calvin; but even to our smaller capacities, the subject appears to be one not readily exhausted, but rich with unfathomable joy.

III. We must now come to our third point, which is, OUR CONVERSATION IS IN HEAVEN, our walk and acts are such as are consistent with our dignity *as citizens of heaven.* Among the old Romans, when a dastardly action was proposed it was thought a sufficient refusal to answer "Romanus sum, —I am a Roman." Surely it should be a strong incentive to every good thing if we can claim to be freemen of the Eternal City. Let our lives be conformed to the glory of our citizenship. In heaven they are holy, so must we be—so are we if our citizenship is not a mere pretence. They are happy, so must we be rejoicing in the Lord always. In heaven they are obedient, so must we be, following the faintest monitions of the divine will. In heaven they are active, so should we be, both day and night praising and serving God. In heaven they are peaceful, so should we find a rest in Christ and be at peace even now. In heaven they rejoice to behold the face of Christ, so should we be always meditating upon him, studying his beauties, and desiring to look into the truths which he has taught. In heaven they are full of love, so should we love one another as brethren. In heaven they have sweet communion one with another, so should we, who though many, are one body, be every one members one of the other. Before the throne they are free from envy and strife, ill-will, jealousy, emulation, falsehood, anger, so should we be: we should, in fact, seek while we are here to keep up the manners and customs of the good old fatherland, so that, as in Paris, the Parisian soon says, "There goes John Bull," so they should be able to say in this land, "There goes a heavenly citizen, one who is with us, and among us, but is not of us." Our very speech should be such that our citizenship should be detected. We should not be able to live long in a house without men finding out what we are. A friend of mine once went across to America, and landing I think at Boston, he knew nobody, but hearing a man say, when somebody had dropped a cask on the quay, "Look out there, or else you will make a Coggeshall job of it." He said, "You are an Essex man I know, for that is a proverb never used anywhere but in Essex: give me your hand;" and they were friends at once. So there should be a ring of true metal about our speech and conversation, so that when a brother meets us, he can say "You are a Christian, I know, for none but Christians speak like that, or act like that." "Thou also wast with Jesus of Nazareth, for thy speech bewrayeth thee." Our holiness should act as a sort of freemasonry by which we know how to give the grip to the stranger, who is not a real stranger, but a fellow citizen with us, and of the household of faith. Oh! dear friends, wherever we wander, we should never forget our beloved land. In Australia, on the other side the world, or in the Cape of Good Hope, or wherever else we may be exiled, surely every Englishman's eye must turn to this fair island; and with all her faults, we must love her still. And surely let us be where we may, our eyes must turn to heaven, the happy land unstained by shadow of fault; we love her still, and love her more and more, praying for the time when our banishment shall expire, and we shall enter into our fatherland to dwell there for ever and ever. Shenstone says, "The proper means of increasing the love we bear our native country, is to reside some time in a foreign land." Sure am I that we who cry, "Woe is me, for I dwell in Mesech, and sojourn in the tents of Kedar!" are sure to add, "O that I had wings like a dove, for then would I fly away, and be at rest."

IV. The text says, "Our conversation is in heaven," and I think we may read it, as though it said, "OUR COMMERCE IS IN HEAVEN." We are trading on earth, but still the bulk of our trade is with heaven. We trade for trinkets in this land, but our gold and silver are in heaven. We commune with heaven, and how? Our trade is with heaven by *meditation,* we often think of God our Father, and Christ our Brother; and, by the Spirit, the Comforter, we are brought in contemplative delight, to the general assembly and Church of the firstborn, whose names are written in heaven. Brethren, do not our *thoughts* sometimes burn within us, when we trade with that blessed land? When I have sent the ships of understanding and consideration to that land of Ophir, which is full of gold, and they have come back again laden with all manner of precious things, my thoughts have been enriched, my soul has longed to journey to that good land. Black and stormy art thou, O sea of death, but I would cross thee to reach that land of Havilah, which hath dust of gold. I know that he who is a Christian will never have his mind long off that better land. And do you know we sometimes trade with heaven in our *hymns.* They tell us of the Swiss soldiery in foreign countries, that there is a song which the band is forbidden to play, because it reminds them of the cowbells of their native hills. If the men hear it, they are sure to desert, for that dear old song revives before their eyes the wooden chalets and the cows, and the pastures of the glorious Alps, and they long to be away. There are some of our hymns that make us homesick, until we are hardly content to stop, and therefore, well did our poet end his song,

> "Filled with delight, my raptured soul,
>   Can here no longer stay.
> Though Jordan's waves around us roll,
>   Fearless we launch away."

I feel the spirit of Wesley, when he said—

> "O that we now might see our guide!
>   O that the word were given!
> Come, Lord of hosts, the waves divide,
>   And land us all in heaven."

In times of high, hallowed, heavenly harmony of praise, the songs of angels seem to come astray, and find their way down to us, and then our songs return with them, hand in hand, and go back to God's throne, through Jesus Christ.

We trade with heaven, I hope, too, not only thus by meditation, and by thought, and by song, but *by hopes and by loves*. Our love is toward that land. How heartily the Germans sing of the dear old fatherland; but they cannot, with all their Germanic patriotism, they cannot beat the genial glow of the Briton's heart, when he thinks of his fatherland too. The Scotchman, too, wherever he may be, remembers the land of "brown heath and shaggy wood." And the Irishman, too, let him be where he will, still thinks the "Emerald Isle" the first gem of the sea. It is right that the patriot should love his country. Does not our love fervently flame towards heaven? We think we cannot speak well enough of it, and indeed here we are correct, for no exaggeration is possible. When we talk of that land of Eschol, our mouths are watering to taste its clusters; already, like David, we thirst to drink of the well that is within the gate; and we hunger after the good corn of the land. Our ears are wanting to have done with the discords of earth, that they may open to the harmonies of heaven; and our tongues are longing to sing the melodious sonnets, sung by flaming ones above. Yes, we do love heaven, and thus it is that we prove that our commerce is with that better land.

Brethren, just as people in a foreign land that love their country always are glad to have plenty of letters from the country, I hope we have much *communication with the old fatherland*. We send our prayers there as letters to our Father, and we get his letters back in this blessed volume of his Word. You go into an Australian settler's hut, and you find a newspaper. Where from, sir? A gazette from the south of France, a journal from America? Oh no, it is a newspaper from England, addressed to him in his old mother's handwriting, bearing the postage stamp with the good Queen's face in the corner; and he likes it, though it be only a newspaper from some little pottering country town, with no news in it; yet he likes it better, perhaps, than the "Times" itself, because it talks to him about the village where he lived, and consequently touches a special string in the harp of his soul. So must it be with heaven. This book, the Bible, is the newspaper of heaven, and therefore we must love it. The sermons which are preached are good news

from a far country. The hymns we sing are notes by which
we tell our Father of our welfare here, and by which he
whispers into our soul his continued love to us. All these are
and must be pleasant to us, for our commerce is with
heaven. I hope, too, we are sending a good deal home. I like
to see our young fellows when they go out to live in the bush,
recollect their mother at home. They say "She had a hard
struggle to bring us up when our father died, and she
scraped her little together to help us to emigrate." John and
Tom mutually agree, "the first gold we get at the diggings we
will send home to mother." And it goes home. Well, I hope
you are sending a great many things home. Dear friends, I
hope as we are aliens here, we are not laying up our treasure
here, where we may lose it, but packing it off as quickly as
we can to our own country. There are many ways of doing it.
God has many banks; and they are all safe ones. We have
but to serve his Church, or serve the souls which Christ has
bought with his blood, or help his poor, clothe his naked, and
feed his hungry, and we send our treasures beyond sea in a
safe ship, and so we keep up our commerce with the skies.

V. Time has gone; those clocks will strike when they ought
not. There is a great reason why we should live like aliens
and foreigners here, and that is, CHRIST IS COMING SOON.
The early Church never forgot this. Did they not pant and
thirst after the return of their ascended Lord? Like the
twelve tribes, day and night they instantly watched for
Messiah. But the Church has grown weary of this hope.
There have been so many false prophets who tell us that
Christ is coming, that the Church thinks He never will come;
and she begins to deny, or to keep in the background the
blessed doctrine of the second advent of her Lord from
heaven. I do not think the fact that there have been many
false prophets should make us doubt our Lord's true word.
Perhaps the very frequency of these mistakes may show that
there is truth at the bottom. You have a friend who is ill, and
the doctor says he cannot last long; he must die; you have
called a great many times expecting to hear of his departure,
but he is still alive; now the frequent errors of the physicians
do not prove that your friend will not die one of these days,
and that speedily too. And so, though the false prophets have
said, "Lo, here," and "Lo, there," and yet Christ has not
come, that does not prove that his glorious appearing will

never arrive. You know I am no prophet. I do not know anything about 1866; I find quite enough to do to attend to 1862. I do not understand the visions of Daniel or Ezekiel; I find I have enough to do to teach the simple word such as I find in Matthew, Mark, Luke, and John, and the Epistles of Paul. I do not find many souls have been converted to God by exquisite dissertations about the battle of Armageddon, and all those other fine things; I have no doubt prophesyings are very profitable, but I rather question whether they are so profitable to the hearers, as they may be to the preachers and publishers. I conceive that among religious people of a certain sort, the abortive explanations of prophecy issued by certain doctors gratify a craving which in irreligious people finds its food in novels and romances. People have a panting to know the future; and certain divines pander to this depraved taste, by prophesying for them, and letting them know what is coming by-and-bye. I do not know the future, and I shall not pretend to know. But I do preach this, because I know it, that *Christ will come,* for he says so in a hundred passages. The Epistles of Paul are full of the advent, and Peter's too, and John's letters are crowded with it. The best of saints have always lived on the hope of the advent. There was Enoch, he prophesied of the coming of the Son of Man. So there was another Enoch who was always talking of the coming, and saying, "Come quickly." I will not divide the house to-night by discussing whether the advent will be pre-millennial or post-millennial, or anything of that, it is enough for me that *he will come,* and "in such an hour as ye think not, the Son of Man will come." To-night he may appear, while here we stand; just when we think that he will not come, the thief shall break open the house. We ought, therefore, to be always watching. Since the gold and silver that you have will be worthless at his advent; since your lands and estates will melt to smoke when he appeareth; since, *then* the righteous shall be rich, and the godly shall be great, lay not up your treasure here, for it may at any time vanish, at any time disappear, for Christ may at any moment come.

I think the Church would do well to be always living as if Christ might come to-day. I feel persuaded she is doing ill if she works as if he would not come till 1866, because he may come before, and he may come this moment. Let her always be living as if he would come *now,* still acting in her Master's sight, and watching unto prayer. Never mind about the last vials, fill your own vial with sweet odours and offer it before the Lord. Think what you like about Armageddon; but forgot not to fight the good fight of faith. Guess not at the precise era for the destruction of Antichrist, go and destroy it yourself, fighting against it every day; but be looking forward and hastening unto the coming of the Son of Man; and let this be at once your comfort and excitement to diligence—that the Savior will soon come from heaven.

Now, I think you foreigners here present—and I hope there are a great many true aliens here—ought to feel like a poor stranded mariner on a desolate island, who has saved a few things from the wreck and built himself an old log hut, and has a few comforts round about him, but for all that he longs for home. Every morning he looks out to sea, and wonders when he shall see a sail; many times while examining the wide ocean to look for a ship, he has clapped his hands, and then wept to find he was disappointed; every night he lights his fire that there may be a blaze, so that if a ship should go by, they may send relief to the stranded mariner. Ah! that is just the way we ought to live. We have heard of one saint who used to open his window every morning when he woke, to see if Christ had come; it might be fanaticism, but better to be enthusiastic than to mind earthly things. I would have us look out each night and light the fire of prayer, that it may be burning in case the ships of heaven should go by, that blessings may come to us poor aliens and foreigners who need them so much. Let us wait patiently till the Lord's convoy shall take us on board, that we may be carried into the glories and splendour of the reign of Christ, let us always hold the log hut with a loose hand, and long for the time when we shall get to that better land where our possessions are, where our Father lives, where our treasures lie, where all our brethren dwell. Well said our poet—

> "Blest scenes, through rude and stormy seas
> I onward press to you."

My beloved friends, I can assure you it is always one of the sweetest thoughts I ever know, that I shall meet with you in heaven. There are so many of you members of this Church, that I can hardly get to shake hands with you once in a year; but I shall have plenty of time then in heaven. You will know your pastor in heaven better than you do now. He loves you now, and you love him. We shall then have more time to recount our experience of divine grace, and praise God together, and sing together, and rejoice together concerning him by whom we were helped to plant, and sow, and through whom all the increase came.

> "I hope when days and years are past,
> We all shall meet in heaven,
> We all shall meet in heaven at last,
> We all shall meet in heaven."

But we shall not all meet in glory; not all, unless you repent. Some of you will certainly perish, unless you believe in Christ. But why must we be divided? Oh! why not all in heaven? "Believe in the Lord Jesus Christ, and thou shalt be saved." "He that believeth and is baptized shall be saved, but he that believeth not shall be damned." Trust Christ, sinner, and heaven is thine, and mine, and we are safe for ever. Amen.

13

The Glorious Hereafter And Ourselves

"Now he that hath wrought us for the selfsame thing is God, who also hath given unto us the earnest of the Spirit."
2 Corinthians 5:5

It is a very comforting thing to be able to see the work of God in our own hearts. We can clearly enough perceive the effects of the fall, the workings of our inward corruption are always sufficiently perceptible. We have not to search long for the foul handiwork of Satan within us, for his temptations vex us day by day, and too often wound us to our hurt. The evil influences of the world are also exceedingly apparent to the eye of self-examination. It is, therefore, consoling to the highest degree when, amidst all these marrings of the vessel by the hand of evil, we can see growing traces of the Great Artist's hand still fashioning the clay upon the wheel, and undoing the mischief of his enemies. It is a sweet thing to be able to say with the apostle that God has wrought us to the grandest of all designs. When the Creator of the world puts his all-wise hand to the work of our new creation, we are favoured in the highest degree, and ought to be filled with gratitude.

It appears from the text that the apostle found the indications of the divine work in a groan. Observe, "We that are in this tabernacle do groan, being burdened." In that groan of his burdened soul he saw the working of the eternal God, and he exclaimed, "He that hath wrought us for the selfsame thing is God." Believers may trace the finger of God in their holy joys, when the soul, like the lark, mounts up

towards heaven and carols her song of gratitude as she
mounts; yet, just as surely is the Holy Spirit present in their
sorrows for sin, their inward conflicts, their hungerings and
thirstings after righteousness, their deep-fetched sighs, and
their groanings which cannot be uttered. My brethren, so
long as it is the work of God it is comparatively a small
matter to us whether our heart's utterance be song or sigh;
let us be assured that it is wrought by the Spirit, and either
the one or the other is a token for good. If it is but proven
that "the Lord is there," we hear a voice which saith, "It is I,
be not afraid."

Our text brings before us a great work of God with a
distinct object—our being "clothed upon with our house
which is from heaven;" and looking at the words minutely,
we see that the one design is accomplished by three great
processes. The Lord has wrought in us *desires after* the
heavenly glory. "He that hath wrought us to the selfsame
thing is God." The apostle had twice over spoken of groaning
after the heavenly house, and we understand him here to
affirm that this groaning was wrought in him by God.
Secondly, the Lord has wrought in us a *fitness for* the eternal
world, for so the text may be understood. "He that has *fitted*
us for" the heavenly inheritance of which the Spirit is the
earnest. Then thirdly, God has given to believers, in addition
to desires after and fitness for, *an earnest of* the glory to be
revealed, which earnest is the Holy Ghost. Let us speak of
these three things as the Holy Ghost may instruct us.

I. God's work is seen in our souls in causing us exciting,
vehement DESIRES AFTER being "clothed upon with our
house which is from heaven."

This earnest desire, of which the apostle has been
speaking in the preceding verses, is made up of two things—
a painful groaning and sense of being burdened while we are
in this present life, and a supreme longing after our
promised portion in the world to come. Dissatisfaction with
the very idea of finding a continuing city here, amounting
even to groaning, is the condition of the Christian's mind.
"We look not at the things which are seen," they are not
worth a glance; they are temporal, and therefore quite unfit
to be the joy of an immortal spirit. The Christian is the most
contented man *in* the world, but he is the least contented
with the world. He is like a traveller in an inn, perfectly

satisfied with the inn and its accommodation, considering it as an inn, but putting quite out of all consideration the idea of making it his home. He baits by the way, and is thankful, but his desires lead him ever onward towards that better country where the many mansions are prepared. The believer is like a man in a sailing vessel, well content with the good ship for what it is, and hopeful that it may bear him safely across the sea, willing to put up with all its inconveniences without complaint; but if you ask him whether he would choose to live on board in that narrow cabin, he will tell you that he longs for the time when the harbour shall be in view, and the green fields, and the happy homesteads of his native land. We, my brethren, thank God for all the appointments of providence; whether our portion be large or scant we are content because God has appointed it: yet our portion is not here, nor would we have it here if we might!

> "We've no abiding city here,
> Sad truth were this to be our home."

No thought would be more dreadful to us than the idea of having our portion in this life, in this dark world which refused the love of Jesus, and cast him out of its vineyard. We have desires which the whole world could not fulfill, we have insatiable yearnings which a thousand empires could not satisfy. The Creator has made us to pant and long after himself, and all the creatures put together could not delight our souls without his presence.

> "Hopeless of joy in aught below,
> We only long to soar,
> The fulness of his love to feel,
> And lose his smile no more."

In addition to this dissatisfaction, there reigns within the regenerate heart a supreme longing after the heavenly state. When believers are in their right minds, their aspirations after heaven are so forcible that they contemn death itself. When faith is weak, then the pains and the groans of dying make a black cloud of forebodings which darken the spirit, and we shrink from the thought of departing; but when we know that our Redeemer liveth, and look forward to the resurrection and to the glory to be revealed, we cry—

> "Oh, if my Lord would come and meet,
> My soul should stretch her wings in haste,
> Fly fearless through death's iron gate,
> Nor fear the terrors as she passed."

Whatever the separation of the soul from the body may involve of pain or mystery, the believer feels that he could dare it all, to enter at once into the unfading joys of the glory-land. Sometimes the heir of heaven grows impatient of his bondage, and like a captive who, looking out of the narrow window of his prison, beholds the green fields of the unfettered earth, and marks the flashing waves of the ocean, ever free, and hears the songs of the uncaged tenants of the air, weeps as he views his narrow cell, and hears the clanking of his chains. There are times when the most patient of the Lord's banished ones feel the home sickness strong upon them. Like those beasts which we have sometimes seen in our menageries, which pace to and fro in their dens, and chafe themselves against the bars—unresting, unhappy, bursting out every now and then into fierce roarings, as though they yearned for the forest or the jungle; even so we also chafe and fret in this our prison-house, longing to be free. As by the waters of Babylon the sons of Zion sat them down and wept, even so do we. Dwelling in Kedar's tents and sojourning with Mesech, we long for the wings of a dove that we might fly away and be at rest.

> "O my sweet home, Jerusalem,
> Would God I were in thee!
> Would God my woes were at an end,
> Thy joys that I might see."

Having thus seen that the groaning wrought in us by God is made up of dissatisfaction with this world and anxious desire for the world to come, we may profitably consider it yet a little further. What is it that makes the Christian long for heaven? What is that within him which makes him restless till he reach the better land? It is, first, *a desire for the unseen.* The carnal mind is satisfied with what the eyes can see, the hands can handle, and the taste enjoy, but the Christian has a spirit within him which has passions and appetites which the senses cannot gratify. This spirit has been created, developed, enlightened, and instructed by the

Holy Ghost, and it lives in a world of unseen realities, of which unregenerate men have no knowledge. While in this sinful world and earthly body, the spirit feels like a citizen exiled from his native land; it stands upon the outmost borders of its own region, and longs to penetrate into the centre of spiritual things. Hampered with this body of clay, the spirit, which is akin to angels, cries after liberty; it longs to see the Great Father of Spirits, to commune with the bands of the pure spirits for ever surrounding the throne of God, both angels and glorified men; it longs, in fact, to dwell in its true element. A spiritual creature, begotten from above, can never rest till it is present with the Lord. Oh! to see the things which we have heard of in metaphor and simile, to enjoy them really with our spirits, the harps, the crowns, the palms—what must it be to possess such joys? The streets of transparent gold, the river of the water of life, the glassy sea, the throne of the Great King—what must all these be? Until these joys and glories be all our own our souls will ever cry and sigh.

Moreover, the Christian spirit *pants after holiness.* He who is born again of incorruptible seed, finds his worst trouble to be sin. While he was in his natural state be loved sin, and sought pleasure in it, but now being born of God and made like to God, he hates sin, the mention of it vexes his ears, the sight of it in others causes him deep sorrow, but the presence of it in his own heart is his daily plague and burden. If he could be clean rid of sin this mortal body might not be to him a load, but because the tendencies of the animal passions are always towards evil, he longeth to be rid of this vile body, that he may be clothed upon with his house which is from heaven, from which all these passions will be expelled. Oh, to be without the tendency to sin, without the possibility to sin! What bliss the prospect affords! My brethren, if we could be placed in the meanest and most destitute condition, and yet could be perfect, we would prefer it to being sinful, even though we should reign in the palaces of kings. Our spirit, therefore, crieth after the immortal state, because sin will be for ever banished from it.

In the Christian's spirit there is also *a sighing after rest.* "There remaineth a rest for the people of God," as though God had put in us the longing for what he has prepared; we labour daily to enter into that rest. Brethren, we long for rest, but we cannot find it here. "This is not our rest." We cannot find rest even within ourselves. Wars and fightings are continuous within the regenerate spirit; the flesh lusteth against the spirit, and the spirit warreth against flesh. As long as we are here it must be so. We are in the camp of war, not in the chamber of ease. The trumpet must sound, and the clash of arms must be heard, and we must go to our watch-tower, and continue there both night and day, for we are militant as yet, and not triumphant. Our soul pines to be at rest. When shall the powers of our spirit indulge themselves to the full without the fear of falling into sin? When shall my memory recollect nothing but what will glorify God? When shall my judgment always rightly balance all events? When shall my desires be after nothing but my Lord? When shall my affections cling to nought but him? O when shall I possess the rest of the sinless, the rest of the satiated, the rest of the secure, the rest of the victorious? This longing for rest helps to inflame the Christian's desires for the house not made with hands.

This divinely-wrought desire is made up of another element, namely, *a thirst for communion with God*. Here, at the nearest, our state is described as being "absent from the Lord." We do enjoy fellowship with God, for "Truly our fellowship is with the Father and with his Son Jesus Christ," but it is remote and dark. "We see through a glass darkly," and not as yet face to face. We have the smell of his garments from afar, and they are perfumed with myrrh, and aloes, and cassia, but as yet the King is in his ivory palaces, and the gate of pearl is between us and him. O that we could come at him! O that he would even now embrace us, and kiss us with the kisses of his mouth. The more the heart loves Christ, the more it longs for the greatest possible nearness to him. Separation is very painful to a bride whose heart is burning for the bridegroom's presence; and such are we, longing to hear the most sweet voice of our Spouse and to see the countenance which is as Lebanon, excellent as the cedars. For a saved soul to long to be where its Saviour is, is no unnatural desire! To be with him is far better than earth's best, and it would be strange if we did not long for it. God, then, hath wrought in us this in all its forms, he has made us to dread the thought of having our portion in this life, he has created in us a supreme longing for our heavenly home, has taught us to value unseen and eternal things, to pant after holiness, to sigh after sinless rest, and to yearn after closer fellowship with God in Christ Jesus.

My brethren, if you have felt a desire such as I have described, give the glory of it to God; bless and love the Holy Spirit who hath wrought this selfsame thing in you, and ask him to make the desires yet more vehement, for they are to his glory.

Bear with a word in praise of this God-wrought groaning. This desire after the world to come is above ordinary nature. All flesh is grass, and the grass loves to strike its root deep into the earth; it has no tendrils with which to clasp the stars. Man by nature would be content to abide on earth for ever. If you long for a holy and spiritual state, your desire is not of nature's creation. God has wrought it in you. Yea, I will venture to say that the desire for heaven is contrary to nature; for as there is an inertia in matter which makes it indisposed to move, so is there in human nature an indisposition to leave the present for the future. Like the limpet, we stick to the rock on which we crawl. We cling to earth like the ivy to the wall. We are afraid to set sail upon that unknown sea of eternity, and therefore shiver on the shore. We dread to leave "the warm precincts of this house of clay," and hovel as this body is, we count it dear. It is the Lord who forbids our lying among the pots, and gives us the wings of a dove to mount aloft. As soon would a clod seek the sun as a soul seek its God, if a miracle of grace were not wrought upon it.

While they are contrary to the old nature, such aspirations *prove the existence of the new nature.* You may be quite sure that you have the nature of God in you if you are pining after God; and if your longings are of a spiritual kind, depend upon it you are a spiritual man. It is not in the animal to sigh after mental enjoyments, neither is it in the mere carnal man to sigh after heavenly things. What your desires are, that your soul is. If you are really insatiably hungering after holiness and after God, there is within you that which is like to God, that which is essentially holy, there is indeed a work of the Holy Ghost within your hearts.

I shall detain you awhile to notice the means by which the Holy Spirit quickens these desires within our spirits. This desire after a portion in the unseen world is first infused in us by *regeneration*. Regeneration begets in us a spiritual nature, and the spiritual nature brings with it its own longings and desires; these longings and desires are after perfection and God. Imagine an angel imprisoned in a stable: it is perfectly certain that it would be discontented with the place where the horned oxen lay. If it felt that the divine will commanded it to tarry there for awhile, I doubt not that the bright visitant would contentedly put up with the confinement; but if it had liberty to leave the society of beasts, how gladly would the bright spirit ascend to its native place. Yes, heaven is the place for angels, the true abode of holy spirits; and we, too, since our spiritual nature is born from above, long to be there, nor shall we be content until we are.

These desires are further assisted by *instruction*. The more the Holy Ghost teaches us of the world to come the more we long for it. If a child had lived in a mine it might be contented with the glimmer of candle light; but if it should hear of the sun and the green fields, and the stars, you may depend upon it the child would not be happy until it could ascend the shaft and behold for itself the brightness of which it had heard; and as the Holy Ghost reveals to us the world to come we feel longings within us, mysterious but mighty, and we sigh and cry to be away where Jesus is.

These desires are farther increased by *sanctified afflictions*. Thorns in our nest make us take to our wings; the embittering of this cup makes us earnestly desire to drink of the new wine of the kingdom. We are very much like our poor, who would stay at home in England and put up with their lot, hard though it be; but when at last there comes a worse distress than usual, then straightway they talk of emigrating to those fair and boundless fields across the Atlantic, where a kindred nation will welcome them with joy. So here we are in our poverty, and we make the best of it we can; but a sharp distress wounds our spirit, and then we say we will away to Canaan, to the land that floweth with milk and honey, for there we shall suffer no distress, neither shall our spirits hunger any more.

Heavenly desires are still further inflamed by *communion with Christ*. The sweets as well as the bitters may be made to increase our longings after the world to come. When a man has once known what fellowship with Jesus is then he pines to enjoy it for ever; like the Gauls on this side the Alps who, when they had once drank the Italian wines, said one to another, "It must be a fair land where they grow such wine as this, come, brethren, let us draw our swords and cross the Alps and take the vineyards for ourselves." Thus does the love of Jesus set us longing to be with him.

> "Since I have tasted of the grapes,
> I ofttimes long to go
> Where my dear Lord the vineyard keeps,
> And all the clusters grow."

Communion with Christ sharpens the edge of our desire for heaven.

And so, to close this vein of thought, does *elevation of soul*. The more we are sanctified and lifted above the grossness of earthliness into conformity with Jesus, the more we long for the world to come. A peasant at the plough is quite content to mix with his fellow labourers, but suppose he forms a passion for the study of the stars, feels a poet's frenzy, or develops mathematical powers, or learns the science of flowers, or in any way discovers the treasure hidden in the field of learning, he will be sure to be uneasy in ignorance, and will pine for books and education. He dreams of schools, and colleges, and libraries. His fellow ploughmen laugh at him, and count him but a fool. If they have enough to eat and drink and clothe themselves, they are content therein, but he has wants for which the village has neither sympathy nor supply. His elevation of mind has brought with it groanings, to which, had he grovelled like his fellows, he would have been a stranger. So is it with the regenerated man, in proportion as he is elevated by the Holy Spirit by growth in grace. The higher he rises the more he longs to rise. To him that hath it is given, and he desireth to have in abundance; with a sacred covetousness he panteth after yet higher degrees of grace, and after glory itself.

Thus have I opened up to you the desire which the Holy Spirit works in us. "He that hath wrought us for the selfsame thing is God.

II. Our second subject of discourse is THE FITNESS FOR HEAVEN which is wrought in us.

Calvin's interpretation of the text is, "He that hath fitted us for the selfsame thing is God." Ah! how true is this. There

is no fitness whatever in man by nature for communion with
his God; it must be a divine work within him. The Father
works in us fitness for heaven by separating us in the
everlasting decree to be his own. Heaven is the place of
God's own abode; we must be God's own people to be fit to be
there. He fits us by adopting us into his family, by justifying
us through the righteousness of Jesus Christ, by preserving
us by his power. The Son of God has an equal share in the
working of this fitness; he fits us by blotting out our
iniquities, and by transferring to us his righteousness, by
taking us into marriage union with himself. The Holy Spirit
also, for ever to be blessed, hath his share in this work. It is
he who first infuses the new nature, he who gives us
spiritual food for the new nature, giving us to feed upon the
flesh and blood of Christ; he who instructs and develops that
new nature, and through the blood of Jesus makes the man
meet to be a partaker of the inheritance of the saints in light.
Glory be unto the Father, and to the Son, and to the Holy
Ghost, who thus in blessed union hath "wrought us for the
selfsame thing."

Now, let me describe with great brevity the work of the
Holy Spirit in preparing us for glory. As we have already
hinted—and we must necessarily traverse much the same
ground—fitness for heaven, as wrought in us by the Spirit,
consists, first, in the possession of a spiritual nature.
Heaven is pre-eminently a spiritual region, and those who
have no nature begotten from above would not by any
possibility be able to enjoy the bliss of heaven. They would
be quite out of their element. It could not be a heaven to
them. A bee in a garden in the midst of the flowers is at
home, and gathers honey from all their cups and bells; but
open the gate and admit a swine, and it sees no beauty in
lilies and roses, and gillyflowers; and therefore it proceeds to
root, and tear, and spoil in all directions. Such would an
unregenerate man be in heaven. While holy saints shall find
bliss in everything in the paradise of God, an ungodly sinner
would be at war with everything in that holy region.

Fitness for heaven lies much in a holy nature. Now, a love
of heaven is as contrary to fallen humanity as light to
darkness. Do you not feel it so? Left to yourselves, O saints
of God, do you not know that you would go back to Egypt? Do
you not feel that the old nature lusts after evil? Well, then,

as you cannot possibly inherit heaven unless you delight in holiness, you owe this fitness for the perfect state to the Holy Spirit. Fitness for heaven lies in a capacity to delight in God. I have always loved that first question and answer in the Assembly's Catechism, "What is the chief end of man? The chief end of man is to glorify God and to enjoy him for ever." Not to enjoy yourself for ever, not even to enjoy the harps of gold and the angelic society, and the feasts of the beatified, but to enjoy God for ever. Now, if a man has as yet no delight in God, and takes no solace in thoughts of him, he has no fitness for heaven, and cannot get there; but if you delight in God, it is God that hath "wrought you to this selfsame thing."

Fitness for heaven will lie very much in love to the saints. Those who do not love the people of God on earth, would find their company very irksome for ever. Here the unrighteous can manage to endure the company of the godly, because it can be diluted with an admixture of graceless men, but up there the people shall be all righteous, and their conversation shall be all of Christ and of things divine; such society and such converse would be weariness itself to godless hearts. My hearer, if you delight in the company of the saints, and if the more spiritual their conversation the more you enjoy it, then you have been wrought to this selfsame thing by the work of the Holy Ghost in your soul, and you may bless the Lord for it.

Joy in service is another sweet preparation for heaven. Heaven is sinless service. They serve God day and night in his temple, service without weariness, service without imperfection, service without cessation. Now do you delight to serve God? If so, you have a fitness for heaven evidently; but as you once abhorred that service, and were the bondslave of the Prince of Darkness, if you now long and wish to glorify your God, you have been wrought thereto by the Holy Spirit's power.

Conformity to Christ Jesus, again, is another preparation for heaven. Much of heaven consists in being like Christ. It is the very object of divine grace that we should be conformed to his image, that he should be the firstborn among many brethren. Now, if you are growing by his grace somewhat like Christ, if you desire to be like him, imitating his tender, loving, brave, prayerful, obedient, self-sacrificing spirit, you have some fitness for the skies; but that fitness was not there by nature; you were once as unlike Christ as possible. God hath wrought all this in you.

I am afraid that I go from one point to another rather too rapidly, but the gist of it all is this. Heaven is the world of spirits, the land of holiness, the house of God, and if we have any capacity for the enjoyment of heaven, it has been wrought in us by God. The unfitness of unrenewed souls for heaven, may be illustrated by the incapacity of certain uneducated and coarse-minded persons for elevated thoughts and intellectual pursuits. When a little child, I lived some years in my grandfather's house. In his garden there was a fine old hedge of yew of considerable length, which was clipped and trimmed till it made quite a wall of verdure. Behind it was a wide grass walk, which looked upon the fields, the grass was kept mown, so as to make pleasant walking. Here, ever since the old Puritanic chapel was built, godly divines had walked and prayed and meditated. My grandfather was wont to use it as his study. Up and down it he would walk when preparing his sermons, and always on Sabbath-days when it was fair, he had half an hour there before preaching. To me it seemed to be a perfect paradise, and being forbidden to stay there when grandfather was meditating, I viewed it with no small degree of awe. I love to think of the green and quiet walk at this moment; but I was once shocked and even horrified by hearing a farming man remark concerning this *sanctum sanctorum,* "It' ud grow a many 'taturs if it wor ploughed up." What cared he for holy memories? What were meditation and contemplation to him? Is it not the chief end of man to grow potatoes and eat them? Such, on a larger scale, would be an unconverted man's estimate of joys so elevated and refined as those of heaven. Alphonse Karr tells a story of a servant-man who asked his master to be allowed to leave his cottage and sleep over the stable. What was the matter with his cottage? "Why, sir, the nightingales all around the cottage make such a 'jug, jug, jug' at night, that I cannot bear them." A man with a musical ear would be charmed with the nightingales' song, but here was a man without a musical soul who found the sweetest notes a nuisance. This is a feeble image of the incapacity of unregenerate man for the enjoyments of the world to come, and as he is incapable of enjoying them, so is he incapable of

longing for them. But if you and I have grown out of all taste
for the things of sin and time, and are sighing for holy, godly
joys, we have therein an evidence that God has wrought in
us by his grace, and will continue to do so till we are made
perfect and immortal.

III. The text informs us that in addition to working in us
desires and fitness for glory, the Lord has graciously given to
us an EARNEST OF GLORY.

An earnest, as you all know, is unlike a pledge, in some
respects. A pledge has to be returned when the matter which
it ensures is obtained; but an earnest is a part of the thing
itself. A man has so much wage to take on Saturday night,
he receives a part of it in the middle of the week, it is an
earnest of the full payment—a part of the payment itself. So
the Holy Spirit is a part of heaven itself. The work of the
Holy Spirit in the soul is the bud of heaven. Grace is not a
thing which will be taken away from us when we enter glory,
but which will develop into glory. Grace will not be
withdrawn as though it had answered its purpose, but will
be matured into glory. What is meant by the Holy Spirit
being given to us as an earnest? I believe it signifies, first,
that the very dwelling of the Holy Ghost within our soul is
the earnest of heaven. My brethren, if God himself
condescends to make these bodies his temples, is not this
akin to heaven's honours? Only put away sin, and the
indwelling of the Holy Ghost would make even this earthly
state to be heavenly to us. O my brethren, ye little know
what a weight of glory is contained in the indwelling of the
Holy Spirit. If you did but know it and believe in it always,
the sorrows of this life would become trivial, and as for the
frowns of men you would deride them. God dwelleth in you.
You walk among the sons of men unknown and despised, yet
as angels see you you are the objects of their wonder. Rejoice
that in this, then, you have an earnest of heaven.

But everything the Holy Spirit works in us is an earnest of
heaven. When the Holy Ghost brings to us the joys of hope,
this is an earnest. While singing some glowing hymn
touching the New Jerusalem, our spirit shakes off all her
doubts and fears, and anticipates her everlasting heritage.
When we enjoy the full assurance of faith, and read our title
clear to mansions in the skies, when faith, looking simply to
the finished work of Christ, knows whom she has believed,

and is persuaded that he is able to keep that which she has committed to him, this is an earnest of heaven. Is not heaven security, confidence, peace? The security, confidence, peace which spring from faith in Jesus Christ, are part and parcel of the heaven of the blessed. Heaven is the place of victory, and, my dear friends, when we are victorious over sin, when the Holy Spirit enables us to overcome some propensity, to get down our anger, to crush our pride, to mortify the flesh with its affections and lusts, then in that conscious victory over sin, we enjoy an earnest of the triumph of heaven. And once more, when the Holy Spirit gives us to enjoy fellowship with Jesus Christ, and with one another, when in the breaking of bread we feel the union which exists between Christ and his members, we have a foretaste of the fellowship of heaven. Do not say then, that you know nothing of what heaven is. "Eye hath not seen, nor ear heard, neither have entered into the heart of man, the things which God hath prepared for them that love him," but "he hath revealed them unto us by his Spirit." Spiritual natures do know what heaven is, in the sense of knowing from the drop what the river must be like, of understanding from the beam what the sun must be. Its fulness you cannot measure, its depth you cannot fathom, its unutterable bliss you cannot tell; but still you know of what character the glory will be, you know that pure are the joys of the blessed, and all their dwellings peace, you know that fellowship with Christ and with holy spirits makes up much of heaven, and you know this because the earnest of the Spirit is a part and parcel of the thing itself.

I conclude with a practical remark or two. If these things be so, what emotions are most fitting for us? Answer: first, O believers in Jesus, *be thankful,* overflow with thankfulness. Remember these things are not your own productions, no flowers of your own garden, but they have been planted in your soul by another hand, and watered by a superior power. Give all the glory to his holy name, for to him all the glory belongs. Not a good desire in you was self-originated, no part of your fitness for paradise was self-formed. Grace hath done it, grace hath done it all. Adore and bless the Holy Spirit who hath wrought all your works in you, for you are "His workmanship, created in Christ Jesus unto good works, which God hath before ordained that we should walk in them." Be ye thankful. As the birds created to sing, pour out their song; as the flowers, the handiwork of God, load the air with their perfume; so sing you, and let your lives be all fragrant with gratitude to him who has wrought you to the selfsame thing.

Another emotion we ought all to feel who have this wrought in us is that of *reverence*. When a scholar knows that all he has learned has been taught him by his master, he looks up from his master's feet into his master's face with respectful reverence and esteem. O reverence the Holy Ghost. Let us in our public ministry and in our private meditations always stand in awe of him. I am afraid we too much forget him, let us reverence him especially by obedience to his faintest monitions. As the leaves of the aspen tremble to the faintest breath of the wind, so may we tremble to the faintest breath of God's Holy Spirit. Let us prize the word because he wrote it; let us love the ordinances because he puts life and power into them. Let us love his indwelling, and never grieve him lest he hide his face from us. "He that hath wrought us to the selfsame thing is God." Vex not his Spirit, but anxiously ask that he would continue his work, and complete it in righteousness.

Lastly, our heart ought to feel great *confidence* this morning. If the good thing had been wrought by ourselves, we might be sure that it would fail before long. Nothing of mortal man was ever perfect. But if he that hath begun the good work be God, there is no fear that he will forsake or leave his work undone. They shall never say of him, "He began to build and was not able to finish." No war of his was ever undertaken and then given up because he had not counted the cost. God has begun, God will complete. His promise is "Yea and amen," and never was forfeited yet. Therefore let us be well assured, and let our hearts be glad. Dear hearers, the unhappy thing about this is that there are so many who have no desires for the blessed hereafter, no fitness for it, no earnest of it. Ah, then, the prophecies that are within you, what do they foretell? No yearning for heaven, does not that foretell that there is no heaven for you? No fitness for the presence of God; what does that say? Why, that in the presence of God you shall not rest. Earnest of the Spirit! Why, you almost laugh at the idea. Ah, then, no earnest is a proof that there is no reward for you. But what then? Will you be annihilated? Will you pass out of this existence and cease to be? Dark as were that prospect, ay, dark as midnight, yet were it brighter than the fate which the word of God allots you. There will be darkness, but you shall live in it; there will be death, but in it you must ceaselessly exist; for if the righteous be promised "life eternal," it is also written, "these shall go away into everlasting punishment." God save you from such woe by leading you to trust the Saviour. Then you will confess with us, "He that hath wrought us for the selfsame thing is God," and unto God be the glory. Amen.

14

The Tent Dissolved And
The Mansion Entered

"**For we know that if our earthly house of this tabernacle were dissolved, we have a building of God, an house not made with hands, eternal in the heavens.**" 2 Corinthians 5:1

Paul ranks among the bravest of the brave. We note also with admiration how the hero of so many dangers and conflicts, who could glow and burn with fervour, was yet among the calmest and quietest of spirits. He had learned to live beyond those present circumstances which worry and disturb; he had stolen a march upon the shadows of time, and entered into possession of the realities of eternity. He looked not on the things which are seen, but he set his whole regard on the things which are not seen; and by this means he entered into a deep and joyful peace which made him strong, resolute, steadfast, immovable. I would to God that we had all acquired Paul's art of being "always confident,"— his habit of having the inward man renewed day by day. The most of us are far too like the insect of the summer hour, which sports away its life of moments among the flowers, and lo! all is over. Are we not too apt to live in the immediate present which is revealed by the senses? The ox projects no thought upward or beyond: to stand in the cool brook or lie down in the fat pasturage is its all in all; even thus is it with the mass of men, their souls are tethered to their bodies, imprisoned within the circumstances of the day. If we could be completely delivered from the thraldom of things seen and felt, and could feel the full influence of the invisible and the eternal, how much of heaven we might enjoy before the celestial shores are reached!

Paul's life was rough and stormy, yet who might not desire it? Had there been no life to come, he would have been of all men the most miserable, for he was one of the poorest, most persecuted, most despised, most slandered, most wearied, and most suffering of mortals: and yet if I had to put my finger upon happy lives I should not hesitate to select among the foremost the life of the Apostle Paul, for whom to live was Christ. It is also to be specially noted as to his happiness that he had a reason for it. My text begins with the word, "For." Paul is always argumentative, the leaning of his mind is in that direction; hence, if he is cast down he has a reason for it, and if he is calm he can show just cause for his peace. Some religionists are deliriously happy, but they cannot tell you why. They can sing and shout, and dance, but they can give no reason for their excitement. They see an enthusiastic crowd, and they catch the infection: their religion is purely emotional; I am not going to condemn it, yet show I unto you a more excellent way. The joy which is not created by substantial causes is mere froth and foam, and soon vanishes away. Unless you can tell why you are happy you will not long be happy. If you have no principle at the back of your passion your passion will burn down to a black ash, and you will look in vain for a living spark. Some professors have not enough emotion, their hearts are too small, though I cannot say that their heads are too large; but there are others whose hearts are their main force, who are soon on fire, blazing away like shavings and brushwood when first the flame lights upon them; but their brains are an uncertain quantity, never sufficient to manage the furnace of their emotions. It was not so with Paul: he was a well-balanced man. If able to defy the present and rejoice in prospect of the future, he had a solid reason for so doing. I like a man who is fervent and enthusiastic, and yet in his fervour is as reasonable as if he were some cool logician. Let the heart be like a fiery, high-mettled steed, but take care that it is curbed and managed by discretion. An instructed Christian man is rational even in his ecstasies: ready to give a reason for the hope that is in him, when that hope seems to rise above all reason. He is glad, gladdest of the glad, but he knows the why and the wherefore of his gladness; and so he can bear the cruel tests to which the world exposes spiritual joy. The true believer's peace can answer the cavils of men or devils; it can justify itself in its opposition to all appearances. This is a house built upon a foundation, a tree which has a firmly settled root, a star fixed in its sphere; and thus it is infinitely superior to the house upon the sand, the tree plucked up, the fleeting vapour of mere emotion. May God, the Holy Spirit, instruct us so that we may know the truth out of which solid happiness is sure to grow!

I see in the text before us, first of all, *a catastrophe which Paul saw to be very possible*—"If our earthly house of this tabernacle were dissolved"; secondly, *the provision which he surely knew to be made* should that catastrophe occur—"We have a building of God, a house not made with hands, eternal in the heavens"; and thirdly, I shall dwell for a minute or two upon *the value of this knowledge to Paul and to the rest of us in our present trying condition.*

I. First, then, consider THE CATASTROPHE WHICH PAUL SAW TO BE VERY POSSIBLE: "If our earthly house of this tabernacle were dissolved."

He did not fear that he himself would be dissolved: he had not the slightest fear about that. The catastrophe which he looked forward to is known among us by the name of "death"; but he calls it the dissolving of the earthly house of his tabernacle; the taking down of his tent-house body. He does not say, "If I were to be destroyed," or "If were to be annihilated"; he knows no supposition of that character; he feels assured that he himself is perfectly safe. There is latent within the text an element of deep quiet as to his real self. "*We* know that if *our* earthly house of this tabernacle were dissolved, *we* have a building of God." The "we" is all unharmed and unmoved; if our house were dissolved *we* should not be undone; if we were to lose this earthly tent we have "a building of God, eternal in the heavens." The real man, the essential self, is out of harm's way; and all that he talks about is the falling to pieces of a certain tabernacle or tent in which for the present he is lodging. Many people are in a great fright about the future, yet here is Paul viewing the worst thing that could happen to him with such complacency that he likens it to nothing worse than the pulling down of a tent in which he was making shift to reside for a little season. He was afraid of nothing beyond that, and if that happened he had expectations which reconciled him to the event, and even helped him to anticipate it with joy.

Paul was not absolutely sure that his body would be dissolved. He hoped that he might be alive and remain at the coming of the Lord, and then he would be changed and be for ever with the Lord, without passing through death. Still, he was willing to leave this in the Lord's hands, and when he saw it to be possible that he should be numbered among the blessed dead who die in the Lord he did not shrink from the prospect, but bravely found a metaphor which set forth the little fear which he entertained concerning it.

The apostle perceived that the body in which he lived was *frail in itself.* Paul was accustomed to make tents. I do not suppose he ever manufactured any very large or sumptuous ones—probably he did not own capital enough for that, but he was a tent worker and mender. The use of tents was common enough among the Roman people in Paul's day. The gentry delighted in bright pavilions which they could set up at pleasure, and the commoner folk found pleasure in spending a part of their time under canvas. Whilst he was sitting writing this letter it is most likely that Paul had a tent or two to repair lying near his hand, and this suggested to him the language of the verse before us. When a tent is newly placed it is but a frail structure, very far removed from the substantiality of a house; in that respect it is exactly like this feeble corporeal frame of ours, which is crushed before the moth. Paul felt that his body would not need any great force to overthrow it; it was like the tent, which the Midianite saw in his dream, which only needed to be struck by a barley cake, and lo! it lay along. A house of solid masonry may need a crowbar and a pick to start its stones from their places, but feebler tools will soon overturn a tent and make a ruin of it. The body is liable to dissolution from causes so minute as to be imperceptible—a breath of foul air, an atom of poisonous matter, a trifle, a mere nothing, may end this mortal life. I hope that you and I duly remember the frailty of our bodies. We are not so foolish as to think that because we are in robust health to-day we must necessarily live to old age. We have had among ourselves lately abundant evidence that those who appear to be the healthiest are often the first to be taken away, while feeble persons linger on among us, whose lives are a continued wonder and a perpetual struggle. When we think of the brittle ware whereof our bodies are made it is not strange that they should soon be broken. Is it not a wonderful thing that we continue to live? much more wonderful than that we should die? Dr. Watts has wisely said—

> "Our life contains a thousand springs,
> And dies if one be gone;
> Strange! that a harp of thousand strings
> Should keep in tune so long."

Some small affair interferes with a minute valve or organ of secretion, mischief is engendered by it, the whole current of life is hindered and by-and-by death ensues. It is a very delicate process by which dust remains animated; a thousand things can stay that process, and then our body is dissolved. Paul, therefore, because he saw his body to be frail as a bubble, looked forward to the time when the earthly house of his soul would be dissolved.

When he was writing this epistle *he had many signs about him that his body would be dissolved.* His many labours were telling upon him; he was worn down with fatigue, he was spent in his Master's service. He was so full of the heavenly fire that he could never rest: after he had evangelized one city he was forced to hasten to another; if he was driven out of one village he hurried to the next, for he was eager to deliver the message of salvation. He wore himself out with labour, and he felt, therefore, that the day would come when his body would give way under the intense excitement of his life-agony. In addition to this he endured cold and hunger, and nakedness, and sickness, and infirmities brought upon him by his missionary self-sacrifice. He had a hard time of it as to physical endurance, and I should think there was scarcely a limb of the man that did not suffer in consequence of the imprisonments, scourgings, stonings, and other hardships which he had suffered. He felt that one of these days in all probability the house of his tent would come down through the violence of his persecutors. Once he most touchingly spoke of himself as "such an one as Paul the Aged"; and aged men cannot get away from the consciousness that their body is failing. Certain crumbling portions warn the old man that the house is dilapidated; the thatch which has grown thin or blanched tells its tale. There are signs about the aged which warn them that their earthly house was not built to stand for ever; it is a tabernacle or tent set up for a temporary purpose, and it shows signs of waxing old, and being ready to pass away. Hence, then, Paul was led to feel that both from the natural frailty of the body, and also from the injuries which it had already sustained, there was before him the evident probability that the earthly house of his tabernacle would be dissolved.

Besides, Paul's frail body had been *subject to exceeding great perils.* I saw the other day an encampment of gipsies out upon the common; many of this wandering race were sitting under a coarse covering sustained by sticks, I should exaggerate if I called them poles; and I could not help feeling that such an abode was all very well on a warm day, but not at all desirable when the east-wind was blowing, or a shower of sleet was driving along, or a deluge of rain descending. The apostle's body was a tent which was subjected to great stress of weather. God had not screened him; though one of the most precious men that ever lived, yet he was exposed to more danger than almost any other of the Lord's servants. Here is his own account of the matter;—"Thrice was I beaten with rods, once was I stoned, thrice I suffered shipwreck, a night and a day I have been in the deep; in journeying often, in perils of waters, in perils of robbers, in perils by mine own countrymen, in perils by the heathen, in perils in the city, in perils in the wilderness, in perils in the sea, in perils among false brethren; in weariness and painfulness, in watchings often, in hunger and thirst, in fastings often, in cold and nakedness." Well might he reckon that ere long his poor shepherd's shanty would give way under such rude blasts.

Besides, Paul knew that *so many others whom he had known and loved had already died,* and he gathered from this that he would himself die. There used to sit in this house a brother who has often assured me that he should not die, and that if any Christian man did die it was because he grieved the Lord. I am sorry to say that I have missed that brother for many months; I hope he has not yet disproved his own theory; but I am sure that he will do so sooner or later unless our Lord should hasten his advent. Whenever I meet with an enthusiast who boasts that he shall never die, I find it best to let him wait and see. One fine old Irish clergyman has frequently sought to instruct me in the art of being immortal, and he has been grieved and angry because I never set much store by the long life which he offered me. Though an old man, he assured me that he should never die; he expected in a short time to throw out all the infirmities of his years in the form of a rash, and then he should be as vigorous as ever. Alas! the good rector is buried, and his crazy brain is at rest. It is appointed unto men once to die. I should have thought that since so many of the excellent of the earth have fallen asleep, nobody would ever have been so mad as to raise a question about its being the common lot. Our crowded cemeteries supply ten thousand arguments why each one of us may expect to die in due time. This earthly house of our tabernacle will be dissolved; all things unite to warrant the belief.

Now, brethren, this was all that Paul did expect on the sad side; and truly it is not much. Is it? Certain Swiss peasants not very long ago were feeding their flocks on one of the lofty upland valleys. On one side of the pasturage stood a number of *châlets,* or wooden huts, in which they were accustomed to live during the summer, poor shelters which were left as soon as the winter set in. One day they heard a strange rumbling up in the lofty Alps, and they understood what it meant; it meant that a mass of rock or snow or ice had fallen, and would soon come crushing down in the form of an avalanche. In a brief space their fears were realized, for they saw a tremendous mass come rushing from above, bearing destruction in its course. What did it destroy? Only the old, crazy *châlets:* that was all. Every man of the shepherds was safe, and untouched: the event was rather to them a matter which caused a Te Deum to be sung in the village church below than a subject for mourning and sorrow. They said, "The avalanche is terrible, but it has not slain the aged mother, nor crushed the babe in its cradle: it has injured none of us, but only buried a few hovels which we can soon rebuild." Their case is a picture of ours. The avalanche of death will fall; but O ye saints, when it comes this is all it will do for you—your earthly house will be dissolved! Will you fret over so small a loss? No evil will come nigh to you; the poor hut of the body will be buried beneath the earth, but as for yourself, what will you have to do but to sing an everlasting Te Deum unto him who delivered you from death and danger, and raised you to his own right hand?

It would not long affect a man if his tent should be overthrown; he would shake himself clear of it and come forth; it would not otherwise disturb him. So death shall not affect us for the worse, but for the better; the dissolution of this hampering frame shall give us liberty. To-day we are like birds in the egg; so long as the shell is whole we are not free: death breaks the shell. Does the fledgling lament the dissolution of the shell? I never heard of a bird in its nest pining over its broken shell; no, its thoughts run otherwise: to wings, and flight, and sunny skies. So let it be with us. This body will be dissolved: let it be so; it is meet it should be. We have been glad of it while we have needed it, and we thank God for the wondrous skill displayed in it; but when we no longer require it we shall escape from it as from imprisonment, and never wish to return to its narrow bounds. Death, as it pulls away our sackcloth canopy, will reveal to our wondering eyes the palace of the King wherein we shall dwell for ever, and, therefore, what cause have we to be alarmed at it? I have set out the whole catastrophe before you, and surely no believer trembles in view of it.

II. So now we pass on to the second head, THE PROVISION OF WHICH THE APOSTLE PAUL MOST SURELY KNEW. He knew that if his tent dwelling was overthrown he would not be without a home; he knew that he would not have to open his eyes in a naked condition, and cry, "Woe's me, whither am I to fly? I have no dwelling place." No, he knew that if this tent-house were gone he had "a building of God." Paul was not afraid of going to purgatory: though of late some even among Protestants have in a modified form revived that grim fiction, and have told us that even believers will have much to bear before they will be fit for eternal happiness. The apostle held no such opinion; but, on the contrary, he wrote—"We know that if our earthly house of this tabernacle were dissolved, we have a building of God." He did not expect to be roasted alive for the next thousand years, and then to leap from purgatory to Paradise; but he did expect to go, as soon as ever his earthly house was dissolved, into his eternal house which is in the heavens. He had not even the thought of lying in a state of unconsciousness till the resurrection. He says, "We know that if the earthly house of this tabernacle were dissolved, we have (we have already) a building of God." He says not "we shall have it," but "we have

it"; "we know that we have it." The picture seems to me to be
as though one of you should dwell in his garden in a tent for
a while. Somebody inquires what would happen if a gale of
wind should blow your tent away in the night. "Oh," say you,
"I have a house over yonder; I should go within doors and
live there." What a comfort to know that, whatever occurs to
our temporary gear, we have a fixed and settled abode to
which we can at once repair. This makes us feel independent
of all dangers, and helps us joyfully to welcome the
inevitable, come when it may.

What did the apostle mean, however? for this text is said to
be a very difficult one. He meant, first—the moment his soul
left its body it would at once enter into that house of which
Jesus said, "In my Father's house are many mansions: if it
were not so, I would have told you." Do you want to know
about that house? Read the Book of the Revelation, and
learn of its gates of pearl, its streets of gold, its walls of
rarest gems, of the river which windeth through it, and of
the trees which bear their fruit every month. If after that
you desire to know more concerning this house, I can but
give you the advice which was given by John Bunyan in a
similar case. One asked of honest John a question which he
could not answer, for the matter was not opened in God's
word; and therefore honest John bade his friend live a godly
life, and go to heaven, *and see for himself.* Believe no
dreams, but bide thy time, believing in the Lord Jesus, and
thou shalt shortly know all about the house not made with
hands, eternal in the heavens.

Paul, however, did mean that in the fulness of time he
would again be clothed upon with a body. He regarded the
waiting time as so short that he almost overlooked it, as men
forget a moment's pause in a grand march. Ultimately, I say
he expected to be housed in a body: the tent-house which
was blown down and dissolved would be developed into a
building, so rich and rare as to be fitly called "a building of
God, a house not made with hands." This also is our
prospect. At this present in this mortal body we groan being
burdened, for our spirit is liberated from bondage, but our
body is not yet emancipated, although it has been bought
with a price. We are "waiting for the adoption, to wit, the
redemption of our body," and so "the body is dead because of
sin; but the Spirit is life because of righteousness." Our soul

has been regenerated, but the body waits for the process, which in its case is analogous to regeneration, namely, the resurrection from the dead. Disembodied saints may have to wait a few thousand years, more or less, dwelling in the Father's house above; but there shall come eventually the sounding of the trumpet and the raising of the dead, and then the perfected spirit shall dwell in a body adapted to its glory. The certainty of the resurrection raises us above the dread which would otherwise surround the dissolution of our body. A child sees a man throwing precious metal into a melting pot, and he is sad because fair silver is being destroyed; but he that knows the business of the refiner understands that no loss will come of the process; only the dross of that silver will be taken away, and the pure molten mass poured out into a comely mould will yet adorn a royal table. Well, my brethren, are we not assured that to lose this vile body is clear gain since it will be fashioned according to the glorious body of the Lord Jesus?

Let us pass on to *consider how Paul could say he knew this.* This wonderfully enlightened nineteenth century has produced an order of wise men who glory in their ignorance. They call themselves "Agnostics," or know-nothings. When I was a boy it would have seemed odd to me to meet with a man who gloried in being an ignoramus, and yet that is the Latin for that Greek word "Agnostic." Is it not singular to hear a man boastfully say, "I am an ignoramus"? How different is our apostle! He says "we know." Whence came this confidence? How did he know?

First, Paul knew that he had a Father in heaven, for he felt the spirit of sonship; he knew also that his Father had a house, and he was certain that if ever he lost the tent in which he lived he should be sure to be welcomed into his own Father's house above. How do our children know that if ever they are in need of a house they can come home to us? Did they learn that from their tutors at school? No, their childhood's instinct teaches them that our house is their home, just as chickens run under the mother-hen without needing to be trained. Because they are our children they feel that as long as we have a house they have a house too; Paul, therefore, unhesitatingly said, "We know"; and brethren, we know the same through like confidence in our Father's love. In the house of the many mansions we feel quite sure of a hearty welcome in due time. Shut out from our Father's home we cannot be! Houseless wanderers while our royal Father dwells in his palace we cannot be! We are not merely hopeful on this matter, but certain; and therefore we say, "I know."

Paul knew, again, that he had an elder brother, and that this brother had gone before to see to the lodging of the younger brethren. Paul remembered that Jesus had said, "I go to prepare a place for you, and if I go and prepare a place for you, I will come again, and receive you unto myself, that where I am ye may be also." So Paul had no question whatever; if the Lord had gone to prepare a place there would be a place for him; for he never knew his divine Lord set about anything and fail therein. Can we not all trust our Forerunner? Have we any doubts of him who has entered within the veil as our representative? No; as we are sure that Jesus has passed into the heavens on our behalf, so are we sure that when this tent-house body is dissolved, there remains a rest and home for our souls.

Doubtless, Paul also thought of the Holy Ghost, that blessed One who deigns to live with us in this frail house of clay, which is in many ways an uncomfortable and unsuitable abode for him by reason of the sin which has defiled it. He condescends to dwell in these mortal bodies, and, therefore, when we leave our earthly house he will leave it too; and we are persuaded that a place will be found where we may still abide in fellowship. As our bodies have been honoured to entertain the Holy Ghost, we may be sure that in our hour of need he will find an abode for us. He has been our guest, and in his turn he will be our host; this we know, for we know the love of the Spirit. He who has made our body his temple will find a rest for our souls. Thus, from the Father, the Son, and the Holy Ghost, we gather assurance that we shall not wander to and fro unhoused, even though this mortal frame should be dissolved.

Besides, let me tell you something. Paul knew that when he died there was a Paradise prepared, for he had been there already. You remember how he locked up that story till he could keep it no longer, and, then, fifteen years after its occurrence, he let out the blessed secret. Let me read his words, "I knew a man in Christ above fourteen years ago, (whether in the body, I cannot tell; or whether out of the body, I cannot tell: God knoweth;) such an one caught up to the third heaven. And I knew such a man, (whether in the body, or out of the body, I cannot tell: God knoweth;) how that he was caught up into paradise, and heard unspeakable words, which is not lawful for a man to utter." He says he was taken up to the third heaven; it was, therefore, idle to tell Paul that there was no home for him hereafter, for he had seen the place. "Well" say you, "I have not seen it." No; but you fully believe the witness of Paul, do you not? For my own part I am sure that Paul would not say that which is false, and inasmuch as he went into the third heaven or paradise, and saw it, I believe that there is such a place. Remember that this is the place to which the Lord Jesus admitted the dying thief, saying, "To-day shalt thou be with me in paradise." This is the place where Jesus is, and where we shall be with him for ever, when the earthly house of this tabernacle shall be dissolved.

Yet, again, dear brothers and sisters, you and I know that when this earthly tabernacle is dissolved there will be a new body for us, because our Lord Jesus Christ has risen from the dead. In my mind the ultimate answer to my deepest unbelief is the fact of the rising of Jesus from the dead. No matter of history is anything like so well attested as the fact that our Lord was crucified, dead and buried, and that he did upon the third day rise again from the dead. This I unhesitatingly accept as a fact, and this becomes my anchorage. Inasmuch as Jesus is the representative of all who are in him, it is as certain that the believer will rise as that Jesus has risen. The apostle says, "We know," and remembering these grand truths I am sure that his words are not a bit too strong. Nay, if I knew any word in the English language which would express more assurance than the word to know, I would use it this morning for myself. Much more, then, might the apostle use it for himself.

This we are also sure of, namely, that if our Lord Jesus be alive and in a place of rest he will never leave his chosen and redeemed ones without house or home. Where he has found a throne his people shall find a dwelling. Delightful is our old-fashioned ditty—

> "And when I shall die, Receive me, I'll cry,
> For Jesus has loved me, I cannot tell why;
> But this I do find, we two are so joined,
> He won't be in glory and leave me behind."

There is such an attachment between Christ and the believer; yea, more, such a vital, essential, indissoluble, tender marriage union that separation is impossible. As no man among us would ever be content to see his wife in prison if he could set her free, or to leave her outside in the cold when he could bring her to his fireside in comfort, so Christ, to whom our soul is espoused in eternal wedlock, will never rest until he has brought every one of his own beloved to be with him where he is, that they may behold his glory, the glory which the Father hath given him. No believer in Jesus has any doubts about that. I am sure you can all say, as Paul did, "We know that if our earthly house of this tabernacle were dissolved, we have a building of God, an house not made with hands."

"Ah," says one, "but how is a man to know that *he* has an interest in all this? Suppose I do know that the children of God are thus favoured, how am I to know that I am one of them?" I invite you to self-examination on this point. Dost thou believe in the Lord Jesus Christ with all thine heart? Then it is written, "He that believeth in me though he were dead yet shall he live. He that liveth and believeth in me shall never die." Having believed in Christ the apostle knew that he was safe; for the promises are to believers, and if any man be a believer every promise of the covenant belongs to him. We obtain further assurance of this by our possessing the new life. Dear friend, have you entered into a new world? Do you feel within you a new heart and a right spirit? Have old things passed away, and have all things become new? Are you a new creature in Christ Jesus? Then it is all right with you: that new life cannot die, your new-born nature must inherit everlasting bliss. "Fear not, little flock; it is your Father's good pleasure to give you the kingdom." In addition to this, do you commune with God? do you speak with Christ? None perish who commune with the Father and the Son. Jesus cannot say at the last "I never knew you; depart from me;" for he does know you, and you know him. "Oh," say you, "he knows enough of me, for I am always begging." Just so, go on with that trade; be always a spiritual mendicant. The Lord of love will never cast away a pleading suppliant: he who frequents the throne of grace shall infallibly reach the throne of glory. Beside, does not "the Spirit itself also bear witness with our spirit that we are

the children of God?" And if children and heirs, are we afraid
of being left naked in the world to come? I hope that many of
us have now reached the full assurance of faith, so that we
believe and are sure. Can you not say each one for himself,—
"I know whom I have believed, and I am persuaded that he
is able to keep that which I have committed to him until that
day"? These are the ways in which believers know that they
are believers, and then by the word of God they know that
all things are theirs, so that if their earthly house should fail
they would be received into everlasting habitations.

III. Lastly, as to THE VALUE OF THIS KNOWLEDGE TO US.
To be sure that when this body dies all is well, is not that
worth knowing? Secularists twit us with taking men's minds
away from the practical present that they may dream over a
fancied future. We answer that the best help to live for the
present is to live in prospect of the eternal future. Paul's
confident belief that if his body should be dissolved he would
be no loser, kept him from fainting. He knew what the worst
would be, and he was prepared for it. Great storms were out,
but the apostle knew the limit of his possible loss, and so
was ready. All we can lose is the frail tent of this poor body.
By no possibility can we lose more. When a man knows the
limit of his risk it greatly tends to calm his mind. The
undiscoverable and the unmeasured are the worst in-
gredients of dread and terror: when you can gauge your
fears, you have removed them. Our apostle felt that he had
been sent into the world with the great design of glorifying
God, winning souls, and building up saints, and he was fully
resolved to keep to the ministry which he had received. He
argues with himself that his most dangerous course would
be to faint in his life-service, for perseverance in his calling
could bring with it no greater risk than death, and that he
summed up as losing a tent and gaining a mansion. The
Roman emperor might strike off his head, or a mob might
stone him to death, or he might be crucified like his Master:
but he made light of such a fate! It was to him only the
coming down of the old tent; it did not affect his undying
spirit; he smiled and sang, "For our light affliction, which is
but for a moment, worketh for us a far more exceeding and
eternal weight of glory."

The prospect of his heavenly house made his present trials
seem very light; for he felt like a man who sojourns for a

night at a poor inn, but puts up with it gladly because he
hopes to be home on the morrow. If we were trying tent life
for a season we should probably cry out, "A fearful draught
comes in at that corner! How damp it is under foot! How
cramped up one feels!" Yet we should smile over it all, and
say, "It will not be for long. We shall soon be in our house at
home." Ah, brethren, an hour with our God will make up for
all the trials of the way. Wherefore, be of good courage, and
press on.

This changed for Paul the very idea of death; death was
transformed from a demon into an angel: it was but the
removal of a tottering tent that he might enter into a
permanent palace. Some of God's own children are much
troubled through fear of death, because they do not know
what it is. If they were better taught they would soon
discover in their present source of sorrow a subject for song.
I would like here to say that I have known some of my
Master's doubting and fearing servants die splendidly. Do
you remember how Mr. Feeble-mind, when he crossed the
river, went over dry-shod. Poor soul, he thought he should
surely be drowned, and yet he scarcely wet the soles of his
feet. I have known men of God go like Jacob all day long
weary and faint, feeling banished from their Father's house;
and yet when they have laid their head down for their final
sleep they have had visions of angels and of God. The end of
their journey has made amends for the rough places of the
way. It shall be so with you, brother believer. There is
usually a dark place in every Christian's experience: I have
seen some travel in sunlight almost the whole of the way,
and then depart in gloom, and I have thought none the
worse of them for it; and I have seen others struggle forward
through a fog for the first part of their pilgrimage, and then
come out into cloudless day. At one period or another
beneath these lowering skies the shadow falls across our
way, but surely "light is sown for the righteous, and gladness
for the upright in heart."

As I have thought of some of my dear brothers and sisters
that I have seen die very sweetly, and I have remembered
that they were, in life, lowly and self-distrustful, I have
compared them to persons who, when they drink their tea,
forget to stir the sugar at the bottom of the cup. How doubly
sweet the drink becomes as they near the bottom: they have

more sweetness than they can well bear. Would it not be wise to stir the tea at once and enjoy the sweetness from the brim to the bottom? This is the benefit of faith as to the future, for it flavours the present with delight. But what if saints should miss immediate comfort for awhile, how richly will they be compensated! What will it be to open your eyes in heaven! What a joy to fall asleep on the bed of languishing and to wake up amid the celestial Hallelujahs! "What am I? Where am I? Ah, my God! my Christ! my heaven! my all! I am at home." Sorrow and sighing shall flee away. Does not this view of things give a transfiguration to death? O you poor unbelievers, how I pity you, since you have no such glorious hopes. O that you would believe in the Lord Jesus and enter into life eternal. Faith had such an effect upon Paul that it made him always calm, and brave. Why should he be afraid of a man that could not do him harm? Even if his persecutor killed him he would do him a service. What had he to fear? This made Paul wise and prudent. He could use his judgment, for he was not fluttered. He was not like some of you that are only a little ill, and straightway you are filled with fright, and so you make yourselves worse than you otherwise would be, so that the doctor has to contend with an affrighted mind as well as a diseased body. He who is calm, restful, happy is already on the road to a cure. He is quiet because he is in his Father's hands, and whether he lives or dies all is well; and this conviction helps the physician to remove his bodily malady. I say again, there is no way to live like learning to die, and he who can afford to be careless whether he lives or dies is the man who will so live as to die triumphantly. Oh, that all of you felt the quiet which comes of trusting in the Lord Jesus. How sad to know that you may die at any moment, and to be unprepared for the change! I do not wonder that you are unhappy: you have good reason for being so. Oh that you were wise, and would make the future sure by faith in the risen Lord.

In Martin Luther's time, and before his era, men who had lived evil lives were often in great fear when they came to die, and in their terror they would send to a monastery and procure a monk's dress in which to be buried. What a foolish fancy! Yet so it was that they hoped to fare better in the day of judgment for being wrapped in brown serge, and covered with a cowl! Be ours a better garment. Here is a wish of holy

Rutherford—"His believed love shall be my winding sheet, and all my grave-clothes; I shall roll up my soul, and sew it up in the web of his sweet and free love." Is not that your idea? It is surely mine! If we are laid to sleep in such a cerecloth, there will be no fear of our waking. It will happen to us as to the man who was laid in Elisha's grave, and at once arose as soon as he touched the prophet's bones. No man can lie dead if wrapped up in the love of Christ, for his love is life. He that has touched the love of Christ has touched the heart of the life of God, and he must live. So let us give ourselves up to that divine love, and trusting in our Lord, let us go onward to eternal bliss till the day break and the shadows flee away: let us triumph and rejoice that there is prepared for us a "building of God, a house not made with hands, eternal in the heavens."

15

The Hope Of Future Bliss

"As for me, I will behold thy face in righteousness: I shall be satisfied, when I awake, with thy likeness." **Psalm 17:15**

It would be difficult to say to which the gospel owes most, to its friends or to its enemies. It is true, that by the help of God, its friends have done much for it; they have preached it in foreign lands, they have dared death, they have laughed to scorn the terrors of the grave, they have ventured all things for Christ, and so have glorified the doctrine they believed; but the enemies of Christ, unwittingly, have done no little, for when they have persecuted Christ's servants, they have scattered them abroad, so that they have gone everywhere preaching the Word; yea, when they have trampled upon the gospel, like a certain herb we read of in medicine, it hath grown all the faster: and if we refer to the pages of sacred writ how very many precious portions of it do we owe, under God, to the enemies of the cross of Christ! Jesus Christ would never have preached many of his discourses had not his foes compelled him to answer them; had they not brought objections, we should not have heard the sweet sentences in which he replied. So with the book of Psalms: had not David been sorely tried by enemies, had not the foemen shot their arrows at him, had they not attempted to malign and blast his character, had they not deeply distressed him, and made him cry out in misery, we should have missed many of those precious experimental utterances we here find, much of that holy song which he penned after

his deliverance, and very much of that glorious statement of
his trust in the infallible God. We should have lost all this,
had it not been wrung from him by the iron hand of anguish.
Had it not been for David's enemies, he would not have
penned his Psalms; but when hunted like a partridge on the
mountains, when driven like the timid roe before the
hunter's dogs, he waited for awhile, bathed his sides in the
brooks of Siloa, and panting on the hill-top a little, he
breathed the air of heaven and stood and rested his weary
limbs. Then was it that he gave honour to God; then he
shouted aloud to that mighty Jehovah, who for him had
gotten the victory. This sentence follows a description of the
great troubles which the wicked bring upon the righteous,
wherein he consoles himself with the hope of future bliss.
"As for me," says the patriarch, casting his eyes aloft; "As for
me," said the hunted chieftain of the caves of Engedi—"As
for me," says the once shepherd boy, who was soon to wear a
royal diadem—"As for me, I will behold thy face in
righteousness; I shall be satisfied, when I awake with thy
likeness."

In looking at this passage to-night, we shall notice first of
all, the *spirit of it;* secondly, the *matter of it;* and then,
thirdly, we shall close by speaking of *the contrast which is
implied in it.*

I. First, then, the SPIRIT OF THIS UTTERANCE, for I always
love to look at the spirit in which a man writes, or the spirit
in which he preaches; in fact, there is vastly more in that
than in the words he uses.

Now, what should you think is the spirit of these words?
"As for me, I will behold thy face in righteousness: I shall be
satisfied, when I awake, with thy likeness."

First, they breathe the spirit of a man *entirely free from
envy.* Notice, that the Psalmist has been speaking of the
wicked. "They are inclosed in their own fat: with their mouth
they speak proudly." "They are full of children, and leave the
rest of their substance to their babes." But David envies
them not. "Go," says he, "rich man, in all thy riches—go,
proud man, in all thy pride—go, thou happy man, with thine
abundance of children; I envy thee not; as for me, my lot is
different: I can look on you without desiring to have your
possessions; I can well keep that commandment, 'Thou shalt
not covet,' for in your possessions there is nothing worth my

love; I set no value upon your earthly treasures; I envy you not your heaps of glittering dust; for my Redeemer is mine." The man is above envy, because he thinks that the joy would be no joy to him—that the portion would not suit his disposition. Therefore, he turns his eye heavenward, and says, "As for me, I shall behold thy face in righteousness." Oh! beloved, it is a happy thing to be free from envy. Envy is a curse which blighteth creation; and even Eden's garden itself would have become defaced, and no longer fair, if the wind of envy could have blown on it; envy tarnisheth the gold; envy dimmeth the silver; should envy breathe on the hot sun, it would quench it; should she cast her evil eye on the moon, it would be turned into blood, and the stars would fly astonished at her. Envy is accursed of heaven; yea, it is Satan's first-born—the vilest of vices. Give a man riches, but let him have envy, and there is the worm at the root of the fair tree; give him happiness, and if he envies another's lot, what would have been happiness becomes his misery, because it is not so great as that of some one else. But give me freedom from envy; let me be content with what God has given me, let me say, "Ye may have yours, I will not envy you—I am satisfied with mine;" yea, give me such a love to my fellow creatures that I can rejoice in their joy, and the more they have the more glad I am of it. My candle will burn no less brightly because theirs outshines it. I can rejoice in their prosperity. Then am I happy, for all around tends to make me blissful, when I can rejoice in the joys of others, and make their gladness my own. Envy! oh! may God deliver us from it! But how, in truth, can we get rid of it so well as by believing that we have something that is not on earth, but in heaven? If we can look upon all the things in the world and say, "As for me, I will behold thy face in righteousness; I shall be satisfied by-and-bye!" then we cannot envy other men, because their lot would not be adapted to our peculiar taste. Doth the ox envy the lion? Nay, for it cannot feed upon the carcase. Doth the dove grieve because the raven can gloat itself on carrion? Nay, for it lives on other food. Will the eagle envy the wren his tiny nest? Oh, no! So the Christian will mount aloft as the eagle, spreading his broad wings, he will fly up to his eyrie amongst the stars, where God hath made him his nest, saying, "As for me, I will dwell here; I look upon the low places of this earth with contempt; I envy not your greatness, ye mighty emperors; I desire not your fame, ye mighty warriors; I ask not for wealth, O Croesus; I beg not for thy power, O Caesar; as for me, I have something else; my portion is the Lord." The text breathes the spirit of a man free from envy. May God give that to us!

Then, secondly, you can see that there is about it the air of a man who is *looking into the future*. Read the passage thoroughly, and you will see that it all has relation to the future; because it says, "As for me, I *shall.*" It has nothing to do with the present: it does not say, "As for me I do, or I am, so-and-so," but "As for me, I *will* behold thy face in righteousness; I *shall* be satisfied, when I awake." The Psalmist looks beyond the grave into another world; he overlooks the narrow death-bed where he has to sleep, and he says, "When I awake." How happy is that man who has an eye to the future; even in worldly things we esteem that man who looks beyond the present day; he who spends all his money as it comes in will soon bring himself to rags. He who lives on the present is a fool; but wise men are content to look after future things. When Milton penned his book he might know, perhaps, that he should have little fame in his lifetime; but he said, "I shall be honoured when my head shall sleep in the grave." Thus have other worthies been content to tarry until time has broken the earthen pitcher, and suffered the lamp to blaze; as for honour, they said, "We will leave that to the future, for that fame which comes late is often most enduring," and they lived upon the "shall" and fed upon the future. "I shall be satisfied" by-and-bye. So says the Christian. I ask no royal pomp or fame now; I am prepared to wait, I have an interest in reversion; I want not a pitiful estate here—I will tarry till I get my domains in heaven, those broad and beautiful domains that God has provided for them that love him. Well content will I be to fold my arms and sit me down in the cottage, for I shall have a mansion of God, "a house not made with hands, eternal in the heavens." Do any of you know what it is to live on the future—to live on expectation—to live on what you are to have in the next world—to feast yourselves with some of the droppings of the tree of life that fall from heaven—to live upon the manna of expectation which falls in the wilderness, and to drink that stream of nectar which gushes from the throne of God? Have you ever gone to the great Niagara of hope, and drank the spray with ravishing delight; for the very spray of heaven is glory to one's soul! Have you ever lived on the future, and said, "As for me I *shall* have somewhat, by-and-bye?" Why, this is the highest motive that can actuate a man. I suppose this was what made Luther so bold, when he stood before his great audience of kings and lords, and said, "I stand by the truth that I have written, and will so stand by it till I die; so help me God!" Methinks he must have said, "I *shall* be satisfied by-and-bye; I am not satisfied now, but I *shall* be soon." For this the missionary ventures the stormy sea; for this he treads the barbarous shore; for this he goes into inhospitable climes, and risks his life, because he knows there is a payment to come by-and-bye. I sometimes laughingly tell my friends when I receive a favour from them, that I cannot return it, but sent it up to my Master in heaven, for they shall be satisfied when they awake in his likeness. There are many things that we may never hope to be rewarded for here, but that shall be remembered before the throne hereafter, not of debt, but of grace. Like a poor minister I heard of, who, walking to a rustic chapel to preach, was met by a clergyman who had a far richer berth. He asked the poor man what he expected to have for his preaching. "Well," he said, "I expect to have a crown." "Ah!" said the clergyman, "I have not been in the habit of preaching for less than a guinea, anyhow." "Oh!" said the other, "I am obliged to be content with a crown, and what is more, I do not have my crown now, but I have to wait for that in the future." The clergyman little thought that he meant the "crown of life that fadeth not away!" Christian! live on the future; seek nothing here, but expect that thou shalt shine when thou shalt come in the likeness of Jesus, with him to be admired, and to kneel before his face adoringly. The Psalmist had an eye to the future.

And again, upon this point, you can see that David, at the time he wrote this, was *full of faith*. The text is fragrant with confidence. "As for me," says David, no *perhaps* about it; "I *will* behold thy face in righteousness; I *shall* be satisfied when I awake up in thy likeness." If some men should say so now, they would be called fanatics, and it would be considered presumption for any man to say, "I *will* behold thy face, I *shall* be satisfied;" and I think there are many now in this world who think it is quite impossible for a man to say to a certainty, "I know, I am sure, I am certain." But, beloved, there are not one or two, but there are thousands and thousands of God's people alive in this world who can say with an assured confidence, no more doubting of it than of their very existence, "I *will* behold thy face in righteousness; I shall be satisfied, when I awake in thy likeness." It is possible, though perhaps not very easy, to attain to that high and eminent position wherein we can say no longer do I *hope,* but I *know;* no longer do I trust, but I am persuaded; I have a happy confidence; I am sure of it; I am certain; for God has so manifested himself to me that now it is no longer "if" and "perhaps," but it is positive, eternal, "shall." "I *shall* be satisfied when I awake in thy likeness." How many are there here of that sort? Oh! if ye are talking like that, ye must expect to have trouble, for God never gives strong faith without fiery trial; he will never give a man the power to say that "shall" without trying him; he will not build a strong ship without subjecting it to very mighty storms; he will not make you a mighty warrior, if he does not intend to try your skill in battle. God's swords must be used; the old Toledo blades of heaven must be smitten against the armour of the evil one, and yet they shall not break, for they are of true Jerusalem metal, which shall never snap. Oh! what a happy thing to have that faith to say "I shall." Some of you think it quite impossible, I know; but it "is the gift of God," and whosoever asks it shall obtain it: and the very chief of sinners now present in this place may yet be able to say long before he comes to die, "I shall behold thy face in righteousness." Methinks I see the aged Christian. He has been very poor. He is in a garret where the stars look between the tiles. There is his bed. His clothes ragged and torn. There are a few sticks on the hearth; they are the last he has. He is sitting up in his chair; his paralytic hand quivers and shakes, and he is evidently near his end. His last meal was eaten yester-morn; and as you stand and look at him, poor, weak, and feeble, who would desire his lot? But ask him, "Old man, wouldst thou change thy garret for Caesar's palace? Aged Christian, wouldst thou give up these rags for wealth, and cease to love thy God?" See how indignation burns in his eyes at once! He replies, "'As for me, I *shall,'* within a few more days, 'behold his face in righteousness; I *shall* be satisfied' soon; here I never shall

be. Trouble has been my lot, and trial has been my portion,
but I have 'a house not made with hands, eternal in the
heavens.'" Bid high; bid him fair; offer him your hands full of
gold; lay all down for him to give up his Christ. "Give up
Christ?" he will say, "no, never!"

> "While my faith can keep her hold,
> I envy not the miser's gold."

Oh! what a glorious thing to be full of faith, and to have the
confidence of assurance, so as to say, "I *will* behold thy face;
I *shall* be satisfied when I awake with thy likeness."

Thus much concerning the spirit of David. It is one very
much to be copied and eminently to be desired.

II. But now, secondly, THE MATTER OF THIS PASSAGE. And
here we will dive into the very depths of it, God helping us;
for without the Spirit of God I feel I am utterly unable to
speak to you. I have not those gifts and talents which qualify
men to speak; I need an afflatus from on high, otherwise I
stand like other men and have nought to say. May that be
given me; for without it I am dumb. As for the matter of this
verse, methinks it contains a double blessing. The first is a
beholding—"I will behold thy face in righteousness;" and the
next is a satisfaction—"I shall be satisfied when I awake
with thy likeness."

Let us begin with the first, then. David expected that he
should *behold God's face*. What a vision will that be, my
brethren! Have you ever seen God's hand? I have seen it,
when sometimes he places it across the sky, and darkens it
with clouds. I have seen God's hand sometimes, when the
cars of night drag along the shades of darkness. I have seen
his hand when, launching the thunder-bolt, his lightning
splits the clouds and rends the heavens. Perhaps ye have
seen it in a gentler fashion, when it pours out the water and
sends it rippling along in rills, and then rolls into rivers. Ye
have seen it in the stormy ocean—in the sky decked with
stars, in the earth gemmed with flowers; and there is not a
man living who can know all the wonders of God's hand. His
creation is so wondrous that it would take more than a
life-time to understand it. Go into the depths of it; let its
minute parts engage your attention; next take the telescope,
and try to see remote worlds, and can I see all God's
handiwork—behold all his hand? No, not so much as one

millionth part of the fabric. That mighty hand wherein the callow comets are brooded by the sun, in which the planets roll in majestic orbits; that mighty hand which holds all space, and grasps all beings—that mighty hand, who can behold it? but if such be his hand, what must his face be? Ye have heard God's voice sometimes, and ye have trembled; I, myself, have listened awe-struck, and yet with a marvellous joy, when I have heard God's voice, like the noise of many waters, in the great thunderings. Have you never stood and listened, while the earth shook and trembled, and the very spheres stopped their music, while God spoke with his wondrous deep bass voice? Yes, ye have heard that voice; and there is a joy marvellously instinct with love which enters into my soul, whenever I hear the thunder. It is my Father speaking, and my heart leaps to hear him. But you never heard God's loudest voice. It was but the whisper when the thunder rolled. But if such be the voice, what must it be to behold his face? David said, "I will behold thy face." It is said of the temple of Diana, that it was so splendidly decorated with gold, and so bright and shining, that a porter at the door always said to every one that entered, "Take heed to your eyes, take heed to your eyes; you will be struck with blindness unless you take heed to your eyes." But oh! that view of glory! That great appearance. The vision of God! to see him face to face, to enter into heaven, and to see the righteous shining bright as stars in the firmament; but best of all, to catch a glimpse of the eternal throne! Ah! there he sits! 'Twere almost blasphemy for me to attempt to describe him. How infinitely far my poor words fall below the mighty subject! But to behold God's face. I will not speak of the lustre of those eyes, or the majesty of those lips, that shall speak words of love and affection; but to behold his face! Ye who have dived into the Godhead's deepest sea, and have been lost in its immensity, ye can tell a little of it! Ye mighty ones, who have lived in heaven these thousand years, perhaps ye know, but ye cannot tell, what it is to see his face. We must each of us go there, we must be clad with immortality. We must go above the blue sky, and bathe in the river of life: we must outsoar the lightning, and rise above the stars, to know what it is to see God's face. Words cannot set it forth. So there I leave it. The hope the Psalmist had was, that he might see God's face.

But there was a *peculiar sweetness mixed with this joy,* because he knew that he should behold God's face *in righteousness.* "I shall behold thy face in righteousness." Have I not seen my Father's face here below? Yes, I have, "through a glass darkly." But has not the Christian sometimes beheld him, when in his heavenly moments earth is gone, and the mind is stripped of matter? There are some seasons when the gross materialism dies away, and when the ethereal fire within blazes up so high that it almost touches the fire of heaven. There are seasons, when in some retired spot, calm and free from all earthly thought, we have put our shoes from off our feet, because the place whereon we stood was holy ground; and we have talked with God! even as Enoch talked with him so has the Christian held intimate communion with his Father. He has heard his love-whispers; he has told out his heart, poured out his sorrows and his groans before him. But after all he has felt that he has not beheld his face in righteousness. There was so much sin to darken the eyes, so much folly, so much frailty, that we could not get a clear prospect of our Jesus. But here the Psalmist says, "I will behold thy face in righteousness." When that illustrious day shall arise, and I shall see my Saviour face to face, I shall see him "in righteousness." The Christian in heaven will not have so much as a speck upon his garment; he will be pure and white; yea, on the earth he is

"Pure through Jesus' blood, and white as angels are."

But in heaven that whiteness shall be more apparent. Now, it is sometimes smoked by earth, and covered with the dust of this poor carnal world; but in heaven he will have brushed himself, and washed his wings, and made them clean; and then will he see God's face in righteousness. My God! I believe I shall stand before thy face as pure as thou art thyself; for I shall have the righteousness of Jesus Christ; there shall be upon me the righteousness of a God. "I shall behold thy face in righteousness." O Christian, canst thou enjoy this? Though I cannot speak about it, dost thy heart meditate upon it? To behold his face for ever; to bask in that vision! True, thou canst not understand it; but thou mayest guess the meaning. To behold his face in righteousness!

The second blessing, upon which I will be brief, is

satisfaction. He will be satisfied, the Psalmist says, when he wakes up in God's likeness. Satisfaction! this is another joy for the Christian when he shall enter heaven. Here we are never thoroughly satisfied. True, the Christian is satisfied from himself; he has that within which is a well-spring of comfort, and he can enjoy solid satisfaction. But heaven is the home of true and real satisfaction. When the believer enters heaven I believe his *imagination* will be thoroughly satisfied. All he has ever thought of he will there see; every holy idea will be solidified; every mighty conception will become a reality; every glorious imagination will become a tangible thing that he can see. His imagination will not be able to think of anything better than heaven; and should he sit down through eternity, he would not be able to conceive of anything that should outshine the lustre of that glorious city. His imagination will be satisfied. Then his *intellect* will be satisfied.

> "Then shall I see, and hear, and know,
> All I desired, or wished, below."

Who is satisfied with *his* knowledge here? Are there not secrets we want to know—depths in the arcana of nature that we have not entered? But in that glorious state we shall know as much as we want to know. The *memory* will be satisfied. We shall look back upon the vista of past years, and we shall be content with whatever we endured, or did, or suffered on earth.

> "There, on a green and flowery mount,
> My wearied soul shall sit,
> And with transporting joys recount
> The labours of my feet."

Hope will be satisfied, if there be such a thing in heaven. We shall hope for a future eternity, and believe in it. But we shall be satisfied as to our hopes continually: and the whole man will be so content that there will not remain a single thing in all God's dealings, that he would wish to have altered; yea, perhaps I say a thing at which some of you will demur—but the righteous in heaven will be quite satisfied with the damnation of the lost. I used to think that if I could see the lost in hell, surely I must weep for them. Could I hear their horrid wailings, and see the dreadful contortions of their anguish, surely I must pity them. But there is no such sentiment as that known in heaven. The believer shall be there so satisfied with all God's will, that he will quite forget the lost in the idea that God has done it for the best, that even their loss has been their own fault, and that he is infinitely just in it. If my parents could see me in hell they would not have a tear to shed for me, though they were in heaven, for they would say, "It is justice, thou great God, and thy justice must be magnified, as well as thy mercy;" and moreover, they would feel that God was so much above his creatures that they would be satisfied to see those creatures crushed if it might increase God's glory. Oh! in heaven I believe we shall think rightly of men. Here men seem great things to us; but in heaven they will seem no more than a few creeping insects that are swept away in ploughing a field for harvest; they will appear no more than a tiny handful of dust, or like some nest of wasps that ought to be exterminated for the injury they have done. They will appear such little things when we sit on high with God, and look down on the nations of the earth as grasshoppers, and "count the isles as very little things." We shall be satisfied with everything; there will not be a single thing to complain of. "I *shall* be satisfied."

But when? "I shall be satisfied when I awake with thy likeness." But not till then. No, not till then. Now here a difficulty occurs. You know there are some in heaven who have not yet waked up in God's likeness. In fact, none of those in heaven have done so. They never did sleep as respects their souls; the waking refers to their bodies, and they are not awake yet—but are still slumbering. O earth! thou art the bedchamber of the mighty dead! What a vast sleeping-house this world is! It is one vast cemetery. The righteous still sleep; and they are to be satisfied on the resurrection morn, when they awake. "But," say you, "are they not satisfied now? They are in heaven: is it possible that they can be distressed?" No, they are not; there is only one dissatisfaction that can enter heaven—the dissatisfaction of the blest that their bodies are not there. Allow me to use a simile which will somewhat explain what I mean. When a Roman conqueror had been at war, and won great victories, he would very likely come back with his soldiers, enter into his house, and enjoy himself till the next day, when he would go out of the city and then come in again in triumph. Now, the saints, as it were, if I might use such a phrase, steal into heaven without their bodies; but on the last day, when their bodies wake up, they will enter in their triumphal chariots. And, methinks, I see that grand procession, when Jesus Christ, first of all, with many crowns on his head, with his bright, glorious body, shall lead the way. I see my Saviour entering first. Behind him come the saints, all of them clapping their hands, all of them touching their golden harps, and entering in triumph. And when they come to heaven's gates, and the doors are opened wide to let the king of glory in, now will the angels crowd at the windows, and on the house-tops, like the inhabitants in the Roman triumphs, to watch them as they pass through the streets, and scatter heaven's roses and lilies upon them, crying, "Hallelujah! Hallelujah! Hallelujah! the Lord God Omnipotent reigneth!" "I shall be satisfied" in that glorious day, when all his angels shall come to see the triumph, and when his people shall be victorious with him.

One thought here ought not to be forgotten; and that is, the Psalmist says we are to wake up in the *likeness of God*. This may refer to the soul; for the spirit of the righteous will be in the likeness of God as to its happiness, holiness, purity, infallability, eternity, and freedom from pain; but specially, I think, it relates to the body, because it speaks of the awaking. The body is to be in the likeness of Christ. What a thought! It is—and alas! I have had too many such to-night—a thought too heavy for words. I am to awake up in Christ's likeness. I do not know what Christ is like, and can scarcely imagine. I love sometimes to sit and look at him in his crucifixion. I care not what men say—I know that sometimes I have derived benefit from a picture of my dying crucified Saviour; and I look at him with his crown of thorns, his pierced side, his bleeding hands and feet, and all those drops of gore hanging from him; but I cannot picture him in heaven, he is so bright, so glorious; the God so shines through the man; his eyes are like lamps of fire; his tongue like a two-edged sword; his head covered with hair as white as snow, for he is the Ancient of days, he binds the clouds round about him for a girdle; and when he speaks, it is like the sound of many waters! I read the accounts given in the book of Revelation, but I cannot tell what he is; they are

Scripture phrases, and I cannot understand their meaning; but whatever they mean, I know that I shall wake up in Christ's likeness. Oh; what a change it will be, when some of us get to heaven! There is a man who fell in battle with the word of salvation on his lips; his legs had been shot away, and his body had been scarred by sabre thrusts; he wakes in heaven, and finds that he has not a broken body, maimed and cut about, and hacked and injured, but that he is in Christ's likeness. There is an old matron, who has tottered on her staff for years along her weary way; time has ploughed furrows on her brow; haggard and lame, her body is laid in the grave. But oh! aged woman, thou shalt arise in youth and beauty. Another has been deformed in his life-time, but when he wakes, he wakes in the likeness of Christ. Whatever may have been the form of our countenance, whatever the contour, the beautiful shall be no more beautiful in heaven than those who were deformed. Those who shone on earth, peerless, among the fairest, who ravished men with looks from their eyes, they shall be no brighter in heaven than those who are now passed by and neglected: for they shall all be like Christ.

III. But now to close up, HERE IS A VERY SAD CONTRAST IMPLIED. We shall all slumber. A few more years and where will this company be? Xerxes wept, because in a little while his whole army would be gone; how might I stand here and weep, because within a few more years others shall stand in this place, and shall say, "The fathers, where are they?" Good God! and is it true? Is it not a reality? Is it all to be swept away? Is it one great dissolving view? Ah! it is. This sight shall vanish soon; and you and I shall vanish with it. We are but a show. This life is but "a stage whereon men act;" and then we pass behind the curtain, and we there unmask ourselves, and talk with God. The moment we begin to live we begin to die. The tree has long been growing that shall be sawn to make you a coffin. The sod is ready for you all. But this scene is to appear again soon. One short dream, one hurried nap, and all this sight shall come o'er again. We shall all awake, and as we stand here now, we shall stand together, perhaps, even more thickly pressed. But we shall stand on the level then—the rich and poor, the preacher and hearer. There will be but one distinction—righteous and wicked. At first we shall stand together. Methinks I see the scene. The sea is boiling; the heavens are rent in twain; the clouds are fashioned into a chariot, and Jesus riding on it, with wings of fire, comes riding through the sky. His throne is set. He seats himself upon it. With a nod he hushes all the world. He lifts his fingers, opens the great books of destiny, and the book of our probation, wherein are written the acts of time. With his fingers he beckons to the hosts above. "Divide," said he, "divide the universe." Swifter than thought all the earth shall part in sunder. Where shall I be found when the dividing comes? Methinks I see them all divided; and the righteous are on the right. Turning to them, with a voice sweeter than music, he says, "Come! Ye have been coming—keep on your progress! Come! it has been the work of your life to come, so continue. Come and take the last step. 'Come, ye blessed of my Father, inherit the kingdom prepared for you from before the foundation of the world.'" And now the wicked are left alone; and turning to them, he says, "Depart! Ye have been departing all your life long; it was your business to depart from me; ye said, 'Depart from me, I love not thy ways.' You have been departing, keep on, take the last step!" They dare not move. They stand still. The Saviour becomes the avenger. The hands that once held out mercy, now grasp the sword of justice; the lips that spoke lovingkindness, now utter thunder; and with a deadly aim, he lifts up the sword, and sweeps amongst them. They fly like deer before the lion; and enter the jaws of the bottomless pit.

But never, I hope, shall I cease preaching, without telling you what to do to be saved. This morning I preached to the ungodly, to the worst of sinners, and many wept—I hope many hearts melted—while I spoke of the great mercy of God. I have not spoken of that to-night. We must take a different line sometimes; led, I trust, by God's Spirit. But oh! ye that are thirsty, and heavy laden, and lost and ruined, mercy speaks yet once again to you! Here is the way of salvation. "He that believeth and is baptized shall be saved." "And what is it to believe?" says one; "is it to say I know Christ died for me?" No, that is not to believe, it is part of it, but it is not all. Every Arminian believes that; and every man in the world believes it who holds that doctrine, since he conceives that Christ died for every man. Consequently that is not faith. But faith is this: to cast yourself on Christ.

As the negro said, most curiously, when asked what he did to be saved; "Massa," said he, "I fling myself down on Jesus, and dere I lay; I fling myself flat on de promise, and dere I lay." And to every penitent *sinner* Jesus says, "I am able to save to the uttermost;" throw thyself flat on the promise, and say, "Then, Lord, thou art able to save *me.*" God says, "Come now, let us reason together; though your sins be as scarlet they shall be white as snow, and though they be red like crimson they shall be as wool." Cast thyself on him, and thou shalt be saved. "Ah!" says one, "I am afraid I am not one of God's people; I cannot read my name in the book of life." A very good thing you can't; for if the Bible had everybody's name in it, it would be a pretty large book; and if your name is John Smith, and you saw that name in the Bible, if you do not believe God's promise now, you would be sure to believe that it was some other John Smith. Suppose the Emperor of Russia should issue a decree to all the Polish refugees to return to their own country; you see a Polish refugee looking at the great placards hanging on the wall, he looks with pleasure, and says, "Well, I shall go back to my country." But some one says to him, "It does not say Walewski." "Yes," he would reply, "but it says Polish refugees: Polish is my Christian name, and refugee my surname, and that is me." And so, though it does not say your name in the Scriptures, it says lost sinner. Sinner is your Christian name, and lost is your surname; therefore, why not come? It says, "lost sinner;"—is not that enough? "This is a faithful saying, and worthy of all acceptation, that Jesus Christ came into the world to save sinners of whom I am chief." "Yes, but," another one says, "I am afraid I am not elect." Oh! dear souls, do not trouble yourselves about that. If you believe in Christ you *are* elect. Whoever puts himself on the mercy of Jesus is elect; for he would never do it if he had not been elect. Whoever comes to Christ, and looks for mercy through his blood, is elect, and he shall see that he is elect afterwards; but do not expect to read election till you have read repentance. Election is a college to which you little ones will not go till you have been to the school of repentance. Do not begin to read your book backwards, and say Amen before you have said your paternoster. Begin with "Our Father," and then you will go on to "thine is the kingdom, the power, and the glory;" but begin with "the kingdom," and you will have hard work to go back to "Our Father." We must begin with faith. We must begin with—

> "Nothing in my hands I bring."

As God made the world out of nothing, he always makes his Christians out of nothing; and he who has nothing at all to-night, shall find grace and mercy, if he will come for it.

Let me close up by telling you what I have heard of some poor woman, who was converted and brought to life, just by passing down a street, and hearing a child, sitting at a door, singing—

> "I am nothing at all
> But Jesus Christ is all in all."

That is a blessed song; go home and sing it; and he who can rightly apprehend those little words, who can feel himself vanity without Jesus, but that he has all things in Christ, is not only far from the kingdom of heaven, but he is there in faith, and shall be there in fruition, when he shall wake up in God's likeness.

16

Creation's Groans And The Saint's Sighs

"For we know that the whole creation groaneth and travaileth in pain together until now. And not only they, but ourselves also, which have the firstfruits of the Spirit, even we ourselves groan within ourselves, waiting for the adoption, to wit, the redemption of our body."   **Romans 8:22-23**

My venerable friend, who, on the first Sabbath of the year, always sends me a text to preach from, has on this occasion selected one which it is very far from easy to handle. The more I have read it, the more certainly have I come to the conclusion that this is one of the things in Paul's epistles to which Peter referred when he said, "Wherein are some things hard to be understood." However, dear friends, we have often found that the nuts which are hardest to crack have the sweetest kernels, and when the bone seems as if it could never be broken, the richest marrow has been found within. So it may by possibility be this morning; so it will be if the Spirit of God shall be our instructor, and fulfil his gracious promise to "lead us into all truth."

The whole creation is fair and beautiful even in its present condition. I have no sort of sympathy with those who cannot enjoy the beauties of nature. Climbing the lofty Alps, or wandering through the charming valley, skimming the blue sea, or traversing the verdant forest, we have felt that this world, however desecrated by sin, was evidently built to be a temple of God, and the grandeur and the glory of it plainly declare that "the earth is the Lord's and the fulness thereof." Like the marvelous structures of Palmyra of Baalbek, in the far off east, the earth in ruins reveals a magnificence which betokens a royal founder, and an extraordinary purpose. Creation glows with a thousand beauties, even in its present fallen condition; yet clearly enough it is not as when it came from the Maker's hand—the slime of the serpent is on it all—this is not the world which God pronounced to be "very good." We hear of tornadoes, of earthquakes, of tempests, of volcanoes, of avalanches, and of the sea which devoureth its thousands: there is sorrow on the sea, and there is misery on the land; and into the highest palaces as well as the poorest cottages, death, the insatiable, is shooting his arrows, while his quiver is still full to bursting with future woes. It is a sad, sad world. The curse has fallen on it since the fall, and thorns and thistles it bringeth forth, not from its soil alone, but from all that comes of it. Earth wears upon her brow, like Cain of old, the brand of transgression. Sad would it be to our thoughts if it were always to be so. If there were no future to this world as well as to ourselves, we might be glad to escape from it, counting it to be nothing better than a huge penal colony, from which it would be a thousand mercies for both body and soul to be emancipated. At this present time, the groaning and travailing which are general throughout creation, are deeply felt among the sons of men. The dreariest thing you can read is the newspaper. I heard of one who sat up at the end of last year to groan last year out; it was ill done, but in truth it was a year of groaning, and the present one opens amid turbulence and distress. We heard of abundant harvests, but we soon discovered that they were all a dream, and that there would be scant in the worker's cottage. And now, what with strifes between men and masters, which are banishing trade from England, and what with political convulsions, which unhinge everything, the vessel of the state is drifting fast to the shallows. May God in mercy put his hand to the helm of the ship, and steer her safely. There is a general wail among nations and peoples. You can hear it in the streets of the city. The Lord reigneth, or we might lament right bitterly.

The apostle tells us that not only is there a groan from creation, but this is shared in by God's people. We shall notice in our text, first, *whereunto the saints have already attained;* secondly, *wherein we are deficient;* and thirdly, *what is the state of mind of the saints in regard to the whole of the matter.*

I. WHEREUNTO THE SAINTS HAVE ATTAINED.

We were once an undistinguished part of the creation, subject to the same curse as the rest of the world, "heirs of wrath, even as others." But distinguishing grace has made a difference where no difference naturally was; we are now no longer treated as criminals condemned, but as children and heirs of God. We have received a divine life, by which we are made partakers of the divine nature, having "escaped the corruption which is in the world through lust." The Spirit of God has come unto us so that our "bodies are the temples of the Holy Ghost." God dwelleth in us, and we are one with Christ. We have at this present moment in us certain priceless things, which distinguish us as believers in Christ from all the rest of God's creatures. *"We have,"* says the text, not "we hope and trust sometimes we have," nor yet "possibly we may have," but "we have, we know we have, we are sure we have." Believing in Jesus, we speak confidently, we have unspeakable blessings given to us by the Father of spirits. Not we *shall have,* but *we have.* True, many things are yet in the future, but even at this present moment, we have obtained an inheritance; we have already in our possession a heritage divine, which is the beginning of our eternal portion. This is called "the first-fruits of the Spirit," by which I understand the first works of the Spirit in our souls. Brethren, we have repentance, that gem of the first water. We have faith, that priceless, precious jewel. We have hope, which sparkles, a hope most sure and steadfast. We have love, which sweetens all the rest. We have that work of the Spirit within our souls which always comes before admittance into glory. We are already made "new creatures in Christ Jesus," by the effectual working of the mighty power of God the Holy Ghost. This is called the first-fruit because *it comes first.* As the wave-sheaf was the first of the harvest, so the spiritual life, which we have, and all the graces which adorn that life are the first gifts, the first operations of the Spirit of God in our souls. We *have* this.

It is called "first-fruits," again, because *the first-fruits were always the pledge of the harvest.* As soon as the Israelite had plucked the first handful of ripe ears, they were to him so many proofs that the harvest was already come. He looked forward with glad anticipation to the time when the wain should creak beneath the sheaves, and when the harvest-

home should be shouted at the door of the barn. So,
brethren, when God gives us "Faith, hope, charity—these
three," when he gives us "whatsoever things are pure, lovely,
and of good report," as the work of the Holy Spirit, these are
to us the prognostics of the coming glory. If you have the
Spirit of God in your soul, you may rejoice over it as the
pledge and token of the fulness of bliss and perfection "which
God hath prepared for them that love him."

It is called "first-fruits," again, because *these were always
holy to the Lord.* The first ears of corn were offered to the
Most High, and surely our new nature, with all its powers,
must be regarded by us as a consecrated thing. The new life
which God has given to us is not ours that we should ascribe
its excellence to our own merit: the new nature is Christ's
peculiarly; as it is Christ's image and Christ's creation, so it
is for Christ's glory alone. That secret we must keep
separate from all earthly things; that treasure which he has
committed to us we must watch both night and day against
those profane intruders who would defile the consecrated
ground. We would stand upon our watch-tower and cry aloud
to the Strong for strength, that the adversary may be
repelled, that the sacred castle of our heart may be for the
habitation of Jesus, and Jesus alone. We have a sacred
secret, which belongs to Jesus, as the first-fruits belong to
Jehovah.

Brethren, the work of the Spirit is called "first-fruits,"
because *the first-fruits were not the harvest.* No Jew was ever
content with the first-fruits. He was content with them for
what they were, but the first-fruits enlarged his desires for
the harvest. If he had taken the first-fruits home, and said,
"I have all I want," and had rested satisfied month after
month, he would have given proof of madness, for the
first-fruit does but whet the appetite—does but stir up the
desire it never was meant to satisfy. So, when we get the
first works of the Spirit of God, we are not to say, "I have
attained, I am already perfect, there is nothing further for
me to do, or to desire." Nay, my brethren, all that the most
advanced of God's people know as yet, should but excite in
them an insatiable thirst after more. My brother with great
experience, my sister with enlarged acquaintance with
Christ, ye have not yet known the harvest, you have only
reaped the first handful of corn. Open your mouth wide, and

God will fill it! Enlarge thine expectations—seek great
things from the God of heaven—and he will give them to
thee; but by no means fold thine arms in sloth, and sit down
upon the bed of carnal security. Forget the steps thou hast
already trodden, and reach forward towards that which is
before, looking unto Jesus.

Even this first point of what the saint has attained will
help us to understand why it is that he groans. Did I not say
that we have not received the whole of our portion, and that
what we have received is to the whole no more than one
handful of wheat is to the whole harvest, a very gracious
pledge, but nothing more? Therefore it is that we groan.
Having received something, we desire more. Having reaped
handfuls, we long for sheaves. For this very reason, that we
are saved, we groan for something beyond. Did you hear that
groan just now? It is a traveller lost in the deep snow on the
mountain pass. No one has come to rescue him, and indeed
he has fallen into a place from which escape is impossible.
The snow is numbing his limbs, and his soul is breathed out
with many a groan. Keep that groan in your ear, for I want
you to hear another. The traveller has reached the hospice.
He has been charitably received, he has been warmed at the
fire, he has received abundant provision, he is warmly
clothed. There is no fear of tempest, that grand old hospice
has outstood many a thundering storm. The man is perfectly
safe, and quite content, so far as that goes, and exceedingly
grateful to think that he has been rescued; but yet I hear
him groan because he has a wife and children down in
yonder plain, and the snow is lying too deep for travelling,
and the wind is howling, and the blinding snow flakes are
falling so thickly that he cannot pursue his journey. Ask him
whether he is happy and content. He says, "Yes, I am happy
and grateful. I have been saved from the snow. I do not wish
for anything more than I have here, I am perfectly satisfied,
so far as this goes, but I long to look upon my household, and
to be once more in my own sweet home, and until I reach it,
I shall not cease to groan." Now, the first groan which you
heard was deep and dreadful, as though it were fetched from
the abyss of hell; that is the groan of the ungodly man as he
perishes, and leaves all his dear delights; but the second
groan is so softened and sweetened, that it is rather the note
of desire than of distress. Such is the groan of the believer,

who, though rescued and brought into the hospice of divine
mercy, is longing to see his Father's face without a veil
between, and to be united with the happy family on the
other side the Jordan, where they rejoice for evermore.
When the soldiers of Godfrey of Bouillon came in sight of
Jerusalem, it is said they shouted for joy at the sight of the
holy city. For that very reason they began to groan. Ask ye
why? It was because they longed to enter it. Having once
looked upon the city of David, they longed to carry the holy
city by storm, to overthrow the crescent, and place the cross
in its place. He who has never seen the New Jerusalem, has
never clapped his hands with holy ecstasy, he has never
sighed with the unutterable longing which is expressed in
words like these—

> "O my sweet home, Jerusalem,
> Would God I were in thee!
> Would God my woes were at an end,
> Thy joys that I might see!"

Take another picture to illustrate that the obtaining of
something makes us groan after more. An exile, far away
from his native country, has been long forgotten, but on a
sudden a vessel brings him the pardon of his monarch, and
presents from his friends who have called him to
remembrance. As he turns over each of these love-tokens,
and as he reads the words of his reconciled prince, he asks
"When will the vessel sail to take me back to my native
shore?" If the vessel tarries, he groans over the delay; and if
the voyage be tedious, and adverse winds blow back the
barque from the white cliffs of Albion, his thirst for his own
sweet land compels him to groan. So it is with your children
when they look forward to their holidays; they are not
unhappy or dissatisfied with the school, but yet they long to
be at home. Do not you recollect how, in your schoolboy days,
you used to make a little almanack with a square for every
day, and how you always crossed off the day as soon as ever
it began, as though you would try and make the distance
from your joy as short as possible? You groaned for it, not
with the unhappy groan that marks one who is to perish, but
with the groan of one who, having tasted of the sweets of
home, is not content until again he shall be indulged with
the fulness of them. So you see, beloved, that because we

have the "first-fruits of the Spirit," for that very reason, if for no other, we cannot help but groan for that blissful period which is called "the adoption, to wit, the redemption of the body."

II. Our second point rises before us—WHEREIN ARE BELIEVERS DEFICIENT? We are deficient in those things for which we groan and wait. And these appear to be four at least.

The first is, that *this body of ours is not delivered.* Brethren, as soon as a man believes in Christ, he is no longer under the curse of the law. As to his spirit, sin hath no more dominion over him, and the law hath no further claims against him. His soul is translated from death unto life, but the body, this poor flesh and blood, doth it not remain as before? Not in one sense, for the members of our body, which were instruments of unrighteousness, become by sanctification, the instruments of righteousness unto the glory of God; and the body which was once a workshop for Satan, becomes a temple for the Holy Ghost, wherein he dwells; but we are all perfectly aware that the grace of God makes no change in the body in other respects. It is just as subject to sickness as before, pain thrills quite as sharply through the heart of the saint as the sinner, and he who lives near to God, is no more likely to enjoy bodily health than he who lives at a distance from him. The greatest piety cannot preserve a man from growing old, and although in grace, he may be "like a young cedar, fresh and green," yet the body will have its grey hairs, and the strong man will be brought to totter on the staff. The body is still subject to the evils which Paul mentions, when he says of it that it is subject to corruption, to dishonour, to weakness, and is still a natural body.

Nor is this little, for the body has a depressing effect upon the soul. A man may be full of faith and joy spiritually, but I will defy him under some forms of disease to feel as he would. The soul is like an eagle, to which the body acts as a chain, which prevents its mounting. Moreover, the appetites of the body have a natural affinity to that which is sinful. The natural desires of the human frame are not in themselves sinful, but through the degeneracy of our nature, they very readily lead us into sin, and through the corruption which is in us, even the natural desires of the

body become a very great source of temptation. The body is
redeemed with the precious blood of Christ, it is redeemed
by price, but it has not as yet been redeemed by power. It
still lingers in the realm of bondage, and is not brought into
the glorious liberty of the children of God. Now this is the
cause of our groaning and mourning, for the soul is so
married to the body that when it is itself delivered from
condemnation, it sighs to think that its poor friend, the body,
should still be under the yoke. If you were a free man, and
had married a wife, a slave, you could not feel perfectly
content, but the more you enjoyed the sweets of freedom
yourself, the more would you pine that she should still be in
slavery. So is it with the Spirit, it is free from corruption and
death; but the poor body is still under the bondage of
corruption, and therefore the soul groans until the body
itself shall be set free. Will it ever be set free? O my beloved,
do not ask the question. This is the Christian's brightest
hope. Many believers make a mistake when they long to die
and long for heaven. Those things may be desirable, but they
are not the ultimatum of the saints. The saints in heaven are
perfectly free from sin, and, so far as they are capable of it,
they are perfectly happy; but a disembodied spirit never can
be perfect until it is reunited to its body. God made man not
pure spirit, but body and spirit, and the spirit alone will
never be content until it sees its corporeal frame raised to its
own condition of holiness and glory. Think not that our
longings here below are not shared in by the saints in
heaven. They do not groan, so far as any pain can be, but
they long with greater intensity than you and I long, for the
"adoption, to wit, the redemption of the body." People have
said there is no faith in heaven, and no hope; they know not
what they say—in heaven it is that faith and hope have their
fullest swing and their brightest sphere, for glorified saints
believe in God's promise, and hope for the resurrection of the
body. The apostle tells us that "they without us cannot be
made perfect;" that is, until our bodies are raised, theirs
cannot be raised, until we get our adoption day, neither can
they get theirs. The Spirit saith Come, and the bride saith
Come—not the bride on earth only, but the bride in heaven
saith the same, bidding the happy day speed on when the
trumpet shall sound, and the dead shall be raised
incorruptible, and we shall be changed. For it is true,

beloved, the bodies that have mouldered into dust will rise again, the fabric which has been destroyed by the worm shall start into a nobler being, and you and I, though the worm devour this body, shall in our flesh behold our God.

> "These eyes shall see him in that day,
>   The God that died for me;
> And all my rising bones shall say,
>   'Lord, who is like to thee?'"

Thus we are sighing that our entire manhood, in its trinity of spirit, soul, and body, may be set free from the last vestige of the fall; we long to put off corruption, weakness, and dishonour, and to wrap ourselves in incorruption, in immortality, in glory, in the spiritual body which the Lord Jesus Christ will bestow upon all his people. You can understand in this sense why it is that we groan, for if this body really is still, though redeemed, a captive, and if it is one day to be completely free, and to rise to amazing glory, well may those who believe in this precious doctrine groan after it as they wait for it.

But, again, there is another point in which the saint is deficient as yet, namely, *in the manifestation of our adoption*. You observe the text speaks of waiting for the adoption; and another text further back, explains what that means, waiting for the manifestation of the children of God. In this world, saints are God's children, but you cannot see that they are so, except by certain moral characteristics. That man is God's child, but though he is a prince of the blood royal, his garments are those of toil, the smock frock or the fustian jacket. Yonder woman is one of the daughters of the King, but see how pale she is, what furrows are upon her brow! Many of the daughters of pleasure are far more fair than she! How is this? The adoption is not manifested yet, the children are not yet openly declared. Among the Romans a man might adopt a child, and that child might be treated as his for a long time; but there was a second adoption in public, when the child was brought before the constituted authorities, and in the presence of spectators its ordinary garments which it had worn before were taken off, and the father who took it to be his child put on garments suitable to the condition of life in which it was to live. "Beloved, now are we the sons of God, and it doth not yet appear what we shall

be." We have not yet the royal robes which become the
princes of the blood; we are wearing in this flesh and blood
just what we wore as the sons of Adam; but we know that
when *he* shall appear who is the "first born among many
brethren," we shall be like him; that is, God will dress us all
as he dresses his eldest son—"We shall be like him, for we
shall see him as he is." Cannot you imagine that a child
taken from the lowest ranks of society, who is adopted by a
Roman senator, will be saying to himself, "I wish the day
were come when I shall be publicly revealed as the child of
my new father. Then, I shall leave off these plebeian
garments, and be robed as becomes my senatorial rank."
Happy in what he has received, for that very reason he
groans to get the fulness of what is promised him. So it is
with us to-day. We are waiting till we shall put on our proper
garments, and shall be manifested as the children of God. Ye
are young princes, and ye have not been crowned yet. Ye are
young brides, and the marriage day is not come, and by the
love your spouse bears you, you are led to long and to sigh
for the marriage day. Your very happiness makes you groan;
your joy, like a swollen spring, longs to leap up like some
Iceland Geyser, climbing to the skies, and it heaves and
groans within the bowels of your spirit for want of space and
room by which to manifest itself to men.

There is a third thing in which we are deficient, namely,
liberty, the glorious liberty of the children of God. The whole
creation is said to be groaning for its share in that freedom.
You and I are also groaning for it. Brethren, we are free! "If
the Son therefore shall make you free, ye shall be free
indeed." But our liberty is incomplete. When Napoleon was
on the island of St. Helena, he was watched by many guards,
but after many complaints, he enjoyed comparative liberty,
and walked alone. Yet, what liberty was it? Liberty to walk
round the rock of St. Helena, nothing more. You and I are
free, but what is our liberty? As to our spirits, we have
liberty to soar into the third heaven, and sit in the heavenly
places with Christ Jesus; but as for our bodies, we can only
roam about this narrow cell of earth, and feel that it is not
the place for us. Napoleon had been used to gilded halls, and
all the pomp and glory of imperial state, and it was hard to
be reduced to a handful of servants. Just so, we are kings—
we are of the blood imperial; but we have not our proper

state and becoming dignities—we have not our royalties
here. We go to our lowly homes; we meet with our brethren
and sisters here in their earth built temples; and we are
content, so far as these things go, still, how can kings be
content till they mount their thrones? How can a heavenly
one be content till he ascends to the heavenlies? How shall a
celestial spirit be satisfied until it sees celestial things? How
shall the heir of God be content till he rests on his Father's
bosom, and is filled with all the fulness of God?

I wish you now to observe that we are linked with the
creation. Adam in this world was in liberty, perfect liberty;
nothing confined him; paradise was exactly fitted to be his
seat. There were no wild beasts to rend him, no rough winds
to cause him injury, no blighting heats to bring him harm;
but in this present world everything is contrary to us.
Evidently we are exotics here. Ungodly men prosper well
enough in this world, they root themselves, and spread
themselves like green bay trees: it is their native soil; but
the Christian needs the hothouse of grace to keep himself
alive at all—and out in the world he is like some strange
foreign bird, native of a warm and sultry clime, that being
let loose here under our wintry skies is ready to perish. Now,
God will one day change our bodies and make them fit for
our souls, and then he will change this world itself. I must
not speculate, for I know nothing about it; but it is no
speculation to say that we look for new heavens and a new
earth wherein dwelleth righteousness; and that there will
come a time when the lion shall eat straw like an ox, and the
leopard shall lie down with the kid. We expect to see this
world that is now so full of sin as to be an Aceldama, a field
of blood, turned into a paradise, a garden of God. We believe
that the tabernacle of God will be among men, that he will
dwell among them, and they shall see his face, and his name
shall be in their foreheads. We expect to see the New
Jerusalem descend out of heaven from God. In this very
place, where sin has triumphed, we expect that grace will
much more abound. Perhaps after those great fires of which
Peter speaks when he says, "The heavens being on fire shall
be dissolved, and the elements shall melt with fervent heat,"
earth will be renewed in more than pristine loveliness.
Perhaps since matter may not be annihilated, and probably
cannot be, but will be as immortal as spirit, this very world

will become the place of an eternal jubilee, from which
perpetual hallelujahs shall go up to the throne of God. If
such be the bright hope that cheers us, we may well groan
for its realisation, crying out,

> "O long-expected day, begin;
> Dawn on these realms of woe and sin."

I shall not enlarge further, except to say that *our glory* is not
yet revealed, and that is another subject of sighing. "The
glorious liberty" may be translated, "The liberty of glory."
Brethren, we are like warriors fighting for the victory; we
share not as yet in the shout of them that triumph. Even up
in heaven they have not their full reward. When a Roman
general came home from the wars, he entered Rome by
stealth, and slept at night, and tarried by day, perhaps for a
week or two, among his friends. He went through the
streets, and people whispered, "That is the general, the
valiant one," but he was not publicly acknowledged. But, on
a certain set day, the gates were thrown wide open, and the
general, victorious from the wars in Africa or Asia, with his
snow-white horses bearing the trophies of his many battles,
rode through the streets, which were strewn with roses,
while the music sounded, and the multitudes, with glad
acclaim, accompanied him to the Capitol. That was his
triumphant entry. Those in heaven, have, as it were, stolen
there. They are blessed, but they have not had their public
entrance. They are waiting till their Lord shall descend from
heaven with a shout, with the trump of the archangel, and
the voice of God; then shall their bodies rise, then shall the
world be judged; then shall the righteous be divided from the
wicked; and then, upstreaming in marvelous procession,
leading captivity captive for the last time, the Prince at their
head, the whole of the blood-washed host, wearing their
white robes, and bearing their palms of victory, shall march
up to their crowns and to their thrones, to reign for ever and
ever! After this consummation the believing heart is
panting, groaning, and sighing.

Now, I think I hear somebody say, "you see these godly
people who profess to be so happy and so safe, they still
groan, and they are obliged to confess it." Yes, that is quite
true, and it would be a great mercy for you if you knew how
to groan in the same way. If you were half as happy as a

groaning saint is, you might be content to groan on for ever. I showed you, just now, the difference between a groan and a groan. I will shew you yet again. Go into yonder house. Listen at that door on the left, there is a deep, hollow, awful groan. Go to the next house, and hear another groan. It seems to be, so far as we can judge, much more painful than the first, and has an anguish in it of the severest sort. How are we to judge between them? We will come again in a few days: as we are entering the first house we see weeping faces and flowing tears, a coffin, and a hearse. Ah, it was the groan of death! We will go into the next. Ah, what is this? Here is a smiling cherub, a father with a gladsome face: if you may venture to look at the mother, see how her face smiles for joy that a man is born into the world to cheer a happy and rejoicing family. There is all the difference between the groan of death and the groan of life. Now, the apostle sets the whole matter before us when he said, "The whole creation groaneth," and you know what comes after that, "travaileth." There is a result to come of it of the best kind. We are panting, longing after something greater, better, nobler, and it is coming. It is not the pain of death we feel, but the pain of life. We are thankful to have such a groaning.

The other night, just before Christmas, two men who were working very late, were groaning in two very different ways, one of them saying, "Ah, there's a poor Christmas day in store for me, my house is full of misery." He had been a drunkard, a spendthrift, and had not a penny to bless himself with, and his house had become a little hell; he was groaning at the thought of going home to such a scene of quarrelling and distress. Now, his fellow workman, who worked beside of him, as it was getting very late, wished himself at home, and therefore groaned. A shopmate asked, "What's the matter?" "Oh, I want to get home to my dear wife and children. I have such a happy house, I do not like to be out of it." The other might have said, "Ah, you pretend to be a happy man, and here you are groaning." "Yes," he could say, "and a blessed thing it would be for you if you had the same thing to groan after that I have." So the Christian has a good Father, a blessed, eternal home, and groans to get to it; but, ah! there is more joy even in the groan of a Christian after heaven, than in all the mirth and merriment, and

dancing, and lewdness of the ungodly when their mirth is at
its greatest height. We are like the dove that flutters, and is
weary, but thank God, we have an ark to go to. We are like
Israel in the wilderness, and are footsore, but blessed be
God, we are on the way to Canaan. We are like Jacob looking
at the wagons, and the more we look at the wagons, the more
we long to see Joseph's face; but our groaning after Jesus is
a blessed groan, for

> "'Tis heaven on earth, 'tis heaven above,
> To see his face, and taste his love."

III. Now I shall conclude with WHAT OUR STATE OF MIND IS.
A Christian's experience is like a rainbow, made up of
drops of the griefs of earth, and beams of the bliss of heaven.
It is a chequered scene, a garment of many colours. He is
sometimes in the light and sometimes in the dark. The text
says, "we groan." I have told you what that groan is, I need
not explain it further. But it is added, "We groan *within
ourselves.*" It is not the hypocrite's groan, when he goes
mourning everywhere, wanting to make people believe that
he is a saint because he is wretched. We groan *within
ourselves.* Our sighs are sacred things; these griefs and sighs
are too hallowed for us to tell abroad in the streets. We keep
our longings to our Lord, and to our Lord alone. We groan
within ourselves. It appears from the text that this groaning
is universal among the saints: there are no exceptions; to a
greater or less extent we all feel it. He that is most endowed
with worldly goods, and he who has the fewest; he that is
blessed in health, and he who is racked with sickness; we all
have in our measure an earnest inward groaning towards
the redemption of our body.

Then the apostle says we are "waiting," by which I
understand that we are not to be petulant, like Jonah or
Elijah, when they said, "Let me die," nor are we to sit still
and look for the end of the day because we are tired of work;
nor are we to become impatient, and wish to escape from our
present pains and sufferings till the will of the Lord is done.
We are to groan after perfection, but we are to wait patiently
for it, knowing that what the Lord appoints is best. Waiting
implies being ready. We are to stand at the door expecting
the Beloved to open it and take us away to himself.

In the next verse we are described as hoping. We are saved

by hope. The believer continues to hope for the time when death and sin shall no more annoy his body; when, as his soul has been purified, so shall his body be, and his prayer shall be heard, that the Lord would sanctify him wholly, body, soul, and spirit.

Now, beloved, the practical use to which I put this, I am afraid somewhat discursive, discourse of this morning is just this. Here is a test for us all. You may judge of a man by what he groans after. Some men groan after wealth, they worship Mammon. Some groan continually under the troubles of life; they are merely impatient—there is no virtue in that. Some men groan because of their great losses or sufferings; well, this may be nothing but a rebellious smarting under the rod, and if so, no blessing will come of it. But the man that yearns after more holiness, the man that sighs after God, the man that groans after perfection, the man that is discontented with his sinful self, the man that feels he cannot be easy till he is made like Christ, that is the man who is blessed indeed. May God help you, and help me, to groan all our days with that kind of groaning. I have said before, there is heaven in it, and though the word sounds like sorrow, there is a depth of joy concealed within.

> "Lord, let me weep for nought but sin,
>   And after none but thee;
> And then I would, O that I might,
>   A constant weeper be."

I do not know a more beautiful sight to be seen on earth than a man who has served his Lord many years, and who, having grown grey in service, feels that, in the order of nature, he must soon be called home. He is rejoicing in the first-fruits of the Spirit which he has obtained, but he is panting after the full harvest of the Spirit which is guaranteed to him. I think I see him sitting on a jutting crag by the edge of Jordan, listening to the harpers on the other side, and waiting till the pitcher shall be broken at the cistern, and the wheel at the fountain, and the spirit shall depart to God that made it. A wife waiting for her husband's footsteps; a child waiting in the darkness of the night till its mother comes to give it the evening's kiss, are portraits of our waiting. It is a pleasant and precious thing so to wait and so to hope.

I fear that some of you, seeing ye have never come and put your trust in Christ, will have to say, when your time comes to die, what Wolsey is said to have declared, with only one word of alteration:—

"O Cromwell, Cromwell!
Had I but served my God with half the zeal
I served *the world,* he would not, in mine age,
Have left me naked to mine enemies."

Oh, before those days fully come, quit the service of the master who never can reward you except with death! Cast your arms around the cross of Christ, and give up your heart to God, and then, come what may, I am persuaded that "Neither death, nor life, nor angels, nor principalities, nor powers, nor things present, nor things to come. Nor height, nor depth, nor any other creature, shall be able to separate us from the love of God, which is in Christ Jesus our Lord." While you shall for awhile sigh for more of heaven, you shall soon come to the abodes of blessedness where sighing and sorrow shall flee away.

The Lord bless this assembly, for Christ's sake. Amen.

17

The Elders Before The Throne

"And round about the throne were four and twenty seats: and upon the seats I saw four and twenty elders sitting, clothed in white raiment; and they had on their heads crowns of gold."
"The four and twenty elders fall down before him that sat on the throne, and worship him that liveth for ever and ever, and cast their crowns before the throne, saying, Thou art worthy, O Lord, to receive glory and honour and power: for thou hast created all things, and for thy pleasure they are and were created."

Revelation 4:4, 10-11

The universe of God is one; heaven and earth are not so separate as unbelief has dreamed. As the Lord hath but one family, written in one register, redeemed with one blood, quickened by one Spirit, so this whole household abides in one habitation evermore. We who are in the body abide in the lower room which is sometimes dark and cold, but bears sufficient marks that it is a room in God's house; for it is to the eye of our faith often lit up with heavenly lustre, and we, even we, while we are yet here, are by blessed earnests made partakers of the inheritance of the saints in light. It is the same house, I say; but ours is the lower room, while our glorified brethren are up there, in the upper story, where the sunlight streams in everlastingly, where no chilling winds or poisonous breath can ever reach. It was well said that God's great house seems to have two wings; the one was a hospital and the other a palace. We are as yet in the wing on the left hand side, which is the hospital. We came into it sick even unto death, leprous to our very core, polluted from head to foot, having no soundness in us anywhere; and in this hospital we are undergoing the process of cure—a cure which is already certain, which is soon to be perfected; and then we shall pass from the hospital, the lazar-house, into the palace, where "without spot or wrinkle, or any such thing," we shall be recognised as the aristocracy of God, princes of the blood-royal of the universe, "sons of God, and joint-heirs with Christ Jesus." Still it is but one building: one roof covers the whole, both lazar-house and palace; one family, we dwell in it—one Church, above, beneath, though now divided by the narrow partition of death.

Now, to a great extent there is a likeness between the lower room and the upper room. As on earth we prepare for heaven, so the state of the saints on earth is heaven foreshadowed. In many respects the condition of the child of God on earth is a type of his condition in heaven; and I may say without fear of question that what the character of the saints is above, that should be the character of the saints below. We may very safely take for our example those glorified spirits. We need not be afraid that we shall be led astray by imitating them, by learning their occupations, or by attempting to share their joys. Surely the things in heaven are patterns of the things on earth, and as *they* are before the throne so ought we to be, and so shall we be in proportion as we live up to our privileges, and receive the likeness and image of our Lord Jesus Christ.

Brethren, beloved, it is upon this subject that I want to speak this morning. God is making heaven very near to us. We are now so large a Church that according to the laws of mortality, we lose five or six every month by death, and frequently two or three are removed in a week. We can hardly hope to meet together upon a single Sabbath without hearing that another of the stars is set. Some little time ago we went to the grave with an excellent elder of our Church, who had long known the Master, and had served him well: and now, during the coming week, it will be our lot to perform the same mournful office for another brother who has been in Christ, I suppose, these forty or fifty years, and who has served this Church for some little time with industry and zeal, but this week has been removed from our midst to join "the general assembly and church of the firstborn whose names are written in heaven." The veil grows thinner and thinner, and our faith in the unseen grows stronger. As the advanced guard of the army wade through the stream, and we hear their triumphant shouts upon the other shore, this world fades away, and that better land stands out in stronger and more glorious reality than it did before. Come, let us talk to one another by the way this morning of that better land, and let us encourage each other's hearts to make ourselves through God such as *they* are who sit upon their thrones, and to make *this* land, through the Spirit, such as that land is where God sheds his light for ever.

With regard to the spirits before the throne, we shall have three things to say this morning. First, a little *concerning their state and enjoyments;* then, further, concerning *their occupations and spirit;* and a few words with regard to *their testimony and precepts to us, as, speaking from the upper spheres, they urge us to follow their example.*

I. First, then, brethren with regard to THE STATE AND ENJOYMENTS OF THE SPIRITS BEFORE THE THRONE. In John's vision you perceive that the Church of Christ is represented by the four-and-twenty elders who sat round the throne. We are to look upon them as being the representatives of the great body of the faithful gathered to their eternal rest.

Mark, then, in the first place, that the saints in heaven are represented as *"elders,"* which we take to refer not merely to the office of the eldership, as it is exercised among us, although it seems most fitting that the officers should be the representatives of the whole body, but the reference is rather to the fulness of growth of believers before the throne. Here we have elders, and those who are elders in office should be chosen, because they have had spiritual experience, are well taught in the things of the kingdom of heaven and are therefore elders by grace as well as elders by office; but in all our Churches we have many who are babes in Christ, who as yet can only receive the elements of the gospel. We have many others who are young men, strong, but not matured. They have the vigour of manhood, but they have not yet the ripeness of advanced age. The elders in the Church are those who by reason of years have had their senses exercised; they are not the saplings of the forest, but the well-rooted trees; they are not the blades of corn up-springing, but the full corn in the ear awaiting the reaper's sickle. Such are the saints before the throne. They have made wondrous strides in knowledge; they understand now the heights and depths, the lengths and breadths of the love of Christ, which still surpasses even *their* knowledge. The meanest, if there be such differences, the meanest of the glorified understands more of the things of God than the greatest divine on earth. The rending of the veil of death is the removal of much of our ignorance. It may be that the saints in heaven progress in knowledge—that is possible, but it is certain that at the time of their departure they made a wondrous spring; they are babes no longer; they are children and infant beginners no more; God teacheth them in one five minutes, by a sight of the face of Jesus, more than they could have learned in threescore years and ten while present in the body and absent from the Lord. Their heresies are all cleared away with their sins; their mistakes are all removed; the same hand which wipes away all tears from their eyes wipes away all motes from their eyes too. Then they become sound in doctrine, skillful in teaching; they become masters in Israel by the sudden infusion of the wisdom of God by the Holy Ghost. They are "elders" before the throne. They are not unripe corn gathered green and damp, but they are all fully ripe, and they come to the garner as shocks of corn come in their season.

Perhaps they are represented as elders to show the dignity and gravity which shall surround saints of God in heaven. We sometimes hear complaints made about the younger members of Churches, that they are somewhat light in their conversation. Well, this has always been the fault of young people, and, as I said the other day, when one complained, I could not make lambs into sheep, and while they were lambs I suppose they would show some playfulness. It seems to be the natural failing of young people to be overflowing with mirth, and sometimes overtaken with levity. But there is a gravity which is very becoming in Christians, and there is a solidity which is extremely comely in the young believer; and I think when we make a profession of our faith in Christ, though we are not to cast away our cheerful faces, but to be more happy than ever we were before, yet we must put away all unseemly levity, and walk as those who are looking for the coming of the Son of Man, hearing this voice in our ears, "What manner of persons ought we to be in all holy conversation and godliness!" Now that fault can never be brought against the Church of God before the throne; there they are elders, glorious, blissful, happy, but yet serene and majestic in their joy. Theirs is not the prattling joy of the child, but the deep silent bliss of the full-grown man. As the senators in the Roman senate sat down in solemn grandeur, so that even the invading barbarians were overawed by their majestic bearing, so let our holy tranquility and joyful serenity cast an influence over the foes of our religion. Look upwards, Christians. There are the elders before the throne, representatives of what you and I, and all of us who trust in Christ, shall soon be; let us be laying aside childish things; let us be getting ready for the elder's dignity; let us leave the toy, the trifle, the plaything, to those who know not the immortal manhood of believers, and let us go on unto perfection, growing in grace and in the knowledge of our Lord and Saviour Jesus Christ.

In passing, I may observe, that the number of *four-and-twenty* is somewhat puzzling. There have been different attempts made to account for it. They say that this was the number of the Sanhedrin; but that is not clear. Others think that as the number twelve was the symbol of the Jewish Church, in the twelve tribes, so twelve more may have been added to represent the accession of the Gentile Church; or it may show the multiplication of the Church, that though small, so that it is numbered by twelve, its number, while still definite and complete, is now larger than it was before. But, still better, I think, as there were twenty-four courses of Levites, who were porters at the gate of the temple, and twenty-four courses of priests who offered sacrifice, so the number twenty-four is made use of to show that the service of God in his temple is complete, that there are as many as will be wanted, that every part of the divine service will be taken up, and around that altar which smokes before God eternally there shall be a full complement of those who shall bow before him, and do him homage.

But, secondly, you will notice that these elders are said to be *around the throne*. We suppose, as near as we can catch the thought of John, sitting in a semi-circle, as the Jewish Sanhedrin did around the Prince of Israel. It is a somewhat singular thing that in the passage in Canticles, where Solomon sings of the king sitting at his table, the Hebrew has it "a round table." From this, some expositors, I think without straining the text, have said, "There is an equality among the saints." In heaven they are not some sitting at the head, and some sitting lower down, but there is an equality in the position and condition of glorified spirits. Certainly that idea is conveyed by the position of the four-and-twenty elders. We do not find one of them nearer than the other, but they all sat round about the throne. We believe, then, that the condition of glorified spirits in heaven, is that of nearness to Christ, clear vision of his glory, constant access to his court, and familiar fellowship with his person. Nor do we think that there is any difference before the throne between one saint and another. We believe that all the people of God, apostles, martyrs, ministers, or private and obscure Christians, shall all have the same place *near the throne,* where they shall for ever gaze upon their exalted Lord, and for ever be satisfied in his love. There shall not be some at a distance, far away in the remote streets of the celestial city, and others in the broad thoroughfares; there shall not be some near the centre, and others far away on the verge of the wide circumference; but they shall all be near to Christ, all ravished with his love, all eating and drinking at the same table with him, as equally his favourites and his friends.

Now, brothers and sisters, as we bade you imitate the saints in their eldership and perfection, so would we exhort you to imitate them in their nearness to Christ. Oh, let us be on earth as the elders are in heaven, sitting round about the throne. May Christ be the centre of this Church! May he be the centre of your thoughts, the centre of your life. If an angel should fly across this assembly this morning, when he came back to heaven, could he say, "I saw them in the house of God, sitting around the throne. Their eyes were gazing on the slaughtered Lamb; their hearts were loving and praising *him;* they were desiring to do *him* homage and to pay *him* reverence?" And what think you of to-morrow, and the other days of the week? Will it be true of you that you are sitting before the throne? Brothers and sisters, we are out of our proper place, when we are looking after anything but Christ. "We are not our own; we are bought with a price." Why live as if we were our own? He is our husband, our soul is espoused to him. Oh! how can we live at such a distance from him? He is our life; he makes us live, he makes us blest: how can we be so much forgetful of him? How can our hearts be such strangers to their beloved? Jesus! draw us nearer to thyself! Oh to be nearer to thy throne, Lord, even while we are here! O take thou us up to thee, or else come thou down to us. Say unto us, "Abide in me, and I in you;" and permit our souls to say, "His left hand is under my head, and his right hand doth embrace me."

> "Abide with me from morn till eve,
> For without thee I cannot live;
> Abide with me when night is nigh,
> For without thee I dare not die."

A third point of likeness strikes us at once. It seems that the elders sitting around the throne were represented to the illuminated eye of John as *"clothed in white raiment."* Not in raiment of party-colours, whereon there were some spots, and yet some signs of whiteness. They are without fault before the throne of God; they have "washed their robes and made them white in the blood of the Lamb," and the Spirit of God also has so thoroughly renewed them, that they are "without spot or wrinkle, or any such thing;" they have been presented holy and unblamable before the throne of God. Brothers and sisters, in this too, they are an example to us. Oh that the Spirit of God might keep the members of this Church, that our garments might be always white. Perfection we must not hope to see here; but oh, we must aim after it. If one should never unite with a Christian Church till he found one which is perfect and free from all fault, then such a man must be a schismatic for ever, for with no Christian people could he ever join. Yet, this is what we aspire unto—to be faultless before God. We desire so to walk, and so to act among men, that our conduct may never bring a slur upon our profession—that our language, our actions, our motives, everything that is about us, may witness to the fact that we have been with Jesus, and have learned of him. O brothers and sisters, it is impossible for one pastor, assisted even by the most earnest of elders, to oversee so large a flock as this. Let me ask, have you kept your garments white this last week? Oh, if you have stained them, I beseech you, repent, bitterly repent before God; and if any of you have backslidden, I pray you, do not be hypocrites; let your guilt be fully confessed before God. If you cannot honour this Church, do not dishonour it; if you cannot glorify Christ by your walk and conversation, at least do not trample under foot his blood, and put his cross to an open shame. There is nothing which can so injure a Church, and cut the sinews of its strength, as the unholiness of its members. When we are "fair as the moon, and clear as the sun," then we shall be "terrible as an army with banners;" but not till then. Those blots upon the escutcheon, those spots upon the garment, are soon perceived by a lynx-eyed world; and then they turn round and say, "Ah! these are your Christians; this is your religion!" The sons of Belial make excuses for their own conscience, and go on in their sin, hardened by our mistakes. Oh, let this be your prayer, I exhort you, you who are mighty in prayer, never forget this day and night, "Lord, keep thy people; hold thou them up." I can say it has been at all times the bitterest draught I have ever had to drink, when any who have professed the name of Christ have turned back unto vanity. To bury you is but a blessed duty in comparison with noting and correcting backsliding and apostacy. I know my prayer for myself has been, a hundred times, "A speedy death, a soon and sudden sleeping beneath the green turf, or even a painful, agonizing, languishing decay, upon a bed of pain, rather than you should live to see your pastor stain his profession, and fall from his integrity." If it be so with the minister, it must be so with each of you. Better for you that you depart at once than that you should live bearing the name of Christ, to make that name a reproach and a bye-word among the heathen. Lord, help thou us, that we, like thy saints above, may be clothed in white garments.

Further, to carry on the parallel. You perceive that these elders *exercised a priesthood.* Indeed, their being clothed in white garments, while it is an emblem of their purity, also represents them as being priests unto God. They themselves expressly sing in the 10th verse of the 5th chapter, "Thou hast made us unto our God kings and priests." They exercise the office of the priesthood, as you perceive, by the double offering of prayer and praise. They hold in their hands the censers full of sweet incense, and the harps which give forth melodious sounds. Brethren, in the wilderness of old they were not all priests. One special tribe, and one family out of that tribe, alone, could exercise that office; the rest of the people stood in the outer court. As for the most holy place, into that only came the high priest, and he only once a year, so much exclusion was there in that age of shadows. But now all believers are priests; we have all a right to stand in the priest's place, to offer sacrifice and incense. Nay, more, through Christ we enter into that which is within the veil, and stand in the most holy place, and look at the bright light from the Shekinah, fearing not that we shall die, but having boldness and confidence through the new and living way, the rent body of Christ. The saints before the throne are represented as all of them in the holy place, round the throne, all officiating, every one of them presenting sacrifice. Brethren, what are *we* doing? Let us look up to them as the priests of God, and then ask ourselves, are *we* celebrating his worship too? Brother, did you this morning, before you came up to this house, lift up your hand with the bowl of incense in it, in your earnest prayer for a blessing upon his people? Have you this day in our sacred song, been laying your fingers mystically among the strings of your golden harp? What did you do last week, my brethren? What *were* you? Can you say that you were a priest? Or, must you not blush that you were rather a buyer and a seller, or a thinker and a writer, than a priest unto our God? And yet this is our high calling; this is our blessed vocation. Our earthly calling is but little honour to us, nor should it engross our richest thoughts; our heavenly calling is of the most importance; it is that which is to last for ever; it is that which should have the cream of our soul's attention. We are priests. Oh! brethren, if we have failed in the past, may God give us grace for the future! and during the coming days of the next work-day week, may he help us, that our buyings and our sellings, our travellings and our tarryings at home, may all be the exercise of priesthood! You know, you can make "the bells upon the horses" holiness to the Lord, and the very pots of your house can be as the bowls upon the altar; you need not go out of your everyday callings to be priests, but be priests in your callings. Sanctify the Lord God in your workshops, in your fields, in your market-places, in your exchanges; and whatsoever ye do, whether ye eat, or drink, or whatever ye do, do it all in the name of the Lord Jesus, who hath made you priests and kings unto him.

I know there is a sad tendency among us all to leave the priesthood to some peculiar clan. Mark you, members of this Church, I will be no priest for you. It is as much as I can do to exercise the priesthood to which God calls me on my own account, to offer my own thanks and my own petitions. I will have none of your responsibilities; you must be priests for yourselves. You cannot shift this burden off, nor would you wish, I am sure, if ye be true-hearted. Ye say ye are poor, ye are unknown, ye have no talent. Ye need it not, these cannot make you priests. How came the sons of Aaron to the priesthood? By birth. So with you. You have been "born not of the will of the flesh, nor of the will of man, nor of blood, but of God," and the priesthood is the inalienable inheritance of the new birth. Exercise your office, then, be ye who ye may, O ye beloved of the Lord. In the name of him who hath "begotten you again unto a lively hope, by the resurrection of Jesus Christ from the dead," live as men sanctified for divine service, who cannot and must not be servants of men and slaves of sin.

Once more, and I think I shall have said enough upon this first point. There is yet another likeness between the saints in heaven and those on earth. You perceive that these *had on their heads crowns of gold.* They reigned with Christ. He was a king, and he made them kings with him. As in the old Persian court the princes of the blood wore crowns, so in the court of heaven the princes of the blood, the brethren of the Lord, are crowned too. They are royal senators; they sit upon thrones, even as he has overcome, and sits down with his Father on his throne. These thrones they have to show their dominion, their rights and jurisdiction. Know ye not that we shall judge angels, and that when Christ shall come he will bring his people with him, and they will sit upon his throne as co-assessors with him? Then the wicked, the persecutors, the revilers of God's people, shall be brought to judgment, and the saints whom they despised shall be their Judges? So that when Christ shall say, "Depart, ye cursed," there shall be heard the thundering assent of the ten thousands of his saints, as they say "Amen," and confirm from their hearts the sentence of the all-righteous Judge. Therefore do these elders sit upon their thrones.

Now, beloved, let us imitate them in this. "Oh!" say you, "but I cannot wear a crown as they do." Nevertheless, you are a king; for they who are Christ's are kings. Take care, brother, that thou wearest thy crown, by reigning over thy lusts. Reign over thy sins. Reign over thy passions. Be as a king in the midst of all that would lead thee astray. Christ Jesus has broken the neck of thy sin; put thy foot upon it; keep it under; subdue it. Be king in the dominions of thine

own being. In the world at large act a king's part. If any
would tempt thee to betray Christ for gain, say, "How can I?
I am a king. How shall I betray Christ?" Let the nobility of
your nature come out in your actings. Forgive in a royal
manner, as a king can forgive. Be ready to give to others as
God hath helped you, as a king gives. Let your liberality of
spirit be right royal. Let your actions never be mean,
sneaking, cowardly, dastardly. Do the right thing, and defy
the worst. Dare all your foes in the pursuit of that which is
right, and let men see while they look upon you that there is
a something under your homely appearance which they
cannot understand. Men make a deal of fuss about the blood
of the aristocracy; I dare say it is not very different from the
blood of crossing-sweepers. But there is a great deal of
difference between the life-blood of the saints and the life-
blood of the proudest prince; for they who love Christ have
fed upon his flesh, and have drunk of his blood, and have
been made partakers of the divine nature. These are the
royal ones; these are the aristocrats; these are the nobility,
and all are mean beside. Christians, perhaps some of you
have not reigned as kings during the last week. You have
been either murmuring, like poor whining beggars, or you
have been scraping, like dunghill rakers, with your
covetousness, or you have been sinning, like idle boys in the
street, who roll in the mire. You have not lived up to your
kingship. Now I pray you, ask God's grace that during the
week to come you may say of sin, "I cannot touch it, I am a
king; I cannot demean myself with it;" that you may say of
this earth's dross, "I cannot go down and scrape that; my
heritage is above;" that ye may be able to say of everything
that is low and mean, "Shall such a man as I do this? How
can I come down from the elevated position to which God has
called me, to act as others act, from their motives and with
their ends?" Let, then, the state of the saints above, while it
is the theme of our delightful thought, while we anticipate
the time when we shall fully partake of it, be also an
example to us while in these lands below.

II. Briefly upon our second point—THE OCCUPATION AND
SPIRIT OF THOSE GLORIFIED ONES, AS THEY SHOULD BE
IMITATED BY US BELOW.

Notice their occupation. First of all it is one of *humility*. At
the tenth verse in our fourth chapter we perceive it is

written, "They fall down before him." They are kings, but yet they fall down—they wear royal crowns, but yet they prostrate themselves. They are second to none in God's universe; they stand as first in the peerage of creation; yet before the king they have no honour and no esteem, but as if they were slaves and menials, they cast themselves upon their faces before his throne, having nothing of their own whereof to glory, but boasting alone in Him. The more holy, the more humble. Where holiness is in perfection, there humility is in perfection too. The cherubim veil their faces with their wings, while they cry, "Holy, holy, holy, Lord God of Sabbaoth." So do these elders, taking the same posture of humility, they bow before the throne.

Brothers and sisters, are we as humble as we should be? If we think we are, we at once betray our pride. But let us understand how unseemly anything but humility must be to us. We are yet on earth; if they in heaven boast not, how dare we? We are yet sinful and erring; if the spotless ones bow what shall we do? If we threw dust and ashes on our head, and acknowledged ourselves to be the vilest of the vile, yet were the words not too coarse for us, nor the action too humiliating. Far hence from us be the pride which would let us exalt ourselves. Pride is natural to us all brethren, we cannot get rid of it, even though we strive against it. What shall we say of those who nurture it—whose very carriage and walk betray the pride of their hearts? What shall we say of the pride which finds root in the purse, or that which shows itself in outward array and garments? What shall we say of the pride of station and of rank, which will not permit the professedly Christian man to speak with his poorer brother? Oh! these are damnable things. I hope we despise, and are rid of these; but is there a subtler pride—a pride which apes humility—a pride which comes in after prayer, or after preaching, or after anything that is done for Christ? Let us strive against it, and be it our constant and daily endeavour to fall before the throne, "While less than nothing we can boast, and vanity confess."

But as they fall before the throne in humility, you will note that they express their *gratitude*. It is said they cast their crowns before the throne. They know where they got them from, and they know to whom to ascribe the praise. Their crowns are their own, and, therefore, they wear them on their heads; their crowns were Jesus' gift, and, therefore, they cast them at his feet. They wear their crown, for he hath made them kings, and they cannot refuse the dignity; but they cast the crown at his feet, for they are only kings by right received from him, and acknowledge him thus to be King of kings and Lord of lords. It was a custom, you know, in imperial Rome, for those kings who held dominion under the emperor, on certain occasions to take off their crowns and lay them down before the emperor, so that when he bade them put them on again, they had fully recognised that their rights of kingship flowed only through him. So do they who are before the throne. With what rapture, with what joy, with what delight, do they cast their crowns there! To think they have a crown, and a crown to cast before him! Brothers and sisters, I am afraid when you and I get any graces, or have been made useful in Christ's cause, we are glad for the thing's sake; but we are not right, if so; we should be glad because we have something to cast at *his* feet. Have you faith? I must thank *him* for faith, I must lay it at his feet, and say, "Jesus, use my faith for thy glory, for thou art its author and finisher." If you and I shall by divine grace persevere to the end, and shall arrive at heaven, it will be a joy to think that we are saved, but we will lay it all at the door of love divine. Will you wear a crown, believer? Will you accept jot or tittle of the glory? O no, ye will each of ye disown anything like the Arminian's proud boast of free self-will. It will be grace, grace, grace alone in heaven. There will be no division and no discord in that eternal hymn. We will cast our crowns at once before him, and we will say, "Not unto us, not unto us, but unto thy name be all the praise." We imitate them, then, in this—in our gratitude mingled with humility.

Further, I well perceive that these elders spent their time in *joyous song*. How glorious was that strain—"Thou art worthy to take the book, and to open the seals thereof: for thou wast slain, and hast redeemed us to God by thy blood, out of every kindred, and tongue, and people, and nation." These elders knew that the time was come when all earth and heaven should be more than usually glad. They, with the four living creatures, whom we take to be the representatives of some special order of presence-angels, about whom we know but little, led the strain; and as the music rolled through the aisles of heaven, distant angels, who were in all parts of God's dominion keeping watch and ward, stood still and listened till they had caught the strain; and then they joined with loudest notes, till from north and south, and east and west, from the highest star and from the uttermost depths, there came up the blessed refrain from ten thousand times ten thousand, and thousands of thousands, "Worthy is the Lamb that was slain to receive power, and riches, and wisdom, and strength, and honour, and glory, and blessing;" till, as these angelic ones sent up the song, the inferior creatures caught the divine infection, and in heaven and earth, the sea and the uttermost depths thereof, the voice was heard, and all creatures responded, while the universe echoed with the song, "Blessing, and honour, and glory, and power, be unto him that sitteth upon the throne, and unto the Lamb for ever and ever." This is the occupation of saints before the throne; be it yours, brothers and sisters. Let us, as God's redeemed, sing with all our hearts, and let us enlist others in the strain. Let us remember that we are to be leaders in the hymn of God's works. We are to begin with, "Bless the Lord, O my soul;" but we are not to end there. We are to go on bidding all God's works praise him, till we come to a climax like that of David, "Bless the Lord, ye hosts, ye ministers of his that do his pleasure; bless the Lord, all his works, in all places of his dominion; bless the Lord, O my soul." The world is the organ—we are the players. We are to put our fingers upon the notes, and wake the universe to thunders of acclaim. We are not to rest with our own feeble note, but we must wake even the dumb earth itself, till all the planets, listening to our earth, and joining her song, shall sing forth the music of the ages. God give you, brothers and sisters, to imitate the saints thus. Some of you perhaps are good hands at groaning; perhaps some of you have come up here to-day mourning and murmuring; lay these things aside; take up your proper vocation, and now smite the strings of your harp; magnify the Lord; let the day of jubilee come to your spirits. Ye saints of God, rejoice; yea, in your God exceedingly rejoice.

Yet once again, these saints not only offered praise, but *prayer.* This was the meaning of the bowls, which are so foolishly translated vials. A vial is precisely the opposite of the vessel that was intended: the vial is long and narrow, whereas, this is broad and shallow. A bowl is meant, full of incense, covered over with a lid, and perforated with holes, through which the smoke of the incense rises. This does not mean that the four-and-twenty elders offer the prayers of the saints below, but their own prayers. Some have thought, Is there any prayer in heaven? Certainly, there is room for prayer in heaven. If you want proof, we have it in the chapter which follows the one out of which we have been reading this morning—the ninth verse of the sixth chapter— "I saw under the altar the souls of them that were slain for the word of God, and for the testimony which they held: and they cried with a loud voice, saying, How long, O Lord, holy and true, dost thou not judge and avenge our blood on them that dwell on the earth?" There is prayer. Perhaps the prayers of the saints are the major portion of that perpetual litany which goeth up to heaven. But leaving that for a moment, let us imitate them. If *they* pray, how much more reason have we? If they plead for the universal Church, they who enjoy the rest of God, how should we pray who are still in this land of temptation and of sin, who see the perils of our brethren, know their weaknesses and their afflictions. Let us draw near unto God; let us never cease day and night to offer intercession for the whole company of the elect.

I must not forget, however, here, that these elders before the throne were ready not only for prayer and praise, but for *all kinds of service.* You remember there was one of them, when John wept, who said, "Weep not." Depend upon it that elder had been occupied in visiting the sick when he was on earth; and often when he had gone into their cottages and found them sorrowing, he had said unto them, "Weep not;" and the good man had not lost his character when he went to heaven, although it had been spiritualized and perfected; and seeing John weeping, he said to him, "Weep not." Ah! those saints before the throne, if there were mourners there, would comfort them, I know; and if they could be sent down here to visit any of the sorrowing children of God, they would be too glad to do it. Then there was, you remember, another of the elders, who said to John, for his instruction, "Who are these that are arrayed in white robes, and whence came they? And I said unto him, Sir, thou knowest. And he said to me, "These are they that came out of great tribulation." I venture to believe that this elder used to teach a catechumen class on earth; that he had been in the habit of teaching young people, and he put the question to John first, as he had been in the habit aforetime of putting it to young disciples on earth. The saved ones would be ready to teach us now, if they could; and they do to-day bear testimony for Christ, for to the ages to come God through his Church makes known to principalities and powers the exceeding riches of his grace.

Now, those before the throne are willing *to comfort the weeper or to instruct the ignorant.* Let us do the same! and may it be ours to wipe the tear from many an eye, to chase the darkness of ignorance from many a young heart. Have you been doing that lately brothers and sisters? If not, mend your ways; be more earnest in these two good works, visit the fatherless, the widow, the suffering, the mourning, and to teach the ignorant and those that are out of the way.

III. And now, lastly, WHAT IS THEIR WORD AND LESSON TO US THIS MORNING? Bending from their shining thrones, being dead they yet speak; and they say to us thus:

First, by way of encouragement, brethren, *follow on.* Be not dismayed. We fought the same battles that you fight, and passed through the like tribulations; yet we have not perished, but enjoy the eternal reward. Press on; heaven awaits you; vacant thrones are here for you—crowns which no other heads can wear—harps that no other hands must play. Follow courageously, faithfully, trusting in him who hath begun the good work in you, and who will carry it on.

Hear them, again, as they say, mark the footsteps that we trod; for only in one way can you reach our rest. We have washed our robes, and made them white in the blood of the Lamb. They say to all the world, "If ye would be clean wash there too. None but Jesus can save your souls. Trust in him; repose in his atonement; confide in his finished work; flee to his sacrificial blood. You shall be saved by faith in him, even as we have been."

"I asked them whence their victory came; they with united breath
Ascribed their conquest to the Lamb, their triumph to his death."

Friends! are ye trusting in Christ? My hearers, many of you are perfect strangers to me this morning, I ask you, are you putting your trust in Christ? Have you come under the shadow of his cross, to find a refuge from his vengeance? If not, no golden crown can be for you; no harp of gold; but, whoever thou mayest be, if thou will believe in Christ Jesus, and put thy soul into his hand, thou shalt be a partaker of the glories which he hath laid up for them that love him.

Lastly, they say to us, as they look down from the battlements of heaven, Are ye getting ready to join our ranks, to take up our occupations, and to sing our song? Answer for yourself, my brother, as I must answer for myself. Are you living for your own pleasure? Then you must die; for "he that soweth to the flesh, shall of the flesh reap corruption." Are you living for Christ? Then shall you live; "because he lives you shall live also." Are you a priest to God today? You shall bear the golden bowl in heaven. Are you instead thereof a servant of your own body, your own lusts, your own gain, your own pleasure? Then the lowest depths must be your portion. Heaven is "a prepared place for a prepared people." Are we prepared? Brothers, sisters, can we say, "We hope in Christ; he is our only trust;" and do we endeavour to live to him? and though with many failings and frailties, yet still can we say, "For me to live is Christ?" Oh! if it be so,

"Come, death, and some celestial band, to bear our souls away!"

But if it be not so, then our end must be destruction, because our God has been our belly.

18

The Beatific Vision

"...we shall see him as he is."   1 John 3:2

It is one of the most natural desires in all the world, that when we hear of a great and a good man, we should wish to see his person. When we read the works of any eminent author, we are accustomed to turn to the frontispiece to look for his portrait. When we hear of any wondrous deed of daring, we will crowd our windows to see the warrior ride through the streets. When we know of any man who is holy and who is eminently devoted to his work, we will not mind tarrying anywhere, if we may but have a glimpse of him whom God has so highly blessed. This feeling becomes doubly powerful when we have any connection with the man; when we feel, not only that he is great, but that he is great for us; not simply that he is good, but that he is good to us; not only that he is benevolent, but that he has been a benefactor to us as individuals. Then the wish to see him rises to a craving desire, and the desire is insatiable until it can satisfy itself in seeing that unknown, and hitherto unseen donor, who has done such wondrously good deeds for us. I am sure, my brethren, you will all confess that this strong desire has arisen in your minds concerning the Lord Jesus Christ. We owe to none so much; we talk of none so much, we hope, and we think of none so much: at any rate, no one so constantly thinks of us. We have I believe, all of us who love his name, a most insatiable wish to behold his person. The thing for which I would pray above all others, would be for ever to behold his face, for ever to lay my head upon his breast, for ever to know that I am his, for ever to dwell with him. Ay, one short glimpse, one transitory vision of his glory, one brief glance at his marred, but now exalted and beaming countenance, would repay almost a world of trouble. We have a strong desire to see him. Nor do I think that that desire is wrong. Moses himself asked that he might see God. Had it been a wrong wish arising out of vain curiosity, it would not have been granted, but God granted Moses his desire: he put him in the cleft of the rock, shaded him with his hands, bade him look at the skirts of his garments, because his face could not be seen. Yea, more; the earnest desire of the very best of men has been in the same direction. Job said, "I know that my Redeemer liveth, and though worms devour this body, yet in my flesh shall I see God :" that was his desire. The holy Psalmist said, "I shall be satisfied when I awake in thy likeness;" "I shall behold thy face in righteousness." And most saints on their death-beds have expressed their fondest, dearest, and most blessed wish for heaven, in the expression of longing "to be with Christ, which is far better." And not ill did our sweet singer of Israel put the words together, when he humbly said, and sweetly too:—

> "Millions of years my wondering eyes
> Shall o'er thy beauties rove;
> And endless ages I'll adore
> The glories of thy love."

We are rejoiced to find such a verse as this, for it tells us that our curiosity shall be satisfied, our desire consummated, our bliss perfected. "WE SHALL SEE HIM AS HE IS." Heaven shall be ours, and all we ever dreamed of him shall be more than in our possession.

By the help of God's mighty Spirit, who alone can put words in our mouths, let us speak first of all concerning *the glorious position*—"AS HE IS;" secondly, *his personal identity*—"we shall see HIM as *he is;*" thirdly, *the positive vision*—"we SHALL SEE him as he is;" and fourthly, *the actual persons*—"WE shall see him as he is."

I. First then, THE GLORIOUS POSITION. Our minds often revert to Christ as he was, and as such we have desired to see him. Ah! how often have we wished to see the babe that slept in Bethlehem! How earnestly have we desired to see the man who talked with the woman at the well! How frequently have we wished that we might see the blessed Physician walking amongst the sick and dying, giving life with his touch, and healing with his breath! How frequently too have our thoughts retired to Gethsemane, and we have wished our eyes were strong enough to pierce through eighteen hundred and fifty years which part us from that wondrous spectacle, that we might see him as he was! We shall never see him thus; Bethlehem's glories are gone for ever; Calvary's glooms are swept away; Gethsemane's scene is dissolved; and even Tabor's splendours are quenched in the past. They are as things that were; nor shall they ever have a resurrection. The thorny crown, the spear, the sponge, the nails—these are not. The manger and the rocky tomb are gone. The places are there, unsanctified by Christian feet, unblessed, unhallowed by the presence of their Lord. We shall never see him as he was. In vain our fancy tries to paint it, or our imagination to fashion it. We cannot, must not, see him as he was; nor do we wish, for we have a larger promise, "We shall shall see him as he *is*." Come, just look at that a few moments by way of contrast, and then I am sure you will prefer to see Christ as he *is*, rather than behold him as he was.

Consider, first of all, that we shall not see him *abased in his incarnation,* but *exalted in his glory.* We are not to see the infant of a span long; we are not to admire the youthful boy; we are not to address the incipient man; we are not to pity the man wiping the hot sweat from his burning brow; we are not to behold him shivering in the midnight air; we are not to behold him subject to pains, and weaknesses, and sorrows, and infirmities like ours. We are not to see the eye wearied by sleep; we are not to behold hands tired in labour; we are not to behold feet bleeding with arduous journeys, too long for their strength. We are not to see him with his soul distressed; we are not to behold him abased and sorrowful. Oh! the sight is better still. We are to see him exalted. We shall see the head, but not with its thorny crown.

> "The head that once was crowned with thorns,
> Is crown'd with glory now."

We shall see the hand, and the nail-prints too, but not the nail; it has been once drawn out, and for ever. We shall see his side, and its pierced wound too, but the blood shall not issue from it. We shall see him not with a peasant's garb around him, but with the empire of the universe upon his shoulders. We shall see him, not with a reed in his hand, but grasping a golden sceptre. We shall see him, not as mocked and spit upon and insulted, not bone of our bone, in all our agonies, afflictions, and distresses; but we shall see him exalted; no longer Christ the man of sorrows, the acquaintance of grief, but Christ the Man-God, radiant with splendour, effulgent with light, clothed with rainbows, girded with clouds, wrapped in lightnings, crowned with stars, the sun beneath his feet. Oh! glorious vision! How can we guess what *he is?* What words can tell us? or how can we speak thereof! Yet whate'er he is, with all his splendour unveiled, all his glories unclouded, and himself unclothed— *we shall see him as he is.*

Remember again: we are not to see Christ as he was, the *despised,* the *tempted one.* We shall never see Christ sitting in the wilderness, while the arch-traitor says to him, "If thou be the Son of God command that these stones be made bread." We shall not see him standing firmly on the temple's pinnacle, bidding defiance to the evil one who bids him cast himself down from his towering height. We shall not see him erect on the mountain of temptation, with the earth offered to him if he will but crouch at the feet of the demon. Nay; nor shall we see him mocked by Pharisees, tempted by Sadducees, laughed at by Herodians. We shall not behold him with the finger of scorn pointed at him. We shall never see him called a "drunken man, and a wine-bibber." We shall never see the calumniated, the insulted, the molested, the despised Jesus. He will not be seen as one from whom we shall hide our faces, who "was despised, and we esteemed him not." Never shall these eyes see those blessed cheeks dripping with the spittle; never shall these hands touch that blessed hand of his while stained with infamy. We shall not see him despised of men and oppressed; but *"we shall see him as he is."*

> "No more the bloody spear,
> The cross and nails no more;
> For hell itself shakes at his name,
> And all the heavens adore."

No tempting devil near him; for the dragon is beneath his feet. No insulting men; for lo! the redeemed cast their crowns before his feet. No molesting demons; for angels sound his lofty praise through every golden street; princes bow before him; the kings of the isles bring tribute; all nations pay him homage, while the great God of heaven and earth shining on him, gives him mighty honour. We shall see him, beloved, not abhorred, not despised and rejected, but worshipped, honoured, crowned, exalted, served by flaming spirits, and worshipped by cherubim and seraphim. "We shall see him as he is."

Mark again. We shall not see the Christ *wrestling with pain,* but Christ *as a conqueror.* We shall never see him tread the winepress alone, but we shall see him when we shall cry, "Who is this that cometh from Edom, with dyed garments from Bozrah? this that is glorious in his apparel, travelling in the greatness of his strength?" We shall never see him as when he stood foot to foot with his enemy: but we shall see him when his enemy is beneath his feet. We shall never see him as the bloody sweat streams from his whole body; but we shall see him as he hath put all things under him, and hath conquered hell itself. We shall never see him as the wrestler; but we shall see him grasp the prize. We shall never see him scaling the rampart; but we shall see him wave the sword of victory on the top thereof. We shall not see him fight; but we shall see him return from the fight victorious, and shall cry, "Crown him! Crown him! Crowns become the victor's brow." *"We shall see him as he is."*

Yet again. We shall never see our Saviour under his father's *displeasure;* but we shall see him *honoured by his Father's smile.* The darkest hour of Christ's life was when his Father forsook him—that gloomy hour when his Father's remorseless hand held the cup to his Son's own lips, and bitter though it was said to him, "Drink my Son—ay, drink;" and when the quivering Saviour, for a moment, having man within him—strong in its agonies for the moment, said, "My Father, if it be possible, let this cup pass from me." Oh! it was a dark moment when the Father's ears were deaf to his Son's petitions, when the Father's eyes were closed upon his Son's agonies. "My Father," said the Son, "Canst thou not remove the cup? Is there no way else for thy severe justice? Is there no other medium for man's salvation?" There is none! Ah! it was a terrible moment when he tasted the wormwood and the gall; and surely darker still was that sad mid-day-midnight, when the sun hid his face in darkness, while Jesus cried "My God, my God, why hast thou forsaken me?" Believer, thou wilt never see that sick face; thou wilt never see that wan, wan forehead; thou wilt never see that poor scarred brow; thou wilt never see those tearful eyes; thou wilt never see that pale emaciated body; thou wilt never see that weary, weary heart! thou wilt never see that exceedingly sorrowful spirit; for the Father never turns his face away now. But what wilt thou see? Thou wilt see thy Lord lit up with his Father's light as well as with his own; thou wilt see him caressed by his beloved Parent; thou wilt see him sitting at his Father's right hand, glorified and exalted for ever. *"We shall see him as he is."*

Perhaps I have not shown clearly enough the difference between the two visions—the sight of what he was and what he is. Allow me then, a moment more, and I will try and make it clearer still. When we see Christ as he was, how *astonished* we are! One of the first feelings we should have, if we could have gone to the Mount of Olives and seen our Saviour sweating there, would have been, astonishment. When we were told that it was the Son of God in agonies, we should have lifted up our hands, and there would have been no speech in us at the thought. But then, beloved, here is the difference. The believer will be as much astonished when he sees Jesus' glories as he sits on his throne, as he would have been to have seen him in his earthly sufferings. The one would have been astonishment, and horror would have succeeded it; but when we see Jesus as he is, it will be *astonishment without horror*. We shall not for one moment feel terrified at the sight, but rather

> "Our joys shall run eternal rounds,
> Beyond the limits of the skies.
> And earth's remotest bounds."

If we could see Jesus as he was, we should see him with *great awe*. If we had seen him walking on the water, what awe should we have felt! If we had seen him raising the dead, we should have thought him a most majestic Being. So we shall feel awe when we see Christ on his throne; but the first kind of awe is awe compounded with fear, for when they saw Jesus walking on the water they cried out and were afraid; but when we shall see Christ as he is, we shall say,

> "Majestic sweetness sits enthroned
> Upon his awful brow."

There will be no fear with the awe—but it will be *awe without fear*. We shall not bow before him with trembling, but it will be with joy; we shall not shake at his presence, but rejoice with joy unspeakable.

Futhermore, if we had seen Christ as he was, we should have had great *love* for him; but that love would have been compounded with *pity*. We should stand over him, and say,

> "Alas! and did my Saviour bleed,
> And did my Sovereign die?
> Would he devote that sacred head
> For such a worm as I?"

We shall love him quite as much when we see him in heaven, and more too, but it will be *love without pity;* we shall not say "Alas!" but we shall shout—

> "All hail, the power of Jesus' name;
> Let angels prostrate fall:
> Bring forth the royal diadem,
> And crown him Lord of all."

Once again. If we had seen Jesus Christ as he was here below, there would have been *joy* to think that he came *to save us;* but we should have had *sorrow* mingled with it to think that we *needed saving.* Our sins would make us grieve that he should die; and "alas!" would burst from us even with a song of joy. But when we see him, there it will be *joy without sorrow;* sin and sorrow itself will have gone; ours will be a pure, unmingled, unadulterated joy.

Yet more. If we had seen our Saviour as he was, it would have been a *triumph* to see how he conquered, but still there would have been *suspense* about it. We should have feared lest he might not overcome. But when we see him up there it will be *triumph without suspense.* Sheathe the sword; the battle's won. 'Tis over now. "'Tis finished," has been said. The grave has been past; the gates have been opened; and now, henceforth, and for ever, he sitteth down at his Father's right hand, from whence also he shall come to judge the quick and the dead.

Here, then, is the difference. "We shall see him as he is."
We shall feel astonishment without horror, awe without
fear, love without pity, joy without sorrow, triumph without
suspense. That is the glorious position. Poor words, why fail
ye? Poor lips, why speak ye not much better? If ye could, ye
would; for these are glorious things ye speak of. "WE SHALL
SEE HIM AS HE IS."

II. Now secondly, we have PERSONAL IDENTITY. Perhaps
while I have been speaking, some have said, "Ah! but I want
to see *the* Saviour, the Saviour of Calvary, the Saviour of
Judea, the very one that died for me. I do not so much pant
to see the glorious Saviour you have spoken of; I want to see
that very Saviour who did the works of love, the suffering
Saviour; for him I love." Beloved, you shall see him. It is the
same one. There is personal identity. "We shall see him."
"Our eyes shall see him and not another." "We shall see HIM
as he is." It is a charming thought that we shall see the very,
very Christ; and the poet sung well, who said—

> "Oh! how the thought that I shall know
> The man that suffered here below,
> To manifest his favour,
> For me, and those whom most I love,
> Or here, or with himself above,
> Does my delighted passion move,
> At that sweet word "for ever."
> For ever to behold him shine,
> For evermore to call him mine,
> And see him still before me.
> For ever on his face to gaze,
> And meet his full assembled rays,
> While all the Father he displays,
> To all the saints for ever."

That is what we want—to see the same Saviour. Ay, it will
be the same Lord we shall see in heaven. Our eyes shall see
him and not another. We shall be sure it is he; for when we
enter heaven we shall know him by his *manhood and
Godhead.* We shall find him a man, even as much as he was
on earth. We shall find him man and God too, and we shall
be quite sure there never was another Man-God; we never
read or dreamed of another. Don't suppose that when you
get to heaven you will have to ask "Where is the man Christ

Jesus?" You will see him straight before you on his throne, a man like yourselves.

> "Bright *like a man* the Saviour sits;
> The God, how bright he shines."

But then you will know Christ by his *wounds*. Have you never heard of mothers having recognized their children years after they were lost by the marks and wounds upon their bodies? Ah! beloved, if we ever see our Saviour we shall know him by his wounds. "But," you say, "They are all gone." Oh no; for he

> "Looks like a Lamb that once was slain,
> And wears his priesthood still."

The hands are still pierced, though the nails are not there; the feet have still the openings through them; and the side is still gaping wide; and we shall know him by his wounds. We have heard of some who on the battle-field have been seeking for the dead; they have turned their faces up and looked at them, but knew them not. But the tender wife has come, and there was some deep wound, some sabre cut that her husband had received upon his breast, and she said "It is he; I know him by that wound." So in heaven we shall in a moment detect our Saviour by his wounds, and shall say "It is he; it is he—he who once said, 'They have pierced my hands and my feet.'"

But then, beloved, Christ and we are not strangers; for we have often seen him in this glass of the Word. When by the Holy Spirit our poor eyes have been anointed with eye-salve, we have sometimes caught a sufficient glimpse of Christ to know him by it. We have never seen him except reflectedly. When we have looked on the Bible, he has been above us and looked down upon it; and we have looked there as into a looking glass, and have seen him "as in a glass darkly." But we have seen enough of him to know him. And oh, methinks when I see him, I shall say, "That is the bridegroom I read of in Solomon's Song; I am sure it is the same Lord that David used to sing of. I know that is Jesus, for he looks even now like that Jesus who said to the poor woman, 'Neither do I condemn thee,'—like that blessed Jesus who said *'Talitha Cumi,'*—'Maid, I say unto thee, arise.'" We shall know him, because he will be so much like the Bible Jesus, that we shall recognize him at once.

Yet more, we have known him better than by Scripture
sometimes—by close and intimate *fellowship* with him. Why,
we meet Jesus in the dark sometimes; but we have sweet
conversation with him, and he puts his lips against our ear,
and our lip goes so close to his ear, when we hold converse
with him. Oh! we shall know him well enough when we see
him. You may trust the believer for knowing his Master
when he finds him. We shall not need to have Jesus Christ
introduced to us when we go to heaven; for if he were off his
throne and sitting down with all the rest of the blessed
spirits, we should go up to him directly, and say—"Jesus, I
know thee." The devil knew him, for he said, "Jesus I know;"
and I am sure God's people ought to know him. "Jesus, I
know thee," we shall say at once, as we go up to him. "How
dost thou know me?" saith Jesus. "Why sweet Jesus, we are
no strangers, thou hast manifested thyself to me as thou
dost not unto the world; thou hast given me sometimes such
tokens of thy gracious affection; dost thou think I have
forgotten thee? Why, I have seen thy hands and thy feet
sometimes by faith, and I have put my hand into thy side,
like Thomas, of old; and thinkest thou that I am a stranger
to thee? No, blessed Jesus; if thou wert to put thine hand
before thine eyes, and hide thy countenance I should know
thee then. Wert thou blindfolded once more, mine eyes
would tell thee, for I have known thee too long to doubt thy
personality." Believer, take this thought with thee: "we shall
see *him*," despite all the changes in his position. It will be
the same person. We shall see the same hands that were
pierced, the same feet that were weary, the same lips that
preached, the same eyes that wept, the same heart that
heaved with agony; positively the same, except as to his
condition. "We shall see *him*." Write the word HIM as large as
you like. "We shall see *him* as he is."

III. This brings us to the third point—THE POSITIVE
NATURE OF THE VISION. "We *shall see* him as he is." This is
not the land of sight; it is too dark a country to see *him,* and
our eyes are not good enough. We walk here by faith, and not
by sight. It is pleasant to believe his grace, but we had
rather see it. Well, "We *shall see* him." But perhaps you
think, when it says, "We shall see him," that it means, we
shall know more about him; we shall think more of him; we

shall get better views of him by faith. Oh, no, it does not at all. It means what it says—positive sight. Just as plainly as I can see my brother there, just as plainly as I can see any one of you, shall I see Christ—with these very eyes too. With these very eyes that look on you shall I look on the Saviour. It is not a fancy that we shall see him. Do not begin cutting these words to pieces. Do you see that gas lamp? You will see the Saviour in the same fashion—naturally, positively, really, actually. You will not see him dreamily, you will not see him in the poetical sense of the word—see, you will not see him in the metaphorical meaning of the word; but positively, you shall "see him as he is." "See him:" mark that. Not think about him, and dream about him; but we shall positively "see him as he is." How different that sight of him will be from that which we have here. For here we see him *by reflection.* Now, I have told you before, we see Christ "through a glass darkly:" then we shall see him face to face. Good Doctor John Owen, in one of his books, explains this passage, "Here we see through a glass darkly;" and he says that means, "Here we look through a telescope, and we see Christ only darkly through it." But the good man had forgotten that telescopes were not invented till hundreds of years after Paul wrote; so that Paul could not have intended telescopes. Others have tried to give other meanings to the word. The fact is, glass was never used to see through at that time. They used glass to see *by,* but not to see *through.* The only glass they had for seeing was a glass mirror. They had some glass which was no brighter than our black common bottle glass. "Here we see through a glass darkly." That means, by means of a mirror. As I have told you, Jesus is represented in the Bible; there is his portrait; we look on the Bible, and we see it. We see him "through a glass darkly." Just as sometimes, when you are looking in your looking glass, you see somebody going along in the street. You do not see the person; you only see him reflected. Now, we see Christ reflected; but then we shall not see him in the looking-glass; we shall positively see his person. Not the reflected Christ, not Christ in the sanctuary, not the mere Christ shining out of the Bible, not Christ reflected from the sacred pulpit; but "we shall see him as he is."

Again: *how partially we see Christ here.* The best believer only gets half a glimpse of Christ. While here one Christian sees Christ's glorious head, and he delights much in the hope of his coming; another beholds his wounds, and he always preaches the atonement: another looks into his heart, and he glories most in immutability and the doctrine of election; another only looks at Christ's manhood, and he speaks much concerning the sympathy of Christ with believers; another thinks more of his Godhead, and you will always hear him asserting the divinity of Christ. I do not think there is a believer who has seen the whole of Christ. No. We preach as much as we can do of the Master; but we cannot paint him wholly. Some of the best paintings, you know, only just give the head and shoulders; they do not give the full-length portrait. There is no believer, there is no choice divine, that could paint a full-length portrait of Christ. There are some of you who could not paint much more than his little finger; and mark, if we can paint the little finger of Jesus well, it will be worth a life-time to be able to do that. Those who paint best cannot paint even his face fully. Ah! he is so glorious and wondrous, that we cannot fully portray him. We have not seen him more than partially. Come, beloved; how much dost thou know of Christ? Thou wilt say, "Ah! I know some little of him; I could join with the spouse, when she declares that he is altogether lovely; but I have not surveyed him from head to foot, and on his wondrous glories I cannot fully dwell." Here we see Christ partially; there we shall see Christ entirely, when "we shall see him as he is."

Here, too, *how dimly we see Christ!* It is through many shadows that we now behold our Master. Dim enough is the vision here; but there "we shall see him as he is." Have you never stood upon the hill-tops, when the mist has played on the valley? You have looked down to see the city and the streamlet below; you could just ken yonder steeple, and mark that pinnacle; you could see that dome in the distance; but they were all so swathed in the mist that you could scarcely discern them. Suddenly the wind has blown away the mist from under you, and you have seen the fair, fair valley. Ah! it is so when the believer enters heaven. Here he stands and looks upon Christ veiled in a mist—upon a Jesus who is shrouded; but when he gets up there, on Pisgah's brow, higher still, with his Jesus, then he shall not see him dimly, but he shall see him brightly. We shall see Jesus then "without a veil between"—not dimly, but face to face.

Here, too, *how distantly we see Christ!* Almost as far off as
the farthest star! We see him, but not nigh; we behold him,
but not near to us; we catch some glimpse of him; but oh!
what lengths and distances lie between! What hills of guilt—
a heavy load! But then we shall see him closely; we shall see
him face to face; as a man talketh with his friend, even so
shall we then talk with Jesus. Now we are distant from him;
then we shall be near to him. Away in the highlands, where
Jesus dwells, there shall our hearts be too, when heart and
body shall be "present with the Lord."

And oh! *how transitory is our view of Jesus!* It is only a
little while we get a glimpse of Christ, and then he seems to
depart from us. Our chariots have sometimes been like
Amminadib's; but in a little while the wheels are all gone,
and we have lost the blessed Lord. Have you not some hours
in your life felt so to be in the presence of Christ, that you
scarcely knew where you were? Talk of Elijah's chariots and
horses of fire; you were on fire yourself; you could have made
yourself into a horse and chariot of fire, and gone to heaven
easily enough. But then, all of a sudden, did you never feel
as if a lump of ice had fallen on your heart, and put the fire
out, and you have cried, "Where is my beloved gone? Why
hath he hidden his face? Oh! how dark! how dim!" But,
Christians, there will be no hidings of faces in heaven!
Blessed Lord Jesus! there will be no coverings of thine eyes
in glory; Is not thine heart a sea of love, where all my
passions roll? And there is no ebb-tide of thy sea, sweet
Jesus, there. Art thou not everything? There will be no
losing thee there—no putting thy hand before thine eyes up
there; but without a single alteration, without change or
diminution, our unwearied, unclouded eyes, shall
throughout eternity perpetually behold thee. "We shall see
him as he is!" Blest sight! Oh! that it were come!

Then do you know, there will be another difference. When
"we shall see him as he is;" how much better that sight will
be than what we have here! When we see Christ here, we see
him to our profit; when we see him there, we shall see him *to
our perfection.* I bear my Master witness, I never saw him
yet, without being profited by him. There are many men in
this world whom we see very often, and get very little good
by, and the less we see of them the better; but of our Jesus
we can say, we never come near him without receiving good

by him. I never touched his garments yet, without feeling that my fingers did smell of myrrh, and aloes, and cassia out of the ivory palaces. I never did come near his lips, but what his very breath shed perfume on me. I was never near my Master yet, but what he slew some sin for me. I never have approached him, but his blessed eyes burned a lust out of my heart for me. I have never come near to hear him speak, but I felt I was melting when the Beloved spoke; being conformed into his image. But, then beloved, it will not be to improve us, it will be to perfect us, when we see him there. "We shall be like him; for we shall see him as he is." Oh! that first sweet look on Christ, when we shall have left the body! I am clothed in rags: he looks upon me, and I am clothed in robes of light. I am black; he looks upon me, and I forget the tents of Kedar, and become white as the curtains of Solomon. I am defiled; sin has looked upon me, and there is filth upon my garments: lo, I am whiter than the driven snow, for he hath looked upon me. I have evil wishes and evil thoughts, but they have fled like the demon before his face, when he said, "Get thee hence, Satan; I command thee to come out of the man." "We shall be like him; for we shall see him as he is." I know, beloved, the Saviour seems to you like a great ship, and I like some small boat, trying to pull the ship out of the harbour. It is how I feel myself. I have the oars, I am trying to pull; but it is such a glorious big ship, that I cannot pull it out. There are some subjects the rudder of which I can take hold of and guide anywhere; they will come out of any harbour, let the passage be ever so narrow; but this is a noble ship—so big that we can hardly get it out to sea. It needs the Holy Ghost to blow the sails for you, and your whole souls to dwell upon it, and desire to think of this wondrous sight; and then I hope you will go away dissatisfied with the preacher, because you will feel that the subject had altogether mastered him and you also.

IV. Lastly, here are THE ACTUAL PERSONS: "*We* shall see him as he is." Come, now, beloved! I do not like dividing you; it seems hard work that you and I should be split asunder, when I am sure we love each other with all our hearts. Ten thousand deeds of kindness received from you, ten thousand acts of heart-felt love and sympathy, knit my heart to my people. But oh! beloved, is it not obvious, that when we say, "*we* shall see him," that word "we" does not signify all of us—does not include everybody here! *"We* shall see him as he is!" Come, let us divide that "we" into "I's." How many "I's" are there here, that will "see him as he is?"

Brother, with snow upon thy head, wilt thou "see him as he is?" Thou hast had many years of fighting, and trying, and trouble: if thou ever dost "see him as he is," that will pay for all. "Yes," sayest thou, "I know in whom I have believed." Well, brother, thine old dim eyes will need no spectacles soon. To "see him as he is," will give thee back thy youth's bright beaming eye, with all its lustre and its fire. But are thy grey hairs full of sin? and doth lust tarry in thy old cold blood? Ah! thou shalt see him, but not nigh; thou shalt be driven from his presence. Would God this arm were strong enough to drag thee to a Saviour; but it is not. I leave thee in his hands. God save thee!

And thou, dear brother, and thou, dear sister, who hast come to middle age, struggling with the toils of life, mixed up with all its battles, enduring its ills, thou art asking, it may be, shalt thou see him! The text says, *"We* shall;" and can you and I put our hands on our hearts and know our union with Jesus? If so, *"We* shall see him as he is." Brother! fight on! Up at the devil! Strike hard at him! Fear not! that sight of Christ will pay thee. Soldier of the cross, whet thy sword again, and let it cut deep. Labourer! toil again; delve deeper; lift the axe higher, with a brawnier and stouter arm; for the sight of thy Master at last will please thee well. Up, warrior! Up the rampart, for victory sits smiling on the top, and thou shalt meet thy Captain there! When thy sword is reeking with the blood of thy sins, it will be a glory indeed to meet thy master, when thou art clothed with triumph, and then to "see him as he is."

Young man, my brother in age, the text says, *"We* shall see him as he is." Does "we" mean that young man there in the aisle? Does it mean you, my brother, up there? Shall *we* "see him as he is?" We are not ashamed to call each other brethren in this house of prayer. Young man, you have got a mother and her soul dotes upon you. Could your mother come to you this morning, she might take hold of your arm, and say to you, "John, we shall 'see him as he is;' it is not I, John, that shall see him for myself alone, but you and I shall see him together, *'we* shall see him as he is.'" Oh! bitter, bitter thought that just now crossed my soul! O heavens! if

we ever should be sundered from those we love so dearly
when the last day of account shall come! Oh! if we should not
see him as he is! Methinks to a son's soul there can be
nought more harrowing than the thought, that it possibly
may happen that some of his mother's children shall see
God, and he shall not! I had a letter just now from a person
who thanks God that he read the Sermon, "Many shall come
from the east and from the west;" and he hopes it has
brought him to God. He says, "I am one out of a large family,
and all of them love God except myself; I don't know that I
should have thought of it, but I took up this sermon of yours,
and it has brought me to a Saviour." Oh! beloved, think of
bringing the last out of nine to a Saviour! Have not I made a
mother's heart leap for joy? But oh! if that young man had
been lost out of the nine, and had seen his eight brothers and
sisters in heaven, while he himself was cast out, methinks
he would have had nine hells—he would be nine times more
miserable in hell, as he saw each of them, and his mother
and his father, too, accepted, and himself cast out. It would
not have been "we" there with the whole family.

What a pleasant thought it is, that we can assemble
to-day, some of us, and can put our hands round those we
love, and stand, an unbroken family—father, mother, sister,
brother, and all else who are dear, and can say by humble
faith, *"We* shall see him as he is"—all of us, not one left out!
Oh! my friends, we feel like a family at Park Street. I do feel
myself, when I am away from you, that there is nothing like
this place, that there is nothing on earth which can
recompense the pain of absence from this hallowed spot.
Somehow or other, we feel knit together by such ties of love!
Last Sabbath I went into a place where the minister gave us
the vilest stuff that ever was brewed. I am sure I wished I
was back here, that I might preach a little godliness, or else
hear it. Poor Wesleyan thing! He preached works from
beginning to end, from that very beautiful text—"They that
sow in tears shall reap in joy!" telling us that whatever we
sowed, that we should reap, without ever mentioning
salvation for sinners, and pardon required even by saints. It
was something like this: "Be good men and women, and you
shall have heaven for it; whatsoever you sow you are sure to
reap; and if you are very good people, and do the best you
can, you will all go to heaven, but if you are very bad and

wicked, then you will have to go to hell; I am sorry to tell you
so, but whatever you sow that shall you reap." Not a morsel
about Jesus Christ, from beginning to end; not a scrap.
"Well," I thought, "they say I'm rather hard on these
Arminian fellows; but if I do not drive my old sword into
them worse than ever, now I have heard them myself again,
then I am not a living man!" I thought they might have
altered a little, and not preach works so much; but I am sure
there never was a sermon more full of salvation by works
preached by the Pope himself, than that was. They do
believe in salvation by works, whatever they may say, and
however they may deny it when you come to close quarters
with them; for they are so everlastingly telling you to be
good, and upright, and godly, and never directing you first to
look to the bleeding wounds of a dying Saviour; never telling
you about God's free grace, which has brought you out of
enormous sins; but always talking about that goodness,
goodness, goodness, which never will be found in the
creature.

Well, beloved, somehow or other, wherever we go, we seem
that we must come back here.

> "Here our best friends, our kindred dwell;
> Here God our Saviour reigns."

And the thought of losing one of you grieves me almost as
much as the thought of losing any of my relatives. How often
have we looked at one another with pleasure! How often
have we met together, to sing the same old songs to the same
old tunes! How often have we prayed together! And how
dearly we all of us love the sound of the word "Grace, grace,
grace!" And yet there are some of you that I know in my
heart, and you know yourselves, will not see him, unless you
have a change—unless you have a new heart and a right
spirit. Well, would you like to meet your pastor at the day of
judgment, and feel that you must be parted from him
because his warnings were unheeded and his invitation cast
to the wind? Thinkest thou, young man, that thou wouldst
like to meet me at the day of judgment, there to remember
what thou hast heard, and what thou hast disregarded? And
thinkest thou, that thou wouldst like to stand before thy
God, and to remember how the way of salvation was
preached to thee—"Believe on the Lord Jesus Christ, and be

baptized, and thou shalt be saved,"—and that thou didst disregard the message? That were sad indeed. But we leave the thought with you, and lest you should think that if you are not worthy you will not see him—if you are not good you will not see him—if you do not do such-and-such good things you will not see him—let me just tell you, whosoever, though he be the greatest sinner under heaven—whosoever, though his life be the most filthy and the most corrupt—whosoever he is, though he has up till now been the most abandoned and profligate—whosoever believeth in the Lord Jesus Christ shall have everlasting life; for God will blot out his sins, will give him righteousness through Jesus, accept him in the beloved, save him by his mercy, keep him by his grace, and at last present him spotless and faultless before his presence with exceeding great joy.

My dear friends, it is a sweet thought to close with now; that with a very large part of you I can say, *"We* shall see him as he is." For you know when we sit down at the Lord's table, we occupy the whole ground floor of this chapel, and I believe that half of us are people of God here, for I know that many members cannot get to the Lord's table in the evening. Brethren, we have one heart, one soul—"One Lord, one faith, one baptism." We may be sundered here below a little while; some may die before us, as our dear brother Mitchell has died; some may cross the stream before the time comes for us; but we shall meet again on the other side of the river."We shall see him as he is."

19

A Door Opened In Heaven

"After this I looked, and, behold, a door was opened in heaven..."
Revelation 4:1

How highly favoured was the apostle John! While his Master was on earth he was the favoured disciple, permitted to lean his head upon his bosom, as a token of the most familiar and loving intercourse. After our Lord had ascended, he had the same heart towards John, and, finding him alone amidst the wild rocks of Patmos, he visited him on the Lord's-day, and revealed himself to him in a most glorious manner. Brethren and sisters, if heaven should offer any one thing which we might choose, if ever the Lord should appear to us as he did to Solomon, and say, "Ask what thou wilt, and it shall be given thee," be it ours to make request that we may enjoy the closest possible fellowship with the Wellbeloved. If we might choose our portion among the sons of men, we could not select a happier, a holier, a more honourable lot, than to abide in hallowed fellowship with Jesus, even as did the beloved disciple. Remember John has not this privilege reserved unto himself. The innermost circle of fellowship is not for the seer of Patmos alone; there is room upon the bosom of Christ for other heads than his; the innermost heart of Jesus is large enough to hold more than one beloved. Despair not of gaining the choicest place! It is not easy to ascend into the hill of the Lord, and to stand in his holy place, but if thou be pure in heart, if thou be fervent in spirit, if thou be purged from earthly dross, and if thou surrender thyself as a chaste virgin unto Christ, thou mayest—even *thou* mayest yet attain unto his rare and choice privilege of abiding in Christ, and enjoying without ceasing, his love shed abroad in thy heart by the Holy Ghost.

Leaving John, however, to whom the door in heaven was so remarkably opened that his vision of the spiritual world excelled all others, we will content ourselves with gathering up the crumbs from his table while we muse upon one of the descriptions which fell from his pen. John says, "A door was opened in heaven," and I believe the first meaning of the statement is that he was permitted to gaze into the secret and mysterious spirit-land, and to behold things which have not at any other time been seen of mortal eyes. That, I think, to be the first meaning; yet, if we append another sense to it, we shall not be departing from the truth, even if we depart from the immediate connection of the text. We shall regard this door opened in heaven in three ways. First, there is *a door of intercourse* between God and man; secondly, and more closely the meaning of the text, *a door of observation* has been opened with regard to the glories of the saints; and thirdly, by-and-by, to each of us there will be *a door of entrance* opened, by which we shall enter in through the golden gate into the city.

I. First, then, a DOOR OF INTERCOURSE has been opened in heaven.

The angels fell. Far back in the ancient ages, Lucifer, the son of the morning, rebelled against his liege Lord, and led a multitude of subordinate spirits to revolt. These, having proved traitors, were expelled from heaven, hurled like lightning from the battlements of glory down into the depths of woe. For them no door was opened in heaven. Mysterious as is the fact, it is nevertheless clear that no mercy was shown to fallen angels. He who will have mercy upon whom he will have mercy, and will have compassion on whom he will have compassion, suffered those once bright and illustrious spirits who had revolted, to continue in their revolt without a proclamation of pardon to suggest repentance; he allowed them to continue in their revolt, delivered unto chains of darkness to be reserved unto judgment. Man also, soon after his creation, broke his Maker's law, placing himself thereby in the same position as the fallen angels. Man had no greater claim upon God's mercy than the devils! Nay, if anything, if claim could be, he had less, seeing the restoration of so insignificant a being was far less important than the rekindling of the stars of heaven, while his destruction would be far less loss than the overthrow of the angelic spirits. Yet the Lord in his sovereignty, for reasons that he knoweth, but which he hath not revealed to us, was pleased to look upon the sons of men with singular favour, determining that in them his grace should be revealed. The devils, as vessels of wrath, are reserved unto judgment; but the sons of men, as vessels of mercy, are prepared for glory. Against angels who kept not their first estate, heaven is straitly shut up; but for men, a door is opened in heaven. Herein is matchless grace, combined with absolute sovereignty, furnishing us with a display of election upon the largest scale, against the truth of which none can raise debate; for whatever objectors may affirm against the choice of some men and not of others, they cannot deny but that God hath chosen men rather than angels; neither can they explain any more than we can, the reason why the Saviour took not up angels, but took up the seed of Abraham. Beyond all question, it is to the praise of divine grace that we are able to declare that for the human race a door is opened in heaven.

A door of intercourse was virtually opened in the covenant of grace, when the sacred persons of the divine Trinity entered into solemn league and compact that the chosen should be redeemed, that an offering should be presented by which sin should be atoned for and God's broken law should be vindicated. In that covenant council chamber where the sacred Three combined to plan the salvation of the chosen, a door was virtually opened in heaven, and it was through that door that the saints who lived and died before the coming of Christ passed into their rest. It was this door which was at the head of the ladder which Jacob saw, through which the angels ascended and descended, keeping up communion between God and man. Blessed be God, the effect of the Saviour's blood reached backward as well as forward. Before it was shed, the anticipation of the blood-shedding availed with God for the salvation of his people.

But, dear brethren, the door was actually and evidently opened when our Lord Jesus came down to the sons of men to sojourn in their flesh. What, doth the Infinite veil himself in an infant's form? Doth the pure and holy God dwell here on earth amongst unholy men? Doth God speak through those lips of tenderness, and doth God's light beam through those eyes of love? It is even so. The Son of Mary was the Son of God, and he that suffered, he that bore our sicknesses, he upon whom our sins were laid, was no other than God over all. The Word which was God, and was in the beginning with God, was made flesh and tabernacled among us. Surely there was a door opened in heaven then, for if the Godhead comes into actual union with manhood, man and God are no more divided by bars and gates. It cannot be impossible that manhood should go up to God, seeing God has come down to man. If God condescendeth thus, it must be with a motive and a reason, and there is hope for poor humanity; there are stars in the darkness of our fallen state. Immanuel, God with us, the Virgin's child, the Son of the Highest, is he among us? Then a door is opened in heaven indeed. The angels knew this, for through the open door they came trooping forth with songs of joy and gladness, hailing the birth of the Prince of Peace; and doubtless the spirits of the just, as they peered through the opened lattice, were glad to behold the union of earth with heaven.

But the door, dear brethren, was not opened even then effectually and completely, for Christ, when he came into the world, had to stand, though in himself pure and holy, in the position of a sinner. "The Lord hath laid upon him the iniquity of us all." Now, where sin is, there is a shutting out from God, and Christ was officially, as our substitute, shut out so long as sin laid upon him. When the transgression of his people was laid on him, and he was numbered with the transgressors, the veil hung down before even him. But oh, remember well how bravely he removed that which hindered! He came up to the cross with the load of sin upon him, a load that would have staggered all the angels, and bowed a universe of human beings to the lowest hell. Up to that cross he came, and there he bare the consequences of his people's guilt. The transgressions of his people were laid on him, and for those iniquities was he smitten; but he bore all the smiting, he drank the cup of wrath to the dregs, and shouting, "It is finished," he took the great veil that hung up between earth and heaven, and, with one gigantic pull, he rent it from the top to the bottom, never to be put together

again, to make an open way between God and man. The veil
is rent in twain, heaven is laid open to all believers.

But though our Lord himself, to prove how he had rent
that veil, passed through it up to the most holy place, as to
his soul, yet you will remember, beloved, that he left his
body behind him. That holy thing slumbered in the grave,
where it could not see corruption; it was not taken up into
the excellent glory, but remained here for forty days. Then,
when the appointed weeks were finished, Jesus once again
entered heaven; this time taking possession of it for our
bodies as well as for our souls. How wondrously David
foretold the glorious opening of the gates, when he sang the
ascent of the illustrious hero! He rose amid attending angels,
ascending not in phantom form, but in a real body, and, as
he neared the heavenly portals, holy angels sang, "Lift up
your heads, O ye gates, and be ye lift up, ye everlasting
doors, that the King of Glory may come in!" When on their
hinges of diamond, those pearly gates revolved, and Jesus
entered, then, once for all and for ever the door was opened
in heaven, by which the chosen people shall all of them
ascend into the joy of their Lord. At this very hour, as if to
show us that he openeth and no man shutteth, we see the
door most certainly open, because he has promised to come
again, and, therefore, the door cannot be shut, for he is
coming quickly. His promise ringeth in our ears, "Behold, I
come as a thief! Blessed is he that watcheth and keepeth his
garments;" yea, blessed are they which are called unto the
marriage-supper of the Lamb. Yet again saith he, "Behold, I
come quickly, and my reward is with me." Expect him then,
and as you expect him, learn that a door is still open in
heaven.

Beloved, there is no little comfort in the belief that
heaven's gates are opened, because then our prayers,
broken-winged as they are, shall enter there. Though they
seem as if they could not mount because of a clogging weight
of sorrow, yet shall they enter through that door. Our sighs
and tears shall pass. There is no boom across the harbour's
mouth; our poor half shipwrecked prayers shall sail into the
haven safely. The ports of the glory-land are not blockaded;
we have access by Jesus Christ unto the Father; and there is
free trade with heaven for poor broken-hearted sinners.
Here is consolation, because our songs also shall reach the

throne through the opened door. How delightful it is to sing
God's praise alone, but much more in company when all our
hearts and voices keep tune together in sacred melodies of
adoration! But what must our songs be compared with the
chorus of the ten thousand times ten thousand! We might
fear that ours would be unable to scale the walls of the New
Jerusalem, but, lo, a door is opened for their entrance.
Moreover, there is access for sinners to God; Jesus came to
seek and to save that which was lost. You are not shut out of
your Father's house, poor prodigal. The door is opened. You
have not to stand and knock by the month together with
processes of repentance and reformation. A door is opened.
Christ is that door. If you come to Christ you have come to
God; if you trust in Jesus you are saved. The door to the ark
was wide enough to admit the hugest beasts as well as the
tiniest animals, and the door into God's mercy is wide
enough to let in the greatest sinner as well as the more
refined moralist. He that cometh to Christ cometh to heaven;
he is sure of heaven who is sure of Christ. Let me cheer
every one here who fears that the gate is barred against him.
The door is still open. While there is life there is hope. Thou
canst not climb to heaven and see thy name left out in the
roll, therefore think not that it is left out. Thou canst not
turn to the list of souls who will perish for ever: believe not,
therefore, that thy name is among them, but rather, since
the silver trumpet rings out the invitation, "Come, labouring
and heavy laden, come to Christ, and he will give you rest!"
accept the invitation, and you shall find that the God who in
mercy gave it, gave you power to comply with it, and gave
you the will to accept it, will by no means cast you out.

II. Now we must turn to the second view of the text, which
is the one proper to it from its connection. "A door was
opened in heaven," it was A DOOR OF OBSERVATION.

It is very little that we can know of the future state, but we
may be quite sure that we know as much as is good for us.
We ought to be as content with that which is not revealed as
with that which is. If God wills us not to know, we ought to
be satisfied not to know. Depend on it, he has told us all
about heaven that is necessary to bring us there; and if he
had revealed more, it would have served rather for the
gratification of our curiosity than for the increase of our
grace. Yet, brethren, much concerning heaven, much I mean

comparatively, may be guessed by spiritual men. There are times when to all who love the Lord, doors are opened in heaven, through which they can by spiritual illumination, see somewhat of the city of the Great King.

And first, a door is opened in heaven whenever we are elevated by the help of God's Spirit to high and ravishing thoughts of the glory of God. Sometimes by investigating the works of nature, we obtain a glimpse of the infinite. More often by beholding the grace and mercy revealed in Jesus Christ, our hearts are warmed towards that blessed One who made us, who sustains us, who redeemed us, to whom we owe all things. My brethren, what joy have we felt in the thought of his presence! it has been bliss to feel that our Father is with us when we are alone, covering us with his feathers in danger, hiding us in peace beneath his shield and buckler in times of alarm. How delightful has it been to serve him, to have a consciousness of doing him some service, poor and imperfect as it is! I think I know of no delight on earth that is higher than that of knowing that you really are with all your heart adoringly serving God. And what a delight it is, dear brethren, when you can feel in your own soul that you are reconciled to God, that there is no opposition between your desires and God's will, or if there should be, yet not in your heart of hearts, for your soul desires to be perfectly at one with him who made it. How glad we feel when God is glorified, how happy when his saints are honouring his name! What a hallowed thrill shoots through us when another sinner is embraced within the arms of divine mercy! Oh, to see God's kingdom come, and his will done on earth as it is in heaven! brethren, if we might but see this, our prayers would be ended; there is nothing more that we could want if we could once see the whole earth filled with the knowledge of the Lord. This is our greatest joy beneath the sky, to know the Lord to be present, to feel that we are one with him, to catch some glimpses of his glory, and to see that glory appreciated amongst the sons of men, while we also are helping to spread it abroad. Now, if it be so happy a thing to obtain some gleamings of the glory, what will it be when we shall be near to him, and shall behold him face to face? What will be our joy when everything that now separates us from God shall be taken away; when inbred sin, that mars our fellowship, shall be utterly rooted up; when, instead of a little casual and imperfect service, we shall serve him day and night in his temple; when we shall no longer behold sin rampant, but shall see holiness universal all around; when there shall be no idle words to vex our ears, no cursing without, and no thought of sin within to molest us; when the hymn of his glory shall for ever make glad our ear, and our tongue shall joyously help to swell the strain world without end? Why, brethren, we have true views of heaven when our soul is blessed with nearness of access to her Father and her God. The unspiritual know not this. If I talked to them of harps, and streets of gold, and palms of victory, they might admire the imagery, but of the inner meaning they would know nothing; yet these are your harps, and these your palms, and these your songs, and these your white robes—the beholding of the glory of the Lord, and being transformed into it. To be made like unto your God in purity and true holiness, this is heaven indeed.

A door is opened in heaven, secondly, whenever the meditative spirit is able to perceive *Christ Jesus* with some degree of clearness. It is true we here see him as in a glass, darkly; but that sight, dark as it is and dim, is transporting to our souls. Do you not know what it is to sit under his shadow with great delight, and to find his fruit sweet unto your taste? The first day you knew Christ, and he spake your pardon to you, why, it was a marriage-day to your soul.

Since that he has opened to you coffers containing priceless treasures: he has taken you into the inner rooms of his treasury, where the richest and best blessings are stored up; and thus your sense of Christ's excellence has been a growing one. You thought him good at first, but now you know him to be better than the best. Now he is "the chief among ten thousand, and the altogether lovely." I am sure, beloved, nothing can so carry you out of yourself above your cares and your present troubles, as to feel that your Beloved is yours, and that you are his. Why, your spirit, like David, dances before the ark of the Lord, when the full beauties of a precious Christ are perceived by your heart. Imagine, then, what must it be to see the Redeemer face to face! To hear but the King's silver trumpets sounding in the distance, doth make the heart to dance, but what must it be to see the King in his beauty in the streets of his own metropolis, where he rideth forth in constant triumph? Have you not known the day when a word from him would have made your spirits like the chariots of Amminadib? what will be your ecstacy when you hear not a few words, but listen continually to him whose lips are like lilies dropping sweet-smelling myrrh! A stray kiss of those lips has ravished you beyond description, but what will it be when those cheeks that are as beds of spices, as sweet flowers, shall for ever be near you, when the full marriage of your soul with the royal spouse shall be come indeed, to your ineffable delight! Perhaps this is a door through which you have often gazed, if so, take not away your eyes, man; take not away your eyes, but through this window of agate, through this gate of carbuncle, gaze ever at the person of your blessed Lord, for in him you may see heaven fully revealed.

We sometimes get a door opened in heaven when we enjoy *the work of the Holy Spirit* in our souls. The Holy Spirit has breathed over our hearts, and turned tumult and storm into peace profound, like the peace of God's own self. He has given us more than quiet resting, he has filled us with high and exulting thoughts of God, until whether we were in the body or out of the body we could not tell; and then there has come with these great thoughts a flush of joy, as though a well of honey had sprung up at our feet, as though soft breezes from the celestial beds of spices were fanning our cheek. We knew that we were one with Christ by indissoluble, vital union; we grasped the promise, we knew it to be true; we were sure that all covenant blessings were our own; the spirit of sonship was within us; we cried, "Abba, Father!" Faith rejoiced exceedingly, bright-eyed hope laughed for joy, love tuned her harp; the Holy Ghost made a paradise within our hearts, and he himself walked in the garden of our soul in the cool of the day. Right well do some of us know what the Holy Ghost can do for us. We have felt his joy not only in prosperous moments, but in our very darkest times, when our troubles have been multiplied and griefs have threatened to overwhelm us. Now, if such it be to enjoy the presence of the Spirit, brethren, what must it be to dwell in the land where we shall never vex him with our sins, where we shall never quench his sacred influences with our negligences, where we shall never miss the delightful, sensible conscious enjoyment of his love shed abroad in our

souls? Ah, if we could always be as we sometimes are! I find
it comparatively easy to climb the hill top, but the difficulty
is to abide there. We slide down to the valley again so soon,
but in glory we shall for ever sit on the top of Amana, with
our forehead bathed in the light that streams from an
unsetting sun, filled with all the fulness of God, and that for
ever and ever. O you that know anything of the blessed
Spirit, there is a door opened in heaven for you in his
gracious operation, look through it and rejoice at what you
see.

Further, brethren, a door is often opened in heaven in *the
joys of Christian worship.* As I was reading over and over
again yesterday the forty-second psalm, I could not but note
how David dotes on the sunny memories of sacred seasons
when he went with the multitude with the voice of joy and
praise, with the multitude that kept holyday; he remembered the times when he went up to the house of the
Lord in the company of his people. Now, it is not always a
delightful thing to go to a place of worship, for some places
are very much used for sleeping in, and in some others it
might be better to be asleep than awake. Many services are
so dull, that men attend them as a stern duty, but they find
no pleasure in them; but where there is unity, harmony,
heartiness, zeal, where the song rolls up with mighty peals
like thunder, where the gospel is preached affectionately and
faithfully, and the Holy Ghost bedews the whole like the
dews that fell on Hermon, oh! it is sweet to be there. Do you
not feel sometimes your Sabbaths to be the most blessed
portions of your life below the skies? And the assemblies of
God's people, what are they to you? Are they not the house of
God and the very gate of heaven! Yes, but, if it be sweet
to-day to mingle now with Christians in their praise and
prayer, when we are so soon to separate and go our way, how
passing sweet that place must be where the saints meet in
eternal session of worship, where the King is always with
them, where there is never a dreary service, where the song
never, never, never ceases, where no discord mars it, and no
harp is hung upon the willows:

> "There no tongue can silent be,
> All shall join the harmony."

Why, if there were no other door in heaven than these

blessed Sabbath gatherings, and the sweet enjoyments of the assemblies of the saints, surely this would be enough to make us long to be there.

Another door is opened in heaven in *the fellowship which we enjoy with the saints on earth.* "They that feared the Lord spake often one to another," and thus they obtained one of the most delightful joys to be had this side the golden gate. Though we love all the saints, have we not some who are our peculiars, to whom we take the doors of our heart right off their hinges and say to them, "Come in, for in sympathy and experience I am one with you, come in and converse with me." Brethren, if common Christian communion be very sweet, and I know that as church members we have found it so, how much sweeter it will be to meet with the more eminent of the saints! What meetings heaven will see! I imagine Saul meeting Stephen. He aided the persecutors who stoned the martyred Stephen, and yet out of the ashes of a Stephen there springs a Paul! What a grip of the hand they will give each other on the other side of Jordan! When holy bright spirits meet, why, I would sooner far watch their salutations than the occultations of the moons of Jupiter; it will be grand to see these celestial bodies casting their shadows as it were for awhile athwart each other, as they come into the closest contact in the skies. And do not you delight to think that you shall meet the apostles, that you shall meet David and Abraham, that you shall have communion with Luther and Calvin, Wesley and Whitfield, and men of whom the world was not worthy? Some have doubted whether there will be recognition in heaven; there is no room for doubt, for it is called "my Father's house;" and shall not the family be known to each other? We are to "sit down with Abraham, and Isaac, and Jacob," and we shall therefore know these patriarchal saints; we shall not sit down with men in iron masks, and see none but great unknowns; but we shall "know even as we are known." Doubtless even before the body rises, there will be marks and peculiarities of constitution about disembodied spirits by which we shall be able to detect them, and shall hold felicitous intelligent intercourse with them. Ah! well, ye grey-headed saints, your best friends have gone before ye, and the thought of seeing them may well make you long to be on the wing. Your dearest ones are on the hither side of

Jordan, they went to their heritage a long while ago; they
abide in the land of the living, while you still linger in the
land of the dying. Press forward! set loose by earth. Let
immortal fingers beckon you towards the dwelling places of
the saints in the land of the hereafter. How the prospect of
future communion ought to make the saints love one
another, because ours is no earthly love which must end at
the grave; our union and communion in Christ will outlast
both sun and moon. Our love in Christ Jesus will rather
ripen in another world, than be dissolved like that of merely
carnal relationship; we need not be afraid of having too
much of it. How kindly affectionate we ought to be to one
another! we are to live together in heaven, never let us
quarrel on earth. I read a story the other day of an elder of a
Scotch kirk, who at the elder's meeting had angrily disputed
with his minister, until he almost broke his heart. The night
after, he had a dream which so impressed him, that his wife
said to him in the morning, "Ye look very sad, Jan; what is
the matter wi' ye?" "And well I am," said he, for I have
dreamed that I had hard words with our minister, and he
went home and died, and soon after I died too; and I
dreamed that I went up to heaven, and when I got to the
gate, out came the minister, and put out his hands to
welcome me, saying, "Come along, Jan, there's nae strife up
here, I'm so glad to see ye." So the elder went down to the
minister's house to beg his pardon, and found in very truth
that he was dead. He was so smitten by the blow, that within
two weeks he followed his pastor to the skies; and I should
not wonder but what his minister did meet him, and say,
"Come along, Jan, there's nae strife up here." Brethren, why
should there be strife below? Let us love each other, and by
the fact that we are co-heirs of that blessed inheritance, let
us dwell together as partakers of a common life, and soon to
be partakers of a common heaven.

Brethren, I think I may add, a door has often been opened
in heaven to us *at the communion-table.* Astronomers select
the best spots for observatories; they like elevated places
which are free from traffic, so that their instruments may
not quiver with the rumbling of wheels; they prefer also to
be away from the smoke of manufacturing towns, that they
may discern the orbs of heaven more clearly. Surely, if any
one place is fitter to be an observatory for a heaven-mind

than another, it is the table of communion.

> "I have been there, and still will go,
> 'Tis like a little heaven below."

Christ may hide himself from his people in preaching, as he did from his disciples on the road to Emmaus, but he made himself known unto them in breaking of bread. Prize much the solemn breaking of bread. That ordinance has been perverted, it has been travestied and profaned; and hence some tender Christians scarcely value it at its right account. To those who will use it rightly, examining themselves, and so coming to that table, it is, indeed, a divine observatory— a place of calm retirement from the world. The elements of bread and wine become the lenses of a far-seeing optic-glass, through which we behold the Saviour; and I say again, if there be one spot of earth clear from the smoke of care, it is the table where saints have fellowship with their Lord. A door is often opened in heaven at this banquet, when his banner over us is love; but if it be so sweet to enjoy the emblem, what must it be to live with Christ himself, and drink the wine new with him in the kingdom of our Father!

Another door that is opened in heaven is *the delights of knowledge.* It is a charming thing to know of earthly science, but it is more delightful far to know spiritual truth. The philosopher rejoices as he tracks some recondite law of nature to its source, and discovers callow principles of matter as they nestle beneath a long hidden mystery; but to hunt out a gospel truth, to track the real meaning of a text of Scripture, to get some fresh light upon one of the offices of the Redeemer, to see a precious type stand out with a fresh meaning, to get to know him and the power of his resurrection experimentally, to have the truth engraven upon the soul as though by the finger of God; oh! this is happiness. It is certainly one of the greatest delights of the Christian to sit at the feet of Jesus with Mary, and learn of him, to be educated in the college of Corpus Christi, and to find the *schola crucis* to be *schola lucis,* because of the light which streams from the cross. But, brethren, if the little knowledge we gain here be so sweet, what will our knowledge be when the intellect shall be expanded, when the mental eye shall be clarified, and when truth shall be perceived not through a veil of mist and cloud, but in full meridian light. If the dawn be bright, what will the midday be? If to-day our little travels in the domains of revelation have so enriched us, how rich shall we be when, like Columbus, we spread the sail for the unknown land, traversing seas of knowledge unnavigated before? What will it be, beloved, to make discoveries of the glory of Christ, and then to make known to the principalities and powers in the heavenly places, the manifold wisdom of God in the person of the Wellbeloved? There is a door opened in heaven to every thoughtful, studious reader of the word, and to every experienced Christian. If you are learning of Christ, the joy of knowledge gives you some idea of heaven.

Another door of heaven may be found in the *sweets of victory*. I mean not the world's victory, where there are garments rolled in blood, and wringing of hands, and wounds and death, but I refer to victory over sin, self, and Satan. How grand a thing to get a passion down and hold it by the throat, strangling it despite its struggles! It is fine work to hang up some old sin as an accursed thing before the Lord, just as they hung up the Canaanitish kings before the face of the sun; or if you cannot quite kill the lust, it is honourable work to roll a great stone at the cave's mouth, and shut in the wretches till the evening comes, when they shall meet their doom. It is a joyous thing when by God's grace under temptation you are kept from falling as you did on a former occasion, and so are made conquerors over a weakness which was your curse in past years. It is a noble thing to be made strong through the blood of the Lamb so as to overcome sin. The delights of holiness are as deep as they are pure. To be acquiring by divine grace spiritual strength, is no mean blessing. But what will it be to be in heaven, when every sin shall be conquered, when Satan himself shall be under our feet? Ah, if I once have him under my foot, how will I exult and rejoice over that old dragon who has tormented the saints of God these many years! Let us once but see sin and hell led captives, how will we sing hosanna to the Lord mighty in battle, and how will we exult and rejoice as we participate in his victory! It is coming; the victory is surely coming. We shall stand upon the mountain's brow with him and chant the lay of victory. At the battle of Dunbar, when Cromwell and his men fought up hill, and step by step achieved the victory, their watchword was the

Lord of hosts, and they marched to the battle singing—

> "O Lord our God, arise, and let
> Mine enemies scattered be,
> And let all them that do thee hate
> Before thy presence flee."

When they had won the day, the grand old leader, saint and soldier in one, bade his men halt and sing with him; and there they poured forth a psalm with such lusty music, that the old German Ocean might well have clapped its hands in chorus, "Sing unto the Lord, for he hath triumphed gloriously." But what a song will that be when we, the followers of Christ, having long fought up hill, wrestling against sin, shall at last see death and hell overcome, and with our Leader standing in our midst, shall raise the last great hallelujah to God and the Lamb, which hallelujah shall roll on for ever and ever. God grant us each to be there! Each little victory here helps us to see as through a door to the grand ultimate triumph, which may God hasten in his own time.

III. I might thus have continued, but time fails altogether; and therefore I must only add two or three sentences concerning THE DOOR OF ENTRANCE.

A door will soon be opened in heaven for each one of us who have believed in Christ Jesus. Christian, the message will soon come to thee, "The Master is come, and calleth for thee." Ready-to-Halt, the post will come to town for thee with the token, "The golden bowl is broken, and the silver cord is loosed." Father Honest must find it true that the daughters of music shall be brought low, and Valiant-for-Truth must learn that the pitcher is broken at the fountain. Gird up, then, your loins for the last time, and go down to the river with courage. It flows, as some say, cold and icy as death at the foot of the celestial hill; remember, however, it will be deeper or shallower to you according to your faith, and if your faith can keep from staggering, you shall pass through that stream dryshod, and in the river's midst you shall sing the loudest song of all your life. You shall then be nearer to heaven, and heaven shall flood your spirit and drown out death. Soon, I say, that door will open; surely you do not want to postpone the day. What is there amiss between you and your Husband that you wish to tarry away from him? What, do you love to be an exile from your own country? Do you love to be banished from the "city that hath foundations," of which you are a citizen? Surely, if your spirit be as it should be, you will say—

> "Like a bairn to its mither, a wee birdie to its nest,
> I would fain be ganging home to my Saviour's breast;
> For he gathers in his bosom witless, worthless lambs like me,
> And he carries them himself to his ain countrie."

Beloved, never try to forget your departure. Thoughts of mortality are incessant with me. But, alas! sometimes they are painful, and I chide myself that it ever should be painful to think of being where Jesus is. No, no, it is not that; it is that naughty doubt and fear that flits across my soul and darkens it; for it must be bliss to be with Jesus, and therefore it must be a secondary bliss to think of being where he is. It is greatly wise to talk with our last hours. It is well often to perform in meditation a rehearsal of the coronation scene, when the crown shall be on our head, and the palm in our hand, anticipate, I pray you, the glory which is surely yours if you are in Christ. But O make sure that you are in Christ. Get two grips of him! O hold him by a strong, but humble, confidence! Fling away all other hopes, they are vanity. Bind yourself to his dear cross, the one plank on which you can swim to glory. Never mariner was drowned on that:—

> "None but Jesus, none but Jesus,
> Can do helpless sinners good."

God bless you for the Redeemer's sake. Amen.

20

The Bliss Of The Glorified

"They shall hunger no more, neither thirst any more; neither shall the sun light on them, nor any heat."   **Revelation 7:16**

We cannot too often turn our thoughts heavenward, for *this is one of the great cures for worldliness.* The way to liberate our souls from the bonds that tie us to earth is to strengthen the cords that bind us to heaven. You will think less of this poor little globe when you think more of the world to come. This contemplation will also serve to *console us for the loss,* as we call it, *of those who have gone before.* It is their gain, and we will rejoice in it. We cannot have a richer source of consolation than this, that they who have fallen asleep in Christ have not perished; they have not lost life, but they have gained the fulness of it. They are rid of all that molests us here, and they enjoy more than we as yet can imagine. Cheer your hearts, ye mourners, by looking up to the gate of pearl, by looking up to those who day without night surround the throne of their Redeemer. It will also *tend to quicken our diligence* if we think much of heaven. Suppose I should miss it after all! What if I should not so run that I may obtain! If heaven be little, I shall be but a little loser by losing it; but if it be indeed such that the half could never be told us, then may God grant us diligence to make our calling and election sure, that we may be certain of entering into this rest, and may not be like the many who came out of Egypt, but who perished in the wilderness and never entered into the promised land. All things considered,

I know of no meditation that is likely to be more profitable
than a frequent consideration of the rest which remaineth
for the people of God. I ask, then, for a very short time that
your thoughts may go upward to the golden streets.

And, first, we shall think a little of *the blessedness of the
saints* as described in the simple words of our text; then we
will say a few words as to *how they came by that felicity;* and
thirdly, *draw some practical lessons from it.* First, then, we
have here:—

I. A DESCRIPTION OF THE BLESSEDNESS OF THE GLORIFIED.

We have not the full description of it here; but we have
here a description of certain *evils from which they are free.*
You notice they are of two or three kinds—first, *such as
originate within*—"They shall hunger no more, neither thirst
any more"—they are free from inward evils; secondly, *such
as originate without*—"Neither shall the sun light on them,
nor any heat." They are altogether delivered from the results
of outward circumstances. Take the first: "They shall hunger
no more, neither thirst any more." We are never so to strain
Scripture for a spiritual sense as to take away its natural
sense, and hence we will begin by saying this is no doubt to
be understood physically of the body they will have in glory.
Whether there will be a necessity for eating and drinking in
heaven, we will not say, for we are not told, but anyhow it is
met by the text, "The Lamb that is in the midst of the throne
shall feed them"—if they need food—"and lead them to living
fountains of water"—if they need to drink. Whatever may be
the necessities of the future, those necessities shall never
cause a pang. Here, the man who is hungry may have to ask
the question, "What shall I eat?"; the man who is thirsty may
have to say, "What shall I drink?"; and we have all to ask,
"Wherewithal shall we be clothed?" But such questions shall
never arise there. They are abundantly supplied. Children of
God have been hungry here: the great Son of God, the head
of the household was hungry before them; and they need not
wonder if they have fellowship with him in this suffering.
Children of God have had to thirst here: their great Lord and
Master said, "I thirst"; they need not wonder, therefore, if in
his affliction they have to take some share. Should not they
who are to be like their head in heaven be conformed unto
him on earth? But up yonder there is no poverty, and there
shall be no accident that shall place them in circumstances

of distress. "They shall hunger no more, neither thirst any more."

While we take this physically, there is no doubt that *it is to be understood mentally.* Our minds are also constantly the victims of hungerings and thirstings. There are on earth various kinds of this hunger and thirst—in a measure evil, in a measure also innocent. There are many men that in this world are *hungering after wealth,* and the mouth of avarice can never be filled. It is as insatiable as the horse-leech, and for ever cries, "Give, give!" But such hunger was never known in heaven, and never can be, for they are satisfied there; they have all things and abound. All their enlarged capacities can desire they already possess, in being near the throne of God and beholding his glory; there is no wealth which is denied them. Here, too, some of the sons of men hunger *after fame,* and oh! what have not men done to satisfy this? It is said that hunger breaks through stone walls; certainly ambition has done it. Death at the cannon's mouth has been a trifle, if a man might win the bubble reputation. But in heaven there is no such hunger as that. Those who once had it, and are saved, scorn ambition henceforth. And what room would there be for ambition in the skies? They take their crowns and cast them at their Saviour's feet. They have their palm-branches, for they have won the victory, but they ascribe the conquest to the Lamb, their triumph to his death. Their souls are satisfied with his fame. The renown of Christ has filled their spirit with everlasting contentment. They hunger no more, nor thirst any more, in that respect. And oh! what hunger and thirst there has been on earth by those of tender and large heart *for a fit object of love!* I mean not now the common thing called "love," but the friendship which is in man's heart, and sends out its tendrils wanting something to which to cling. We must—we are born and created for that very purpose— we must live together; we cannot develop ourselves alone. And oftentimes a lonely spirit has yearned for a brother's ear, into which to pour its sorrows; and doubtless many a man has been brought to destruction and been confined to the lunatic asylum whose reason might have been saved had there been some sympathetic spirit, some kind, gentle heart that would have helped to bear his burden. Oh! the hunger and the thirst of many a soul after a worthy object of confidence. But they hunger and they thirst, up there, no more. Their love is all centred on their Saviour. Their confidence, which they reposed in him on earth, is still in him. He is their bosom's Lord, their heart's Emperor, and they are satisfied, and, wrapped up in him, they hunger and they thirst no more.

And how many young spirits there are on earth that are *hungering after knowledge,* who would fain get the hammer and break the rock, and find out the history of the globe in the past. They would follow philosophy, if they could, to its source, and find out the root of the matter. Oh! to know, to know, to know! The human mind pants and thirsts for this. But there they know even as they are known. I do not know that in heaven they know all things—that must be for the Omniscient only—but they know all they need or really want to know; they are satisfied there. There will be no longer searching with a spirit that is ill at ease. They may, perhaps, make progress even there, and the scholar may become daily more and more wise; but there shall never be such a hungering and thirsting as to cause their mental faculties the slightest pang. They shall hunger no more, neither thirst any more. Oh! blessed land where the seething ocean of man's mind is hushed, and sleeps in everlasting calm! Oh! blessed country where the hungry spirit, that crieth every hour for bread, and yet for more, and yet for more, and spends its labour for that which satisfieth not, shall be fed with the bread of angels, and be satisfied with favour and full of the goodness of the Lord.

But, dear friends, surely the text also means *our spiritual hungering and thirsting.* "Blessed is the man that hungers and thirsts to-day after righteousness, for he shall be filled." This a kind of hunger that we ought to desire to have; this is a sort of thirst that the more you have of it will be the indication of the possession of more grace. On earth it is good for saints to hunger and to thirst spiritually, but up there they have done even with that blessed hunger and that blessed thirst. To-day, beloved, some of us are *hungering after holiness.* Oh! what would I not give to be holy, to be rid of sin, of every evil thing about me! My eyes—ah! adieu sweet light, if I might also say, "Adieu sin!" My mouth—ah! well would I be content to be dumb if I might preach by a perfect life on earth! There is no faculty I know of that might not be cheerfully surrendered if the surrender of it would deprive us of sin. But they never thirst for holiness in heaven, for this excellent reason, that they are without fault before the throne of God. Does it not make your mouth water? Why this is the luxury of heaven, to be perfect. Is not this—the heaven of heaven, to be clean rid of the root and branch of sin, and not a rag or bone, or piece of a bone of our old depravity left—all gone—like our Lord, made perfect without spot or wrinkle, or any such thing. And here, too, brethren and sisters, we very rightly hunger and thirst *after full assurance and confidence.* Many are hungering after it; they hope they are saved, and they thirst to be assured that they are. But there is no such thirst as that in heaven, for, having crossed the golden threshold of Paradise, no saint ever asks himself, "Am I saved?" They see his face without a cloud between; they bathe in the sea of his love; they cannot question that which they perpetually enjoy. So, too, on earth I hope we know what it is to hunger and thirst *for fellowship with Christ.* Oh! when he is gone from us—if he do but hide his face from us, how we cry, "My soul desires thee in the night"! We cannot be satisfied unless we have the love of God shed abroad in our hearts by the Holy Ghost. But in heaven they have no such thing. There the shepherd is always with the Sheep, the King is ever near them, and because of his perpetual presence their hungering and their thirsting will be banished for ever. Thus much upon those evils, then, that would arise from within. As they are perfect, whatever comes from within is a source of pleasure to them, and never of pain.

And now, dear friends, *the evils that come from without:* let us think of them. We no doubt can appreciate in some measure, though not to the degree which we should if we were in Palestine in the middle of summer—we can appreciate the words, "Neither shall the sun light on them, nor any heat." This signifies that nothing external shall injure the blessed. Take it literally. There shall be nothing in the surroundings of heavenly saints that shall cause glorified spirits any inconvenience. I think we may take it mainly in relation to the entire man glorified; and so let us say that on earth the sun lights on us and many heats in the form of affliction. What *heats of affliction* some here have passed through! Why there are some here who are seldom

free from physical pain. There are many of the best of God's
children that, if they get an hour without pain, are joyful
indeed. There are others that have had a great fight of
affliction. Through poverty they have fought hard. They
have been industrious, but somehow or other God has
marked them out for the scant tables and the thread-worn
garments. They are the children of poverty, and the furnace
heat is very hot about them. With others it has been
repeated deaths of those they have loved. Ah! how sad is the
widow's case! How deep the grief of the fatherless! How
great the sorrow of bereaved parents! Sometimes the arrows
of God fly one after the other; first one falls and then another
until we think we shall hardly have one left. These are the
heats of the furnace of affliction. And at other times these
take the form of ingratitude from children. I think we never
ought to repine so much about the death of a child as about
the ungodly life of a child. A dead cross is very heavy, but a
living cross is heavier far. Many a mother has had a son of
whom she might regret that he did not die even the very
hour of his birth, for he has lived to be the grief of his
parents, and a dishonour to their name. These are sharp
trials—these heats—but you shall have done with them
soon. "Neither shall the sun light on them, nor any heat." No
poverty, no sickness, no bereavement, no ingratitude—
nothing of the kind. They for ever rest from affliction. Heat
sometimes comes in another form—*in the matter of
temptation.* Oh! how some of God's people have been tried—
tried by their flesh! Their constitution, perhaps, has been
hot, impulsive, and they have been carried off their feet, or
would have been but for the interposing grace of God, many
and many a time. They have been tempted, too, in their
position, and they of their own household have been their
enemies. They have been tempted by their peculiar
circumstances; their feet have almost gone many a time. And
they have been tempted by the devil; and hard work it is to
stand against Satanic insinuations. It is hot, indeed, when
his fiery darts fly. Oh! when we shall have once crossed the
river, how some of us who have been much tempted will look
back upon that old dog of hell, and laugh him to scorn
because he will not be able even to bark at us again! Then we
shall be for ever free from him. He worries us now because
he would devour us, but there, as he cannot devour, so shall

he not even worry us. "Neither shall the sun" of temptation "light on them, nor any heat." Happy are the people that are in such a case. The *heats of persecution* have often, too, carried about the saints. It is the lot of God's people to be tried in this way. Through much tribulation of this sort they inherit the kingdom; but there are no Smithfields in heaven, and no Bonners to light up the faggots, no Inquisitions in heaven, no slanderers there to spoil the good man's name. They shall never have the heat of persecution to suffer again. And, once more, they shall not have *the heat of care.* I do not know that we need have it, even here; but there are a great many of God's people who allow care to get very hot about them. Even while sitting in this place to-night while the hymn was going up, "What must it be to be there!" the thoughts of some of you have been going away to your business, or your home. While we are trying to preach and draw your attention upwards, perhaps some housewife is thinking of something she has left out which ought to have been locked up before she came away, or wondering where she left the key. We make any excuses for care through the cares we continually invent, forgetting the words, "Cast all your care on him, for he careth for you." But they have no cares in heaven. "They hunger no more, neither thirst any more; neither shall the sun light on them, nor any heat." Ah! good man, there shall be no ships at sea by-and-bye—no harvests—to trouble you as to whether the good weather will last! Ah! good woman, you shall have no more children that are sickly to fret over, for there you will have all you desire, and be in a family circle that is unbroken, for all the brothers and sisters of God's family shall by-and-bye be there, and so you shall be eternally blest.

We have thus opened up as well as we could the words of the text on the felicity of the saints. Now, very briefly:—

II. HOW DO THEY COME TO BE HAPPY?

Well, it is quite clear that they did not come to it because they were very fortunate people on earth, for if you read another passage of the Word of God you will find, "These are they that came out of great tribulation." Those that have had trial and suffering on earth are amongst those that have the bliss of heaven. Encourage yourselves, you poor and suffering ones. It is quite certain they did not come there from their own merit, for we read, they have "washed their robes"—they wanted washing. They did not keep them always undefiled. There had been spots upon them. They came there not because they deserved to be there, but because of the rich grace of God. How did they come there then? Well, first, they came there *through the Lamb that was slain.* He bore the sun and the heat, and, therefore, the sun doth not light on them, nor any heat. The hot sun of Jehovah's justice shone full upon the Saviour—scorched, and burned, and consumed him with grief and anguish; and because the Saviour suffered, therefore we suffer it no more. All our hopes of heaven are found at the cross.

But they came there next *because the Saviour shed his blood.* They washed their robes in it. Faith linked them to the Saviour. The fountain would not have cleansed their robes if they had not washed in it. Oh! there shall be none come to heaven but such as have by faith embraced what God provides. Dear hearer, judge thyself whether thou art right, therefore. Hast thou washed thy robe and made it white in the Lamb's blood? Is Christ all in all to thee? If not, canst thou hope to be there? And they are there in perfect bliss, we are told. No sun lights on them, nor any heat, because the Lamb in the midst of the throne is with them. How could they be unhappy who see Christ? Is not this the secret of their bliss, that Jesus fully reveals himself to them?

And besides, *they have the love of God to enjoy,* for the last word of the chapter is, "God shall wipe away all tears from their eyes." The blood of Jesus applied, the presence of Jesus enjoyed, and the love of God fully revealed—these are the causes of the bliss of the saved in heaven. But we must close our meditation with the last point, which is:—

III. WHAT THIS TEACHES US.

First, the bliss of the saved in glory teaches us *to long for it.* It is legitimate to long for heaven—not to long to escape from doing our duty here. It is idleness to be always wanting to have done with this world—it is clear sloth—but to be longing to be where Jesus is, is only natural and gracious. Should not the child long to go home from the school? Should not the captive pine for liberty? Should not the traveller in foreign lands long to see his native country? Should not the bride, the married wife, when she has been long away from her husband, long to see his face? If you did not long for heaven, surely you might question whether heaven belonged to you. If you have ever tasted of the joys of the saints, as believers do on earth, you will sing with full soul:—

> "My thirsty spirit faints
> To reach the land I love,
> The bright inheritance of saints,
> Jerusalem above."

You may long for this.

And the next lesson is, *be patient until you get there.* As it will be such a blessed place when you arrive, don't trouble about the difficulties of the way. You know our hymn:—

> "The way may be rough, but it cannot be long."

So

> "Let us fill it with hope, and cheer it with song."

You know how well your horse goes when you turn its head homewards. Perhaps you had to flog him a bit before, but when he begins to know he is going down the long lane which leads home he will soon lift up his ears, and away, away he will go. We ought to have as much sense as horses. Our heads are turned towards heaven. We are steering towards that port—homeward bound. It may be rough weather but we shall soon be in the fair haven where not a wave of trouble shall ever disturb us again. Be patient, be patient. The husbandman has waited for the precious fruits of the earth; you can well wait for the precious things of heaven. You sow in tears, but you shall reap in joy. He has promised you a harvest. He who cannot lie has said the seed-time and harvest shall never cease. They do not cease below; depend upon it, they won't cease above. There is a harvest for you who have been sowing here below.

Our first lesson, then, is, long for this, and then be patient in waiting. But our next lesson is to be, wait your appointed time. And now the next instruction is, *make much of faith.* They entered heaven because they had washed their robes in blood. Make much of the blood and much of the faith by which you have washed. Dear hearers, have you all got faith? It is, as it were, the key of blessedness. "But all men have not faith," says the Apostle. Hast thou faith? Dost thou believe in Christ Jesus? In other words, dost thou trust thyself alone with him? Can you sing with our poet:—

"Nothing in my hand I bring,
Simply to thy cross I cling;
Naked, come to thee for dress,
Helpless, look to thee for grace.
Foul, I to the fountain fly,
Wash me, Saviour, or I die"?

Make much of the faith that will admit you to heaven.

Once more, our text teaches us this lesson—Do any of us want to know what heaven is on earth? Most of us will say, "Aye" to that. Well then, the text tells you *how to find heaven on earth.* You find it in the same way as they find it in heaven. First, be thou washed in the blood of Christ, and that will be a great help towards happiness on earth. It will give thee peace now, "the peace of God that passeth all understanding." Some people think that heaven on earth is to be found in the theatre, and in the ballroom, and in the giddy haunts of fashion. Well, it may be heaven to some, but if God has any love to you, it won't be heaven to you. Wash your robe, therefore, in the Saviour's blood, and there will be the beginning of heaven on earth.

Then next, it appears, if you read the connection of our text, that those who enjoy heaven serve God day and night in his temple. If you want heaven on earth, serve God continually day and night. Having washed your robe first, then put it on, and go out to serve God. Idle Christians are often unhappy Christians. I have met with many a spiritual dyspeptic always full of doubts and fears. Is there a young man here full of doubts and fears who has lost the light he once possessed, and the joy he once had? Dear brother, get to work. In cold weather the best way to be warm is not to get before a fire, but to work. Exercise gives a healthy glow, even amidst the frost. "I am doing something," says one. Yes, with one hand; use the other hand. "Perhaps I should have too many irons in the fire," says one. You cannot have too many. Put them all in, and blow the fire with all the bellows you can get. I do not believe any Christian man works too hard, and, as a rule, if those who kill themselves in Christ's service were buried in a cemetery by themselves, it would be a long while before it would get filled. Work hard for Christ. It makes happy those who are in heaven to serve God day and night, and it will make you happy on earth. Do all you can. Another way is to have fellowship with Christ here.

Read again this chapter. "He that sitteth on the throne shall dwell among them—he shall feed them." Oh! if you want to be happy, live near to Jesus. Poor men are not poor when Christ lives in their house. Truly, sick men have their beds made easy when Christ is there. Has he not said, "I will make his bed in all his sickness"? Only get fellowship with Jesus, and outward circumstances won't distress you. The sun will not light on you, nor any heat. You will be like the shepherd on Salisbury Plain, who said it was good weather, though it rained hard. "It is weather," said he, "that pleases me." "How so?" said a traveller to him. "Well, sir," he said, "it pleases God, and what pleases God pleases me." "Good day!" said one to a Christian man. "I never had a bad day since I was converted," said he. "They are all good now since Christ is my Saviour." Do you not see, then, that if your wishes are subdued, if you do not hunger any more, or thirst any more as you used to do, and if you always live near to Christ, you will begin to enjoy heaven on earth. Begin, then, the heavenly life here below. The Bible says, "For he hath raised us up, and made us sit together in heavenly places in Christ Jesus." The way to live on earth, according to many, is to live on earth, but to look upward to heaven. That is a good way of living, but I will tell you a better, and that is to live in heaven, and look down on earth. The Apostle had learned that when he said, "Our conversation is in heaven." It is good to be on earth, and look up to heaven; it is better for the mind to be in heaven, and to look down upon earth. May we learn that secret. The Lord lead us into it. Then when faith is strong, and love is ardent, and hope is bright, we shall sing, with Watts:—

"The men of grace have found
Glory begun below;
Celestial fruits on earthly ground
From faith and hope may grow."

The Lord grant you a participation in this bliss, beloved, and an abundant entrance into that bliss for ever, for Jesus Christ's sake. Amen.

21

"Let Not Your Heart Be Troubled"

"Let not your heart be troubled: ye believe in God, believe also in me. In my Father's house are many mansions: if it were not so, I would have told you. I go to prepare a place for you. And if I go and prepare a place for you, I will come again, and receive you unto myself; that where I am, there ye may be also. And whither I go ye know, and the way ye know."   John 14:1-4

We may well feel glad that God's people, whose lives are recorded in the Old and New Testaments, were men of like passions with ourselves. I have known many a poor sinner pluck up hope as he has observed the sins and struggles of those who were saved by grace, and I have known many of the heirs of heaven find consolation as they have observed how imperfect beings like themselves have prevailed with God in prayer, and have been delivered in their time of distress. I am very glad that the apostles were not perfect men; they would then have understood all that Jesus said at once, and we should have lost our Lord's instructive explanations; they would also have lived above all trouble of mind, and then the Master would not have said to them these golden words, "Let not your heart be troubled."

It is, however, most evident from our text that it is not according to our Lord's mind that any of his servants should be troubled in heart. He takes no delight in the doubt and disquietude of his people. When he saw that because of what he had said to them sorrow had filled the hearts of his apostles, he pleaded with them in great love, and besought them to be comforted. As when a mother comforteth her child, he cried, "Let not your heart he troubled." Jesus saith the same to you, my friend, if you are one of his downcast ones. He would not have you sad. "Comfort ye, comfort ye my people; speak ye comfortably to Jerusalem," is a command even of the old dispensation, and I am quite sure that under this clearer revelation the Lord would have his people free from heartbreak. Has not the Holy Ghost especially undertaken the work of comfort in order that it may be effectually done? Trials depress the hearts of God's children, for which the most tender ministry fails to afford consolation; and then it is most sweet for the failing comforter to remember the unfailing Comforter, and to commit the case of the sorrowful spirit into the divine hands. Seeing that one Person of the blessed Trinity has undertaken to be the Comforter, we see how important it is that our hearts should be filled with consolation. Happy religion in which it is our duty to be glad! Blessed gospel by which we are forbidden to be troubled in heart!

Is it not a thing greatly to be admired that the Lord Jesus should think so carefully of his friends at such a time? Great personal sorrows may well be an excuse if the griefs of others are somewhat overlooked. Jesus was going to his last bitter agony, and to death itself, and yet he overflowed with sympathy for his followers. Had it been you or I, we should have asked for sympathy for ourselves. Our cry would have been, "Have pity upon me, O my friends, for the hand of God hath touched me!" But, instead of that, our Lord cast his own crushing sorrows into the background, and bent his mind to the work of sustaining his chosen under their far inferior griefs. He knew that he was about to be "exceeding sorrowful, even unto death"; he knew that he should soon be in an agony through bearing "the chastisement of our peace;" but ere he plunged into the deep, he must needs dry the tears of those he loved so well, and therefore he said most touchingly, "Let not your heart be troubled."

While I admire this condescending tenderness of love, I at the same time cannot help adoring the marvellous confidence of our blessed Lord, who, though he knows that he is to be put to a shameful death, yet feels no fear, but bids his disciples trust implicitly to him. The black darkness of the awful midnight was beginning to surround him, yet how brave his word—"Believe also in me!" He knew in that threatening hour that he had come forth from the Father, and that he was in the Father and the Father in him; and so he says, "Ye believe in God, believe also in me." The calm bearing of their Master must have greatly tended to confirm his servants in their faith.

While we see here his confidence as man, we also feel that this is not a speech which a mere man would ever have uttered had he been a good man; for no mere creature would thus match himself with God. That Jesus is a good man few question; that he must be God is therefore proven by these words. Would Jesus bid us trust in an arm of flesh? Is it not written—"Cursed be the man that trusteth in man, and maketh flesh his arm"? Yet the Holy Jesus says, "Ye believe in God, believe also in me." This association of himself with God as the object of human confidence in the time of trouble, betokens a consciousness of his own divine power and Godhead; and it is a mystery in whose difficulties faith takes pleasure, to see in our Lord Jesus the faith of a man for himself, and the faithfulness of God for others.

Come then, dear friends, close up to the text, and may the Spirit of God be with us! I will read the text again very distinctly. Ask that you may feel the words even more powerfully than the apostles felt them; for they had not yet received the Comforter, and so they were not yet led into all truth; in this we excel them as they were that night: let us therefore hopefully pray that we may know the glory of our Lord's words, and hear them spoken into our very soul by the Holy Spirit. "Let not your heart be troubled: ye believe in God, believe also in me. In my Father's house are many mansions: if it were not so, I would have told you. I go to prepare a place for you. And if I go and prepare a place for you, I will come again, and receive you to myself; that where I am, there ye may be also. And whither I go ye know, and the way ye know."

These words are in themselves much better than any sermon. What can our discourse be but a dilution of the essential spirit of consolation which is contained in the words of the Lord Jesus? Now let us, first, *taste of the bitter waters of heart-trouble;* and, secondly, let us *drink deep of the sweet waters of divine consolation.*

I. First, then, LET US TASTE OF THE BITTER WATERS. "Because I have said these things unto you, sorrow hath filled your heart." I would not confine the comfort to any one form of affliction, for it is a balm for every wound; but still it

will be well to enquire what was the particular trouble of the
disciples? It may be that some of us are passing through it
now, or we may be plunged in it ere long.

It was this—*Jesus was to die:* their Lord, whom they
sincerely loved, was about to go from them by a shameful,
painful death. What tender heart could bear to think of that?
Yet he had told them that it would be so, and they began to
remember his former words wherein he had said that the
Son of man would be betrayed into the hands of wicked men,
and would be scourged and put to death. They were now to
pass through all the bitterness of seeing him accused,
condemned, and crucified. In a short time he was actually
seized, bound, carried to the high priest's house, hurried to
Pilate, then to Herod, back again to Pilate, stripped,
scourged, mocked, insulted. They saw him conducted
through the streets of Jerusalem bearing his cross. They
beheld him hanging on the tree between two thieves, and
heard him cry, "My God, my God, why hast thou forsaken
me?" A bitter draught this! In proportion as they loved their
Lord they must have deeply grieved for him: and they
needed that he should say, "Let not your heart be troubled."
To-day those who love the Lord Jesus have to behold a
spiritual repetition of his shameful treatment at the hands
of men; for even now he is crucified afresh by those who
account his cross a stumbling-block and the preaching of it
foolishness. Ah me! how is Christ still misunderstood,
misrepresented, despised, mocked, and rejected of men!
They cannot touch him really, for there he sits enthroned in
the heaven of heavens; but as far as they can, they slay him
over again. A malignant spirit is manifested to the gospel as
once it was to Christ in person. Some with coarse
blasphemies, and not a few with cunning assaults upon this
part of Scripture, and on that, are doing their best to bruise
the heel of the seed of the woman. It is a huge grief to see the
mass of mankind pass by the cross with averted eyes as if
the Saviour's death was nothing—nothing at least to them.
In proportion as you feel a zeal for the Crucified, and for his
saving truth, it is wormwood and gall to live in this age of
unbelief. Christ Jesus is nailed up between the two thieves
of superstition and unbelief, while around him gathers still
the fierce opposition of the rude and the polished, the
ignorant and the wise.

In addition to this, the apostles had for an outlook the expectation that *their Lord would be away from them.* They did not at first understand his saying, "A little while, and ye shall not see me: and again, a little while, and ye shall see me, because I go to the Father." Now it dawned upon them that they were to be left as sheep without a shepherd; for their Master and head was to be taken from them. This was to them a source of dread and dismay: for they said to themselves, "What shall we do without him? We are a little flock; how shall we be defended when he is gone, and the wolf is prowling? When the Scribes and Pharisees gather about us, how shall we answer them? As for our Lord's cause and kingdom, how can it be safe in such trembling hands as ours? Alas for the gospel of salvation when Jesus is not with us!" This was a bitter sorrow: and something of this kind of feeling often crosses our own hearts as we tremble for the ark of the Lord. My heart is sad when I see the state of religion among us. Oh for an hour of the Son of man in these darkening days! It is written, "There shall come in the last days scoffers"; and they have come, but, oh, that the Lord himself were here in person! Oh, that the Lord would pluck his right hand out of his bosom, and show us once again the wonders of Pentecost, to the confusion of his adversaries, and to the delight of all his friends. He has not come as yet! Well-nigh two thousand years have rolled away since he departed, and the night is dark, and there is no sign of dawn. The ship of the church is tossed with tempest, and Jesus is not come unto us. We know that he is with us in a spiritual sense; but, oh, that we had him in the glory of his power! Surely he knows our need and the urgency of the times; yet are we apt to cry, "It is time for thee, Lord, to work; for they make void thy law."

But they felt a third grief, and it was this: that *he was to be betrayed by one of themselves.* The twelve were chosen men, but one of them was a devil and sold his Lord. This pierced the hearts of the faithful—"the Son of man is betrayed." He is not taken by open seizure, but he is sold for thirty pieces of silver by one whom he entrusted with his little store. He that dipped with him in the dish had sold him for paltry gain. This cut them to the heart, even as it did the Master himself; for our Lord felt the treachery of his friend. Of this bitter water the faithful at this hour are made to drink: for

what see we at this day? What see we in various places but
persons that are reputed to be ministers of the gospel whose
main business seems to be to undermine our holy faith, and
batter down the truths which are commonly received in the
Christian church? Certain of them preach as if they were
ordained not of God, but of the devil; and anointed not by the
Holy Spirit, but by the spirit of infidelity. Under the banner
of "advanced thought," they make war upon those eternal
truths for which confessors contended and martyrs bled, and
by which the saints of past ages have been sustained in their
dying hours. It is not an enemy; then we could have borne
and answered it. If the outward and avowed infidel attacks
inspiration, let him do so. It is a free country, let him speak;
but when a man enters our pulpits, opens the sacred volume,
and denies that it is inspired, what does he there? How does
his conscience allow him to assume an office which he
perverts? To make him a shepherd who is a wolf; to make
him a dresser of the vineyard who, with his axe, cuts up the
very roots of the vines;—this is an incomprehensible folly on
the part of the churches. It is a dagger to every believing
heart that Judas should be represented in the Christian
church by so many of the professed ministers of Christ. They
betray their Master with a kiss.

Then there came another pang at the back of this; for one
of them, though true-hearted and loyal, would that night
deny his Lord. Peter, in many respects the leader of the little
company, had been warned that he would act the craven and
vehemently deny his Lord. This is bitterness indeed, of
which those that love the church of God are compelled full
often to drink, to see men whom we cannot but believe to be
the disciples of Jesus Christ carried away by temptation, by
fear of man, or by the fashion of the times, so that Christ and
his gospel are virtually denied by them. The fear of being
thought dogmatic or puritanic closes many a mouth which
ought to be declaring him to be the Son of God with power,
and extolling his glorious majesty in defiance of all that dare
oppose him. The hearts of some who best love Jesus grow
heavy at the sight of the worldliness and lukewarmness of
many of his professed followers. Hence it seems to me to be
a most seasonable hour for introducing you to the sweet
waters of our text, of which I bid you drink till every trace of
bitterness is gone from your mouth: for the Master saith to

you, even to you, "Let not your heart be troubled: ye believe in God, believe also in me."

II. Under our second head LET US DRINK OF THE SWEET WATERS and refresh our souls.

First, in this wonderful text our Master indicates to us the true means of comfort under every sort of disquietude. How puts he it? "Let not your heart be troubled"—*believe*. Kindly look down your Bibles, and you will see that this direction is repeated. He says in the opening of the eleventh verse, "Believe me"; and then, again, in the second clause, "Believe me." I thought as I tried to enter into the meaning of this sacred utterance that I heard Jesus at my side saying thrice to me, "Believe me! believe me! believe me!" Could any one of the eleven that were with him have disbelieved their present Lord? He says, "Believe me! believe me! believe me!"—as if there was great need to urge them to faith in him. Is there no other cure, then, for a troubled heart? No other is required. This is all-sufficient through God. If believing in Jesus you still are troubled, believe in him again yet more thoroughly and heartily. If even that should not take away the perturbation of your mind, believe in him to a third degree, and continue to do so with increasing simplicity and force. Regard this as the one and only physic for the disease of fear and trouble. Jesus prescribes, "Believe, believe, believe in *me!*" Believe not only in certain doctrines, but in Jesus himself—in him as able to carry out every promise that he has made. Believe in him as you believe in God. One has been at times apt to think it easier to believe in Jesus than in God, but this is a thought of spiritual infancy; more advanced believers find it not so. To a Jew this was certainly the right way of putting it, and I think to us Gentiles it is so also, when we have been long in the faith; for we get to believe in God as a matter of course, and faith in Jesus requires a further confidence. I believe in God's power in creation: he can make what he wills, and shape what he has made. I believe in his power in providence, that he can bring to pass his eternal purposes, and do as he wills among the armies in heaven and among the inhabitants of this lower world. I believe concerning God that all things are possible unto him. Just in that way I am called upon to believe in Jesus that he is as omnipotent in power and as sure in his working as the Lord from whom come all the forces of nature; and just as certain to accomplish his purposes as God is to achieve his design in the works of providence. Relying upon the Saviour with the implicit faith which every right-minded man renders towards God, we shall only give our Lord the faith which he justly claims. He is faithful and true, and his power can effect his promise: let us depend trustfully upon him, and perfect peace shall come into our hearts. These disciples knew that the Saviour was to be away from them, so that they could not see him nor hear his voice. What of that? Is it not so with God, in whom we believe? "No man hath seen God at any time"—yet you believe in the invisible God working all things, sustaining all things. In the same manner believe in the absent and invisible Christ, that he is still as mighty as though you could see him walking the waves, or multiplying the loaves, or healing the sick, or raising the dead. Believe him, and sorrow and sighing will flee away.

Believe in him as ever living, even as you believe in the eternity of God. You believe in the eternal existence of the Most High whom you have not seen, even so believe in the everlasting life of the Son of God. Ay, though you see him die, though you see him laid in the grave, yet believe in him that he has not ceased to be. Look for his reappearance, even as ye believe in God. Yea, and when he is gone from you, and a cloud has received him out of your sight, believe that he liveth, even as God liveth; and because he lives, you shall live also. You believe in the wisdom of God, you believe in the faithfulness of God, you believe in the goodness of God; "Even as ye believe in God," saith Jesus, "believe also in me." Faith in Jesus Christ himself as an ever-living and divine Person, is the best quietus for every kind of fear. He is the "King Eternal, Immortal, Invisible," "the Wonderful Coun-sellor, the mighty God, the everlasting Father, the Prince of Peace;" and therefore you may safely rest in him. This is the first ingredient of this priceless comfort.

But now our Lord proceeded to say that though he was going from them *he was only going to his Father's house.* "In my Father's house are many mansions." Ay, but this was sweet comfort. "I am going," said he, "and on my way you will see me scourged, bleeding, mocked, and buffeted; but I shall pass through all this to the joy and rest, and honour of my Father's house." God is everywhere present, and yet as on earth he had a tabernacle wherein he specially manifested himself, so there is a place where he in a peculiar manner is revealed. The temple was a type of that matchless abode of God which eye hath not seen; we call it heaven, the pavilion of God, the home of holy angels and of those pure spirits who dwell in his immediate presence. In heaven God may be said in special to have his habitation, and Jesus was going there to be received on his return to all the honour which awaited his finished service. He was, in fact, going home, as a son who is returning to his father's house, from which he had gone upon his father's business. He was going where he would be with the Father, where he would be perfectly at rest, where he would be above the assaults of the wicked; where he would never suffer or die again; he was going to reassume the glory which he had with the Father or ever the world was. Oh, if they had perfectly understood this, they would have understood the Saviour's words, "If ye loved me, ye would rejoice, because I said, I go unto the Father." Imagination fails to picture the glory of our Lord's return, the honourable escort which heralded his approach to the Eternal City, the heartiness of the welcome of the Conqueror to the skies. I think the Psalmist gives us liberty to believe that, when our Lord ascended, the bright ones of the sky came to meet him, and cried, "Lift up your heads, O ye gates; and be ye lift up, ye everlasting doors; and the King of glory shall come in." May we not believe of bright seraphs and ministering angels that—

"They brought his chariot from on high
To bear him to his throne;
Clapped their triumphant wings, and cried,
'The glorious work is done.'"

"He was seen of angels." They beheld that "joyous re-entry," the opening of the eternal doors to the King of Glory, and the triumph through the celestial streets of him who led captivity captive and scattered gifts among men. They saw the enthronement of Jesus who was made a little lower than the angels for the suffering of death, but was then and there crowned with glory and honour. These are not things of which these stammering lips of mine can speak, but they are things for you to consider when the Spirit of the Lord is upon you. Muse upon them for your delectation.

Jesus has gone by the way of Calvary up to his Father's house: all his work and warfare done, he is rewarded for his sojourn among men as man. All the shame which his work necessitated is now lost in the splendour of his mediatorial reign. Ye people of God, be no more troubled, for your Lord is King, your Saviour reigns! Men may still scoff at him, but they cannot rob him of a ray of glory! They may reject him, but the Lord God omnipotent has crowned him! They may deny his existence, but he lives! They may rebelliously cry, "Let us break his bands asunder, and cast his cords from us," but the Lord hath set his King upon his holy hill of Zion, and none can thrust him from his throne. Hallelujah! "God hath highly exalted him, and given him a name which is above every name: that at the name of Jesus every knee should bow." Wherefore let not your hearts be troubled by the noise of controversy, and the blasphemy and rebuke of an evil age. Though there be confusion as when the sea roareth and the fulness thereof, and the wicked foam in their rage against the Lord and against his anointed, yet the Lord sitteth upon the flood, the Lord sitteth King forever. Again let us say, "Hallelujah!" The Prince hath come unto his own again; he hath entered into his Father's palace; the heavens have received him. Why should we be troubled?

Thirdly, our Lord gave his servants comfort in another way: *he gave them to understand by implication that a great many would follow him to the Father's house.* He did not only assure them that he was going to his Father's house, but he said, "In my Father's house are many mansions." These mansions are not built to stand empty. God doeth nothing in vain; therefore it is natural to conclude that a multitude of spirits, innumerable beyond all count, will rise in due time to occupy those many mansions in the Father's house. Now I see in this great comfort to them, because they doubtless feared that if their Lord was absent his kingdom might fail. How would there be converts if he were crucified? How could they expect, poor creatures as they were, to set up a kingdom of righteousness on the earth? How could they turn the world upside down and bring multitudes to his feet whom he had purchased with his blood, if his conquering right arm was not seen at their head? The Lord Jesus in effect said, "I am going, but I shall lead the way for a vast host who will come to the prepared abodes. Like the corn of wheat which is cast into the ground to die, I shall bring forth much fruit, which shall be housed in the abiding resting-places." This is one part of our comfort at this hour. Little boots it how men fight against the gospel, for the Lord knoweth them that are his, and he will ransom by power those redeemed by blood. He has a multitude according to the election of grace whom he will bring in. Though they seem to-day to be a small remnant, yet he will fill the many mansions. This stands fast as a rock—"All that the Father giveth me shall come to me; and him that cometh to me I will in no wise cast out." They boast that "they will not come unto Christ;" but the Spirit of God foresaw that they would reject the salvation of the Lord. What said Jesus to those like them? "Ye believe not, because ye are not of my sheep, as I said unto you. My sheep hear my voice, and I know them, and they follow me: and I give unto them eternal life." The wicked unbelief of men is their own condemnation; but Jesus loses not the reward of his passion. We fling back into the faces of the despisers of Christ the scorn which they pour upon him, and remind them that those who despise him shall be lightly esteemed, their names shall be written in the earth. What if *they* come not to him? it is their own loss, and well did he say of them, "No man can come to me except the Father which hath sent me draw him." Their wickedness is their inability and their destruction. They betray by their opposition the fact that they are not the chosen of the Most High. But "the redeemed of the Lord shall come to Zion with songs and everlasting joy upon their heads." "He shall see of the travail of his soul, and shall be satisfied." This matter is not left to the free will of man, so that Jesus may be disappointed after all. Oh no, "they will not come unto him, that they may have life;" but they shall yet know that the eternal Spirit has power over the human conscience and will, and can make men willing in the day of his power. If Jesus be lifted up he will draw all men unto him. There shall be no failure as to the Lord's redeeming work, even though the froward reject the counsel of God against themselves. What Jesus has bought with blood he will not lose; what he died to accomplish shall surely be performed; and what he rose again to carry out shall be effected though all the devils in hell and unbelievers upon earth should join in league against him. Oh, thou enemy, rejoice not over the cause of the Messiah; for though it seem to fall it shall arise again!

But our Lord went much further, for he said, *"I go to prepare a place for you."* I think he did not only refer to the many mansions for our spirits, but to the ultimate *place of* our risen bodies, of which I will speak before long. In our Lord's going away, as well as in his continuance in his Father's presence he would be engaged in preparing a place for his own. He was going that he might clear all impediment out of the way. Their sins blocked the road; like mountains their iniquities opposed all passage; but now that he is gone, it may be said, "The breaker is come up before them, and the Lord on the head of them." He hath broken down every wall of partition, and every iron gate he hath opened. The way into the kingdom is opened for all believers. He passed through death to resurrection and ascension to remove every obstacle from our path.

He went from us also to fulfil every condition: for it was absolutely needful that all who entered heaven should wear a perfect righteousness, and should be made perfect in character, seeing no sin can enter the holy city. Now the saints could not be perfected without being washed in his precious blood, and renewed by the Holy Spirit; and so the Saviour endured the death of the cross; and when he arose he sent us the sanctifying Spirit, that we might be fitted for his rest. Thus he may be said to have prepared the place of our rest by removing from its gateway the sin which blocked all entrance.

He went away also that he might be in a position to secure that place for all his people. He entered the glory-land as our Forerunner, to occupy the place in our name, to take possession of heaven as the representative of all his people. He was going that he might in heaven itself act as Intercessor, pleading before the throne, and therefore be able to save to the uttermost all that come to God by him. He was going there to assume the reins of Providence, having all things put under his feet, and having all power given to him in heaven and in earth that he might bless his people abundantly. By being in heaven our Lord occupies a vantage-ground for the sure accomplishing of his purposes of love. As Joseph went down into Egypt to store the granaries, to prepare for Israel a home in Goshen, and to sit upon the throne for their protection, so hath our Lord gone away into the glory for our good, and he is doing for us upon his throne what could not so advantageously have been done for us here.

At the same time, I am inclined to think that there is a special sense in these words over and above the preparing of heaven for us. I think our Lord Jesus meant to say, "I go to prepare a place for you" in this sense—that there would in the end be a place found for their entire manhood. Mark that word, *"a place."* We are too apt to entertain cloudy ideas of the ultimate inheritance of those who attain unto the resurrection of the dead. "Heaven is a state," says somebody. Yes, certainly, it is a state; but it is a *place* too, and in the future it will be more distinctly a place. Observe that our blessed Lord went away in body; not as a disembodied spirit, but as one who had eaten with his disciples, and whose body had been handled by them. His body needed a *"place,"* and he is gone to prepare a place for us, not only as we shall be for a while, pure spirits, but as we are to be ultimately— body, and soul, and spirit. When a child of God dies, where does his spirit go? There is no question about that matter: we are informed by the inspired apostle—"absent from the body, present with the Lord." But that is a spiritual matter, and something yet remains. My spirit is not the whole of myself, for I am taught so to respect my body as to regard it as a precious portion of my complete self—the temple of God. The Lord Jesus Christ did not redeem my spirit alone, but my body too, and consequently he means to have a "place" where I, this person who is here, in the wholeness of my individuality, may rest forever. Jesus means to have a place made for the entire manhood of his chosen, that they may be where he is and as he is. Our ultimate abode will be a state of blessedness, but it must also be *a place* suited for our risen bodies. It is not, therefore, a cloud-land, an airy something, impalpable and dreamy. Oh, no, it will be as really a place as this earth is a place. Our glorious Lord has gone for the ultimate purpose of preparing a suitable place for his people. There will be a place for their spirits, if spirits want place; but he has gone to prepare a place for them as body, soul, and spirit. I delight to remember that Jesus did not go as a spirit, but in his risen body, bearing the scars of his wounds. Come, you that think you will never rise again, you who imagine that the scattering of our dust forbids all

hope of the restoration of our bodies; we shall go where
Christ has gone, and as he has gone. He leads the way in his
body, and we shall follow in ours. Ultimately there shall be
the complete redemption of the purchased possession, and
not a bone shall be left in the regions of death, not a relic for
the devil to glory over. Jesus said to Mary, "Thy brother
shall rise again;" he did not need to say thy brother's spirit
shall live immortally; but thy brother shall "rise again," his
body shall come forth of the tomb. Well might the apostles'
hearts be comforted when they learned the blessed errand
upon which their Lord was going!

The next consolation was *the promise of his sure return:* "If
I go away to prepare a place for you, I will come again."
Listen, then! Jesus is coming again. In the same manner as
he ascended he will return—that is, really, literally, and in
bodily form. He meant no play upon words when he so
plainly said, without proverb, "I will come again," or more
sweetly still, "I go away and come again *unto you.*" This is
our loudest joy-note, "Behold, he cometh!" This is our never-
failing comfort. Observe that the Saviour, in this place, says
nothing about death, nothing about the peace and rest of
believers till he is come; for he looks on to the end. It is not
necessary to put every truth into one sentence; and so our
Lord is content to mention the brightest of our hopes, and
leave other blessings for mention at other times. Here the
consolation is that he will come, come personally to gather
us in. He will not send an angel, nor even a host of cherubim
to fetch us up into our eternal state; but the Lord himself
will descend from heaven. It is to be our marriage-day, and
the glorious Bridegroom will come in person. When the
Bride is prepared for her Husband, will he not come to fetch
her to his home? O beloved, do you not see where our Lord's
thoughts were? He was dwelling upon the happy day of his
ultimate victory, when he shall come to be admired in all
them that believe. That is where he would have his peoples'
thoughts to be; but alas! they forget his advent. The Lord
shall come; let your hearts anticipate that day of days. His
enemies cannot stop his coming! "Let not your heart be
troubled." They may hate him, but they cannot hinder him;
they cannot impede his glorious return, not by the twinkling
of an eye. What an answer will his coming be to every
adversary! How will they weep and wail because of him! As

surely as he lives he will come; and what confusion this will bring upon the wise men who at this hour are reasoning against his Deity and ridiculing his atonement! Again I say, "Let not your heart be troubled" as to the present state of religion; it will not last long. Do not worry yourselves into unbelief though this man may have turned traitor, or the other may have become a backslider, for the wheels of time are hurrying on the day of the glorious manifestation of the Lord from heaven! What will be the astonishment of the whole world when with all the holy angels he shall descend from heaven and shall glorify his people!

For that is the next comfort—*he will receive us.* When he comes he will receive his followers with a courtly reception. It will be their marriage reception; it shall be the marriage supper of the Son of God. Then shall descend out of heaven the new Jerusalem prepared as a bride for her husband. Then shall come the day of the resurrection, and the dead in Christ shall rise. Then all his people who are alive at the time of his coming shall be suddenly transformed, so as to be delivered from all the frailties and imperfections of their mortal bodies: "The dead shall be raised incorruptible, and we shall be changed." Then we shall be presented spirit, soul, and body "without spot, or wrinkle, or any such thing"; in the clear and absolute perfection of our sanctified manhood, presented unto Christ himself. This is the sweetest idea of heaven that can be, that we shall be with Christ, that we shall see him, that we shall speak to him, that we shall commune with him most intimately, that we shall glorify him, that he will glorify us, and that we shall never be divided from him for ever and ever. "Let not your heart be troubled," all this is near at hand, and our Lord's going away has secured it to us.

For this was the last point of the consolation, that when he came and received his people to himself *he would place them eternally where he is, that they may be with him.* Oh, joy! joy! unutterable joy! Can we not now, once for all, dismiss every fear in the prospect of the endless bliss reserved for us?

> "See that glory, how resplendent!
> Brighter far than fancy paints!
> There in majesty transcendent,
> Jesus reigns, the King of saints.
> Spread thy wings, my soul, and fly
> Straight to yonder world of joy.

> Joyful crowds, his throne surrounding,
> Sing with rapture of his love;
> Through the heavens his praises sounding,
> Filling all the courts above.
> Spread thy wings, my soul, and fly
> Straight to yonder world of joy."

The Lord talks to us as if we now knew all about his goings and doings; and so we do as far as all practical purposes are concerned. He says, "Whither I go ye know." He is not gone to a place unknown, remote, dangerous. He has only gone home. "Whither I go ye know." When a mother sends her boy to Australia she is usually troubled because she may never see him again; but he replies, "Dear mother, the distance is nothing now, we cross the ocean in a very few weeks, and I shall speedily come back again." Then the mother is cheered; she thinks of the ocean as a little bit of blue between her and her son, and looks for him to return, if need be. So the Saviour says, "Whither I go ye know." As much as to say—"I told you, I am going to your own Father's house, to the mansions whither your spirits will soon come, and I am going for the blessed purpose of making it ready to receive you in the entirety of your nature. You are thus made to know all about my departure and my business. I am going to a glorious place which eye hath not seen, but my Spirit will reveal it to you. You know where I am going, and you know also the way by which I am going—I am going through suffering and death, through atonement and righteousness: this is the way to heaven for you also, and you will find it all in me. You shall in due time enter heaven by my atonement, by my death, by my sacrifice, for 'I am the way.' You know the way; but remember it is only the way, and not the end. Do not imagine that the wicked can make an end of me; but believe that Christ on the cross, Christ in the sepulchre, is not the end, but the way." This, beloved, is the way for us as well as for our Lord. He could not reach his crown except by the cross, nor his mediatorial glory except by death: but that way once made in his own person is open for all who believe in him. Thus you know where the Lord has gone, and you know the road; therefore, be encouraged, for he is not far away; he is not inaccessible; you shall be with him soon. "Let not your heart be troubled."

Oh, brave Master, shalt thou be followed by a tribe of

cowards? No, we will not lose heart through the trials of the day. Oh, holy Master, thou didst meet thy death with song, for "after supper they sang a hymn:" shall not we go through our griefs with joyful trust? Oh, confident Lord, bidding us believe in thee as in God himself, we do believe in thee, and we also grow confident. Thine undisturbed serenity of faith infuses itself into our souls, and we are made strong. When we hear thee bravely talking of thy decease which thou hadst to accomplish at Jerusalem, and then of thy after-glory, we also think hopefully of all the opposition of ungodly men, and, waiting for thine appearing, we solace ourselves with that blessed hope. Make no tarrying, O our Lord! Amen.

22

Now And Then

"For now we see through a glass, darkly; but then face to face..."
1 Corinthians 13:12

In this chapter the apostle Paul has spoken in the highest terms of charity or love. He accounts it to be a grace far more excellent than any of the spiritual gifts of which he had just before been speaking. It is easy to see that there were good reasons for the preference he gave to it. Those gifts, you will observe, were distributed among godly men, to every man his several portion, so that what one had another might have lacked; but this grace belongs to all who have passed from death unto life. The proof that they are disciples of Christ is found in their love to him and to the brethren. Those gifts, again, were meant to fit them for service, that each member of the body should be profitable to the other members of the body; but this grace is of personal account: it is a light in the heart and a star on the breast of every one who possesses it. Those gifts, moreover, were of temporary use: their value was limited to the sphere in which they were exercised; but this grace thrives at all times and in all places, and it is no less essential to our eternal future state than it is to our present welfare. By all means covet the best gifts, my dear brother, as an artist would wish to be deft with all his limbs and quick with all his senses; but above all, cherish love, as that same artist would cultivate the pure taste which lives and breathes within him—the secret spring of all his motions, the faculty that prompts his skill. Learn to esteem this sacred instinct of love beyond all the choicest endowments. However poor you may be in talents, let the love of Christ dwell in you richly. Such an exhortation as this is the more needful, because love has a powerful rival. Paul may have noticed that in the academies of Greece, as indeed in all our modern schools, knowledge was wont to take all the prizes. Who can tell how much of Dr. Arnold's success, as a schoolmaster, was due to the honour in which he held a good boy in preference to a clever boy? Most certainly Paul could discern in the church many jealousies to which the superior abilities of those who could speak foreign tongues, and those who could prophesy or preach well, gave rise. So, then, while he extols the grace of love, he seems rather to disparage knowledge; at least, he uses an illustration which tends to show that the kind of knowledge we pride ourselves in, is not the most reliable thing in the world. Paul remembered that he was once a child. A very good thing for any of us to bear in mind. If we forget it, our sympathies are soon dried up, our temper is apt to get churlish, our opinions may be rather overbearing, and our selfishness very repulsive. The foremost man of his day in the Christian church, and exerting the widest influence among the converts to Christ, Paul thought of the little while ago when he was a young child, and he thought of it very opportunely too. Though he might have hinted at the attainments he had made or the high office he held, and laid claim to some degree of respect, he rather looks back at his humble beginnings. If there is wisdom in his reflection, there is to my mind a vein of pleasantry in his manner of expressing it. "When I was a child I spake as a child, I understood as a child, I thought as a child: but when I became a man, I put away childish things." Thus he compares two stages of his natural life, and it serves him for a parable. In spiritual knowledge he felt himself to be then in his infancy. His maturity, his thorough manhood, lay before him in prospect. He could easily imagine a future in which he should look back on his present self as a mere tyro, groping his way amidst the shadows of his own fancy. "For now," he says, "we see through a glass, darkly; but then face to face: now I know in part; but then shall I know even as also I am known." Here he employs one or two fresh figures. *"Through a glass!"* What kind of a glass he alluded to, we may not be able exactly to determine. Well; we will leave that question for the critics to disagree about. It is enough for us that the meaning is obvious. There is all the difference between viewing an object through an obscure medium, and closely inspecting it with the naked eye. We must have the power of vision in either case, but in the latter case we can use it to more advantage. "Now we see through a glass, *darkly.*" Darkly—in a riddle! So weak are our perceptions of mind, that plain truths often puzzle us. The words that teach us are pictures which need explanation. The thoughts that stir us are visions which float in our brains and want rectifying. Oh, for clearer vision! Oh, for more perfect knowledge! Mark you, brethren, it is a matter of congratulation that *we do see;* though we have much cause for diffidence, because we do but "see through a glass, darkly." Thank God *we do know;* but let it check our conceit, we know only in part. Beloved, the objects we look at are distant, and we are near-sighted. The revelation of God is ample and profound, but our understanding is weak and shallow.

There are some things which we count very precious now, which will soon be of no value to us whatever. There are some things that we know, or think we know, and we pride ourselves a good deal upon our knowledge; but when we shall become men we shall set no more value upon that knowledge than a child does upon his toys when he grows up to be a man. Our spiritual manhood in heaven will discard many things which we now count precious, as a full grown man discards the treasures of his childhood. And there are many things that we have been accustomed to see that, after this transient life has passed, we shall see no more. Though we delighted in them, and they pleased our eyes while sojourning on earth, they will pass away as a dream when one awaketh; we shall never see them again, and never want to see them; for our eyes in clearer light, anointed with eye-salve, shall see brighter visions, and we shall never regret what we have lost, in the presence of fairer scenes we shall have found. Other things there are that we know now and shall never forget; we shall know them for ever, only in a higher degree, because no longer with a partial knowledge; and there are some things that we see now that we shall see in eternity, only we shall see them there in a clearer light.

So we shall speak upon *some things that we do see* now,

which *we are to see* more fully and more distinctly *hereafter;* then enquire *how it is we shall see them more clearly;* and finish up by considering *what this fact teaches us.*

I. Among the things that we see now, as many of us as have had our eyes enlightened by the Holy Spirit, is OURSELVES.

To see ourselves is one of the first steps in true religion. The mass of men have never seen themselves. They have seen the flattering image of themselves, and they fancy that to be their own facsimile, but it is not. You and I have been taught of God's Holy Spirit to see our ruin in the fall; we have bemoaned ourselves on account of that fall; we have been made conscious of our own natural depravity; we have been ground to the very dust by the discovery; we have been shown our actual sinfulness and how we have transgressed against the Most High. We have repented for this, and have fled for refuge to the hope set before us in the gospel. Day by day we see a little more of ourselves— nothing very pleasing, I grant you—but something very profitable, for it is a great thing for us to know our emptiness. It is a step towards receiving his fulness. It is something to discover our weakness; it is a step essential towards our participation of divine strength. I suppose the longer we live the more we shall see ourselves; and we shall probably come to this conclusion: "Vanity of vanities; all is vanity:" and cry out with Job, "I am vile." The more we shall discover of ourselves, the more we shall be sick of ourselves. But in heaven, I doubt not, we shall find out that we never saw even ourselves in the clearest light, but only as "through a glass, darkly," only as an unriddled thing, as a deep enigma; for we shall understand more about ourselves in heaven than we do now. There we shall see, as we have not yet seen, how desperate a mischief was the Fall, into what a horrible pit we fell, and how fast we were stuck in the miry clay. There shall we see the blackness of sin as we have never seen it here, and understand its hell desert as we could not till we shall look down from yonder starry height whither infinite mercy shall bring us. When we shall be singing, "Worthy is the Lamb that was slain," we shall look at the robes that we have washed in his blood, and see how white they are. We shall better understand then than now how much we needed washing—how crimson were the stains and how precious was that blood that effaced those scarlet spots. There, too, shall we know ourselves on the bright side better than we do now. We know to-day that we are saved, and there is therefore now no condemnation to them that are in Christ Jesus; but that robe of righteousness which covers us now, as it shall cover us then, will be better seen by us, and we shall discern how lustrous it is, with its needlework and wrought gold—how much better than the pearls and gems that have decked the robes of monarchs are the blood and righteousness of Jehovah Jesus, who has given himself for us. Here we know that we are adopted. We feel the spirit of sonship; "we cry, Abba, Father;" but there we shall know better what it is to be the sons of God, for here it doth not yet appear what we shall be; but when we shall be there, and when Christ shall appear, we shall be like him, for we shall see him as he is, and then we shall understand to the full what sonship means. So, too, I know to-day that I am a joint-heir with Christ, but I have a very poor idea of what it is I am heir to; but there shall I see the estates that belong to me; not only see them, but actually enjoy them. A part shall every Christian have in the inheritance undefiled and that fadeth not away, that is reserved in heaven for him, because he is in Christ Jesus; one with Christ—by eternal union one. But I am afraid that is very much more a riddle to us than a matter of understanding. We see it as an enigma now, but there our oneness with Christ will be as conspicuous to us and as plain as the letters of the alphabet. There shall we know what it is to be a member of his body, of his flesh, and of his bones; there shall I understand the mystical marriage bond that knits the believer's soul to Christ; there shall I see how, as the branch springs from the stem, my soul stands in union, vital union, with her blessed Lord Jesus Christ. Thus, one thing that we see now which we shall see in a much clearer light hereafter, is "ourselves."

Here, too, we see the CHURCH, but WE SHALL SEE THE CHURCH MUCH MORE CLEARLY BY-AND-BY.

We know there is a church of God. We know that the Lord has a people whom he hath chosen from before the foundation of the world: we believe that these are scattered up and down throughout our land, and many other lands. There are many of them we do not know, many that we should not particularly like, I daresay, if we did know them,

on account of their outward characteristics; persons of very
strange views, and very odd habits perhaps; and yet, for all
that, the people of the living God. Now, we know this church,
we know its glory, moved with one life, quickened with one
Spirit, redeemed with one blood, we believe in this church,
and we feel attachment to it for the sake of Jesus Christ,
who has married the church as the Bride. But, oh! when we
shall get to heaven, how much more we shall know of the
church, and how we shall see her face to face, and not
"through a glass, darkly." There we shall know something
more of the numbers of the chosen than we do now, it may be
to our intense surprise. There we shall find some amongst
the company of God's elect, whom we in our bitterness of
spirit had condemned, and there we shall miss some who, in
our charity, we have conceived to be perfectly secure. We
shall know better then who are the Lord's and who are not
than we ever can know here. Here all our processes of
discernment fail us. Judas comes in with the apostles, and
Demas takes his part among the saints, but there we shall
know the righteous, for we shall see them; there will be one
flock and one Shepherd, and he that on the throne doth reign
for evermore shall be glorified. We shall understand then,
what the history of the church has been in all the past, and
why it has been so strange a history of conflict and conquest.
Probably, we shall know more of the history of the church in
the future. From that higher elevation and brighter
atmosphere we shall understand better what are the Lord's
designs concerning his people in the latter day; and what
glory shall redound to his own name from his redeemed
ones, when he shall have gathered together all that are
called and chosen and faithful from among the sons of men.
This is one of the joys we are looking for, that we shall come
to the general assembly and church of the firstborn whose
names are written in heaven; and have fellowship with those
who have fellowship with God through Jesus Christ our
Lord.

Thirdly. Is it not possible, nay, is it not certain, that in the
next state WE SHALL SEE AND KNOW MORE OF THE
PROVIDENCE OF GOD THAN WE DO NOW?

Here we see the providence of God, but it is in a glass,
darkly. The apostle says "through" a glass. There was glass
in the apostles' days, not a substance such as our windows

are now made of, but thick, dull coloured glass, not much more transparent than that which is used in the manufacture of common bottles, so that looking through a piece of that glass you would not see much. That is like what we now see of divine providence. We believe all things work together for good to them that love God; we have seen how they work together for good in some cases, and ex- perimentally proved it to be so. But still it is rather a matter of faith than a matter of sight with us. We cannot tell how "every dark and bending line meets in the centre of his love." We do not yet perceive how he will make those dark dispensations of trials and afflictions that come upon his people really to subserve his glory and their lasting happiness; but up there we shall see providence, as it were, face to face; and I suppose it will be amongst our greatest surprises, the discovery of how the Lord dealt with us. "Why," we shall some of us say, "we prayed against those very circumstances which were the best that could have been appointed for us." "Ah!" another will say, "I have fretted and troubled myself over what was, after all, the richest mercy the Lord ever sent." Sometimes I have known persons refuse a letter at the door, and it has happened, in some cases, that there has been something very valuable in it, and the postman has said, afterwards, "You did not know the contents, or else you would not have refused it." And often God has sent us, in the black envelope of trial, such a precious mass of mercy, that if we had known what was in it, we should have taken it in, and been glad to pay for it— glad to give it house room, to entertain it; but because it looked black we were prone to shut our door against it. Now, up there we shall know not only more of ourselves, but perceive the reasons of many of God's dealings with us on a larger scale; and we shall there perhaps discover that wars that devastated nations, and pestilences that fill graves, and earthquakes that make cities tremble, are, after all, necessary cogs in the great wheel of the divine machinery; and he who sits upon the throne at this moment, and rules supremely every creature that is either in heaven, or earth, or hell, will there make it manifest to us that his government was right. It is good to think in these times when everything seems loosening, that "the government shall be upon his shoulder: and his name shall be called Wonderful,

Counsellor, The mighty God, The everlasting Father, The
Prince of Peace." It must come out right in the long run; it
must be well; every part and portion must work together
with a unity of design to promote God's glory and the saint's
good. We shall see it there, and we shall lift up our song with
new zest and joy, as fresh displays of the wisdom and
goodness of God, whose ways are past finding out, are
unfolded to our admiring view.

Fourthly. It is surely no straining of the text to say, that,
though here we know something of THE DOCTRINES OF THE
GOSPEL, AND THE MYSTERIES OF THE FAITH, by-and-by, in a
few months or years at the longest, *we shall know a great
deal more than we do now.* There are some grand doctrines,
brethren and sisters, we dearly love, but though we love
them, our understanding is too feeble to grasp them fully.
We account them to be mysteries; we reverently
acknowledge them, yet we dare not attempt to explain them.
They are matters of faith to us. It may be that in heaven
there shall be counsels of eternal wisdom into which no
saints or angels can peer. It is the glory of God to conceal a
matter. Surely, no creature will ever be able, even when
exalted to heaven, to comprehend all the thoughts of the
Creator. We shall never be omniscient—we cannot be. God
alone knoweth everything, and understandeth everything.
But how much more of authentic truth shall we discern
when the mists and shadows have dissolved; and how much
more shall we understand when raised to that higher sphere
and endowed with brighter faculties, none of us can tell.
Probably, things that puzzle us here will be as plain as
possible there. We shall perhaps smile at our own ignorance.
I have fancied sometimes that the elucidations of learned
doctors of divinity, if they could be submitted to the very
least in the kingdom of heaven, would only cause them to
smile at the learned ignorance of the sons of earth. Oh! how
little we do know, but how much we shall know! I am sure
we shall know, for it is written, "Then shall I know even as
also I have known." We now see things in a mist—"men as
trees, walking"—a doctrine here, and a doctrine there. And
we are often at a loss to conjecture how one part harmonizes
with another part of the same system, or to make out how all
these doctrines are consistent. This knot cannot be untied,
that gnarl cannot be unravelled, but—

"Then shall I see, and hear and know
All I desired or wish'd below;
And every power find sweet employ
In that eternal world of joy."

But, my dear brethren and sisters, having kept you thus
far in the outer courts, I would fain lead you into the temple;
or, to change the figure, if in the beginning I have set forth
good wine, certainly I am not going to bring out that which is
worse; rather would I have you say, as the ruler of the feast
did to the bridegroom, "thou has kept the good wine until
now." HERE WE SEE JESUS CHRIST, BUT WE DO NOT SEE HIM AS
WE SHALL SEE HIM SOON. We have seen him by faith in such
a way, that we have beheld our burdens laid on him, and our
iniquities carried by him into the wilderness, where, if they
be sought for, they shall not be found. We have seen enough
of Jesus to know that "he is altogether lovely;" we can say of
him, he "is all my salvation, and all my desire." Sometimes,
when he throws up the lattice, and shows himself through
those windows of agate and gates of carbuncle, in the
ordinances of his house, at the Lord's Supper especially, the
King's beauty has entranced us even to our heart's
ravishment; yet all we have ever seen is somewhat like the
report which the Queen of Sheba had of Solomon's wisdom.
When we once get to the court of the Great King we shall
declare that the half has not been told us. We shall say,
"mine eyes shall behold, and not another." Brethren, is not
this the very cream of heaven? There have been many
suggestions of what we shall do in heaven, and what we
shall enjoy, but they all seem to me to be wide of the mark
compared with this one, that we shall be with Jesus, be like
him, and shall behold his glory. Oh, to see the feet that were
nailed, and to touch the hand that was pierced, and to look
upon the head that wore the thorns, and to bow before him
who is ineffable love, unspeakable condescension, infinite
tenderness! Oh, to bow before him, and to kiss that blessed
face! Jesu, what better do we want than to see thee by thine
own light—to see thee, and speak with thee, as when a man
speaketh with his friend? It is pleasant to talk about this,
but what will it be there when the pearl gates open? The
streets of gold will have small attraction to us, and the harps
of angels will but slightly enchant us, compared with the
King in the midst of the throne. He it is who shall rivet our

gaze, absorb our thoughts, enchain our affection, and move all our sacred passions to their highest pitch of celestial ardour. We shall see Jesus.

Once again (and here we come into the deep things), beyond a doubt WE SHALL ALSO SEE GOD. It is written that the pure in heart shall see God. God is seen now in his works and in his word. Little indeed could these eyes bear of the beatific vision, yet we have reason to expect that, as far as creatures can bear the sight of the infinite Creator, we shall be permitted to see God. We read that Aaron and certain chosen ones saw the throne of God, and the brightness as it were of sapphire stone—light, pure as jasper. In heaven it is the presence of God that is the light thereof. God's more immediate dwelling in the midst of the new Jerusalem is its peerless glory and peculiar bliss. We shall then understand more of God than we do now; we shall come nearer to him, be more familiar with him, be more filled with him. The love of God shall be shed abroad in our hearts; we shall know our Father as we yet know him not; we shall know the Son to a fuller degree than he has yet revealed himself to us, and we shall know the Holy Spirit in his personal love and tenderness towards us, beyond all those influences and operations which have soothed us in our sorrows and guided us in our perplexities here below. I leave your thoughts and your desires to follow the teaching of the Spirit. As for me, I cower before the thought while I revel in it. I, who have strained my eyes while gazing at nature, where the things that are made show the handiwork of God; I, whose conscience has been awe-struck as I listened to the voice of God proclaiming his holy law; I, whose heart has been melted while there broke on my ears the tender accents of his blessed gospel in those snatches of sacred melody that relieve the burden of prophecy; I, who have recognised in the babe of Bethlehem the hope of Israel; in the man of Nazareth, the Messiah that should come; in the victim of Calvary, the one Mediator; in the risen Jesus, the well-beloved Son—to me, verily, God incarnate has been so palpably revealed that I have almost seen God, for I have, as it were, seen him in whom all the fulness of the Godhead bodily doth dwell. Still I "see through a glass, darkly." Illumine these dark senses, waken this drowsy conscience, purify my heart, give me fellowship with Christ, and then bear me up, translate me to the third heavens; so I may, so I can, so I shall see God. But what that means, or what it is, ah me! I cannot tell.

II. We proposed to enquire, in the second place, HOW THIS VERY REMARKABLE CHANGE SHALL BE EFFECTED? WHY IS IT THAT WE SHALL SEE MORE CLEARLY THEN THAN NOW? We cannot altogether answer the question, but one or two suggestions may help us. No doubt many of these things will be more clearly revealed in the next state. Here the light is like the dawn: it is dim twilight. In heaven it will be the blaze of noon. God has declared something of himself by the mouth of his holy prophets and apostles. He has been pleased, through the lips of his Son, whom he hath appointed heir of all things, to speak to us more plainly, to show us more openly the thoughts of his heart and the counsel of his will. These are the first steps to knowledge. But there the light will be as the light of seven days, and there the manifestation of all the treasures of wisdom shall be brighter and clearer than it is now; for God, the only-wise God, shall unveil to us the mysteries, and exhibit to us the glories of his everlasting kingdom. The revelation we now have suits us as men clad in our poor mortal bodies; the revelation then will suit us as immortal spirits. When we have been raised from the dead, it will be suitable to our immortal spiritual bodies. Here, too, we are at a distance from many of the things we long to know something of, but there we shall be nearer to them. We shall then be on a vantage ground, with the entire horizon spread out before us. Our Lord Jesus is, as to his personal presence, far away from us. We see him through the telescope of faith, but then we shall see him face to face. His literal and bodily presence is in heaven, since he was taken up, and we need to be taken up likewise to be with him where he is that we may literally behold him. Get to the fountain-head, and you understand more; stand in the centre, and things seem regular and orderly. If you could stand in the sun and see the orbits in which the planets revolve round that central luminary, it would become clear enough; but for many an age astronomers were unable to discover anything of order, and spoke of the planets as progressive, retrograde, and standing still. Let us get to God, the centre, and we shall see how providence in order revolves round his sapphire throne. We, ourselves, too, when we get to heaven, shall be better qualified to see than we are now. It would be an inconvenience for us to know here as much as we shall know in heaven. No doubt we have sometimes thought that if we had better ears it would be a great blessing. We have wished we could hear ten miles off; but probably we should be no better off; we might hear too much, and the sounds might drown each other. Probably our sight is not as good as we wish it were, but a large increase of ocular power might not be of any use to us. Our natural organs are fitted for our present sphere of being; and our mental faculties are, in the case of most of us, properly adapted to our moral requirements. If we knew more of our own sinfulness, we might be driven to despair; if we knew more of God's glory, we might die of terror; if we had more understanding, unless we had equivalent capacity to employ it, we might be filled with conceit and tormented with ambition. But up there we shall have our minds and our systems strengthened to receive more, without the damage that would come to us here from overleaping the boundaries of order, supremely appointed and divinely regulated. We cannot here drink the wine of the kingdom, it is too strong for us; but up there we shall drink it new in our heavenly Father's kingdom, without fear of the intoxications of pride, or the staggerings of passions. We shall know even as we are known. Besides, dear friends, the atmosphere of heaven is so much clearer than this, that I do not wonder we can see better there. Here there is the smoke of daily care; the constant dust of toil; the mist of trouble perpetually rising. We cannot be expected to see much in such a smoky atmosphere as this; but when we shall pass beyond, we shall find no clouds ever gather round the sun to hide his everlasting brightness. There all is clear. The daylight is serene as the noonday. We shall be in a clearer atmosphere and brighter light.

III. The practical lessons we may learn from this subject demand your attention before I close. Methinks there is an appeal to our *gratitude*. Let us be very thankful for all we do see. Those who do not see now—ah, not even "through a glass, darkly"—shall never see face to face. The eyes that never see Christ by faith shall never see him with joy in heaven. If thou hast never seen thyself a leper, defiled with sin and abashed with penitence, thou shalt never see thyself redeemed from sin, renewed by grace, a white-robed spirit. If thou hast no sense of God's presence here, constraining thee to worship and love him, thou shalt have no sight of his glory hereafter, introducing thee to the fulness of joy and pleasure for evermore. Oh! be glad for the sight you have, dear brother, dear sister. It is God that gave it to thee. Thou art one born blind; and "Since the world began was it not heard that any man opened the eyes of one that was born blind." This miracle has been wrought on thee; thou canst see, and thou canst say: "One thing I know, that whereas I was blind, now I see."

Our text teaches us that this feeble vision is very *hopeful*. *You shall see better by-and-by*. Oh, you know not how soon—it may be a day or two hence—that we shall be in glory! God may so have ordained it, that betwixt us and heaven there may be but a step.

Another lesson is that of *forbearance* one with another. Let the matters we have spoken of soften the asperity of our debates; let us feel when we are disputing about points of difficulty, that we need not get cross about them, because after all there are limits to our present capacity as well as to our actual knowledge. Our disputes are often childish. We might as well leave some questions in abeyance for a little while. Two persons in the dark have differed about a colour, and they are wrangling about it. If we brought candles in and held them to the colour, the candles would not show what it was; but if we look at it to-morrow morning, when the sun shines, we shall be able to tell. How many difficulties in the word of God are like this! Not yet can they be justly discriminated; till the day dawn, the apocalyptic symbols will not be all transparent to our own understanding. Besides, we have no time to waste while there is so much work to do. Much time is already spent. Sailing is dangerous; the winds are high; the sea is rough. Trim the ship; keep the sails in good order; manage her and keep her off quicksands. As to certain other matters, we must wait till we get into the fair haven, and are able to talk with some of the bright spirits now before the throne. When some of the things they know shall be opened unto us, we shall confess the mistakes we made, and rejoice in the light we shall receive.

Should not this happy prospect excite our *aspiration* and

make us very desirous to be there? It is natural for us to
want to know, but we shall not know as we are known till we
are present with the Lord. We are at school now—children at
school. We shall go to the college soon—the great University
of Heaven—and take our degree there. Yet some of us,
instead of being anxious to go, are shuddering at the thought
of death—the gate of endless joy we dread to enter! There
are many persons who die suddenly; some die in their sleep,
and many have passed out of time into eternity when it has
scarcely been known by those who have been sitting at their
bedsides. Depend upon it, there is no pain in dying; the pain
is in living. When they leave off living here, they have done
with pain. Do not blame death for what it does not deserve;
it is life that lingers on in pain: death is the end of it. The
man that is afraid of dying ought to be afraid of living. Be
content to die whenever the Master's will shall bid thee.
Commit thy spirit to his keeping. Who that hath seen but the
glimpses of his beaming countenance doth not long to see his
face, that is as the sun shining in his strength? O Lord! thy
will be done. Let us speedily behold thee, if so it may
be—only this one word, if so it may be. Do we now see, and
do we expect to see better? Let us bless the name of the Lord,
who hath chosen us of his mercy and of his infinite
lovingkindness. On the other hand, let it cause us great
anxiety if we have not believed in Jesus, for he that hath not
believed in him, dying as he is, will never see the face of God
with joy. Oh! unbeliever, be concerned about your soul, and
seek thou after him, repair thou to him. Oh! that God would
open thy eyes now in this very house of prayer. Blessed for
thee to know in part. Thrice blessed, I say; for as surely as
thou knowest in part now, thou shalt fully know hereafter.
Be it your happy lot to know him, whom to know is life
eternal. God grant it, for Jesus' sake. Amen.

23

The Earnest Of Heaven

"...that holy Spirit of promise, Which is the earnest of our inheritance..."   Ephesians 1:13-14

So then, heaven, with all its glories, is an *inheritance!* Now, an inheritance is not a thing which is bought with money, earned by labour, or won by conquest. If any man hath an inheritance, in the proper sense of that term, it came to him by birth. It was not because of any special merit in him, but simply because he was his father's son that he received the property of which he is now possessed. So is it with heaven. The man who shall receive this glorious heritage will not obtain it by the works of the law, nor by the efforts of the flesh; it will be given to him as a matter of most gracious right, because he has been "begotten again unto a lively hope, by the resurrection of Jesus Christ from the dead;" and has thus become an heir of heaven by blood and birth. They who come unto glory are sons; for is it not written, "The captain of our salvation bringeth many sons unto glory"? They come not there as servants; no servant has any right to the inheritance of his master; let him be never so faithful, yet is he not his master's heir. But because ye are sons—sons by God's adoption, sons by the Spirit's regeneration—because by supernatural energy ye have been born again—ye become inheritors of eternal life, and ye enter into the many mansions of our Father's house above. Let us always understand, then, when we think of heaven, that it is a place which is to be ours, and a state which we are to enjoy as the

result of birth,—not as the result of work. "Except a man be
born again, he cannot see the kingdom of God;" that kingdom
being an inheritance, until he hath the new birth, he can
have no claim to enter it. But is it possible for us, provided
that heaven be our inheritance, and we are God's sons—is it
possible for us to know anything what ever of that land
beyond the flood? Is there power in human intellect to fly
into the land of the hereafter, and reach those islands of the
happy, where God's people rest in the bosom of their God
eternally? We are met at the outset with a rebuff which
staggers us. "Eye hath not seen, nor ear heard, neither hath
entered into the heart of man, the things which God hath
prepared for them that love him." If we paused here we
might give up all idea of beholding from our houses of clay
that goodly land of Lebanon; but we do not pause, for like
the apostle, we go on with the text, and we add "But he hath
revealed it unto us by his Spirit." It *is* possible to look within
the vail; God's Spirit *can* turn it aside for a moment, and bid
us take a glimpse, though it be but a distant one, at that
unutterable glory. There are Pisgahs even now on the
surface of the earth, from the top of which the celestial
Canaan can be beheld, there are hallowed hours in which
the mists and clouds are swept away, and the sun shineth in
his strength, and our eye, being freed from its natural
dimness, beholds something of that land which is very far
off, and sees a little of the joy and blessedness which is
reserved for the people of God hereafter. Our text tells us,
that the Holy Spirit is the earnest of the inheritance; by
which I understand, that he is not only the pledge, for a
pledge is given for security, but when the thing pledged is
given, then the pledge itself is restored—but he is an
earnest, which is a pledge and something more. An earnest
is a part of the thing itself; it is not only a pledge of the
thing, for security, but it is a foretaste of it for present
enjoyment. The word in the Greek has a stronger force than
our word pledge. Again I repeat it: if I promise to pay to a
man somewhat, I may give him land or property *in pledge,*
but if instead thereof I pay him a part of the sum which I
have promised, that is a pledge; but it is more,—it is *an
earnest,* because it is a part of the thing itself. So the Holy
Spirit is a pledge to God's people. Inasmuch as God hath
given them the graces of the Spirit, he will give them the

glory that results therefrom. But he is more: he is a foretaste—he is a sweet antepast of heaven; so that they who possess the Spirit of God possess the first tastes of heaven; they have reaped the first-fruits of the eternal harvest; the first drops of a shower of glory have fallen upon them; they have beheld the first beams of the rising sun of eternal bliss; they have not merely a pledge for security—they have an earnest, which is security and foretaste combined. Understand, then, for this is what I am about to speak of this morning: by the Holy Spirit there is given to the people of God even now, experiences, joys, and feelings, which prove that they shall be in heaven—which do more, which *bring heaven down to them, and make them already able to guess in some measure what heaven must be.* When I have enlarged upon that theme, I shall take the black side of the picture, and remark that *it is possible for men on earth to have both a pledge and an earnest of those eternal pains which are reserved for the impenitent:* a dark subject, but may God grant it may be for our profit and arousing.

I. First, then, THERE ARE SOME WORKS OF THE SPIRIT WHICH ARE PECULIARLY AN EARNEST TO THE CHILD OF GOD, OF THE BLESSINGS OF HEAVEN.

1. And, first, *heaven is a state of rest.* It may be because I am constitutionally idle, that I look upon heaven in the aspect of rest with greater delight than under any other view of it, with but one exception. To let the head which is so continually exercised, for once lie still—to have no care, no trouble, no need to labour, to strain the intellect, or vex the limbs! I know that many of you, the sons of poverty and of toil, look forward to the Sabbath-day, because of the enjoyments of the sanctuary, and because of the rest which it affords you. You look for heaven as Watts did in his song.

> "There shall I bathe my weary soul
> In seas of heavenly rest,
> And not a wave of trouble roll
> Across my peaceful breast."

"There remaineth therefore a rest to the people of God." 'Tis not a rest of sleep, but yet a rest as perfect as though they slept; it is a rest which puts from them all carking care, all harrowing remorse, all thoughts of to-morrow, all straining after a something which they have not as yet. They are

runners no more—they have reached the goal; they are
warriors no more—they have achieved the victory; they are
labourers no more—they have reaped the harvest. "They
rest, saith the Spirit; they rest from their labours, and their
works do follow them."

My beloved, did you ever enjoy on certain high days of your
experience, a state of perfect rest? You could say you had not
a wish in all the world ungratified; you knew yourself to be
pardoned; you felt yourself to be an heir of heaven; Christ
was precious to you; you knew that you walked in the light of
your Father's countenance; you had cast all your worldly
care on him, for he cared for you. You felt at that hour that
if death could smite away your dearest friends, or if calamity
should remove the most valuable part of your possessions on
earth, yet you could say, "The Lord gave and the Lord hath
taken away, blessed be the name of the Lord." Your spirit
floated along the stream of grace, without a struggle; you
were not as the swimmer, who breasts the billows, and tugs
and toils for life. Your soul was made to lie down in green
pastures, beside the still waters. You were passive in God's
hands; you knew no will but his. Oh! that sweet day!

"That heavenly calm within the breast,
Was the sure pledge of glorious rest,
Which for the Church of God remains,
The end of cares, the end of pains."

Nay, it was more than a pledge; it was a part of the rest
itself. It was a morsel taken from the loaf of delights; it was
a sip out of the wine vats of immortal joy; it was silver spray
from the waves of glory. So, then, whenever we are quiet and
at peace—"For we which have believed do enter into rest,"
and have ceased from our own works, as God did from his—
when we can say, "O God, my heart is fixed, my heart is
fixed; I will sing and give praise;"—when our spirit is full of
love within us, and our peace is like a river, and our
righteousness like the wave of the sea;—then we already
know in some degree, what heaven is. We have but to make
that peace deeper, and yet more profound, lasting, and more
continual; we have but to multiply it eternally, and we have
obtained a noble idea of the rest which remaineth for the
people of God.

2. But, secondly, there is a passage in the book of

Revelation, which may sometimes puzzle the uninstructed reader, where it is said concerning the angels, that "They rest not day and night," and as we are to be as the angels of God, it must undoubtedly be true in heaven, that in a certain sense, they rest not day nor night. They always rest, so far as ease and freedom from care is concerned; they never rest, in the sense of indolence or inactivity. In heaven, spirits are always on the wing; their lips are always singing the eternal *hallelujahs* unto the great *Jehovah* that sitteth upon the throne; their fingers are never divorced from the strings of their golden harps; their feet never cease to run in obedience to the eternal will; they rest, but they rest on the wing; as the poet pictured the angel as he flew,—not needing to move his wings, but resting, and yet darting swiftly through the ether, as though he were a flash shot from the eye of God. So shall it be with the people of God eternally; ever singing— never hoarse with music; ever serving—never wearied with their service. "They rest not day and night." Have there never been times with you, when you have had both the pledge and the earnest of this kind of heaven?—ay, when we have preached once, and again, and again, and again, in one day, and some have said, "But the constitution will be destroyed, the mind will be weakened; such toil as this will bring the man low?" But we have been able to reply, "We do not feel it; for the more toil has been cast upon us, the more strength has been given." Have you ever known what it is to have the pastor's work in revival times, when he has to sit hour after hour, seeing convert after convert—when the time for one meal is past, and he has forgotten it, and the time for another meal has come and gone, and he has forgotten that, for he has been so busy and so happy with his feast of ingatherings, that he has been like his Master, and has forgotten to eat bread, and positively did not hunger and did not thirst, because the joy of the service had taken away all fatigue? Just at this hour, our missionaries are engaged throughout Jamaica, in a sweltering sun, preaching the Word. Perhaps there has never been a more glorious revival than that which God has sent to that island—an island which has often been blessed, but which now seems to have received a seven-fold portion. One missionary in writing home, says that he had not been in bed one night for a week, and he had been preaching all day and all night long: and I do not doubt but his testimony to you would be, that at least, during the first part of the labour, it seemed not to be labour. He could sleep on the wing; he could rest while he worked; the joy of success took away from him the feeling of lassitude; the blessed prospect of seeing so many added to the Church of God, had made him forget even to eat bread. Well, then, at such a time as that, he had a foretaste of the rest, and the service too, which remaineth for the people of God. Oh, do not doubt, if you find comfort in serving God— and such comfort that you grow not weary in his service— do not doubt, I say, but that you shall soon join that hallowed throng, who "day without night circle his throne rejoicing," who rest not, but serve him day and night in his temple! These feelings are foretastes, and they are pledges too. They give some inklings of what heaven must be, and they make your title to heaven clear.

3. But let us pass on. Heaven is a place of *communion* with all the people of God. I am sure that in heaven they know each other. I could not perhaps just now prove it in so many words, but I feel that a heaven of people who did not know each other, and had no fellowship, could not be heaven; because God has so constituted the human heart that it loves society, and especially the renewed heart is so made that it cannot help communing with all the people of God. I always say to my Strict Baptist brethren who think it a dreadful thing for baptized believers to commune with the unbaptized, "But you cannot help it; if you are the people of God you must commune with all saints, baptized or not. You may deny them the outward and visible sign, but you cannot keep from them the inward and spiritual grace." If a man be a child of God, I do not care what I may think about him—if I be a child of God I *do* commune with him, and I must, for we are all parts of the same body, all knit to Christ, and it is not possible that one part of Christ's body should ever be in any state but that of communion with all the rest of the body. Well, in glory I feel I may say, we know we shall converse with each other. We shall talk of our trials on the way thither—talk most of all of him who by his faithful love and his potent arm has brought us safely through. We shall not sing solos, but in chorus shall we praise our King. We shall not look upon our fellows there like men in the iron mask, whose name and character we do not know; for there

we shall know even as we are known. You shall talk with the prophets; you shall have conversation with the martyrs; you shall sit again at the feet of the great reformers and all your brethren in faith who have fallen before you, or who have rather entered into rest before; these shall be your companions on the other side the grave. How sweet must that be! How blessed—that holy converse, that happy union, that general assembly and Church of the first-born whose names are written in heaven! Have we anything on earth like this? Ay, that we have, in miniature. We have the pledge of this; for if we love the people of God, we may know that we shall surely be with them in heaven. We have the *earnest* of it; for how often has it been our privilege to hold the highest and sweetest fellowship with our fellow Christians! Why, you and I have often said, "Did not our hearts burn within us, while we talked together by the way, and Christ was with us both?" When we have been together and the doors have been shut, has not the Master said, "Peace be unto you?" When love has gone from heart to heart, and we have all felt knit together as one man; when party names were all forgotten; when all jealousies and bickerings were driven out of doors, and we felt that we were one family, and all did bear the same one name, having "one Lord, one faith, and one baptism;" then it was that we had the earnest, the foretaste, the first drinking of that well of Bethlehem which is on the other side the pearly gate of the celestial city.

4. I have to be brief on each of these points, for there are so many to mention. Part of the bliss of heaven will consist *in joy over sinners saved.* The angels look down from the battlements of the city which hath foundations, and when they see prodigals return they sing. Jesus calleth together his friends and his neighbours, and he saith unto them, "Rejoice with me, for I have found the sheep which was lost." The angels begin the theme; the sacred fire runs through the host, and all the saints above take up the strain. Hark, how they sing before the throne, for it has just been whispered there of some Saul, "Behold, he prayeth!" Hark how their songs get a new inspiration—how their eternal Sabbath seems to be Sabbatised afresh, and "the rest" becomes more joyous far, while they sing of new-born sons added to the family, and new names written in the register of the Church below! Part of the joy of heaven, and no mean part of it, will

be to watch the fight on earth, to see the Conqueror as he marches on, and to behold the trophies of his grace, and the spoils which his hands shall win. Is there anything like this on earth? Ay, that there is, when the Spirit of God gives to *us* joy over sinners saved. The other evening, when some of us sat in Church meeting, what joy was there, when one after another, those who had been plucked from the deepest hell of sin made avowal of their faith in Christ! Some of us look back upon those Church meetings as the gladdest nights we ever spent; when first one and then another has said, "*I* have been plucked as a brand from the burning," and the tale of grace has been told; and a third has stood up and said, "And I, too, was once a stranger wandering far from God, and Jesus sought me." Why, we have some of us gone home and felt that it was heaven below to have been there. We have felt more joy over the conversion of others, we have sometimes thought, than even over our own. It has been such bliss while we have taken the hand of the convert, and the tear has been in both eyes, when the word of gratitude has been spoken, and Jesus Christ has been magnified by lips that once blasphemed him. My brothers and sisters, though the whole world should censure me, I cannot help it; I must tell it, to the praise of God's free grace and boundless love. There are hundreds here that are the most wonderful trophies of grace that ever lived on earth. My heart has been gladdened, and your hearts have been gladdened too. I must not keep it back; I *will* not. It was my Master's work; it is to his honour, it is to his praise. We will tell *that* on earth which we will sing in heaven. They *have* washed their robes, and made them white in the blood of the lamb; and I do believe that the joy we felt when sinners have been converted, has been an earnest and a pledge that we shall be partakers of the like joy in heaven.

5. But to proceed. Here is another earnest of heaven, which is rather a personal matter than one which is drawn from others. Did you ever get a knotty passage in Scripture, which repeated itself in your mind so many times that you could not get rid of it? You borrowed some commentaries; you opened them, and you found that you might enquire within, but get no information whatever upon the particular subject you wished most to be informed about. Commentaries generally are books which are written to

explain those parts of Scripture which everybody
understands, and to make those that are dark more
mysterious than they were before. At any rate, if that was
the aim of the different authors, they have most of them
admirably succeeded. I do not believe in great commentaries
upon the whole Bible, no one man can write such a book, so
that all of it shall be valuable. When a man gives his whole
life-time to some one book, that one is worth reading. When
a man has taken up, as some have done, the Epistle to the
Romans, or the Book of Genesis, and gone on year after year
toiling through it, then such a book has been a monument of
labour, and has been valuable to the Christian student; but,
generally, large commentaries give little information where
most it is needed. Well, disappointed, you have gone back to
your Bible, and have said, "I must not meddle with this text,
it is above me." But it has repeated itself in your ears; you
could not make it out; it has followed you—dogged your
steps; it would not go away from you. At last you thought,
"There was a message from God in that text to you." You
prayed over it; while you were praying, some one word in the
text seemed to lift itself right out of the connexion, and
shone upon you like a star, and in the light of that one word
you could see the meaning of all the words that preceded and
followed; and you rose up from your knees, feeling that you
knew the mind of the Spirit there, and had got a step
forward in Scriptural knowledge. You remember the day,
some of you, when you first learned the doctrines of grace.
When we were first converted, we did not know much about
them; we did not know whether God had converted us, or we
had converted ourselves; but we heard a discourse one day
in which some sentences were used, which gave us the clue
to the whole system, and we began at once to see how God
the Father planned, and God the Son carried out, and God
the Holy Spirit applied, and we found ourselves on a sudden
brought into the midst of a system of truths, which we might
perhaps have believed before, but which we could not have
clearly stated, and did not understand. Well, the joy of that
advance in knowledge was exceeding great. I know it was to
me. I can remember well the day and hour, when first I
received those truths in my own soul—when they were burnt
into me, as John Bunyan says—burnt as with a hot iron into
my soul; and I can recollect how I felt I had grown on a

sudden from a babe into a man—that I had made progress in Scriptural knowledge, from having got a hold once for all of the clue to the truth of God. Well, now, in that moment when God the Holy Spirit increased your knowledge, and opened the eyes of your understanding, you had the earnest, that you shall one day see, not through a glass darkly, but face to face, and by-and-bye you shall know the whole truth, even as you are known.

6. But further than this—to put two or three thoughts into one, for brevity's sake: whenever, Christian, thou hast achieved a victory over thy lusts—whenever after hard struggling, thou hast laid a temptation dead at thy feet— thou hast had in that day and hour a foretaste of the joy that awaits thee, when the Lord shall shortly tread Satan under thy feet. That victory in the first skirmish, is the pledge and the earnest of the triumph in the last decisive battle. If thou hast overcome *one* foe, thou shalt overthrow them all. If the walls of Jericho have been dismantled, so shall every fort be carried, and thou shalt go up a conqueror over the ruins thereof; and when, believer, thou hast known thy security in Christ—when thou hast been able to say, "I *know* that my Redeemer liveth, and I am persuaded that he is able to keep that which I have committed to him"—when you felt sure that earth and heaven might reel, but *his* love could never pass away—when you have sung out the strong lines of Toplady,

> "My name from the palms of his hands
> Eternity will not erase;
> Impress'd on his heart it remains
> In marks of indelible grace;"

when you could put your foot upon a rock, and feel that you stood securely, knowing that you were safe in him, and because he lived, you must live also,—in that hour you had the pledge and the foretaste of that glorious security which should be yours, when you are beyond gunshot of the infernal fiend, beyond even the howling of the infernal dog. O Christian, there are many windows to heaven, through which God looks down on thee; and there are some windows through which thou mayest look up to him. Let these *past* enjoyments be guarantees of thy future bliss; let them be to thee as the grapes of Eshcol were to the Jews in the

wilderness; they were the fruit of the land, and when they
tasted them, they said, "It *is* a land that floweth with milk
and honey." These enjoyments are the products of Canaan;
they are handfuls of heavenly flowers thrown over the wall;
they are bunches of heaven's spices, brought to thee by angel
hands across the stream. Heaven is full of joys like these.
Thou hast but a few of them, heaven is strewn with them.
There thy golden joys are but as stones, and thy most
precious jewels are as common as the pebbles of the brook.
Now thou drinkest drops, and they are so sweet, that thy
palate doth not soon forget them; but there thou shalt put
thy lips to the cup, and drink, but never drain it dry; there
thou shalt sit at the well-head, and drink as much as thou
canst draw, and draw as much as thou canst desire. Now
thou seest the glimmerings of heaven as a star twinkling
from leagues of distance; follow that glimmering, and thou
shalt see heaven no more as a star, but as the sun which
shineth in its strength.

8. Permit me to remark yet once more, there is one
foretaste of heaven which the Spirit gives, which it were
very wrong for us to omit. And now, I shall seem, I dare say,
to those who understand not spiritual mysteries, to be as one
that dreams. There are moments when the child of God has
real fellowship with the Lord Jesus Christ. You know what
fellowship between man and man means. There is as real a
fellowship between the Christian and Christ. Our eyes can
look on *him*. I say not that these human optics can behold
the very flesh of Christ; but I say that the eyes of the soul
can here on earth more truly see Christ, after a spiritual
sort, than ever eyes of man saw him when he was in the
flesh on earth. To-day, your head may lean upon the
Saviour's bosom; to-day, he may be your sweet companion,
and with the spouse you may say, "Let him kiss me with the
kisses of his mouth, for his love is better than wine." I pray
you, think not that I rave now. I speak what I do know, and
testify what I have seen, and what many of you have seen
and known too. There are moments with the believer, when,
whether in the body or out of the body, he cannot tell—God
knoweth—but this he knows, that Christ's left hand is under
his head, and his right hand doth embrace him. Christ hath
shown to him his hands and his side. He could say with
Thomas, "My Lord and my God;" but he could not say much

more. The world recedes, it disappears. The things of time
are covered with a pall of darkness; Christ only stands out
before the believer's view. I have known that some believers,
when they have been in this state, could say with the spouse,
"Stay me with apples, comfort me with flagons, for I am sick
of love." Their love of Christ and Christ's love to them, had
overcome them. Their soul was something in the state of
John, whom we described last Lord's-day morning: "When I
saw *him,* I fell at his feet as dead." A sacred faintness
overcomes my soul; I die—I die to prove the fulness of
redeeming love, the love of Christ to me. Oh, these seasons!
Talk ye not of feasts, ye sons of mirth; tell us not of music, ye
who delight in melodious sound; tell us not of wealth, and
rank, and honour, and the joys of victory. One hour with
Christ is worth an eternity of all earth's joys. May I but see
him, may I but see *his* face, but behold *his* beauties—come
winds, blow ye away all earthly joys I have—this joy shall
well content my soul. Let the hot sun of tribulation dry up all
the water-brooks; but this fresh spring shall fill my cup full
to the brim—yea, it shall make a river of delight, wherein
my soul shall bathe. To be with Christ on earth is the best,
the surest, the most ecstatic foretaste and earnest of the joys
of heaven. Forget not this, Christian! If thou hast ever
known Christ, heaven is thine; and when thou hast enjoyed
Christ, thou hast learned a little of what the bliss of futurity
shall be.

9. I do not doubt, also, that on dying beds men get
foretastes of heaven which they never had in health. When
Death begins to pull down the old clay-house, he knocks
away much of the plaster, and then the light shines through
the chinks. When he comes to deal with our rough garment
of clay he pulls it to rags first; and then it is we begin to get
a better view of the robes of righteousness, the fair white
linen of the saints, with which we are always covered,
though we know it not. The nearer to death, the nearer to
heaven, with the believer; the more sick, the nearer he is to
health. The darkest part of his night is indeed the dawning
of the day; just when he shall think he dies he shall begin to
live; and when his flesh drops from him, then is he prepared
to be clothed upon with his house which is from heaven.
Children of God in dying have said wonderful things, which
it were scarcely lawful for us to utter here. It needs the

stillness of the room; the solemn silence of the last hour; the failing eye, the choked utterance, the pale thin hand, to put a soul into their utterances. I remember when a Christian brother, who had often preached with me the gospel, was sore sick and dying, he was suddenly smitten with blindness, which was a first monition of the approach of death, and he said to me—

> "And when ye see my eyestrings break,
>   How sweet my moments roll;
> A mortal paleness on my cheek,
>   But glory in my soul."

And said it with such emphasis, as a man who, but two or three minutes after, stood before his God, that I can never read those lines without feeling how well the poet must have foreseen a death like his. Ay, there are mystic syllables that have dropped from the lips of dying men that have been priceless as the richest pearls. There have been sights of heaven seen in the midst of Jordan which these eyes cannot see, until this breast shall be chilled in the dread and cold stream. All these things that we have mentioned are the fruits of "that Holy Spirit of promise, which is the earnest of our inheritance until the redemption of the purchased possession."

II. A few minutes only—and, O God! do thou help us!—with all solemnity, I utter a few sentences upon THE BLACK REVERSE OF THE JOYOUS PICTURE I HAVE PRESENTED UNTO YOU.

There is another world, for the wicked, as well as for the righteous. They who believe not in Christ are no more annihilated than those who do believe in him. Immortality awaits us all. We die, but we die not; we live *for ever;* and if we fear not God, that immortality is the most frightful curse that ever fell on a creature—

> "To linger in eternal death,
>   Yet death for ever fly."

Can we tell what that world of woe is? In vain do we talk to you about the pit that is bottomless, and the fire that never can be quenched, and the worm that dieth not. These are but images, and images which are used so often that we fear they are almost threadbare in your estimation, and you will scarcely give an ear to them. Listen, then. If thou be this day without God and without Christ in the world, thou hast in thyself a few sparks of that eternal fire; thou hast already been singed by the vehement heat of that furnace which to some men has been so hot that even when they have passed it on earth, like Nebuchadnezzar's mighty men, they have fallen down, smitten by the heat thereof, ere they came within its flames. Ungodly, unconverted men, have an uneasiness of spirit; they are never contented; they want something; if they have that, they will want something more. They do not feel happy; they see through the amusements which the world presents to them; they are wise enough to see that they are hollow; they understand that the fair cheek is painted; they know that its beauty is but mere pretence; they are not befooled; God has awakened them. They are sensible enough to know that this world cannot fill a man's heart; they know that an immortal spirit is never to be satisfied with mortal joys. They are uneasy; they wish to kill time, it hangs heavy on their hands. They wish they could sleep three and twenty hours out of the four and twenty, or drink half the day. They try if they cannot find some pleasure that may wake up their energies—some new device, some novelty, even though it were novelty of sin, which might give a little excitement to a palate that has lost all power to be pleased. Now, when a man gets into that uneasy state, he may make a guess of what hell will be. It will be that uneasiness intensified, magnified to the extreme: to wander through dry places, seeking rest and finding none; always thirsting, but never having a drop of water to cool that thirst; hungering, but feeding upon wind, and hungering still; longing, yearning, groaning, sighing, conscious of misery, sensible of emptiness, feeling poverty, but never getting aught whereby that poverty may be made rich, or that hunger may be stayed. Ah! ye uneasy ones, may your uneasiness bring you to Christ!

But unconverted men without Christ have another curse, which is a sure foretaste to them of hell. They are uneasy about death. I have my mind now upon a person who trembles like an aspen leaf during a thunderstorm; and I know another man who could bear a storm very well, but if there be the slightest thing the matter with him, if he has a cough, he fears his lungs are affected—if he feels a little

hoarse, he is sure he will have bronchitis, and die; and that
thought of dying, he cannot bear. He will hear you talk about
it, and crack a joke over it, merely for the sake of covering up
his own dismay. He fancies you cannot see through him; but
you can plainly discover that he is as afraid of dying as ever
he can be. I know at this moment a family where the
governess was instructed, when she took the situation, never
to mention the subject of death to the children, or else she
would be instantly discharged. That fear of dying which
haunts some men! Not when their blood boils, and they are
excited—then they could rush to the cannon's mouth; but
when they are cool and steady, and look at it—when it is not
the sword's point, and glory, but dying, mere dying, then
they shiver. Oh how these strong men start, and how they
quail! Full many an infidel has recanted his infidelity then—
given it all up, when he has come to deal with the awful
mysteries of death. But those dreads of death are but the
foreshadows of that darker gloom which must gather round
your spirit, except you believe in Christ. With some men it
has even gone further than this. When a man has long
resisted the invitations of the gospel, long gone from bad to
worse, from sin to sin, a horror, an unspeakable horror, will
seize hold upon him at times, especially if he be a man who
is given to intoxication. Then a delirium will come upon him,
mingled with a remorse, which will make his life intolerable.
It has been my unhappy lot to see one or two such cases of
persons who have been ill, and have been vexed with fears,
fears of a most hideous caste, which you could not remove.
You speak to them about Christ; they say, "What have I to
do with him? I have cursed him hundreds of times." You
speak to them about faith in Christ; "Faith in Christ," they
say, "what is the use of that to me? I am past hope; I am
given up, and I do not care about it either." And then they
collapse—go back again into that dull despair, which is the
sure advance guard of damnation itself. With these men one
may pray; they bid you pray for them, and then they say,
"Get up, sir; it is of no use; God will never hear you for *me*."
They will ask you to go home and pray; but assure you that
it will be useless to do so. You read the Bible to them; "Don't
read the Scriptures," say they; "every text cuts me to the
quick, for I have neglected the Word of God, and all my time
now is past." You tell them that

> "While the lamp holds out to burn,
> The vilest sinner may return."

No, no, *they* cannot. You may tell them that there is hope—
that Jesus Christ calls many at the eleventh hour; you
picture to them the thief on the cross. No, no, they put far
from them all hope, and choose their own delusions, and
perish. Now, such men give the gravest picture of what hell
must be, in these forebodings of the wrath to come. I saw one
man, now in eternity, and where he is God knoweth; I could
not describe to you what I saw that day of him. He said he
would not die, and walked up and down as long as there was
life in him, under the notion, as he said, that if he could walk
about he knew he should not die. He would not die, he said;
he *would* live, he *must* live. "I cannot die," said he, "for I
must be damned if I die; I feel I must;" and that poor wretch,
sometimes giving ear to your admonitions, then cursing you
to your face, bidding you pray, and then blaspheming—
dying with hell commenced, with all the horrors of perdition
just beginning—a sort of infant perdition strangling to be
born within him! Oh! may God deliver you from ever
knowing this vilest premonition of destruction! And how
shall you be delivered, but by this? "Believe in the Lord
Jesus Christ, and thou shalt be saved; for he that believeth
and is baptized shall be saved"—so saith the Scripture—"he
that believeth not shall be damned." Trust Christ and you
are saved, be you whom you may. Come to the foot of the
cross, and cast yourself where his blood is dropping, and you
are saved. Give your heart to him; believe in him; repose
your confidence in him. May the Spirit of God enable you to
do this! May he help you to repent of sin; and having
repented, may he bring you to Christ, as the sin propitiator!
and may you go away this day, saying, "I *do* believe in
Christ; my soul rests in him!" And if you can say that, the joy
and peace in believing, which must follow a simple faith in
Christ, shall be to you the work of "the Holy Spirit of
promise and the earnest of our inheritance, until the
redemption of the purchased possession."

24

"For Ever With The Lord"

"...so shall we ever be with the Lord."   **1 Thessalonians 4:17**

We know that these words are full of consolation, for the apostle says in the next verse, "Wherefore comfort one another with these words." The very words it appears were dictated by the Holy Spirit the Comforter, to be repeated by the saints to each other with the view of removing sorrow from the minds of the distressed. The comfort is intended to give us hope in reference to those who have fallen asleep. Look over the list of those, beloved in the Lord, who have departed from you, to your utmost grief, and let the words of our text be a handkerchief for your tears. Sorrow not as those that are without hope, for they are with the Lord though they are not with you, and by-and-by you shall surely meet them where your Lord is the centre of fellowship for ever and ever. The separation will be very transient; the reunion will be everlasting. These words are also intended to comfort the saints with regard to themselves, and I pray that they may be a cordial to any who are sick with fear, a matchless medicine to charm away the heartache from all believers. The fact that you bear about a dying body is very evident to some of you by your frequent and increasing infirmities and pains, and this, it may be, is a source of depression of spirits. You know that when a few years are gone you must go the way whence you shall not return; but be not dismayed, for you shall not go into a strange country alone and unattended. There is a friend that sticketh closer than a brother, who will not fail you nor forsake you; and, moreover, you are going home; your Lord will be with you while you are departing, and then you will be ever with him. Therefore, though sickness warn thee of the near approach of death, be not in the least dismayed; though pain and weariness should make thy heart and flesh fail, yet doubt not of thy triumph through the Redeemer's blood; though it should sometimes make thy flesh to tremble when thou rememberest thy many sins and the weakness of thy faith, yet be of good cheer, for thy sins and weakness of faith will soon be removed far from thee, and thou shalt be in his presence where there is fulness of joy, and at his right hand, where there are pleasures for evermore. Comfort yourselves, then, both with regard to those who have gone before and in reference to the thought of your own departure.

Observe that the comfort which the apostle here presents to us may be partly derived from the fact of the resurrection, but not chiefly; for he does not so much refer to the words "The dead in Christ shall rise," as to these last—"so shall we ever be with the Lord." It is a great truth that you will rise again; it is a sweeter truth that you will be "ever with the Lord." There is some consolation also in the fact that we shall meet our departed brethren when we all shall be caught up together in the clouds, to meet the Lord in the air. Blissful will be the general assembling of the redeemed, never again to be broken up; the joy of meeting never to part again is a sweet remedy for the bitterness of separation. There is great comfort in it, but the main stress of consolation does not lie even there. It is pleasant to think of the eternal fellowships of the godly above, but the best of all is the promised fellowship with our Lord,—"So shall we ever be with the Lord." Whatever else you draw comfort from, neglect not this deep, clear, and overflowing well of delight. There are other sources of good cheer in connection with the glory to be revealed, for heaven is a many-sided joy; but still none can excel the glory of communion with Jesus Christ, wherefore comfort one another in the first place, and most constantly, with these words, "So shall we ever be with the Lord."

I shall view our text, in order to our comfort at this time, in three lights. I look upon it, first, as a *continuance*—we are with the Lord even now, and we ever shall be; secondly, as *an advancement*—we shall ere long be more fully with the Lord than we are now; and thirdly, as a *coherence*—for we both are and shall be with him in a close and remarkable manner.

I. I regard the text as A CONTINUANCE of our present spiritual state—"So shall we ever be with the Lord." To my mind, and I think I am not incorrect in so expounding, the apostle means that nothing shall prevent our continuing to be ever with the Lord; death shall not separate us, nor the terrors of that tremendous day when the voice of the archangel and the trump of God shall be heard; by divine plan and arrangement all shall be so ordained that "So shall we ever be with the Lord." By being caught up into the clouds, or in one way or another, our abiding in Christ shall remain unbroken. As we have received Christ Jesus the Lord, so shall we walk in him, whether in life or in death.

I understand him to mean that we are with the Lord now, and that nothing shall separate us from him. Even now like Enoch we walk with God, and we shall not be deprived of divine communion. Our fear might be that in the future state something might happen which would become a dividing gulf between us and Christ, but the apostle assures us that it will not be so, there shall be such plans and methods used that "so shall we ever be with the Lord." At any rate, I know that, if this be not *the* truth here intended, it is *a* truth worthy to be expounded, and therefore I do not hesitate to enlarge upon it.

We are with the Lord *in this life* in a high spiritual sense. Read you not, in the epistle to the Colossians, "for ye are dead, and your life is hid with Christ in God"? Were you not "buried with him in baptism, wherein also ye are risen with him through the faith of the operation of God, who hath raised him from the dead"? Do you not know what it is to be dead to the world in him, and to be living a secret life with him? Are you not risen with Christ; ay, and do you not understand in some measure what it is to be raised up together, and made to sit together in the heavenlies in Christ Jesus? If you are not with him, brethren, you are not Christians at all, for this is just the mark of the Christian, that he follows with Christ. It is essential to salvation to be a sheep of Christ's fold, nay more, a partaker of Christ's life, a member of his mystical body, a branch of the spiritual vine. Separated from him we are spiritually dead; he himself has said, "If a man abide not in me, he is cast forth as a branch, and is withered; and men gather them, and cast them into the fire, and they are burned." Jesus is not far from any one of his people; nay, it is our privilege to follow him whithersoever he goeth, and his loving word to us is, "Abide in me, and I in you." May he enable us sweetly to realize this. We are, dear brethren, constantly with Christ in the sense of abiding union with him, for we are joined unto the Lord, and are one spirit. Sometimes this union is very sweetly apparent to ourselves; "We know that we are in him that is true," and in consequence we feel an intense joy, even Christ's own joy fulfilled in us. For the same reason we are at times bowed down with intense sorrow; for being in and with Christ we have fellowship with him in his sufferings, being made conformable with his death: this is such sweet sorrow that the more we experience it the better.

> "Live or die, or work or suffer,
> Let my weary soul abide,
> In all changes whatsoever,
> Sure and stedfast by thy side."

> "Nothing can delay my progress,
> Nothing can disturb my rest,
> If I shall, where'er I wander,
> Lean my spirit on thy breast."

This companionship is, we trust, made manifest to others by its fruits. It ought always so to be; the life of the Christian should be manifestly a life with Christ. Men should take knowledge of us that we have been with Jesus, and have learned of him; they should see that there is something in us which could not have been there if it were not for the Son of God; a temper, a spirit, a course of life, which could not have come by nature but must have been wrought in us through grace which has been received from him in whom dwells a fulness of grace, even our Lord Jesus Christ. Brethren, if we are what we ought to be, our life is spent in conscious communion, growing out of continued union with the Lord Jesus Christ, and if it be so we have that rich assurance which is written by the beloved John, "If that which ye have heard from the beginning shall remain in you, ye also shall continue in the Son, and in the Father."

We are with him, dear friends, in this sense too, that his unchanging love is always set upon us, and our love, feeble though it sometimes may be, never quite dies out. In both senses that challenge of the apostle is true, "Who shall separate us from the love of God which is in Christ Jesus our Lord?" We can say, "I am my beloved's, and his desire is towards me;" and, on the other hand, we also testify, "My beloved is mine, and I am his." He claims us and we claim him: he loves us and we love him. There is a union of heart between us. We are with him, not against him; we are in league with him, enlisted beneath his banner, obedient to his Spirit. For us to live is Christ: we have no other aim.

He is with us by the continued indwelling of the Holy Ghost, who is with us and shall be in us for ever. His anointing abideth on us, and because of it we abide in Christ Jesus. He has sent us the Comforter to represent himself, and through that divine Paraclete he continues to be with us, and so even now we are ever with the Lord.

Our Lord has also promised to be with us whenever we are engaged in his work. That is a grand word of encouragement, "Lo, I am with you alway, even unto the end of the world." Think not, therefore, that it will be the first time of our being with Christ when we shall see him in glory, for even now he manifests himself unto us as he does not unto the world. Has he not often fulfilled his promise, "Where two or three are gathered together in my name, there am I in the midst of them"? We have heard the sound of our Master's feet behind us when we have been going on his errands; we have felt the touch of his hand when we have come to the forefront of the battle for his sake, and we have known that he dwelleth in us by his Spirit, and is with us by the power wherewith he has attended our work, and the deeds which he has wrought by the gospel which we have proclaimed. The Lord Jesus is with his church in her tribulation for his name's sake, and he will ever be so, for he forsaketh not his saints. "Fear not, I am with thee," is as much a word of the Lord under the gospel as in Old Testament times. By the power of his blessed Spirit Jesus abides with us, and through this present dispensation he enables us to be "ever with the Lord."

But, my brethren, the time is coming when *we shall die,*

unless the Lord shall descend from heaven with a shout meanwhile. Assuredly in the article of death we shall still be with the Lord.

> "Death may my soul divide
> From this abode of clay;
> But love shall keep me near thy side
> Through all the gloomy way."

"Yea, though I walk through the valley of the shadow of death, I will fear no evil: for thou art with me; thy rod and thy staff they comfort me." This makes dying such delicious work to the people of God, for then especially is Jesus seen to be near. By death they escape from death, and henceforth it is no more death for them to die. When Jesus meets his saints there seems no iron gate to pass through, but in a moment they close their eyes on earth and open them in glory. Beloved, there should be no more bondage through fear of death, since Christ attends his people even in their descent into the tomb, and strengthens them upon the bed of languishing. This has been a great joy to many departing saints. A dying believer, who was attended by an apothecary who was also a child of God, was observed to be whispering to himself while dying, and his good attendant, wishing to know what were his last words, placed his ear against the dying man's lips, and heard him repeating to himself again and again the words, "For ever with the Lord, For ever with the Lord." When heart and flesh were failing, the departing one knew that God was the strength of his life and his portion for ever, and so he chose for his soft, low-whispered, dying song,—"For ever with the Lord."

After death, we shall abide awhile in the separate, disembodied state, and we shall know as to our soul what it is to be still with the Lord; for what saith the apostle? "Knowing that when we are absent from the body we are present with the Lord." The dying thief was to be that day with Christ in paradise, and such shall be our lot as soon as our souls shall have passed out of this tenement of clay into that wondrous state of which we know so little. Our pure spirits shall "come unto Mount Sion, and unto the city of the living God, the heavenly Jerusalem, and to an innumerable company of angels, to the general assembly and church of the firstborn, which are written in heaven, and to God the

Judge of all, and to the spirits of just men made perfect, and to Jesus the mediator of the new covenant, and to the blood of sprinkling, that speaketh better things than that of Abel." Who is dismayed when such a prospect opens up before him?

Ay, and this body which shall fall asleep, though apparently it shall be destroyed, yet shall it not be so, but it shall only slumber awhile, and then awake again and say, "When I awake I am still with thee." Constantly death is described as sleeping in Jesus; that is the state of the saint's mortal frame through the interregnum between death and resurrection. The angels shall guard our bodies; all that is essential to complete the identity of our body shall be securely preserved, so that the very seed which was put into the earth shall rise again in the beauty of efflorescence which becomes it; all, I say, that is essential shall be preserved intact, because it is still with Christ. It is a glorious doctrine which is stated by the apostle in the first epistle to the Thessalonians, the fifth chapter, at the ninth and tenth verses, "For God hath not appointed us to wrath, but to obtain salvation by our Lord Jesus Christ, who died for us, that, whether we wake or sleep, we should live together with him."

In due time the last trump shall sound and *Christ shall come,* but the saints shall be with him. The infinite providence has so arranged that Christ shall not come without his people, for "Them also that sleep in Jesus shall God bring with him." The saints shall be with him in the advent as they are now. Our souls shall hear the shout of victory and join in it; the voice of the archangel shall be actually heard by all his redeemed, and the trump of God shall be sounded in the hearing of every one of his beloved, for we shall be with Jesus all through that glorious transaction. Whatever the glory and splendour of the second advent, we shall be with Jesus in it. I am not going to give you glimpses of the revealed future, or offer any suggestion as to the sublime history which is yet to be written, but most certainly there is to be a last general judgment, and then we shall be with Christ, assessors with him at that day. Being ourselves first acquitted, we shall take our seat upon the judgment bench with him. What saith the Holy Ghost by the apostle—"Do ye not know that the saints shall judge the world? Know ye not that we shall judge angels?" The fallen angels, to their shame, shall in part receive the verdict of their condemnation from the lips of men, and thus vengeance shall be taken upon them for all the mischief they have done to the sons of men. Oh, think of it: amidst the terror of the tremendous day you shall be at ease, resting in the love of God, and beholding the glory of Christ, and "so shall you ever be with the Lord."

There is, moreover, to be a reign of Christ. I cannot read the Scriptures without perceiving that there is to be a millennial reign, as I believe, upon the earth, and that there shall be new heavens and new earth, wherein dwelleth righteousness. Well, whatever that reign is to be, we shall reign also. "And he that overcometh, and keepeth my works unto the end, to him will I give power over the nations: and he shall rule them with a rod of iron; as the vessels of a potter shall they be broken to shivers; even as I received of my Father." "And hast made us unto our God kings and priests: and we shall reign on the earth." He shall reign, but it will be "before his ancients gloriously." We shall be partakers in the splendours of the latter days, whatever they may be, and "So shall we ever be with the Lord."

The particular incident of the text does not exhaust the words, but you may apply them to the whole story of God's own children. From the first day of the spiritual birth of the Lord's immortals, until they are received up into the seventh heaven to dwell with God, their history may be summed up in these words, "So shall we ever be with the Lord." Whether caught up into the clouds or here below on this poor afflicted earth, in paradise or in the renovated earth, in the grave or in the glory, we shall ever be with the Lord. And when cometh the end, and God alone shall reign, and the mediatorial kingdom shall cease, ages, ages, and ages shall revolve, but "so shall we ever be with the Lord." The saints immortal shall be with their covenant Head, and like him free from sorrow. All tendency to sin shall be gone, and all fear of change or death; their intimate communion will last on for ever:—

> "Blessed state! beyond conception!
> Who its vast delights can tell?
> May it be my blissful portion,
> With my Saviour there to dwell."

I think the text looks like a continuation of what is already begun, only rising to something higher and better. To be with Christ is life eternal: this we have already, and shall continue to have, and "so shall we ever be with the Lord."

II. Secondly, most assuredly, brethren, the text is A GREAT ADVANCEMENT—"So shall we ever be with the Lord."

It is an advancement upon this present state, for however spiritual minded we may be, and however in consequence thereof we may be very near unto our Lord Jesus, yet still we know that while we are present in the body we are absent from the Lord. This life, at its very best, is still comparatively an absence from the Lord, but in the world to come we shall be more perfectly at home. Now we cannot now in the highest sense be with Christ, for we must, according to the apostle's phraseology, "depart, and be with Christ; which is far better"; but there we shall be for ever beholding his face unveiled. Earth is not heaven, though the believer begins the heavenly life while he is upon it. We are not with Christ as to place, nor as to actual sight, but in the glory-land we shall be.

And it is an advancement, in the next place, upon the present state of the departed, for though their souls are with the Lord yet their bodies are subject to corruption. Still does the sepulchre contain the blessed dust of the fathers of our Israel, or scattered to the four winds of heaven the martyr's ashes are with us still. The glorified saints are not as yet consciously "with the Lord" as to their complete manhood, but when the grand event shall occur of which Paul speaks, the body shall be reanimated. This is our glorious hope. We can say with the patriarch Job—"For I know that my redeemer liveth, and that he shall stand at the latter day upon the earth: and though after my skin worms destroy this body, yet in my flesh shall I see God; whom I shall see for myself, and mine eyes shall behold, and not another; though my reins be consumed within me." Know ye not, brethren, that flesh and blood cannot inherit the kingdom of God? That is, as they are; but this corruptible must put on incorruption, and this mortal must put on immortality, and then shall the entire manhood, the perfected manhood, the fully developed manhood, of which this manhood is as it were but a shrivelled seed, be in the fullest and divinest sense for ever with the Lord. This is an advancement even upon the present paradisiacal state of departed saints.

And now let us consider what this glorious condition is to which we shall be advanced. We shall be with the Lord in the strongest possible meaning of that language. So with him that we shall never mind earthly things again, shall have no more to go into city business, or into the workshop, or into the field; we shall have nought to do but to be engaged for ever with him in such occupations as shall have no tendency to take us off from communion with him. We shall be so with him as to have no sin to becloud our view of him; the understanding will be delivered from all the injury which sin has wrought in it, and we shall know him even as we are known. We shall see him as a familiar friend, and sit with him at his marriage feast. We shall be with him so as to have no fear of his ever being grieved and hiding his face from us again. We shall never again be made to cry out in bitterness of spirit, "Oh, that I knew where I might find him." We shall always know his love, always return it, and always swim in the full stream of it, enjoying it to the full. There will be no lukewarmness to mar our fellowship. He shall never have to say to us, "I would thou wert either cold or hot." There shall be no weariness to suspend our ceaseless bliss; we shall never have to cease from fellowship with him, because our physical frame is exhausted through the excessive joy of our heart; the vessel will be strengthened to hold the new wine. No doubts shall intrude into our rest, neither doctrinal doubts nor doubts about our interest in him, for we shall be so consciously with him as to have risen ten thousand leagues above that gloomy state. We shall know that he is ours, for his left hand shall be under our head and his right hand shall embrace us, and we shall be with him beyond all hazard of any removal from him. The chief blessedness seems to me to lie in this, that we shall be with him and with him always. Now we are with the Lord in conscious enjoyment sometimes, and then we are away from him, but there it will be constant, unwavering fellowship. No break shall ever occur in the intimate communion of the saints with Christ. Here we know that our high days and bright Sabbaths, with their sweetest joys, must have their eventides, and then come the work-days with the burden of the week upon them; but there the Sabbath is eternal, the worship endless, the praise unceasing, the bliss unbounded.

"For ever with the Lord." Speak ye of a thousand years of reigning? What is that compared with "for ever with the Lord"? The millennium is little compared with "for ever"—a millennium of millenniums would be nothing to it. There can come no end to us and no end to our bliss, since there can be no end to him—"because I live, ye shall live also."

"For ever with the Lord"—What will it mean? I remember a sermon upon this text by a notable preacher, of which the heads were as follows—"For ever life, for ever light, for ever love, for ever peace, for ever rest, for ever joy." What a chain of delights! What more can heart imagine or hope desire? Carry those things in your mind and you will get, if you can drink into them, some idea of the blessedness which is contained in being for ever with the Lord; but still recollect these are only the fruits, and not the root of the joy. Jesus is better than all these. His company is more than the joy which comes out of it. I do not care so much for "life for ever," nor for "light for ever," as I do for "for ever with the Lord." Oh, to be with him! I ask no other bliss, and cannot imagine aught more heavenly. Why, the touch of the hem of his garment healed the sick woman; the sight of him was enough to give life to us when we were dead! What, then, must it be to be with him actually, consciously, and always? to be with him no more by faith, but in very deed with him for ever? My soul is ready to swoon away with too much joy as she drinks even in her shallow measure into the meaning of this thought, and I dare not venture further. I must leave you to muse your souls into it, for it needs quiet thought and room for free indulgence of holy imagination till you make your soul to dream of this excess of joy. "Eye hath not seen, nor ear heard, neither have entered into the heart of man, the things which God hath prepared for them that love him. But God hath revealed them unto us by his Spirit."

> "O glorious hour! O blest abode!
> I shall be near and like my God;
> And flesh and sin no more control
> The sacred pleasures of my soul."

We love to think of being with Jesus under the aspect which the text specially suggests to us. We are to be for ever with the Redeemer, not as Jesus the Saviour only, but as *the Lord*. Here we have seen him on the cross and lived thereby;

we are with him now in his crossbearing and shame, and it is well; but our eternal companionship with him will enable us to rejoice in him *as the Lord*. What said our Master in his blessed prayer? "I will that they also, whom thou hast given me, be with me where I am; that they may behold my glory." It will be heaven to us to be for ever with him as the Lord. Oh, how we shall delight to obey him as our Lord! How we shall triumph as we see what a lord he is over all the universe! and what a conqueror he is over all his enemies! He will be more and more the Lord to us as we see all things put under him. We shall for ever hail him as King of kings, and Lord of lords. How we will adore him there when we see him in his glory. We do worship him now, and are not ashamed to believe that the Man of Nazareth is "very God of very God;" but oh, how his deity will shine upon us with infinite effulgence when we come to be near him. Thanks be to his name, we shall be strengthened to endure the sight, and we shall rejoice to see ourselves in the full blaze of his glory. Then shall we see what our poet endeavoured to describe when he said—

> " Adoring saints around him stand,
> And thrones and powers before him fall;
> The God shines gracious through the Man,
> And sheds sweet glories on them all."

We shall be for ever with the Lord, and his Lordship shall be most upon our minds. He has been raised into glory and honour, and is no more able to suffer shame.

> "No more the bloody spear,
> The cross and nails no more;
> For hell itself shakes at his word,
> And all the heavens adore."

III. Now we come to our third point, and shall consider what, for want of a better word, I entitle A COHERENCE. Those who are acquainted with the Greek language know that the *"with"* here is not *meta*, which signifies being in the same place with a person, but *sun,* which goes very much further, and implies a coherence, the two who are with each other are intimately connected. Let me show you what I mean. We are to be for ever with the Lord: now, the Christian's life is all along like the life of his Lord, and so it is a life with Christ. He was in all things with his brethren, and grace makes us to be with him. Just hurriedly look at your spiritual experience and your Lord's life, and see the parallel. When you were new born as a Christian you were born as Jesus Christ was, for you were born of the Holy Ghost. What happened after that? The devil tried to destroy the new life in you, just as Herod tried to kill your Lord: you were with Christ in danger, early and imminent. You grew in stature and in grace, and while yet grace was young, you staggered those who were about you with the things you said, and did, and felt, for they could not understand you; even thus when he went up to the temple our Lord amazed the doctors who gathered around him. The Spirit of God rested upon you, not in the same measure, but still as a matter of fact it did descend upon you as it did upon your Lord. You have been with him in Jordan's stream, and have received the divine acknowledgment that you are indeed the son of God. Your Lord was led into the wilderness to be tempted; and you too have been tempted of the devil. You have been with the Lord all along, from the first day until now. If you have been by grace enabled to live as you should, you have trodden the separated path with Jesus; you have been in the world, but not of it, holy, harmless, undefiled, and separate from sinners. Therefore you have been despised; you have had to take your share of being unknown and misrepresented, because you are even as he was in the world. "Therefore the world knoweth us not, because it knew him not." As he was here to serve, you have been with him as a servant, you have carried his yoke and counted it an easy load. You have been crucified to the world with him: you know the meaning of his cross, and delight to bear it after him. You are dead to the world with him, and wish to be as one buried to it. You have already in your measure partaken of his resurrection, and are living in newness of life. Your life-story is still to be like the life-story of your Lord, only painted in miniature. The more you watch the life of Christ the more clearly you will see the life of a spiritual man depicted in it, and the more clearly will you see what the saints' future will be. You have been with Christ in life, and you will be with him when you come to die. You will not die the expiatory death which fell to his lot, but you will die feeling that "it is finished," and you will breathe out your soul, saying, "Father, into thy hand I commend my spirit."

Then our Lord went to paradise, and you will go there too. You shall enjoy a sojourn where he spent his interval in the disembodied state. You shall be with him, and like him, and then like him you shall rise when your third morning cometh. "After two days will he revive us; in the third day he will raise us up, and we shall live in his sight." "Thy dead men shall live, together with my dead body shall they arise." You shall also ascend as Christ did. Do you catch the thought? How did he ascend? In clouds. "A cloud received him out of their sight," and a cloud shall receive you. You shall be caught up into the clouds to meet the Lord in the air, and so shall you be ever with the Lord, in the sense of being like to him, walking with him in experience, and passing through the like events. That likeness shall continue for ever and for ever. Our lives shall run parallel with that of our Lord.

Think then, beloved, we are to be like Christ as to our character: we are to be with the Lord by sharing his moral and spiritual likeness. Conformed to his image, we shall be adorned with his beauty. When the mother of Darius saw two persons entering her pavilion, she being a prisoner bowed to the one whom she supposed to be Alexander. It turned out to be Hyphestion, the King's favourite. Upon discovering that it was Hyphestion the lady humbly begged Alexander's pardon for paying obeisance to the wrong person, but Alexander answered, "You have not mistaken, Madam, for he also is Alexander," meaning that he loved him so much that he regarded him as his other self. Our Lord looks on his beloved as one with himself, and makes them like himself. You remember, brethren, how John bowed down before one of his fellow servants, the prophets in heaven. It was a great blunder to make, but I dare say you and I will be likely to make the same, for the saints are so like their Lord. Know ye not that "we shall be like him when we shall see him as he is"? Christ will rejoice to see them all covered with the glory which his Father has given him. He will not be ashamed to call them brethren. Those poor people of his, who were so full of infirmity, and mourned over it so much, they shall be so like him that they shall be at once seen to be his brethren. Where shall such favoured ones be found?

We shall be with him in the sense that we shall be partakers of all the blessedness and glory which our adorable Lord now enjoys. We shall be accepted together with him. Is he the beloved of the Lord? Does his Father's heart delight in him, as well it may? Behold ye also shall be called Hephzibah, for his delight shall be in you. You shall be beloved of the Father's soul. Is he enriched with all manner of blessings beyond conception? So shall you be, for he has blessed us with all spiritual blessings in Christ Jesus, according as he has chosen us in him. Is Christ exalted? Oh, how loftily is he lifted up to sit upon a glorious high throne for ever! But you shall sit upon his throne with him and share his exaltation as you have shared his humiliation. Oh, the delight of thus being joint heirs with Christ, and with him in the possession of all that he possesses. What is heaven? It is the place which his love suggested, which his genius invented, which his bounty provided, which his royalty has adorned, which his wisdom has prepared, which he himself glorifies; in that heaven you are to be with him for ever. You shall dwell in the King's own palace. Its gates of pearl and streets of gold shall not be too good for you. You who love him are to abide for ever with him, not near him in a secondary place, as a servant lives at the lodge gate of his master's mansion, but with him in the self-same palace in the metropolis of the universe.

In a word, believers are to be identified with Christ for ever. That seems to me to be the very life and essence of the text: with him for ever, that is, identified with him for ever. Do they ask for the Shepherd? They cannot behold him to perfection except as surrounded by his sheep. Will the King be illustrious? How can that be if his subjects are lost? Do they ask for the bridegroom? They cannot imagine him in the fulness of joy without his bride. Will the Head be blessed? It could not be if it were separated from the members. Will Christ be for ever glorified? How can he be if he shall lose his jewels? He is a foundation, and what would he be if all his people were not built upon him into the similitude of a palace? O brethren, there shall be no Christ without Christians; there shall be no Saviour without the saved ones; there shall be no Elder Brother without the younger brethren; there shall be no Redeemer without his redeemed. We are his fulness, and he must have us with him. We are identified with him for ever. Nothing can ever divide us from him. Oh, joy, joy for ever. Hallelujah!

> "Since Christ and we are one,
> Why should we doubt or fear?
> If he in heaven hath fix'd his throne,
> He'll fix his members there."

Two or three practical sentences. One word is this—*This "with the Lord" must begin now.* Do you wish to be for ever with the Lord? You must be with him by becoming his disciple in this life. None come to be with the Lord hereafter who are not with the Lord here in time. See to it, dear hearers, see to it, lest this unspeakable privilege should never be yours. Next, every Christian should seek to be more and more with Christ, for *the growth and glory of your life lies there.* Do you want to have heaven below? Be with Christ below. Do you want to know at once what eternal bliss is? Know it by living now with the Lord.

The next word is, *how plainly then the way of life is to be with the Lord.* If you want to be saved, sinner, you must be "with the Lord." There is no other way for you. Come near to him, and lay hold upon him by faith. Life lies there. Come to him by a humble, tearful faith. Come at once.

And, lastly, *what must it be to be without the Lord?* What must it be to be against the Lord? For it comes to that, "He that is not with me," saith he, "is against me." To be for ever without the Lord, banished from his love, and light, and life, and peace, and rest, and joy! What a loss will this be! What must it be to be for ever against the Lord! Think of it: for ever hating Jesus, for ever plotting against him, for ever gnashing your teeth against him; this is hell, this is the infinite of misery, to be against the Lord of love and life and light. Turn ye from this fatal course. Believe on him: "Kiss the Son, lest he be angry, and ye perish from the way, when his wrath is kindled but a little. Blessed are all they that put their trust in him." Amen.

25

Fear Of Death

"And deliver them who through fear of death were all their lifetime subject to bondage."   **Hebrews 2:15**

It is a very natural thing that man should fear to die, for man was not originally created to die. When Adam and Eve were first placed in the garden of Eden, they were in such a condition that they might have remained there for a myriad of years if they had kept their integrity. There was no reason why unfallen man should die; but now that we have sinned, the seeds of corruption are in this flesh of ours, and it is appointed unto men once to die. Yet, as if the body knew that it was not according to the first decree of heaven that it should go to the earth and to the worm, it has a natural reluctance to return to its last bed. And this fear of death, so far as it is natural, is not wrong. In fact, it subserves a very high purpose in the economy of mankind, for there is many a man who might be tempted to end this mortal life were it not for the fear of death. But to end his life by his own hand would be a dreadful deed; it would prove that he was not the child of God, for "ye know that no murderer hath eternal life abiding in him." I mean, of course, if such a deed were done by anyone in possession of his senses; I am not giving any judgment on those who are not in the possession of reason, and who are not accountable for what they do. If any man in his sober senses were to commit suicide, we could entertain no hope of eternal life for him. Yet many would do so were it not that there is impressed upon them the fear of what would result from thus ending their being.

So far, you see, the fear of death answers a good purpose, and is, in itself, right; but it can very readily go beyond the point where it is right into the region wherein it becomes evil; and I do not doubt that many godly persons have a fear of death about them which is very evil, and which produces very evil effects. Some, no doubt, have been hindered from confessing Christ, and following him fully, through fear of death; not, perhaps, so much now as in the days of the martyrs. Then, there were heroic spirits that went willingly to the stake, or to some other painful form of death which the tyrant of the hour decreed, and cheerfully, with shouts of victory, laid down their lives, which they did not count dear unto them, for the sake of Jesus Christ. But there were timid spirits that shrank from such an ordeal; they loved life, and they feared death, especially in the terrible forms in which it was thrust upon them. This shrinking would be wrong in any one of us; if the fear of death made us dishonour Christ, we should be guilty of deadly sin. If any man resolves to follow Christ, he must not love his own life in comparison with his love to Jesus Christ, but he must be willing even to lay it down for the sake of him who gave up his life upon the cross for us.

Fear of death also causes some Christian people to have to endure many needless sorrows. They are ill, and likely to die, and, instead of being in a calm and serene state of mind, as they ought to be, they are greatly perturbed and distressed. Even while they are well, it sometimes happens that, sitting down, and thinking upon their last hours, they are burdened and depressed. Now this sorrow is a sorrow of the flesh which ought to be avoided; we ought to seek for grace to conquer it so that we may not have the sorrow of the world which worketh death.

This fear of death is very dishonouring to God. It looks as if you could trust him in fair weather, but not in storms; could believe in him while you are well and strong, but could not trust in him when health and strength are failing you. Never forget what David said, "He that is our God is the God of salvation; and unto God the Lord belong the issues from death." We greatly glorify God when we can say with Job, "Though he slay me, yet will I trust in him;" but if we are afraid to die, it looks as if we had not a whole-hearted trust in God, or that perfect love to him which casteth out fear.

And this fear of death also tends very much to dishonour our holy religion in the eyes of those who are not believers in Jesus. The calmness with which the Christian expects his end, or even the holy joy with which he anticipates it, is one of the things which ungodly men cannot comprehend; and even if they will not confess it, they are a good deal impressed by it, and often feel their hearts longing to know that blessed secret which can make Christians look forward to their last days on earth in such a cheery spirit. The Christian who contemplates death with joy is a living sermon. He is a better defence of the gospel than all the works that Butler and Paley, and the other writers of Christian evidences have ever been able to compile. Hence, dear friends, the Church of Christ loses this defence, and the world loses this evidence, when we are troubled by the fear of death. This fear ought not to be found in Christians; and if it ever is, they ought to strive against it until they overcome it.

> "Why should we start, or fear to die?
> What timorous worms we mortals are!
> Death is the gate of endless joy,
> And yet we dread to enter there."

> "The pains, the groans, the dying strife,
> Fright our approaching souls away;
> Still we shrink back again to life,
> Fond of our prison and our clay."

"How are we to get rid of this fear?" asks one. Well, let us never try to get rid of it, as some do, by forgetting all about death. That would be to live as the brutes that perish; they live their little day here without any thought beyond the present. The ox and the sheep go to the slaughter-house without the power to look beyond the present life. I would not like to obtain peace of mind by descending to the level of those "dumb, driven cattle." Yet there are many men whose only peace arises from thoughtlessness; yet that is a sorry peace which cannot endure contemplation and con-sideration. Why, we know men who are bold enough in company, and who can even blaspheme God; but set them down in a room by themselves, compel them to think in solitude even for a single hour, and you could not condemn them to a greater misery. They cannot bear the idea of parting with their present joys; venturing into another world seems to them such a hazardous enterprise that they forget all about it, and shut their eyes to all thoughts beyond this life. It is not in that way that Christians seek to overcome their fear of death. They are thoughtful, and they wish ever to ponder, to consider, and to judge concerning the future as well as the present. They desire to look beyond this mortal state; they ask for brighter vision and clearer eyesight, and do not want to shut their eyes to the future, whatever it may have in store for them.

I am going to try to answer three questions concerning this fear of death. First, *where shall we look to be delivered from it?* Secondly, *what shall we further think of to help us conquer it?* And, thirdly, *what shall we do to overcome it?*

I. First, then, WHERE SHALL WE LOOK TO BE DELIVERED FROM THE FEAR OF DEATH?

The answer is, beloved, that you must look for that where you are bound to look for everything, namely, TO THE LORD JESUS CHRIST, for there is no true deliverance from the fear of death except by looking unto him whose death is the death of death. The verse before our text suggests this when it tells us that Jesus Christ became man, "that through death he might destroy him that had the power of death, that is, the devil; and deliver them who through fear of death were all their lifetime subject to bondage."

How does Christ take away from us the fear of death? He does it, first, *by taking away from us the sin which is the sting of death.* To die forgiven, "accepted in the Beloved," is not really to die, but to depart out of this world unto the Father. Unforgiven sin is that which makes it hard to lay the head upon the dying pillow; but when sin is forgiven, and we know that it is, and we have perfect peace with God, we can even long for that last evening of life to come that we may undress, and sleep in Jesus. Be sure, beloved, that you are forgiven; "make your calling and election sure:" know for a certainty that Jesus Christ's words apply to you, "Verily, verily, I say unto you, he that believeth on me hath everlasting life;" rest completely upon that sacrifice which he once offered upon the cross when he made a full atonement for all who believe in him; understand that he hath washed you from your sins in his blood, and made you kings and priests unto God; and then I do not see how the fear of death can live in you any longer.

> "If sin be pardon'd, I'm secure;
> Death hath no sting beside:
> The law gives sin its damning power;
> But Christ, my ransom, died."

Next, Christ has delivered you from the fear of death *by changing the very character of death itself*. You know what he said to Martha, "Whosoever liveth and believeth in me shall never die;" and believers never do die in the sense in which others die. They die in order to endure the penalty of sin; but for us, that penalty was borne by Christ. All our iniquities were laid upon him, and all the penalty of them was borne by him. Death to the believer is no penalty; it is a development from this time state to another and a higher one; a breaking of the shell that now confines us; a snapping of the cable that holds the vessel to the shore; a severing of the chain that holds the eagle down to the rock. Death releases us so that we may soar away to that land of light and love where Jesus is, as John Newton sings,—

> "In vain my fancy strives to paint
> The moment after death,
> The glories that surround the saint
> When yielding up his breath."

> "One gentle sigh the fetter breaks:
> We scarce can say, 'They're gone!'
> Before the willing spirit takes
> Her mansion near the throne."

Death to the believer is not an execution, it is his deliverance, his manumission, and admission into the glory of God.

Christ has taken away the fear of death from those who truly know him *by assuring us that our soul shall not die or become extinct*. There is a vital principle within us, as he has said, "Because I live, ye shall live also." One of his last solemn declarations was, "Father, I will that they also, whom thou hast given me, be with me where I am; that they may behold my glory." We sorrow not as without hope concerning those who have fallen asleep in Jesus, for we

know that they are for ever with the Lord. "To be absent
from the body, and to be present with the Lord," is the divine
revelation concerning all who are in Christ Jesus by a living
faith; because our souls shall never die, we are not afraid to
venture into the world of spirits.

Then there is that master-doctrine of the Christian faith,
which was not revealed to men in all its fulness until Jesus
came; I mean, *the doctrine of the resurrection of the body.* It
is for this body that we have any fear; corruption, earth, and
worms are its heritage, and it seems a hard thing that these
eyes, which have seen the light, should be blinded in the
mould; that these hands, which have been active in God's
service, should lie still in the grave; and that these limbs,
which have trodden the pilgrim path, should be able to move
no longer. But courage, believer! your body shall rise again.
Laid in the earth it may be, but kept in the earth it cannot
be. The voice of nature bids you die, but the voice of the
Omnipotent bids you live again. For the trumpet shall
sound, and then the bodies of the saints shall rise,—

> "From beds of dust and silent clay,
> To realms of everlasting day."

This is our consolation, that, as Jesus Christ died, and rose
again from the dead, "even so them also which sleep in Jesus
will God bring with him." As we have this double comfort for
soul and body, what more do we want?

Thus I have shown you that, to overcome the fear of death,
we must look to Jesus Christ, on the cross atoning for us, in
the resurrection rising for us, in the glory taking possession
of our home for us, and at the right hand of God preparing
our place for us, possessing all power, and using it so that he
may bring us unto his eternal kingdom; and soon to come
again, in all the glory of the latter days, to raise the bodies of
his people from the dead unless they are still alive at his
coming. This is he who conquers for us the fear of death; it is
to him we are to look; "looking unto Jesus." Let your eyes be
always looking to him, then the fear of death will not make
you subject to bondage.

II. Now, secondly, WHAT SHALL WE THINK OF THAT MAY
FURTHER HELP US TO OVERCOME THIS FEAR OF DEATH?

First, let us remember that, if we are called to die, *we are
called to do no more than Jesus Christ has done before us.*

When my body goes down to the grave, it will not be the first tenant of the sepulchre. Myriads of the saints have been there before, and, best of all, the saints' Master and Lord has slept in the tomb. You remember that Jesus left the napkin folded by itself, that mourners might use it in drying their tears; but the linen clothes, in which he had been wrapped, remained together so that our last bed might be well-sheeted, that our last sleeping-room might not be un-furnished. More than that,—

> "There the dear flesh of Jesus lay,
> And left a long perfume."

Should not the servant be as the Master? Does he ask for more? If the King himself has passed this way, shall his bodyguard, his soldiers, his companions, be afraid to pursue the same downward path? No, beloved; as you follow the track of the Crucified to the tomb of Joseph of Arimathæa, you may yourself walk safely there. If the footprints of the flock have often encouraged us, how much more should the footprints of the Shepherd! So, believers, be not afraid to die, for Jesus died.

Remember, also, that *death will not separate us from the love of Christ, nor from Christ himself.* He is with us now, and he will be with us then; and, after death, we shall be with him for ever. He loves us to-day, and he will love us to-morrow, he will love us all our lives, he will love us in death, and he will love us throughout eternity. It was this truth that Paul proclaimed when he wrote, "I am persuaded, that neither death, nor life, nor angels, nor principalities, nor powers, nor things present, nor things to come, nor height, nor depth, nor any other creature, shall be able to separate us from the love of God, which is in Christ Jesus our Lord." In one of his inventories of the Christian's possessions, he writes, "Life or death, or things present, or things to come"; all are yours; so death is yours if you are in Christ Jesus. If the pangs of death could separate the members of Christ's mystical body from their Head, it would be death indeed; if that grievous sorrow could divide the heart of Jesus from the heart of his elect, then might we dread to die; but it is not so. If death makes any difference to us, the bonds that unite us to Christ shall become still firmer, and the revelation of Christ shall become yet brighter, and Jesus shall be nearer and dearer to us in our departure from earth than he ever was before. "Wherefore comfort one another with these words."

Next, let us recollect that *death will not even separate us from all our friends.* It will take the wife from the husband, and the child from the mother, and we must leave behind us many who have been our comrades in the battle of life. But, especially to you who are growing old, it ought to be a very comforting thought that probably most of your best friends have crossed the river already. If you were to count up those who have been dear to you from your youth up, you would find that the majority have gone on before you as you have advanced in years; and there are some above who, a long way behind our Lord, of course, will be amongst the dearest friends that we hope to see up yonder. The mother will find her babes, who were lent to her for a brief season, and then caught away to heaven, safe on the other shore. And grandparents, and parents, and brothers, and sisters, and many a fellow church-member, with whom we went to the house of the Lord in company, are all there ready to welcome us when we shall be new-comers in the celestial city. Do not, therefore, have a fear of death because of the separation from friends below, but rather cheer yourself with the prospect of a blessed re-union with friends above. You may, perhaps, regret that you have to leave some behind, but think of the friends ahead, and let your spirit rejoice to remember that you are going "to the general assembly and church of the firstborn, which are written in heaven." Again I say to you, "Comfort one another with these words."

I think the fear of death ought to vanish from us when we recollect that *it will be an answer to a great many of our prayers.* I am not sure we always do right to sing such words as these,—

> "Father, I long, I faint to see
> The place of thine abode."

I remember a minister, an old friend of mine, who went into the pulpit, one Sabbath morning, and stood up, and read that verse,—

> "Father, I long, I faint to see
> The place of thine abode;
> I'd leave thine earthly courts, and flee
> Up to thy seat, my God!"

As he uttered those words, he sat down in the seat, fell back, and he had gone to be with his God. We should not venture to say or sing such words as these unless we are fully prepared for such a sudden change as came to my aged friend. But how often you and I have prayed to be rid of troubles! Well, we shall be rid of them, then. How often have we prayed to be rid of sin! We shall be rid of it, then. We have prayed to be delivered from temptation; and we shall be, then. We have asked to be like Jesus; and we shall be, then. We have prayed for a clearer vision of him, and we shall have it, then. Why, our prayers, except when we pray, "Let the whole earth be filled with thy glory," can scarcely go further than when we say, "Let us be with thee where thou art." By our death, the Lord will answer our prayers. One kiss on our lips from his dear mouth will kiss away our soul, and we shall be where we shall see his blessed face in all the splendour of his glory. Then, if death is the answer to your prayers, why need you dread it?

Remember, too, that *death is attended by very special comforts*. I remember a sermon by my grandfather which stuck in my youthful memory, and is fresh in my recollection still. I forget the text, but I think it was, "Grace to help in time of need;" and at the end of the first head the old gentleman said, "But there is one kind of grace that you do not want." Then he went on to a second head, and mentioned another kind of grace, and again he said, "But there is one kind of grace that you do not want." He had five or six heads to his discourse, but at the end of every one of them he said, "But there is one kind of grace that you do not want." We were all wondering what he could mean, when he finished up with this remark, "You do not want dying grace till dying moments come;" there was truth in that observation. I may say to myself, "Do I feel now that I could die calmly or even triumphantly?" I may put the question if I like, but it is hardly a fair one, for I am not yet called to die; yet my experience and observation of others lead me to believe that very remarkable grace is often given to believers in their last hours. I have seen the timid become more strong than the brave, I have seen the retiring become more bold than the courageous; and I have known some, who seemed to be almost dumb before, speak with matchless utterance; and some, whose faces have been lit up with supernatural joy who before appeared to be amongst the doubting and the trembling ones of Christ's family. There are choice revelations, special manifestations, nearer approaches to Christ, wider outlets of love from him, and greater inlets into the soul of the brightness of his presence, in those times, than ever before. When the body is strong, it often seems like a thick wall that shuts out the light; but when disease comes and shakes the tenement, it makes great rifts in wall and roof, and through those rifts the light comes streaming in as it had never come in before. I never can doubt the truth of our holy faith, or the reality of religion, after what I have witnessed at the deathbeds of the Lord's people. I could tell you of one, who died this week, and who had long been a member of this church. She was unconscious in her last hours; but up to the time when unconsciousness came on, it would have been a joy to any of you to see her. She almost incessantly requested her friends that they would sing such songs as—

"Safe in the arms of Jesus."

As long as she could do so, she took her part, joining better than any of them in the real joy of the song, for they were sorrowful at the thought of losing one whom they loved, but she was joyful in the prospect of soon beholding the face of him whom her soul loved so intensely. I believe there is no joy in life that equals the joy of departing believers. You may visit the haunts of folly, if you will, and search for joy there, but you shall not find any joy worth the having. You may go to the palaces of kings, you may go to bridal chambers, you may go where health, and strength, and fame, and honour contribute to worldly mirth; but you shall not find such deep, intense joy anywhere else as you shall find in that room where the death-sweat is on the believer's brow, but the glory of heaven is shining upon his face. I have heard some say that it was worth while to live even for the sake of the joy they have had when they were dying, so there is no cause for a Christian to fear death if such an experience as this awaits him.

But it is not so much the joy of dying that can console us as *the life that is beyond death.* I never like to hear people quote the first part of that text, and omit the latter portion, "Eye hath not seen, nor ear heard, neither have entered into the heart of man, the things which God hath prepared for them that love him. But God hath revealed them unto us by his Spirit: for the Spirit searcheth all things, yea, the deep things of God." Christians know that there is a joy unspeakable and eternal which will be their portion so soon as they shall depart from this world to be with the Father. Well did we sing just now,—

> "Let doubt, then, and danger my progress oppose,
> They only make heaven more sweet at the close:
> Come joy or come sorrow, whate'er may befall,
> An hour with my God will make up for them all."

What will be the sensations of the first hour in heaven? I will not try to picture them, I will leave you to imagine them; but what will be your sensations when you realize that you are not merely to be there for an hour, or a day, or even for seventy years, but for ever and ever. Of him that overcometh, Christ says, "He shall go no more out;" he shall be blessed for ever and ever in the presence of his Lord. The righteous are to go "into life eternal." Take away that word eternal, and you have taken away our all; but while that remains, the heaven of heaven is the fact that it will last for ever and ever!

I cannot stay to speak at length upon all this, but I do entreat every child of God to think much upon these comforting themes; and then, surely, he will be helped to overcome the fear of death.

III. Now, thirdly, WHAT SHALL WE DO, as well as what shall we think of, IN ORDER THAT WE MAY OVERCOME THE FEAR OF DEATH?

I would say, first, *let us die every day.* "I die daily," said the apostle Paul. The man who practices dying every day, the man who has, as it were, a daily rehearsal of it, will not be afraid of the reality when it comes. We are wise to talk of our last hours, to be familiar with the thought of our departure from this world. Every night, when we go to our bed, we ought to have a rehearsal of death. We lay aside our clothes for the night just as we shall have to lay aside our bodies in death. I like that idea best on Saturday night, for then we take off our work-day clothes, and they are put away, and we fall asleep; and then, in the morning, there are our Sabbath-day garments laid ready for us; and oh, what wonderful

Sabbath-day clothes we shall have when we awake in the morning in heaven, and are "arrayed in fine linen: clean and white," which is "the righteousness of saints." So, die daily, brethren, in this fashion; get into the habit of so doing. I remember an old Christian woman, who used to say that she had dipped her feet in the river of death every morning before she left her bedroom, so she did not mind when she was called to go through it, she was so accustomed to "die daily."

The next piece of advice I have to give you is this, *hold very loosely everything on earth.* Have you a great many possessions and friends? Mind that you do not cling too closely to them, for there is danger about them all. As one once observed to a rich man who took him over his parks and gardens, "Ah, sir, these are the things that make it hard to die!" The poor have little enough to leave; and when they go, they have not the regrets which the covetous and avaricious rich man oftentimes has, or the man who has added field to field, and farm to farm, till he owns all the land in the region where he lives. "Must I leave you? Must I leave you?" has often been the miser's cry, as he has tried to clutch his money-bags with his dying fingers. O beloved, hold everything loosely! You are in a dying world, and everything about you is, like yourself, shadowy and fleeting. Do not build your nest here as if you were to abide here for ever. We ought to live in this world like lodgers at an inn. There was a good bishop, who used to say that he should like to die at an inn, because he felt as if he should then be in a similar position both literally and spiritually; and, truly, that is the spirit in which Christians should live here. A man on a journey goes to an inn, to spend a night; he does not trouble himself because the room is not quite to his taste, for he will be off in the morning. You, believer, are only at an inn, so do not fret about the little inconveniences there, for you are to be off in the morning, and you may depend upon it that your Father's carriage will be at the door at the right time, so have everything packed up ready for your departure. Do not go buying a lot of lumber here, for you cannot carry it with you. Have very little, and have it all ready. And a very good thing is to send as much as ever you can on before you. Somebody said, the other day, that the best way to travel was to send all your goods on by the luggage train in advance, and then go yourself by the first-class express passenger train. He explained that he meant that you were to give as much as ever you could away to the poor, and to the Church of God, and so send it on by the luggage train. "What I spent, I *had*," said a man; "what I kept, I *lost*; what I gave away, I *have*;" and truly it is so when believers die. Still is that theirs which they have given to God and to his poor; "but whose is that which they have left behind?" Perhaps some ungrateful heir will sinfully squander it.

I have often admired the difference between a rich man's funeral and a poor man's; it grieves me, sometimes, to think of the rich man's funeral. What do the sons and daughters of the miser think about it? They are most concerned to get home to hear the reading of the will. But when the poor man dies, it is quite another matter. There is his daughter, Jane, who is out at service; she contributes a little towards the cost of the funeral. Then there is a son, John, who has a wife and four or five children, but he pinches himself so as to contribute a little. All the children do something to help; and those are honest tears that they shed for the poor old man, for they have nothing to gain by his departure, and the grief at his funeral will be real and true. But whether you are rich or poor in this world's goods, make sure that you are among "the poor in spirit: for theirs is the kingdom of heaven."

But the main way to overcome the fear of death is *to believe firmly in your Lord*. You will generally find that, in proportion as your faith gets stronger, your fear of death will vanish, and as your faith gets weak, fear will come in to take its place. Realize that Christ is your Saviour, that he loves you, and has given himself for you, and saved you with an everlasting salvation. Realize that he has inscribed your name upon the palms of his hands,—nay, more, that he has graven it upon his heart. Remember that, although a woman may forget her sucking child, your Lord never can forget you; and that he has said, "I will never leave thee, nor forsake thee;" and then will you be able to say, "Yea, though I walk through the valley of the shadow of death, I will fear no evil: for thou art with me; thy rod and thy staff they comfort me."

The next thing I exhort you to do is to *walk much with God*. Never get out of fellowship with him. You cannot have the fear of death while you walk with him. There was a man, you remember, who never died, and the reason was because he walked with God; if any man would escape all dread of death, he must pursue Enoch's path. It is the only way to rise superior to the natural fear that comes upon us all at times.

Next, to get rid of the fear of death, I urge you to *serve God every day with all your might.* Live each day as if it were to be your last day. If any Christian man knew that he had only one more day to live, what a deal of work he would crowd into that day! Then do that every day, since any night when you fall asleep, you may do so for the last time on earth. Press as much service as you can into each day; live at a quick rate; serve the Lord with all your heart, and mind, and soul, and strength, and try to get a full day's work done in every day.

I met, the other day, with a piece of poetry which struck me very forcibly; I wonder whether it will strike you in the same way as I read it:—

> "'My work is done, I lay me down to die;
>   Weary and travel-worn, I long for rest;
> Speak but the word, dear Master, and I fly,
>   A dove let loose, to nestle on thy breast.'
> 'Not yet, my child; a little longer wait,
> I need thy prayerful watch at glory's gate.'"

> "'But, Lord, I have no strength to watch and pray,
>   My spirit is benumbed, and dim my sight;
> And I shall grieve thy wakeful love, as they,
>   Who in the garden slept, that paschal night.'
> 'My child, I need thy weakness, hour by hour,
> To prove, in me, thy strengthlessness is power.'"

> "'Not for myself, I urge the suit,
> But loved ones lose, for me, life's priceless bloom;
> And tender, patient, uncomplaining, mute,
> Wear out their joyance in my darkened room.'
> 'Enough, my child; I need their love to thee;
> Around thy couch they minister to me.'"

> "It is enough, dear Master, yea, Amen;
>   I will not breathe one murmur or reply;
> Only fulfil thy work in me, and then,
> Call me, and bid me answer, 'Here am I.'"
> "My child, the sign I waited for is given:
> Thy work *is* done; I need thee now in heaven."

I admire that utterance of Mr. Whitefield, which I have quoted to you before, "I try to keep all my affairs so arranged that, if I were to die at any time, they would be no trouble to those who come after me." He was so particular in his habits that he would not fall asleep even if he had a pair of gloves out of place; and I like to feel that, as far as it can be, all is right with my own affairs. I do not wonder that some Christian people would be afraid to die now, for they recollect that they have not made their wills. Simple as that remark may seem to be to you, it is a very important matter, for it is a terrible thing for a man to be taken suddenly ill, and instead of having to think about departing to his God he has to send for a lawyer; and when his own wits are scarcely ready for it, he has to be planning about what is to be done for his wife and children, and others whom he wishes to benefit. Get that matter settled as soon as ever you can, and see to everything else that needs attention, so that you may be able to say, "Here am I, standing like a passenger at a railway station, my luggage is all ready, and I am only waiting to step into the carriage, and be gone." Happy man who is in that prepared state, for he need have no fear of death.

And, brethren, if you would get rid of the fear of death, my last word of advice is, *use the telescope very frequently*. Look away up to the eternal hills where your heavenly inheritance lies, for all the glory which Christ has with the Father is yours. You shall sit upon his throne, even as he sits upon the Father's throne. You shall be crowned, even as he is crowned. Look away from this mist and fog, this frost and snow, to the land where the sun goeth no more down, and the days of your mourning shall be for ever ended. Let your spirit rejoice that, as you are one with Jesus, you have already, by faith, taken possession of the land where you shall be no more subject to any pain, or trial, or sorrow, or sin, or death.

Happy are the people who have such a blessed place to go to when they die; but I am afraid there are some here who have not any such prospect before them. To them I will repeat a simple story which I have told to some of you before. I have heard of a certain king who had a jester or "fool" to make fun for him, as kings used to have. But this "fool" was no fool; he had much sense, and he had thought wisely about eternal matters. One day, when he had greatly pleased the king, his majesty gave him a stick, and said to him, "Tom, there is a stick which you are to keep till you see a bigger fool than yourself, and then you may give it to him." One day, his majesty was taken ill, and it was thought that he would die, and many went to see him, and Tom also went, and said, "What is the matter, your majesty?" "I am going, Tom, I am going." "Where are you going?" asked Tom. "I fear it is a very long way," said the king. "And are you coming back, your majesty?" "No, Tom." "You are going to stop a long while, then?" "For ever," said the king. "I suppose your majesty has a palace ready over there." "No." "But I suppose you have provided everything that you will need there if you are going such a long way, and never coming back? I suppose you have sent a good deal on, and got everything provided on ahead?" "No, Tom," said the king, "I have done nothing of the kind." "Here, then, your majesty, take my stick, for you are a bigger fool than I am." And if there is a man here who has made no provision for eternity, and who has no mansion, no abiding-place, no treasure, no Friend, no Advocate, no Helper there, he is a gigantic fool, be he who he may. The Lord give that fool a little sense, and lead him to confess his folly, and to look to Jesus, who is Saviour, Friend, and Heaven all in one. God bless you, for Christ's sake! Amen.

	INDEX OF SERMONS	Text	Volume	Sermon
1	Why They Leave Us	John 17:24	MTP-32	1892
2	Fallen Asleep	1 Corinthians 15:6	MTP-46	2659
3	The Heaven Of Heaven	Revelation 22:4	MTP-14	824
4	Preparation For Heaven	2 Corinthians 5:5	MTP-62	3538
5	"For Ever With The Lord"	Philippians 1:23	MTP-19	1136
6	Heavenly Rest	Hebrews 4:9	NPSP-3	133
7	No Tears In Heaven	Revelation 7:17	MTP-11	643
8	Departed Saints Yet Living	Luke 20:37-38	MTP-31	1863
9	The Hope Laid Up In Heaven	Colossians 1:5	MTP-24	1438
10	The Christian's Manifestation	1 John 3:2	MTP-52	3004
11	The Two Pivots	Ex. 3:6, Heb.11:16	MTP-45	2633
12	Citizenship In Heaven	Philippians 3:20	MTP-8	476
13	The Glorious Hereafter And Ourselves	2 Corinthians 5:5	MTP-16	912
14	The Tent Dissolved And The Mansion Entered	2 Corinthians 5:1	MTP-29	1719
15	The Hope Of Future Bliss	Psalm 17:15	NPSP-1	25
16	Creation's Groans And The Saint's Sighs	Romans 8:22-23	MTP-14	788
17	The Elders Before The Throne	Revelation 4:4, 10, 11	MTP-8	441
18	The Beatific Vision	1 John 3:2	NPSP-2	61
19	A Door Opened In Heaven	Revelation 4:1	MTP-15	887
20	The Bliss Of The Glorified	Revelation 7:16	MTP-62	3499
21	"Let Not Your Heart Be Troubled"	John 14:1-4	MTP-29	1741
22	Now And Then	1 Corinthians 13:12	MTP-17	1002
23	The Earnest Of Heaven	Ephesians 1:13-14	MTP-7	358
24	"For Ever With The Lord"	1 Thessalonians 4:17	MTP-23	1374
25	Fear Of Death	Hebrews 2:15	MTP-55	3125

NPSP New Park Street Pulpit 1855-1860
MTP Metropolitan Tabernacle Pulpit 1861-1917